The Sportsman's Crafts Book

The Sportsman's Crafts Book

Paul C. McNair

Winchester Press

Library of Congress Cataloging in Publication Data
McNair, Paul C
  The sportsman's crafts book.

  Includes index.
  1. Hunting—Implements and appliances.   2. Fishing—
Implements and appliances.   3. Handicrafts.   I. Title.
SK273.M3   688.7'6   78-57523
ISBN 0-87691-263-3

9 8 7 6 5 4 3 2 1

Published by Winchester Press
205 East 42nd Street
New York, N.Y. 10017

WINCHESTER is a Trademark of Olin Corporation used by
Winchester Press, Inc. under authority and control of the
Trademark Proprietor

Printed in the United States of America

DEDICATION

To John Kroplin, for his help, encouragement, and friendship—and to my wife Beverly and son John, for the sacrifices they made to see me through this book.

I wish to acknowledge the contribution of several other backwoodsmen—Bill, Denis, Jim, Jack, Howard, Lou, Ray, and Wes—who allowed me to borrow their ideas.

CONTENTS

The Sportsman's Crafts Book

INTRODUCTION

What marks a well-equipped sportsman? Is he the one who's surrounded by glass-encased racks of custom rods and guns for every occasion? Or the guy with a hatful of flies, tackle boxes brimming with lures, shelves laden with decoys, and drawers crammed with reloading paraphernalia? Maybe. All too often, however, the only result of years of accumulating hunting and fishing gear is a nicely furnished den. While this may have cost him hundreds or thousands of dollars, plus many hours in his workshop, it doesn't represent the total investment in his hobby.

Pursuing that hobby on weekends and vacations, he'll spend money for lodging, kennel fees, and gratuities to natives he's begged for space on duck blinds and hunting stands. Here in the north woods, we've met a lot of sportsmen in this category: we call them tourists, and they're vital to our economy. Businesses cater to them: motels offer a place to sleep, bait shops sell them worms and minnows, local taverns stock the juices to warm their bones, and resorts provide complete outfitting packages including ice-fishing shacks and comfortable chairs. For more personalized attention there are guides to cart around their prized possessions, dockboys to speed-clean their catch, and smokehouse operators to preserve the meat for its return home—all for a fee, of course. Still other merchants profit by charging a premium for needed equipment that sportsmen haven't anticipated, such as anchors, camp heaters, backpacks, and snowshoes.

Unfortunately, not all sportsmen can afford these goods and services. For every well-heeled visitor, there are a dozen avid hunters and anglers who love the outdoors so much they'll make financial sacrifices elsewhere to meet the price of their recreation —which they pay, and pay, and *pay*. Often the wife is drawn into this (though she may be left at home), because the added income from her job—or the pennies that she saves—must contribute to these trips, or to the monthly installments for a four-wheeler or lakeside cabin.

If you're a cost-conscious outdoorsman, you've no doubt discovered how easy it is to save money by making your own accessories. Other books published by Winchester Press cover a wide range of do-it-yourself subjects, from making rods to tying flies to building shooting aids. So why stop there? If you limit your do-it-yourself work to items that can be attached to your rod or gun, you still qualify as a sustaining member of the expensive "Welcome, tourist" club. The "tackle-box" kind of projects may save you a few dollars, but the projects we propose can save you considerably more, because most of them are designed to help you avoid the route traveled by the rest of the tourist traffic.

Using the ideas in this book, you can trap your own minnows and keep them alive, or start your own night-crawler farm. You can erect a permanent or portable ice-fishing shack. You can put up your own duck blind or hunting stand. You can shoulder a backpack, tramp in snowshoes, or drop an anchor made by your own hands. You can keep warm with a homemade heater. You *can*.

Do you lack the confidence to tackle a big project? Then start with a small one, such as our simple worm box or fisherman's chair, and build your way up to the items that appear more complicated. We think you'll find that our directions are much less difficult to follow than the bewildering blueprints and carpentry "in-speak" text of other publications. You can construct anything in this book without knowing what "16-in. O.C." means, or what "O.D." stands for. So take heart—even if you flunked bookends in high-school shop class. I almost did myself; but I also learned an important lesson: my bookends, nicked and poorly finished as they were, worked just as well as the good-looking ones my classmates built.

Remember that since your overall objective as a do-it-yourselfer is to save money, looks are less important than whether or not the things you put together will serve their purpose. In other words, *function* is more important than *fashion.* Minor foul-ups are inevitable, and no reason to give up or throw a hammer through a window! Instead, accept the fact that experienced workmen make mistakes as stupid as yours. So say a few cuss words over them, then make the best of them. Our concrete block smokehouse, for example, was built by a journeyman mason who forgot he was working with 4-inch blocks rather than the 8-inch ones he was accustomed to. Such oversights, discovered in horror, can be remedied with the benefit of a clearer head and some sympathetic advice from your building materials supplier, and the function of your finished product won't suffer from the error. Above all, concentrate on what you're doing, go slowly, and don't be too proud or fussy to utter the skilled laborer's favorite expression: "That's close enough."

Is the cost of materials a hang-up? It shouldn't be. Consider our pickup-mounted accessories, for instance: The lumber bill for our snowmobile carrier is less than a third the amount you'd pay for a trailer. Our cargo box is far less costly than commercially available models. Our plywood camper top, much cheaper to build than to buy in a metal-

and-glass style, can pay for itself several times over by eliminating motel bills. Your outlay for materials is a drop in the bucket when compared with the price tag for store-bought equipment. Besides, our function-over-fashion emphasis gives you the opportunity for further economies by being resourceful with "whatever's handy" materials. You can develop the knack for visualizing discarded items as the inspiration for eventual projects. Before long, you may be setting aside windows for that ice-fishing shack you're going to build someday, or hanging onto an old sink that has plenty of years left for cleaning fish. One man's junk is another man's treasure. And if you don't have brass hinges or galvanized nails, for example, feel free to substitute what you have on hand; it may rust, but it'll do the job. Or if your board widths don't match, or your edges are uneven, so what? We realize this approach has the ring of heresy, but it's practiced all the time. Your work may not measure up to the standards of professional builders, but you aren't charging as much, either. Amateur purists are sure to wince, but who cares?

You'll note that we've recommended power tools for a number of projects in this book, but don't let this discourage you either. Many lumber dealers will trim plywood sheets to measure for a beginning builder who doesn't own a circular saw. If you don't own an electric drill, shame on you! But now that millions of these handy devices have been sold, you probably can borrow one from a neighbor.

We're grateful to a number of self-sufficient backwoodsmen who gave us the ideas described here. Although some items are patterned after high-priced equipment on the market, most are unpatented inventions which, as far as we know, aren't for sale anywhere. Build one of these things, and you'll be the only person in your block with a copy of a backwoods original.

The tourist trade can get along without you!

FOR THE HUNTER

1. HUNTING STAND

A hunting stand is sometimes little more than that: a place to stand. For example, the hunter on the receiving end of a deer drive doesn't always have time to set up housekeeping as his party shifts operations from one patch of woods to the next. He'll simply have to make his stand near the edge of a clearing and, if he's lucky, he'll find a spot that conceals him while providing some wind protection.

Without the help of buddies to flush out the game, a lone hunter often makes better preparations. An experienced nature observer will use his knowledge of animal signs to locate a well-traveled deer crossing, and he'll set up a stand within easy range of it. Then, where possible, he'll choose an alternate site, so he can stay downwind in the event of a change in direction of prevailing breezes. If the stakeout proves successful, you can bet he'll return there year after year, each time with the anticipation of a football fan with first-class 50-yard-line seats for the Super Bowl.

But if a game warden catches him shooting from a permanently installed blind, he can be in for big trouble. In most states, conservation officers take a dim view of these high-ground pillboxes, as well as the platforms they find nailed into trees, and temporary huts made from hacked-off pine boughs and saplings. These setups are not only illegal in many cases, they're unnecessary. Several manufacturers are marketing tree stands which will help you comply with state laws; the easy-to-assemble units can be readily removed before sundown.

A smart investment? Not when homemade varieties are so much less expensive.

We favor the tree-mounted type (provided it can be erected without serious damage to the trunk or limbs). It gives us a wide area of visibility; and since a buck rarely if ever looks up, there's no need for up-front cover. This unobstructed view feature is most appreciated by bow hunters, who need maneuvering room to get off an arrow.

Our lowest-cost, least-work stand is a loose platform of 1 or more 2-inch boards supported by a couple of stout limbs. With this one, as the saying goes, you get what you pay for. It may be just the thing for a big oak you've had your eye on, but it might be useless elsewhere. Some trees (pine and aspen, for example), don't have limbs that can accommodate a shelf of loose boards—even if you're willing to carry a couple of cumbersome 2 x 8's through the woods to another clearing.

We've designed a more adaptable stand you can carry on your back and set up in a jiffy. It's a plywood seat on a frame of 2 x 4's and inch-board scraps, with angle iron teeth and sideguards (cut from a bedspring frame) to prevent it from slipping or swiveling. It hangs from a rope looped around the trunk on an overhead branch or a 2 x 2 block secured to a girdle of hanger iron. We'll show you how to make a rope ladder that will get you high enough to mount the stand.

Besides a saw, hammer, vise, and electric drill, we suggest that you use a reciprocating saw with a metal-cutting blade. A hand hacksaw will make the required cuts in the angle iron, but it will take several hours, skinned knuckles, and a handful of replacement blades. To tell the truth, our iron was cut

Mounted hunting stand can be tied to a limb or to a block of wood that's bolted to a piece of hanger iron wrapped around the tree trunk. Angle-iron teeth dig into the trunk to resist slipping. Painting isn't necessary.

with an acetylene torch by a welder who charged us only $1.

Bill of Materials

1	¹/₂ x 15 x 15″ A-D exterior-grade plywood	platform
2	1 x 3 scraps, 12″ long	frame
2	2 x 4's, 19″ long	frame
	angle iron:	
1	6″	
2	3¹/₂″	
	rope	
11	¹/₄ x 2″ bolts, with washers	
	8d galvanized nails	
	6d galvanized nails	
	hanger iron	
	2 x 2 block	
	wing nut and bolt	

Put each 2 x 4 in a vise and drill a ¹/₂-inch hole 1¹/₂ inches from each end for inserting support ropes. Join the 2 x 4's with 12-inch 1 x 3's, positioned 2 inches from the ends. (You may use only 2 x 4's for framing, but this will add to the weight of the seat.)

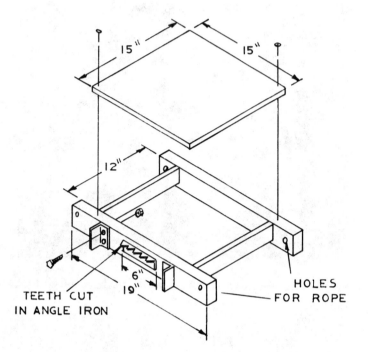

Diagram 1. Simple construction of this tree-mounted hunting stand includes a frame of 2 x 4's and inch-boards, a plywood seat, angle-iron teeth which dig into the tree to resist slippage, angle-iron guards against swiveling, and holes for rope supports.

TEETH CUT
IN ANGLE IRON

HOLES
FOR ROPE

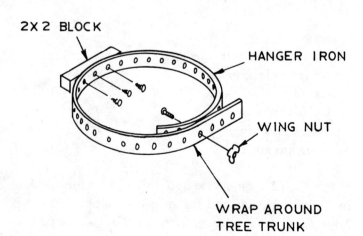

2X2 BLOCK

HANGER IRON

WING NUT

Diagram 2. Rope support, which may be employed when the nearest limb of the tree is too far above or below the desired height for the stand, consists of a block of wood bolted onto a piece of hanger iron.

WRAP AROUND
TREE TRUNK

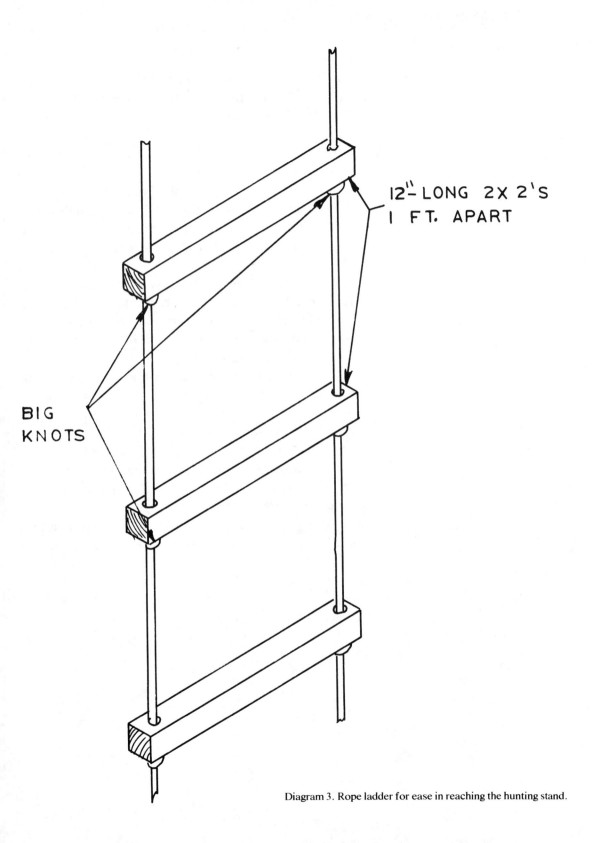

12" LONG 2X 2'S
1 FT. APART

BIG
KNOTS

Diagram 3. Rope ladder for ease in reaching the hunting stand.

Lay the plywood on top of this frame and square it in place by nailing it to each corner. The inch-boards of the frame should rest on 2 x 4 scraps during nailing.

If you're cutting your angle iron from a bed frame, plan your 3½- and 6-inch marks to take advantage of holes already drilled in the metal, if possible. Bolt the 3½ inch pieces to the 2 x 4 at the rear of the seat, one on each end. After cutting teeth in the 6-inch piece, bolt it to the center of the 2 x 4 (Diagram 1).

If no tree limb is handy for your stand's support rope, use four ¼-inch bolts to attach a 6-inch 2 x 2 to the middle of a strip of hanger iron, which in turn is wrapped around the trunk and joined with a bolt and wing nut (Diagram 2).

You can make a rope ladder by drilling holes in the ends of 2 x 2's. Thread the rope through these holes, 1 board at a time, and tie knots big enough to keep the rope from slipping through. Space rungs a foot apart (Diagram 3). To get it into the tree, tie it to a weighted rope, throw the weight over a limb at the desired height for your stand, and secure the rope to a nearby tree.

After you've climbed up to our tree-mounted platform, the so-called "stand" becomes a place to sit down.

2. DUCK BLIND

Have you ever lost out in the annual scramble for space in somebody else's duck blind on the opening day of the season? Are you familiar with the hassle of sloshing around at the water's edge, trying to fashion some makeshift cover before the birds spy you at daybreak? Then maybe this is the year you'll decide to build your own blind.

The type you build will depend on your circumstances, and the way you prefer to set up for shooting. For instance, if you're a lakeside cabin owner whose shoreline is graced with inviting reeds that are visited annually by flocks of ducks, you can install a permanent blind. Or, if you prefer to float your decoys in different spots during the season, a portable one is the answer. We'll show you how to build both types.

Our solid-based platform unit provides room for a 4- to 6-man party to cover incoming birds. It also has channels of water for cleaning birds during lulls between shooting action. Although it's a stationary blind, 2 men can move it to correspond with changes in the lake level. This is really a simple carpentry project for keyhole saw, crosscut handsaw, hammer, brace and bit, level, square, adjustable wrench, and your pair of waders.

Diagram 1. Snow fencing provides a long-lasting frame for attaching camouflage to a post-supported duck blind. A raised floor allows space for a boat underneath.

Bill of Materials

6	6 x 6" posts (cedar or redwood)*	
2	2 x 4's, 48" long	framing
2	2 x 4's, 93" long	framing
1	¹/₂ x 40¹/₂ x 96" marine plywood	deck
	snow fencing, 16' long	camouflage frame
16	¹/₄ x 4" lag screws, with	
	washers	frame fasteners
	16d galvanized nails	
	8d galvanized nails	

*Lengths will depend on the depth of water off your shoreline.

As you might imagine, a photograph of a duck blind will reveal very little about its construction features, because hiding your carpentry work is the name of the game. So we've provided a pen-and-ink illustration, free of camouflage, to show the elements of a serviceable model (Diagram 1). Note that our 4 x 8-foot blind is close to the shoreline (since some state laws forbid duck blinds in open water), and it has clearance for stowing an 8-foot johnboat underneath.

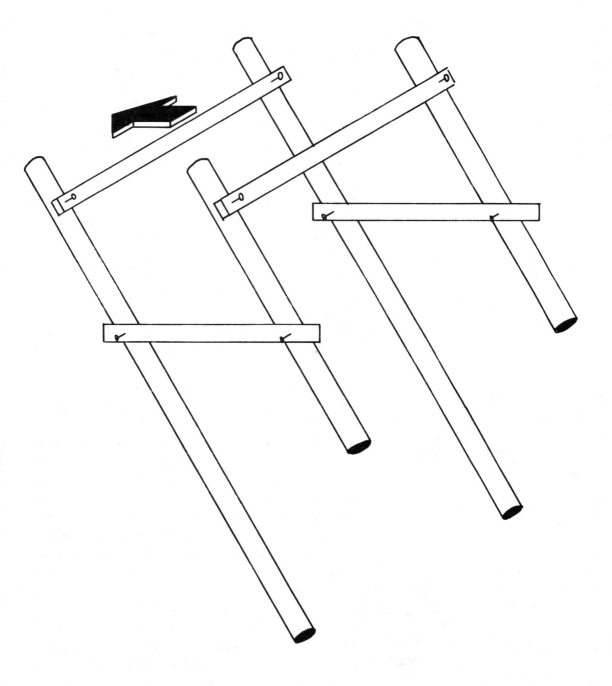

Diagram 2. Temporary frame for dragging the corner posts of a duck blind across the water to the desired setup location.

When you've chosen a setting for the blind, slip on your hip boots, clamp your hunting knife between your teeth, and wade into the reeds with a long 2 x 4 for taking soundings and rough measurements. Cut out an 8-foot-wide area that extends 4 feet or more from shore. Then grab the floating 2 x 4 and begin readings of water depth. Beginning at the deep end of the blind area, stand up the 2 x 4 and push the bottom of it firmly into the lake bed. To estimate the length of posts needed for this end of the blind, figure the depth of water, another 2 feet for easy clearance of a boat under the frame and decking, 4 more feet for snow fencing, and another 6 inches just in case the posts settle deeper into the lake bed. Your 2 posts at the water's edge (again allowing 2 feet for boat clearance and 6 inches for settling) should be at least 6½ feet high. Although this is a "permanent" installation, we advise against setting the posts in concrete, because the added weight will make it difficult to move the blind in or out from the original shoreline when there's a change in water level.

Back on shore, nail together a temporary frame (only 1 spike at each joint) with the 4 posts and four 2 x 4's (Diagram 2). By pulling on the front crosspiece in the direction of the arrow, you can tow this folding frame into the water. Once you've got it in the clearing, stand up the frame so that the front of the structure is farthest from shore. This frame will hold the posts erect while you adjust it to proper height (with 2 x 4's at least 2½ feet above the water's surface) (Diagram 3). Don't drive the spikes all the way home; they're intended only to hold the 2 x 4's in place until you've leveled them and squared up the corners. Use the "3-4-5 carpenter's square" method described in project 5. The lower frame is shown in Diagram 3.

With your brace and ¼-inch bit (for safety's sake, *not* an electric drill), bore 2 holes into one 2 x 4, in line with the middle of the post (Diagram 4),

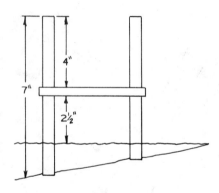

Diagram 3. Positioning corner posts of the duck blind along the shoreline, allowing clearance for a johnboat.

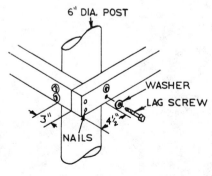

Diagram 4. Attaching outside platform framing with nails and lag screws.

insert the screw bolts, and tighten them with a wrench. Do the same with the adjoining 2 x 4, and repeat this on all 4 corners, making certain the frame remains level as you go along. When all the bolts are tight, drive a couple of spikes into the 2 x 4 joints at each corner.

Floor joists are next. Spike six 45-inch 2 x 4's from front to back. Exact spacing between joists isn't critical here, except in the middle, where we've placed joists on each side of the center poles for better support of the deck (Diagram 5).

Our own deck is pieced together from plywood scraps, cut where necessary to meet at the center of the 2 x 4 joists. If you use a full sheet of plywood, provide for notches—and expansion space—around the rear posts. The underside of this piece may be sealed with a coating of paint before it's nailed on. If you'd rather build your deck with 1 x 4's, you'll also have to frame the rear corner posts with scrap 2 x 4's. And don't nail these 1 x 4 decking boards until you've spread them on the frame to make sure they fit. Again, don't forget to include expansion space between boards and posts. Two 37$\frac{1}{2}$-inch 1 x 4's will fit on each side of the center post at the rear, and eight more 8-footers will complete the span to the front posts, leaving the channels between them for cleaning birds.

We favor snow fencing for the camouflage frame, because it's considerably stronger than chicken-wire netting, and it holds its shape better. Stretching isn't necessary to hang it, but hand-pull it as taut as possible before pounding in the staples (at least 3 per post). A number of items are suitable as camou-flage material, but we suggest that your best choice is the natural cover in your blind's immediate envi-ronment. Best is, we think, reeds and cattails, which can be tied to the fencing's wood slats. In our area, however, the most popular materials are corn-stalks and pine boughs, because they are available and can be tied on and replaced with less bother.

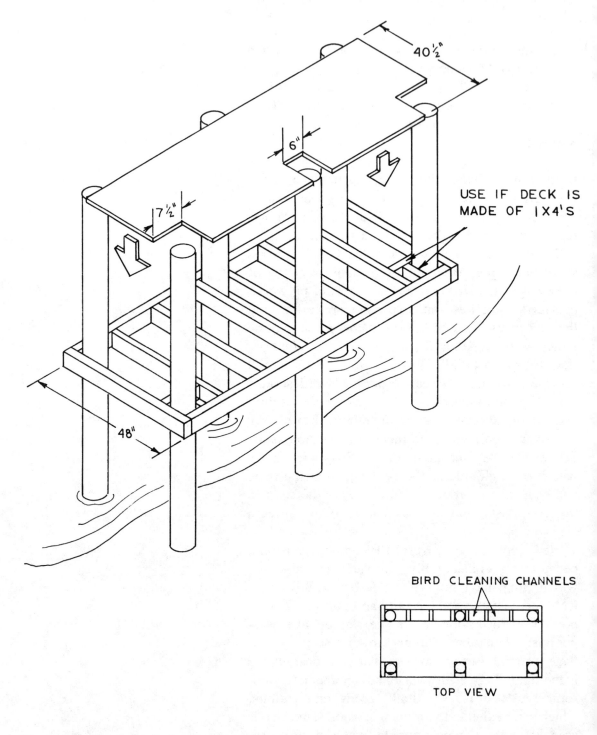

40½"

6"

7½"

USE IF DECK IS
MADE OF 1X4'S

48"

BIRD CLEANING CHANNELS

TOP VIEW

Diagram 5. 2 x 4 framing for the floor of the duck blind. The rear center post (along shoreline) may be sawed flush with the top of the framing if 3-sided camouflage is desired. Downed birds may be lowered with short cords through floor openings to the water when cleaning.

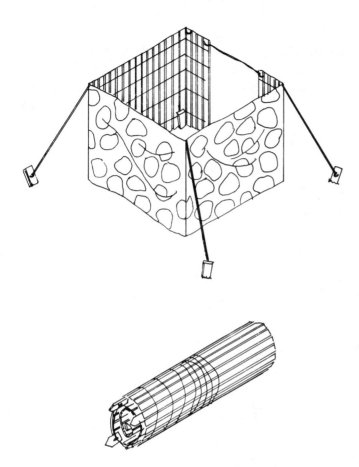

Diagram 6. Portable duck blind for on-land use features snow fencing held upright with staked ropes.

Our portable blind, which sets up in minutes along the shore, also features snow fencing. When you want to shoot elsewhere, it rolls into a bundle that can be carried in one hand. This same roll-up feature lets you store it out of the way between shooting sessions. It may be arranged in a variety of shapes to enclose the hunter, and the fencing's construction of oak slats threaded through heavy-gauge wire enables it to stand with a minimum of support. All that's required is stakes tied to diagonal ropes from the top wire, plus inside support stakes to prevent the bottom of the fence from "toeing in," and a rope tied overhead (Diagram 6). The ropes also serve as wrapping and carrying straps for the rolled-up bundle. Nail a fence staple into each stake, and thread the stakes with one of the ropes, to include all the stakes in the same bundle. Camouflage-colored fabric, which you may order through a specialty yard-goods shop, furnishes quick, portable cover.

3. DOG CRATE

Whether your dog is a sporting hound or just a family friend, building a pet carrier can be the solution to a host of problems when you bring him along on your travels. It's a sure way to prevent a rambunctious rover from pouncing on the driver's lap, or jumping off the back of a pickup to join a passing parade of mutts over a bitch in heat. It also does away with complaints from the wife about dog hairs, muddy paw prints, and doggie-do on the seats. (Purebreds, especially, are hard to control.)

A crate also has its advantages on the hunt. It may be used as a doghouse on overnight outings, to confine the animal in camp. Free to roam, an ambitious animal can spoil the next day's shooting by riling up all the critters in the woods. Rabbit hunters, in particular, will keep their beagles housed until the hunting party arrives at a promising location. This conserves a little hound's energy that otherwise might be spent straining at the end of his leash or scampering around old trails. In winter, some rabbit hunters haul their beagles on sled-mounted carriers to eliminate the possibility of a dog's developing a "cold nose" before reaching a fresh trail.

Dog crates come in various sizes and styles, depending on the dog's size and temperament, as well as where it will ride when it travels. Light-framed chicken wire may be adequate for a small, well-

Pegboard dog crate has an angled front to fit inside a station wagon. Handle for the swing-up door also serves as a handhold for carrying.

Confining this spirited blue-tick coonhound in a dog crate prevents him from roaming the woods until we're ready to release him.

behaved cocker spaniel that respects confinement, but a feisty terrier might scratch it to shreds. Our slanted-front model is designed for traveling inside the rear of a station wagon; it may be scaled down in size for a smaller dog. Its panels, including the roof and floor, were cut from 1 sheet of pegboard (sometimes called perforated hardboard). This material provides plenty of ventilation. The floor may be lined with furniture store remnants of indoor-outdoor carpeting to give the dog a foothold when the vehicle rounds a sharp curve. This perforated board is too drafty for the back of an open pickup on cold winter days, so if that's where your portable doghouse will be riding, substitute solid sheets of plywood or other 1/4-inch paneling and cut ventilation holes near the roof.

To build your dog a mobile home, you'll need hammer, saw, plane, combination square, level, electric drill, screwdriver, and adjustable wrench.

Bill of Materials

1/4" pegboard:

1	20 x 30"	top
1	20 x 36"	bottom
1	20 x 24"	rear
1	20 x 25"	door
2	24 x 30 x 36"	sides

quartered 2 x 4's:

4	22³/₈"	corner posts
4	19¹/₂"	top, bottom framing
2	29¹/₂"	top framing
2	35¹/₂"	bottom framing
2	23"	door framing
2	8"	door framing
1	29³/₄"	top framing, handle support
1	6"	top framing, handle support
2	6" scraps	door pull
	hasp, with bolts and washers	door lock
	Liquid Nails or other glue	
2	brass hinges	
2	³/₁₆ x ³/₈" bolts, with nuts	hinge fasteners
	drawer handle	
2	1/4" hook bolts, with nuts and washers	handle fasteners
2	1¹/₄" flathead brass screws	
10	1" flathead brass screws	

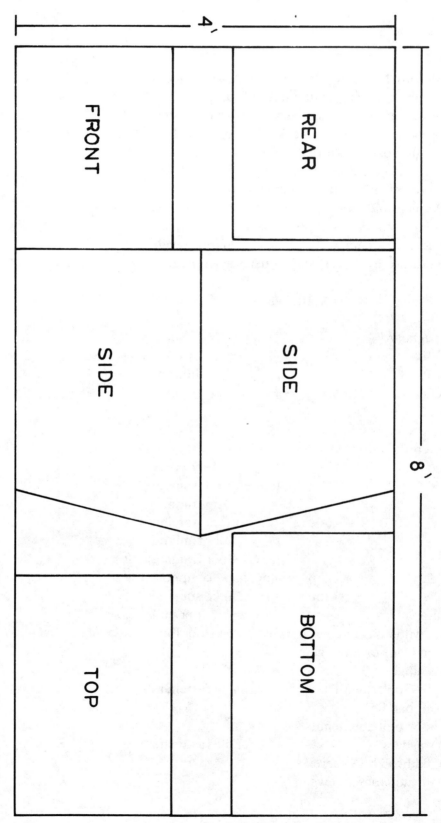

Diagram 1. Cutting pattern for panels of the dog crate.

3/4" flathead brass screws*
6d finishing nails

* Glue will do most of your fastening work on the frame, with at least 3 or 4 screws from pegboard into each piece of the wood frame. Put in more screws, if you wish.

If you're sawing the panels from a full 4 x 8 sheet of material, follow our cutting pattern (Diagram 1), using as narrow a blade as possible. Before assembling these pieces, you may want to plane about 1/16 inch from the top of the rear-and the front-door panels, so these pieces match the height of the side panels.

Framing for our doggie box consists of 2 x 4's which were ripped into quarters; that is, ripped to form rough 2 x 2's, which in turn were ripped in half again (Diagram 2). You may elect to add a few pounds to the crate by framing it with whole 2 x 2's, or to substitute ripped-apart 1 x 4's.

Draw a 1/4-inch border around the inside of the top and bottom panels. Your framing boards, cut on an angle (or mitered) at the ends, will fit inside this border, providing a 1/4-inch gap for setting in the side pieces later. Apply glue to the ends and bottom of the mitered framing boards and fasten them along the inside edge of the penciled border. Tack them together at the corners with 6d finishing nails, and secure them from the outside with 3/4-inch flathead screws. If you're using pegboard paneling, of course, the holes for these screws are predrilled.

Now is the time to make preparations for the crate's carrying handle, which will be mounted later in the center of the top panel. While the underside of the top panel is facing you, glue a 6-inch wood scrap in the middle of the 29³/4-inch board, then lay this longer piece down the center of the panel. Join it to the end framing boards with glue and screws. Drill 1/4-inch holes through these center pieces to accept bolts for the carrying handle.

Since our plan calls for framing with quartered 2 x 4's, our 4 corner posts are 22³/8 inches high. (Your

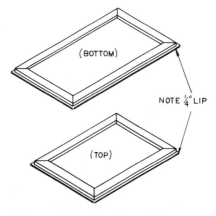

Diagram 2. Framing the crate's top and bottom sheets with quartered 2 x 4's.

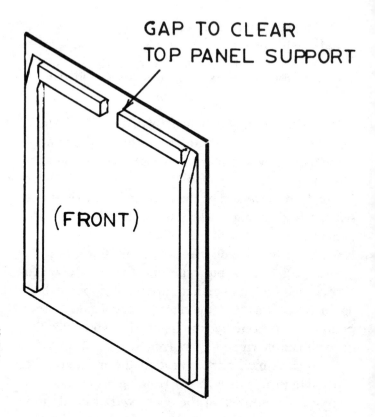

GAP TO CLEAR
TOP PANEL SUPPORT

(FRONT)

Diagram 3. Framing the door of the dog crate. Note the angles at the top of the quartered 2 x 4's, to provide clearance for the roof framing.

measurement may vary slightly, depending on the width of your framing boards.) Stand them up at the corners of your 19½ x 29½-inch top framing and tack them to the top frame with short diagonal braces, nailed temporarily inside the frame. When you're sure that each post is exactly 90 degrees, glue it to the framing. Secure each post with a 1½-inch screw turned in from the outside of the pegboard.

Set this framed top panel on the framed bottom panel. The corner posts should stand flush with the bottom framing at the rear corners and 6½ inches in from the front, flush with the outside edge of the longer framing boards. Again using short braces nailed on temporarily, glue the posts to the bottom framing at 90-degree angles, and later screw them in place from the outside of the pegboard. After the glue dries, remove the temporary braces, then glue and screw the end and side panels in position.

Framing on the inside of the door, besides strengthening it, will prevent the angled ends of the box from sagging inward. One end of each 23-inch framing board should be cut at an angle so it will clear the bottom of the box when the door closes (Diagram 3). Measure down 5 inches from the end of each board that will be attached at the bottom of the door, draw a cutting line to the opposite corner, and saw off the sharp angle. With more glue and screws, attach the 2 boards 1/4 inch from the sides and 1 1/4 inches from the top of the door. Nail two 8-inch framing boards across the top of the door, also 1 1/4 inches from the edge, leaving a gap between the ends to clear the butt of the framing board that runs down the center of the top panel.

The handle for our door is an arrangement of 2 glued-together wood scraps that are joined to the pegboard with washered screws turned in from the inside. You may use a drawer handle instead.

Don't hinge the door until you've bolted the carrying handle to the top of the crate (Diagram 4). Our hinges are screwed to the top of the box, and in addition to a screw on the door side of each hinge, we've put in a 3/16-inch bolt for more strength. If you do likewise, you'll have to bore holes into the top framing, in line with the nuts, to let the door close completely. Install a hasp at the bottom center of the door for a lock.

Your dog will travel more easily in this new home if it has a chance to get accustomed to it for a few days before your next hunting trip.

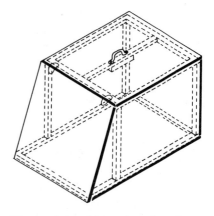

Diagram 4. Attaching pegboard panels to a frame of quartered 2 x 4's for the dog crate.

4. TRAPSHOOTING RANGE

Sounds like quite an undertaking, doesn't it? And depending on your circumstances, building a trap-shooting range of your very own may be out of the question. Property requirements for a regulation-size shooting setup are formidable. You need a se-cluded location that's out of earshot of other prop-erty owners—in short, the kind of ground an out-doorsman might shop for in a vacation place. So this project may be your inspiration to go out and buy a piece of privacy.

Need more convincing to take on such a big-scale job? Consider safety: When you can *build safety into* a trapshooting range, why go on firing your practice rounds where the risk of a shooting acci-dent is greater? If you normally do a lot of target practice, or if you're teaching a youngster to handle a firearm, then a safe outdoor shooting gallery is something you owe yourself—and him, too.

Still not convinced? Think of the financial side of it: You could save a considerable sum on shooting fees paid to a commercial range. Since you'd prob-ably do more shooting on a place of your own, this would sharpen your eye to win bigger purses at tur-key shoots and other trap competitions. Additional fringe benefits might include occasional bottles of booze or other gratuities from friends who make use of the range.

Because we believe this project is worthwhile for the avid shooter, we'll tell you how to go about it. First, the specific requirements. In laying out a trap field, safety-minded shooters prefer a firing area that's at least 200 yards from the nearest building or roadway. Local zoning ordinances may be more restrictive, so check them out before you proceed. If it appears that building codes or nervous neighbors will forbid a permanent installation, you may be able to get by with a temporary setup, which we'll describe later.

A traphouse is the main component of a shooting range. This small building, where the trap is loaded and targets are thrown, is essential for the protection of the trap loader, who is stationed inside this bunker. If your trap house is to be a permanent structure (for which you may need a building permit), you have the option of leaving the far side of it open or installing a drop-open hinged door that can be locked for safer storage of trap equipment and accessories. Before you build it, however, you should stake out the field to make sure the building location and height, along with other critical measurements, are in line with specifications of the Amateur Trapshooting Association.

Tools needed: 100-foot measuring tape, hammer, saw, carpenter's level, shovel, hoe, wheelbarrow, trowel, jointer, electric drill, wrench, ball of string, and chalk.

Concrete trap house of this trapshooting range provides more than ample protection for the person who loads the trap inside. The first firing line is located 16 yards away from the trap.

Bill of Materials

3 cu. yd. of pit-run gravel	drainage
1 perforated drain pipe, 4' or longer	drainage
2½ cu. yds. of foundation-mix gravel	
1 cu. yd. of coarse sand	
6 bags of portland cement	
1 bag of masonry cement	

reinforcement rod, 8' square
6 x 8 x 16" concrete blocks*
6 x 8 x 16" corner blocks (flat on one end) †
6 x 8 x 16" corner blocks (flat on both ends) ‡

2	1 x 6's, 90"	doorway framing, jambs
2	1 x 4's, 88½" long	doorway framing, jambs
2	1 x 6's, 30½" long	doorway framing, jambs
2	1 x 4's, 29" long	doorway framing, jambs
	¾ x 29 x 88½" A-D exterior-grade plywood §	door

8 headless anchor bolts
2 heavy-duty hinges
  heavy-duty hasp
2 bolt locks
  6d nails

*Figure 20 blocks per course below doorway, then 15 per course plus 7 more for trimming to shape the roofline, and a few extras to allow for breakage.
† Figure 4 corner blocks per course below doorway, then 3 per course.
‡ Figure 1 block per 2 courses, to be cut for doorway.
§ Height of door opening will determine size of boards and plywood.

First off, shooting uphill is a no-no, so to avoid costly excavation work, the ground between shotgunner and target should be level—or better yet, sloped slightly downhill. Also, the throwing arm of the trap, when mounted in position, must be exactly the same height as the shooter's feet. We've diagramed a layout of ATA-specified distances (Diagram 1).

In case the details of regulation trapshooting are new to you, the 16-yard firing line is assigned to the best competitors. The poorer the shooter, the farther he must stand from the trap. The principle is that a novice shotgunner, standing a greater distance from the trap, has more room and shooting time to sight in a moving target. As his shooting average improves, he advances to the closer positions.

Following Diagram 1, drive a stake at point *T* (the spot where your trap will be mounted) and pound a nail partway into the top of it. Hook your measuring

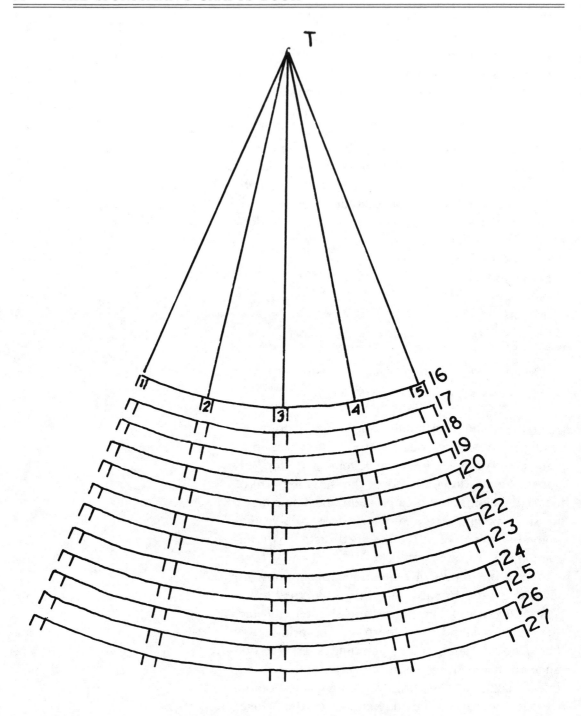

Diagram 1. Firing positions for trap range. Points 1 through 5 are 3 yards apart, and 16 yards from T, the trap position. Arcs 16 through 27 are a yard apart.

tape on the nail and step off 16 yards to position 3 of the diagram. This is the central shooting position along an arched walkway that includes 4 other shooting positions—2 on each side. To stake these other spots exactly 16 yards from the trap, you must function as the pencil point of a compass. With a 9-foot board, measure 3 yards to mark position 4, another 3 yards to position 5, and so on for points 1 and 2 on the other side of the arc.

After the 16-yard line is staked out, you should check the height of this firing line against the proposed level of your trap. Since the trap arm should be on the same plane as the level of your shoes 16 yards away, the ground in between should be level or sloped downhill toward the trap marker. In lieu of surveying instruments, you can determine the correct trap height with a carpenter's level and a long board that's fairly straight. To explain this crude but effective technique (Diagram 2), let's assume you're working with that same 9-foot board. Drive tall, wide stakes (from inch-board scraps) 8 feet apart along a straight line between the trap stake and the one that marks shooting position 3. With temporary nailing, tack the board to the number three stake and, once the board is level, tack the other end to the next stake 8 feet away. Use a pencil to mark the outline of the board as it's tacked on level. Remove the board and move it down to the next stake. Line up one end with the pencil marks on the second stake and tack it on. Level the board again. Tack it to the next stake. Draw a heavy pencil mark on the trap stake where the bottom of the board crosses it. This will give you the exact height of the trap.

Remove all the level-checking stakes except for the trap stake and the one just ahead of it (which will help keep your fix on the trap level after you've removed the trap stake for excavation work later), and while your tape measure is handy, stake out the rest of the shooting positions. Hook the end of the

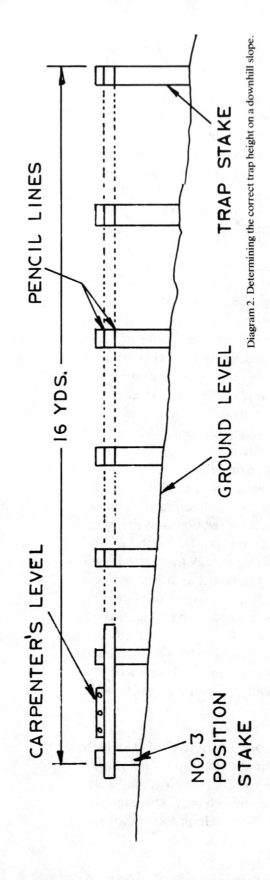

CARPENTER'S LEVEL

PENCIL LINES

16 YDS.

NO. 3 POSITION STAKE

GROUND LEVEL

TRAP STAKE

Diagram 2. Determining the correct trap height on a downhill slope.

tape onto the nail of the trap stake and line up the tape with position 5 of Diagram 1. Drive a stake 27 yards from the trap stake, in line with position 3, and more stakes at 1-yard intervals down to the 16-yard marker. Follow the same procedure for marking positions in line with the number four, three, two, and one stakes along the 16-yard arc.

A slight downhill slope is preferred as a trap-house site, because this assures plenty of clearance for clay targets. However, we must warn you against placing the house on the edge of a steep hillside, where water runoff will eventually erode the ground around the structure. Also, if part of the building is below ground level, you may want a simple drainage system to handle surface water from rainstorms so the poor trap loader won't be bothered by wet feet. We'll show you how to go about that after you've finished your excavation.

First, remove the trap stake. (Don't worry about losing this marker for positioning the trap arm, because the leveling line on the remaining stake ahead of it will help you pinpoint the spot later.)

The bottom of the hole you dig will be lined with a foot-thick layer of gravel (for drainage) and covered with a 3½-inch concrete pad, and your trap device will rest on this slab (or possibly on a concrete block platform above it). Therefore, the hole should be at least 15½ inches deeper than the correct height of the trap arm when installed. This means, of course, that you should buy the trap and measure it before you do any spadework.

We're not ashamed to admit that if we ever had to dig another of these foundation holes, we'd hire it done. Besides the drainage ditch and 9-foot-square space for a slab of concrete, you must give yourself 2 or more feet of working room for striking the footing with a long 2 x 4. And we'd give our trap loader more headroom. A backhoe operator can accomplish in less than an hour what will take you the better part of a week. Typically, this heavy-equip-

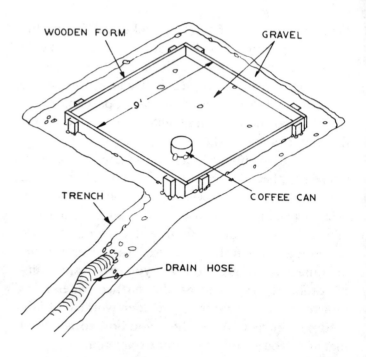

Diagram 3. Gravel-filled opening and trench for drainage and a base for the trap house's 9-foot-square footing and slab floor. Plastic pipe or perforated pipe may be used to channel away surface water from rainstorms.

ment operator tows his trailer-mounted backhoe with a gravel truck, so ask him to deliver enough gravel for a foot-thick layer in your hole and trench. Lay the perforated pipe (holes down) at the end of the trench (Diagram 3) on about 6 inches of gravel and cover it with leaves or straw and more gravel.

The concrete pad means mixing and pouring concrete (see project 5 for mixing instructions). With 2 x 4's nailed to long stakes driven through the gravel into the dirt below, build a 9-foot-square form for the poured concrete. Although the outside dimensions of the trap house will be 8½ x 8½ feet (the maximum allowed by the ATA), the footing should be slightly larger, to provide an ample base for building blocks. Lay a straight 2 x 4 across these form boards to check the form with a level. Work a coffee can (for a drainage hole) into the gravel base, near the corner leading to the trench, so that the rim is about 3 inches above the gravel. Later on, you'll be shaping the poured concrete around the coffee-can rim as you strike the form, so the slab floor will dip slightly in the area around the drainage hole. Therefore, your concrete mixture shouldn't be soupy, or the stuff will merely run into the hole.

As the concrete begins to set, and if you've decided on a shallow crawl space for the trap loader, you'll have to install bolts for mounting the trap. Ours sits higher up, on a raised concrete pad, but the installation method is the same. Obviously, the bolt holes in the base of the trap itself will determine the number and size of anchor bolts you'll need. But to position them accurately, you should make a *template*. Set the trap on a piece of stiff cardboard and mark the bolt openings on it. Punch holes in these markings and set the cardboard in the middle of the concrete—directly in line with the center shooting position (16 yards back). Then push the bolts through the template holes and into the concrete. Don't wait too long, or the bolts won't be seated firmly. Allow enough exposed thread on the bolts to attach nuts later. The cardboard, which also will .help hold the bolts rigid in the soft concrete, may be removed after it hardens. At this point, it's a good idea to cover these protruding bolts with a box; if you don't, you may stub your toes on them while you're laying block.

To mark a 102-inch-square chalk line as a guide for your blocks, drive long stakes though the gravel outside the edges of the concrete pad. Join these 4 stakes with twine, and adjust their position according to the 3-4-5 carpenter's square described in project 5. Chalk the bottom of the string and snap it on the concrete on all 4 sides. Lay your first course of blocks with the chalk line along their outside edge (Diagram 4).

Again, the number of block courses you lay up will depend on the height of your trap-flinging device, and perhaps more on how much room you plan to furnish the trap loader. When you reach the level that will be cleared by the trap arm (or where a person can sit comfortably), your front wall is com-

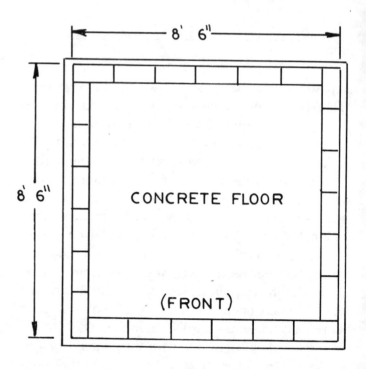

FIRST COURSE

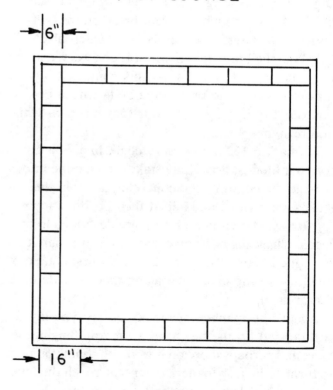

Diagram 4. Block-laying pattern for odd-
and even-numbered courses of the concrete block trap house.

SECOND COURSE

Trap arm's metal base is attached with anchor bolts to a concrete pad. Interior of the trap house should provide room for the trap loader.

pleted. Now is the time to think about inserting anchor bolts to hold the frame for a door across the front. Insert at least 2 doorjamb anchor bolts between the blocks on each side of the opening.

Your block work is finished when you've laid enough courses to give headroom to a seated trap loader (or when your final layer reaches a point between 14½ and 22½ inches above the height of the trap arm). If you're in doubt about this, go ahead and set the trap temporarily in place, because ATA regulations specify that the top of a slanted-roof trap house can't be more than 34 inches or less than 24 inches above the trap arm.

The way you provide for a pitch in the roof (the complicated part of this project) will depend on your choice of materials. Heavy-gauge sheet metal or a span of 2 x 6's is adequate protection for the person in the trap house, and these roofs are easier to put on than concrete. But the model we've photographed provides the ultimate protection of a concrete slab roof (which most of the big boys seem to favor), so we'll show you how this item can be put on. Although our building's roof includes a short overhang, our plan describes a cover that's flush

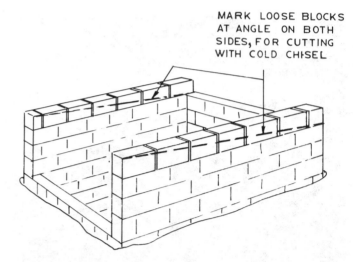

MARK LOOSE BLOCKS
AT ANGLE ON BOTH
SIDES, FOR CUTTING
WITH COLD CHISEL

Diagram 5. Marking blocks for the sloped
roof of the trap house.

with the walls, which is easier for a beginner to handle.

Begin by laying a course of block on both side walls, but don't mortar them in place yet. Snap diagonal chalk lines from one corner of each block course to the other, on both sides of the blocks (Diagram 5). After chalk-marking both sides of each block, set them on the slab floor and cut the blocks with a hammer and cold chisel. A small-head hammer is recommended for pounding blocks, because it will keep you from striking with too much force. Tap lightly along the entire chalk line of each block, rather than pounding through in one spot. By working carefully, you may be able to save intact pieces for the opposite side. Don't worry about blocks that don't break cleanly on the chalk lines, because cracked blocks and chipped-out spots can be joined or filled with a thick mixture of mortar, which can be shaped without the aid of a form to complete the diagonal line.

If you opt instead to rig up triangle-shaped forms on each side, remember to insert foundation bolts to anchor the slab roof.

The concrete roof calls for more poured concrete. At this stage of the project, there's nothing sinful

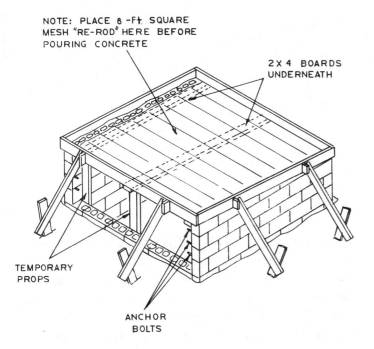

NOTE: PLACE 8-Ft. SQUARE
MESH "RE-ROD" HERE BEFORE
POURING CONCRETE

2 X 4 BOARDS
UNDERNEATH

TEMPORARY
PROPS

ANCHOR
BOLTS

Diagram 6. Supporting the form for the sloped concrete slab roof of the trap house.

about ordering a load of ready-mixed concrete to finish the job. To make it worth the trucker's while, you may want to order additional concrete to be used as markers for firing positions. In that case, dig small holes and build ground-level wood forms for square pads at each position you wish to mark, say, 16, 20, and 25 yards. An even fancier setup (which is sure to make your supplier happy while you run up your costs) could include concrete walkways.

The form for our concrete slab roof resembles one set up for the floor of our smokehouse in project 5. Note that Diagram 6 also includes an 8-foot-square piece of "re-rod" to reinforce the concrete. When mixing concrete for the roof, add water sparingly; the mixture must be thick enough to cling to a form that's on a slight pitch. A too soupy mix will slop off the lower edge of the form. In "finishing" this concrete, work the striking board from side to side, and from the bottom up. Cover the hardening mud with weighted sheets of cardboard for over-

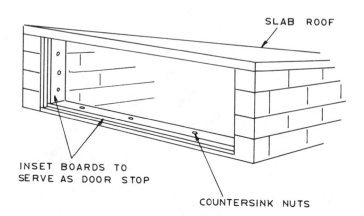

SLAB ROOF

INSET BOARDS TO
SERVE AS DOOR STOP

COUNTERSINK NUTS

Diagram 7. Framing for the trap house's
flop-open door.

night curing. To provide for a door header, you may
insert 2 anchor bolts into the hardening concrete
(through predrilled holes in the front inch-board of
the form). Should you forget this step, you can
make up for the oversight by drilling holes with a
concrete-cutting bit, and inserting bolts from an anchor bolt kit.

Install the trap before you frame the opening.
Then cut two 1 x 6's to fit the top and bottom span
across the front. This distance should be exactly 90
inches, but check it to be sure. Snug the boards
against the protruding bolts, flush with the outside
edge of the blocks, and rap the boards with a hammer. Drill holes where the bolts mark the boards,
then bolt on the timbers. Countersinking the bolt
holes will help prevent tearing your shirt or seat of
your pants when you crawl in and out. The side
framing of inch-boards, installed the same way,
should fit up against the top and bottom boards of
the doorway. For doorjambs (to keep your door
from swinging inside and straining the hinges), bolt
inch-boards or 2 x 4 scraps inside the frame (Diagram 7), inset to allow for the thickness of your
door. In other words, a ³/₄-inch-thick plywood door
means your jambs should be ³/₄ inch from the outside edge of the framing.

While 2-inch-board roofing is more than stout
enough to stop stray shot from a trap load, it's not

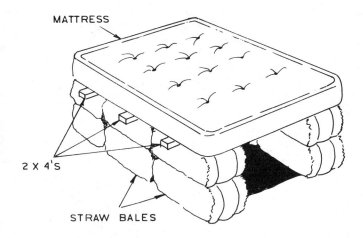

MATTRESS

2 X 4'S

STRAW BALES

Diagram 8. Temporary trap house to protect a trap loader using a hand-operated trap-flinging device. Straw bales and mattress covering are piled over an open pit.

waterproof; furthermore, tar paper or rolled roofing isn't practical, because it will soon be peppered with pellets. That's why we believe roofing is a better alternative. Use heavy-gauge galvanized panels. Allow the panels to overlap each other by 1½ to 2 inches, and nail them to the 2-inch boards, coated afterward on their heads with dabs of roofing tar. If you choose this type of roof, remember to insert plate bolts in concrete-filled holes of your last course of block, as described in project 5.

An 88½-inch sheet of ¾-inch plywood may serve as the door, or you may build one with inch-boards. Hinge it at the bottom, attach a hasp for your padlock, and install sliding bolt locks if you wish.

To test the trap performance for making final adjustments, erect a pole, topped with a "T" bar, 10 feet above the height of the trap arm and 30 feet beyond it. Then send out a dozen clay targets from the trap. The birds should consistently fly over or under the "T" by no more than 2 feet, and drop to the ground 48 to 52 feet from the trap.

If you're not fussy about complying with ATA regulations, a less expensive but still safe trap house can be built with straw bales and old mattresses covering a shoveled-out pit (Diagram 8).

You can add a rifle range dimension to your shooting gallery by hanging up bull's-eyes and ani-

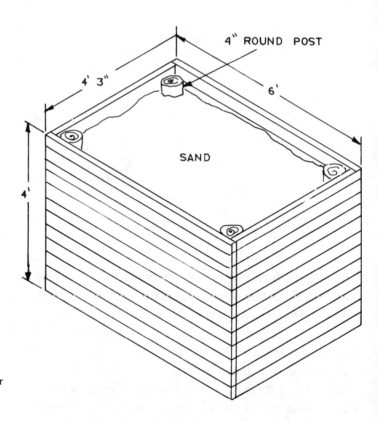

Diagram 9. Simple backstop of 2 x 6's for rifle range.

mal outline targets. But you'll need more than a few bales of straw to stop the high-velocity slugs. Besides a convenient hillside for a background, we recommend a sand-filled box built with 2-inch lumber. This type of backstop is substantial enough to take practice rounds from a .22 pistol or an elephant gun, and it will be in demand for "sighting-in" rifles or scopes as the hunting season approaches (Diagram 9).

Building the backstop is an easy job for saw, hammer, level, spade, wheelbarrow, and posthole digger. Our plan uses finished 2-inch boards, for those who must rely on what's available at discount lumber dealers. However, rough-cut boards are even more suitable—and often cheaper. They can be obtained at a country lumber mill before they're sent through a planer. For framing, 4 x 4's are more convenient to work with than fence posts, but when you have to pry off battered boards for replacement, you'll appreciate the posts. It's your choice.

Bill of Materials

4	4-inch fence posts or 4 x 4's, 66″ long	frame
18	2 x 6's, 72″ long	front, rear
18	2 x 6's, 48″ long	sides
	16d nails	
	sand or dirt	fill
	newsprint or cardboard	targets

The site for your sandbox-backed targets should be on a level spot near the foot of a hill, as extra insurance against an errant slug traveling into the next county. Ideally, there should be no rise or drop in ground level between shooter and target.

Before setting the posts, stake out a 4 x 6-foot area for the box, employing the 3-4-5 carpenter's square method for the corners. Lay a straight 2 x 6 on edge across the length and width of this area and check it with a level. If necessary, shave off some of the sod along the outside outline of the box. Mark a handle of your posthole digger 18 inches up from the tip of the blades. Dig corner holes exactly to that depth (so your backstop box won't appear lopsided), piling dirt inside the rectangle to get a head start on your fill. Drop the posts in the holes and firm them in position by tamping in some of your diggings with the butt of your shovel handle.

The posts must be vertically straight if the 2 x 6's are to meet perfectly at the corners. That's why you should spike them on from the top down. A slight variance in board width may result in a gap at the bottom, but this can be filled with dirt. Working from corner to corner, temporarily nail boards flush with the top of the posts and check them with your level before boarding the rest of the way down the sides. Two nails into each end of a 2 x 6 are sufficient. If you're building this with 4 x 4's instead of

Diagram 10. To make your own animal-outline targets for your rifle-range backstop, photograph these targets on slide film and project them lifesize on pasted-together sheets of cardboard or newspaper. They can then be cut out and used as patterns.

posts, use larger spikes, but allow just enough clearance for a hammer claw under the nailheads.

It doesn't take an artist to draw animal figure outlines to scale; the trick is to photograph the animals on colored slides, and with the aid of a slide projector, trace them life-size on pasted-together sheets of cardboard or newspaper. Or photograph and enlarge the animal outlines that we've provided here (Diagram 10).

A
SPORTSMAN'S
MISCELLANY

5. SMOKEHOUSES

The angler who tosses back all but his trophy-size fish may do so in the name of good sportsmanship, but more than likely there's another reason: his taste for fried fish isn't what it used to be. We made that same discovery about ourselves, but not until our home freezer was half full of wrapped fillets, still months away from the frying pan.

"You should have smoked 'em," an old-timer told me.

The thought intrigued us. We had eaten smoked fish in the past, but only as a delicacy reserved for special festivities. Fancy food that sold for fancy prices. Except for holiday hors d'oeuvres, we left it to the gourmets.

My backwoods friend opened a package of smoke-colored fish slabs and laid them in front of me. "Here," he offered, "try this—it's OK to use your fingers."

I lifted a piece neatly away from the backbone and sampled a bite. The zesty flavor of smoked spiciness surprised my taste buds. A far cry from the oil-soaked morsels that come packed in supermarket tins. A bit on the dry side, but just the right snack to go with a bottle of beer.

"What kind of fish is this?" I asked, reaching hungrily for more.

"Suckers," he replied proudly. "I smoked 'em myself last spring."

It was hard to believe that smoking could make a trash fish such good eating. Gorging myself, I decided to build my own smokehouse—not just for an occasional treat of smoked suckers, but to add a taste variety to the rest of the assorted fish and game in our diet.

There's hardly an item on a sportsman's menu—from catfish to salmon, from oyster to pheasant—that can't be enhanced with the proper amount of smoking. Besides that, smoking is a cheap preservative (before refrigeration, the only one), which works as well for venison jerky as it does for curing the hams and bacon from a wild boar. The trick is to give the meat enough smoke, but not too much. Enough will prevent spoilage; too much will shrink the meat to a dehydrated, inedible char. A successful smoking process calls for the right kind of wood (which we'll tell you about later) and a well-designed unit to provide sufficient smoke with a minimum of heat.

Several models—from campsite-crude to backyard-sophisticated—will fill the bill. And where antipollution laws prohibit the sweet-smelling smoke, there are portable styles as well.

Let's start with the primitive Indian-style model. It's ideal for preserving dressed fish and game over long outings in remote areas, where it's impossible to keep meat by chilling it. You can fashion this smoking device as the Indians did—with a tomahawk and your bare hands. Or you can make it easier on yourself with the aid of three common woodsman's tools—an ax or hatchet, a small bow saw, and a shovel—and complete the entire project in less than 4 hours.

Begin by digging a shovel-width trench about 3 feet long and 3 feet deep on one end, rising to 2 feet deep on the other. While digging, pile the sods along one side of the trench for use later. If you want to smoke-cure your meat without cooking it at the same time, make this trench 6 feet long. This ditch will be your smoke passage. At the lower end of it, dig a 2-foot-diameter hole. This will be your firebox. At the higher end of the trench, dig a 4-foot-square hole, level with the bottom of the smoke passage. The second hole, tapered slightly to the bottom, will be your smoking chamber (Diagram 1).

After digging the square hole, you must furnish it with shelving to hold the meat and allow smoke to circulate. Sticking with the primitive method, cut 6-inch-diameter logs, each 4 feet long, tiered to within 1 or 2 inches from the top of both sides of the hole. Then pound in 2 stakes on each side to secure the logs against the walls, and to make sure the logs will fit the opening.

Now you should decide if you want 1 or 2 shelves. For a single-shelf smoking chamber, lift out all but 1 or 2 of the logs from behind their holding stakes. Then place a row of straight, inch-thick green saplings, spaced across the span between the logs. You'll need about 20 of these 4-foot-long saplings, to provide smoke circulation room between each. Arrange them roughly that way, and lower the other logs back into position to secure the saplings while you do a more even job of spacing. Roll 5-foot logs across the top of the hole and brace them securely with stakes.

For a larger-capacity, double-shelf arrangement, remember to provide smoke circulation space between the top shelf and the meat or fish slabs on the bottom shelf. Also there must be clearance between the meat on the top shelf and the layer of logs covering the chamber. And to avoid tearing up the top shelf to get at the bottom one, make the top one narrower (Diagram 2).

To cover the smoke passage, lay a framework of branches across the trench and top them off with your sods.

Now for the firebox. The object of a smoke-

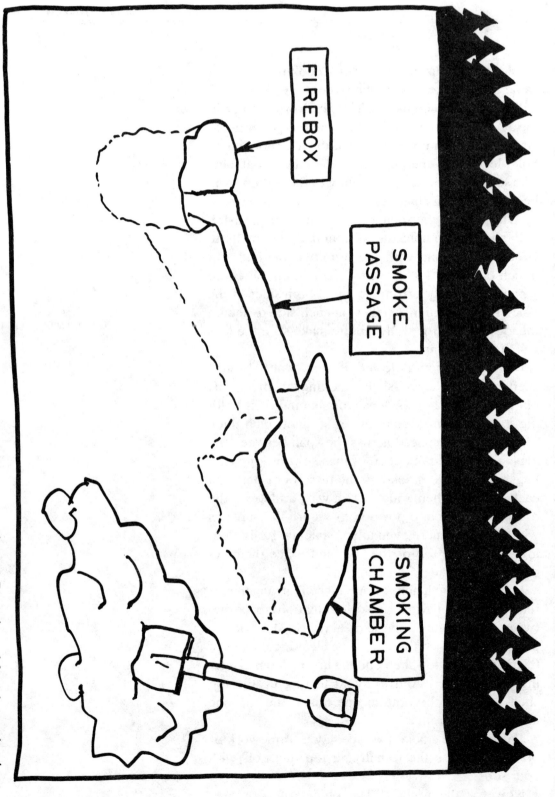

FIREBOX

SMOKE PASSAGE

SMOKING CHAMBER

Diagram 1. Excavation work for underground smoker.

5-FT.-LONG LOGS
COVER HOLE

GREEN
SAPLING
SHELF

4-FT. LOGS LINE
TWO SIDES

STAKES
HOLD
LOGS

ALTERNATE TWO-
SHELF SYSTEM

Diagram 2. Cutaway drawing of log-covered smoking chamber and meat rack. Ideally, you should use the same wood for construction that you use for burning.

Our concrete block smokehouse is built into the side of a small hill. Entrance to the basement level fire pit is at the rear.

house's wood-burning system is threefold: (1) to allow just enough draft intake to keep a fire smoldering or barely flickering, but not roaring; (2) to provide enough ventilation for heat escape, while retaining as much smoke as possible; and (3) to minimize heat in the smoking chamber (unless you plan to cook the meat or fish). The sod-covered trench, serving as a kind of horizontal chimney, will dissipate enough heat to deliver low-temperature smoke. However, to force the smoke into the trench in the first place, you must cover all or most of the firebox. Indians did this with a dampened hide, which doubled for sending smoke signals. You'll do just as well with a basketlike lid of lashed-together saplings covered with sod. Or bring along the metal cover from a discarded trash can.

My friend's smokehouse, much more elaborate, comes complete with baffle and weathertight door. And like most things built to last, it took more time to construct than our temporary backwoods model. When not in use for smoking, it's a multipurpose outbuilding that won't mar the landscape around the weekend cabin. Since this smokehouse is considered a permanent structure, it may require a building permit. If so, show the plans in this book to your building inspector. Although most of this smokehouse project is concrete work, you don't need a cement mason's union card to tackle the job.

Bill of Materials

    5 bags of portland cement
    1 bag of masonry cement
  1½ cu. yds. of foundation-mix gravel
    1 cu. yd. of coarse sand
143 8-inch concrete blocks
 56 8-inch corner blocks (flat on one end)
  9 8-inch concrete half blocks (flat on one end)
 48 firebricks
  6 half firebricks

2 reinforcement rods, ³/₈ by 24"
1 8 x 8" cleanout door

6	2 x 4's, 51" long	rafters
2	2 x 8's, 72" long	side plates
2	2 x 8's, 57" long	front, rear plates
2	2 x 4's, 64" long	doorjambs
6	2 x 4's, 56" long	furring strips

¹/₂" A-D exterior-grade plywood:

2	36 x 72" triangles	gable ends
2	48 x 63"	roof
2	15 x 48"	roof
1	48 x 96"	roof
4	2 x 4's, 13¹/₂" long	floor form
2	2 x 4's, 56" long	floor form
11	1 x 6's, 56" long	floor form

8d nails
16d nails
¹/₂" roofing nails
tar paper
rolled roofing
roofing tar
2 heavy-duty door hinges, with flathead screws
3 furnance registers (about 12" wide)
8 ³/₈" L-shaped bolts, with nuts and washers
20 ³/₈ x 4" headless anchor bolts, with nuts and washers
4 ³/₁₆" roundhead wood screws
¹/₄" staples

For concrete work, you'll need: shovel, wheelbarrow, hoe, ball of string, level, trowel, jointer, stepladder, and chalk. For the carpentry: hammer, circular saw or crosscut handsaw, keyhole saw or saber saw, combination square, screwdriver, linoleum knife, electric drill, and stapler.

The project begins with the footing. Made of poured concrete, this will be the base for your building blocks. Your footing should be approximately 76 inches square (allowing for a foundation that's slightly larger than your building dimensions), so dig

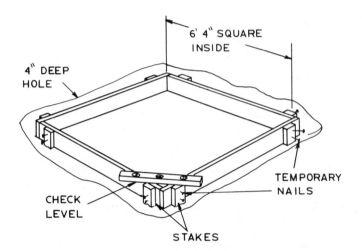

Diagram 3. Building the form for the slab floor of our concrete block smokehouse. Keep your level handy.

a hole about 7 feet square and about 4 inches deep. This will hold a slab of poured concrete as shown in Diagram 3.

Although the footing doesn't have to be perfectly square, it should be level. With 1 x 4 boards (which may be reused for other projects), build a staked frame for your footing. Pound in a corner stake until the footing boards touch the bottom of the hole. Then begin tapping at the other stakes until your level registers a true reading across each corner. Once your form has passed the level inspection, shovel dirt against the outside of the footing boards. This will prevent poured concrete from oozing under the boards.

Before mixing your first batch of concrete, be sure there's enough time left in the day to mix and pour about 7 or 8 wheelbarrow loads of the stuff. And postpone the mixing if the overnight weather forecast calls for below-freezing temperatures. The standard 6-to-1 (gravel-to-cement) formula for making concrete allows enough margin of error for the ingredients to be rough-measured with a shovel. But to avoid waste from spillage, don't heap your shovel during mixing. Another waste-prevention tip: In handling powdered cement, lay the unopened bag on its back, then open it with several stabs of your shovel point. And another: Keep your other ingredients—coarse sand (for mortar) and gravel—piled neatly on tarps or large sheets of cardboard.

After shoveling a total of 12 parts gravel and 2 parts portland cement into the wheelbarrow, mix with a hoe. Then add water, a little at a time, and continue mixing until the mass reaches the right consistency. If the concrete is too soupy to be lifted out with a shovel, mix in small amounts of cement and sand. The right mixture, not too watery, will slide easily out of your wheelbarrow and pour neatly into the form.

When you've filled the form, pick up a straight 2 x 4 and work it back and forth across the top of the footing boards to even off the poured concrete. This is called striking. With all 4 sides and corners struck off, stand guard over your work for an hour or so, because concrete and wet paint offer the same temptation to onlookers. Then cover the hardening concrete with weighted strips of cardboard. This will protect the fresh surface from footprints and windblown debris during the overnight "curing" period. Also, don't forget to rinse the concrete "mud" off such tools as your shovel, hoe, wheelbarrow, and striking board.

You're about to try your hand at laying block (Diagram 4). If this causes you some anxiety, tell

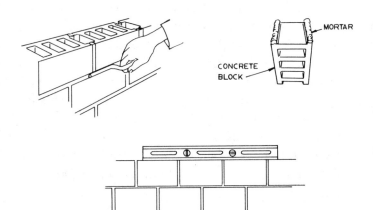

Diagram 4. Block-laying steps include "buttering" the ends with mortar, using a jointer tool to clean excess mortar from the joints, and continual level checking.

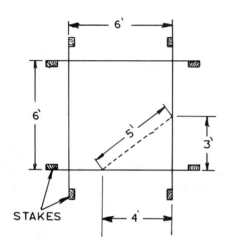

Diagram 5. Squaring the chalk line. Measure 3 feet down one side, 4 feet down the other, and the diagonal measurement across the corner should be 5 feet.

Diagram 6. Block course for first layer of fire-pit level.

yourself that the job isn't as difficult as it looks, and that by doing your own work, you'll save more than $100 in skilled labor cost—assuming you could find a mason who'd be willing to contract such a measly job. The main difference between working with these building blocks and the ones you played with as a child is that now you'll be cementing them with mortar. And because it won't be easy to knock down your blocks and start over, you must take extra care to keep your walls and corners straight, and your blocks level.

Set up a string guide, staked about 2 inches above the slab, with dimensions exactly 6 x 6 feet. If your measurement isn't square, you'll wind up with a trapezoid-shaped foundation with walls that don't join properly at the corners. A simple, foolproof trick will give you square corners; it's called the "3-4-5 carpenter's square." At each corner, measure 3 feet down one side and 4 feet down the other. The diagonal measurement between these points should be exactly 5 feet (Diagram 5).

You'll use the string guide to make a chalk line. Rub chalk into the bottom of the string, then snap the string against the concrete. The result: straight lines from one corner to the next—a sure guide for positioning your blocks. The first course, laid with the blocks along the inside of the chalk line, should follow Diagram 6.

To anchor your first course of blocks, you must cement them to the footing with a special mortar mixture. The formula is 3 parts sand and 1 part masonry cement. Mix only a small batch at one time so it won't harden in your wheelbarrow before you have a chance to use all of it. Add water sparingly, because a mortar mix should be thicker than a footing mix. "Mud" of the right consistency will cling to your trowel or block when you tilt it. Slop some of this mud on a piece of scrap plywood about 18 inches wide.

Beginning at one corner with your trowel, spread mortar about ¹/₂ inch thick in a rectangular outline that matches the bottom of your first block. Firm the block into position and, with your level resting on top of the block, tap the block with the butt of your trowel handle until the bubble registers a level reading from end to end and side to side. Scrape the excess mortar away from the bottom of the block—lightly—and use it to help make a mortar base for your next block. Before setting the second block in place, spread mortar on its end to cement it to the first block. Repeat the mortaring, placement, and leveling steps until the first course of blocks is completed. Your second course (Diagram 7) should include a half block at the rear to provide an opening for the clean-out door (for access to the firebox).

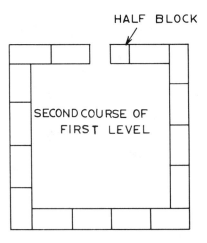

HALF BLOCK

SECOND COURSE OF FIRST LEVEL

Diagram 7. Block course for second layer of fire-pit level. Note 8-inch opening for the clean-out door.

Before laying the third course of blocks, scrape out the mortar joints with a jointer. And when you place the block over the hole for your clean-out door, prop it level with a scrap of wood about 8 inches high. Let the third-course mortar set overnight before your next step: building the fire pit (Diagram 8).

On your slab floor, scratch a pencil mark in line with the center of the clean-out door opening. Then make pencil marks exactly 12 inches on each side of this center mark. Using your carpenter's square at these 2 outside marks, draw 2 straight lines on the floor, perpendicular to the wall, and exactly 32 inches long. Now draw another straight line, joining the 2 ends. This will be your guide for the outside walls of firebrick.

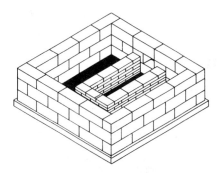

Diagram 8. Building the fire pit inside the basement of the smokehouse.

Mix another batch of mortar and begin laying the firebrick, using mortar at the base of the bricks, between joints, and against the concrete block wall.

Lay a third course of bricks as you did the first one, a fourth course like the second one, and so on until 6 courses are completed. Let the mortar joints set overnight.

While your firebox doesn't need a top, the concrete blocks that surround it need a ceiling. Of course, this ceiling also will serve as the floor of your smoking chamber. This calls for pouring another slab of 6-to-1 concrete mix.

Scrap lumber will come in handy for a temporary floor under this slab. Lay out enough inch-boards to fit snugly against the 4 inside walls. Boards should be cut 56 inches long to cover the span between walls—but double-check both measurements. If you're using 1 x 6's, for example, you may have to rip ½ inch or so off one of the boards. Your main concern here is to guard against gaps between wood and wall, which would let the poured concrete escape. These form boards must be supported by a temporary frame of 2 x 4's: four 13½-inch verticals at the corners, holding up two 56-inch boards that run along 2 of the walls. Tie a rope to the bottom of each vertical 2 x 4, and draw the end of it out the clean-out door opening (so you may collapse the wood form by tugging on the rope).

By following Diagram 9 you'll notice that the inch-boards are about ¼ inch lower than the top of the concrete blocks. This provides for a lip over the inside edge of the block walls.

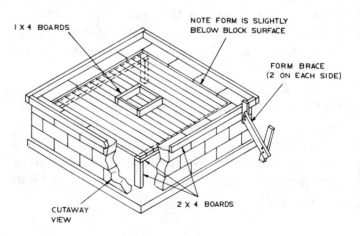

1 X 4 BOARDS

NOTE FORM IS SLIGHTLY BELOW BLOCK SURFACE

FORM BRACE (2 ON EACH SIDE)

2 X 4 BOARDS

CUTAWAY VIEW

Diagram 9. Building the form for the slab floor of the smoking chamber. Note the center form to provide an opening for the floor baffle.

To keep the poured concrete from spilling over the sides, you'll have to build a holding form flush with the outside edge of the block wall. This part can be tricky, and there are several ways of doing it. Our method was to take a temporary frame of 2 x 4's, and support it with scrap 2 x 4's, which we nailed to ground stakes—2 supports on each wall. The wall of this form has to be level, because when this second slab hardens, it will serve as the base for the next course of blocks. But before pouring concrete, remember that now is the time to make room for your baffle. Use 4-inch scrap boards to build a frame that matches the inside dimensions of one of your furnace registers, and tack the frame (nailed lightly from inside) near the center of the temporary floor. Finally, lay your 2 reinforcement rods on the temporary floor between the baffle and doorway.

After all supports and framing is in place, you'll need a platform for mixing and pouring concrete. Stack your still-to-be-used blocks beside one wall. Now the procedure is the same as for the footing: Pour the concrete, strike it, rinse off your equipment, and cover the hardening concrete for the night. To dismantle the form next morning, pull on the tie rope. Then fish out the collapsed boards by reaching through the clean-out and baffle openings. Remove the baffle form and drop the furnace register in its place.

Now you're ready to lay up blocks for the second story (smoking chamber) of the smokehouse, making room for a doorway into the smoking chamber (Diagrams 10 and 11). At this point, begin telling yourself not to forget the bolts for your 2 x 4 doorjambs! On each side of the doorway opening, embed four 4-inch anchor bolts into the mortar between the blocks.

In addition, you'll need to provide for shelving that goes across the doorway. Embed 4-inch anchor bolts between the joints of the 2 facing side walls. These bolts (protruding about 2 inches from the

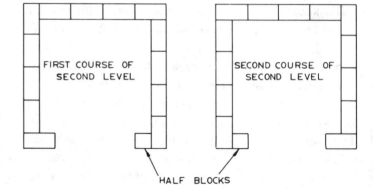

FIRST COURSE OF SECOND LEVEL

SECOND COURSE OF SECOND LEVEL

HALF BLOCKS

Diagram 10. First block layer for doorway opening above slab floor.

Diagram 11. Even-numbered layers of block for the smoking chamber have half blocks on opposite side of doorway.

mortar joints) will hold 2 x 4's, or furring strips, which in turn will support smoking racks in the chamber.

Take your time with this masonry work. It's more important to keep your walls level and square, to remember to embed your bolts, and to guard against falling off your stepladder, than to finish the job in 1 day. And when you have a few dabs of mud left over from a batch of mortar, use it to cement your clean-out door into the fire-pit opening. Your eighth course should include L-shaped plate bolts. Fill block holes with mortar and embed the bolts with about 2 inches showing above the concrete.

Now that your brief career as a block layer is over, it's time for hammer and nails. And you don't have to wear a union button in your cap to do the carpentry either. In fact, measurements are far less critical, because a smokehouse needs a few cracks in the woodwork for the smoke to escape. The more pains you take "for looks," the more you'll be disappointed when the looks are ruined from smoking your first batch of meat.

Once the mortar sets, the bolts on top will help anchor 2 x 8's, or "plates," for the roof. Begin with the 2 plates for the side walls. Mark each board for drilling by placing it on top of the bolts, in line with the outside edge and both ends of the wall, and strike the board with a hammer. Drill the $3/8$-inch

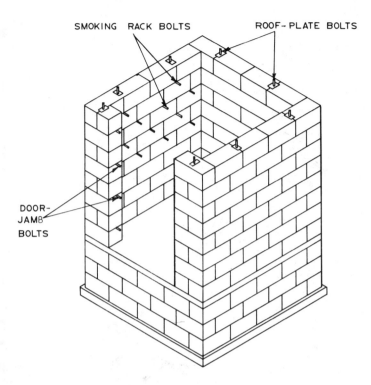

SMOKING RACK BOLTS   ROOF-PLATE BOLTS

DOOR-
JAMB
BOLTS

Diagram 12. Placing bolts in the mortar. Top bolts will secure 2 x 6 plates. Inside-wall bolts will anchor furring strips to support angle-iron racks, and 2-inch boards for doorjambs.

holes and secure the plates with nuts and washers. Do the same with the front and rear plates. Door-jambs next: Fit a 2 x 4 on one side of the doorway and hit it with a hammer against the bolts. The nuts should fit flush with the wood, so countersink the holes. Complete the frame by pounding spikes from the front plate into the top of the doorjambs (Diagram 12).

Next, saw off each end of six 51-inch 2 x 4's at 45-degree angles. Use a combination square to mark the wood for your cuts. These are the rafters for your gable roof, to be joined on each end and in the middle of your side plates. To hold your rafters straight for nailing, tack a board temporarily across the center of the 3 rafters on one side of the roof. Then nail plywood panels to the other side, remove the brace, and finish the roof (Diagram 13).

Sealing the roof is the easy part of this project. Use the linoleum knife to cut lengths of tar paper to

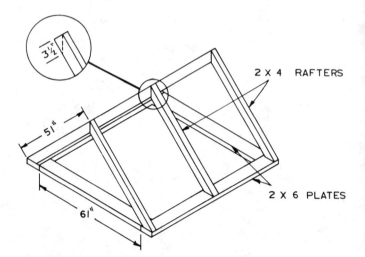

2 X 4 RAFTERS

2 X 6 PLATES

Diagram 13. Framing the smokehouse roof.

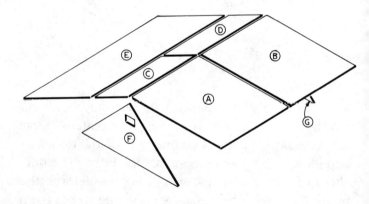

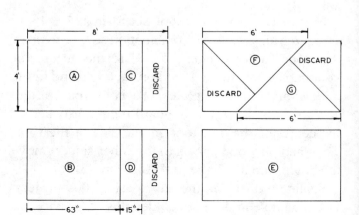

Diagram 14. Cutting plywood for roofing the gable panels of the smokehouse.

cover the roof—up one side and down the other, with considerable overlapping in the center. Space your roofing nails or staples about a foot apart on the bottom, side, and seam edges. Cut lengths of rolled roofing *across* the roof. Line up a strip with the bottom edge of a plywood panel and nail it over the tar paper on the side and bottom edges only, about 4 inches apart. Brush roofing tar along the top edge of this roofing strip before nailing on the second one, which should overlap the first by an inch or 2. Again, nail only the side and bottom edges of the roofing strip. Do the same on the other side of the roof. Center the last sheet over the ridge, to overlap the roofing on both sides, and nail it down completely. Remember to brush tar under each seam.

Now for your gable ends. If you choose tongue-in-groove boards instead of plywood, the most reliable way to fit them is to mark each board for sawing as you nail them up to the peak. But if you're using large triangles cut from plywood (Diagram 14), it will be easier now to install your "chimneys"—the other 2 furnace registers. Although the lip of the register allows some margin of error in measurement, there shouldn't be any if you hold the underside of the register against the siding and outline it with a pencil. Drill a hole *inside* one corner of the outline and use a keyhole saw to cut out the rest of it. Saw with gentle, even strokes to avoid cracking the wood. After you've cut out both openings, drill holes in the rim of each register—one in the middle of each side. Put each register in place and mark holes in the wood to line up with those you drilled in the lip edges of the registers. Screw the registers in place, then enclose the gable ends (Diagram 15).

Only the door remains, and you have several options. Most of us handy sportsmen have learned to be as keen-eyed for useful junk as we are for the flash of a whitetail. So we wouldn't bypass something as valuable as a discarded door. It's a matter of cutting down the door to fit the doorway, and

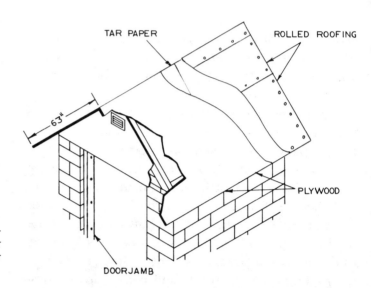

Diagram 15. Cutaway view of roof and gable covering. After smoke exhaust register and doorjambs are installed, it's time for hanging the door.

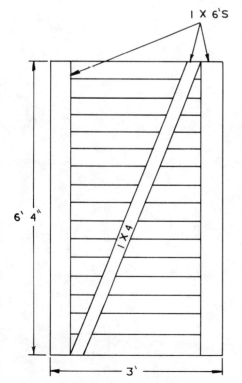

Diagram 16. Basic construction of the smokehouse door.

screwing on the hinges. If you're not blessed with such a find, you can build a door with inch-boards or plywood. Our plan (Diagram 16) uses 1 x 6 cross members nailed to 1 x 6 vertical framing, and a 1 x 4 diagonal brace. As you're nailing the boards together, check occasionally for square corners.

And you've finished.

This permanent smokehouse is for the sportsman whose investment in the outdoor life includes his own backwoods retreat; but a weekend sportsman who starts building one in his suburban backyard might well face a stop-work order. Antipollution laws in and around large cities frown on smoke-producing devices. In that case, a portable smokehouse is the answer. You can operate it on location, whether it be at a rented lakeside cabin, a campsite, or a friend's country place, where antipollution laws aren't so restrictive. And between uses, it stores easily in the garage or on the back porch.

The most popular portable smokehouse is made from a discarded refrigerator. You can find one at a dump or junkyard and adapt it with a few hours of work. The old, latch-type refrigerators are most easily modified. However, if yours is old enough to qualify as a true icebox, you'd be better off to keep it intact or sell it as an antique. If you can lay your hands on an old electric box, strike a blow for child safety by removing the latch mechanism. Later, you can keep the door closed during smoking by wiring or roping it shut, or by setting it on a slight uphill angle so gravity closes it.

The next step, tearing out the rubber seals, may provide enough intake and ventilation for the smoking process.

Check out the interior. You'll have to remove all the shelves and braces. For one thing, the shelves wouldn't be strong enough, if heated, to hold a load of meat. For another, I'm told that some shelf coating gives off noxious fumes at high temperatures. Even though appliance manufacturers may deny this, it's not worth the risk. Remove all plastics and glass, too. If yours is a newer model with the freezer compartment across the top, cut a hole in the bottom of it—large enough for a good-sized grate from an oven or charcoal grill.

Once you've stripped your refrigerator, you're on your own. Because discarded ones don't come in a standard size, there's no way we can diagram the modifications you'll have to make. But we can give you these guidelines:

This smokehouse, made from a discarded refrigerator, has cured and flavored fish for more than 30 years. The smoke is delivered from sawdust and shavings that smolder over a hot plate—all housed in an old brake drum covered with a loose-fitting lid.

1. The bottom of the refrigerator, since it may be your fire pit, should be lined with an inch or 2 of sand (not dirt) so coals won't burn through the metal.
2. Decide how many shelves you want: 2 at least; 3 at most. For each shelf, drill 3 holes in both sides of the refrigerator (or use the ones that remain after stripping). Before drilling, of course, measure up from the bottom so the facing holes are straight across from each other. Pound on the sides of the box to loosen insulation. Plug in your wife's vacuum

cleaner, and stick the nozzle against the holes to suck out any free insulation particles—an nth-degree safety measure. Join the facing holes by bending the ends of 9-gauge wire into one hole, then into the corresponding one on the other side. Three strands of wire—or reinforcement rod—for each shelf frame will hold racks for smoking meat.

3. Installing meat racks is easy. Either borrow the grills from your charcoal burners or your wife's oven. Or keep your eyes peeled for throwaways. Scrub the grills with cleanser and set them on the frames.

These guidelines may be all you need for converting an old-fashioned refrigerator, or you may not be lucky enough to get by with them. So test out the refrigerator-turned-smokehouse to determine if its income-outgo draft is balanced enough to keep the wood smoldering, but not blazing. It's possible, however, that your combination fire pit and smoking chamber will either smother the fire or build up the kind of smoke and heat pressure that could blow the door off!

If your draft is too anemic—or too powerful—to support a steady, smoldering fire, you'll have to pipe in the smoke from an outside source: the handy sportsman's stove described in project 6. Then buy enough 3-inch stovepipe joints to aim the pipe into the bottom of the refrigerator storage space.

Now put on a pair of cheap gloves and pull out the insulation that's packed inside the refrigerator wall. Remove as many gobs of the itchy stuff as you can reach, then insert a vacuum cleaner nozzle to suck out any loose particles.

If you need to vent the refrigerator, a small furnace register is the best device, because its lever will allow you to regulate the smoke exhaust. Cut a square hole to match the inside dimensions of the register, so its lip edges rest over the top of the hole.

Then cut a corresponding hole in the ceiling of the refrigerator. Again, carefully and thoroughly clean out the packed insulation. A register also may be attached to the side of an older, dome-topped model, using sheet metal screws.

Give the interior a final once-over with the vacuum cleaner, then a thorough scrubbing. Leave the door open for air drying.

About the smoking process: Choice of wood is important. Best types for smoke-flavoring are maple, cherry, apple, hickory, and hackberry. Select smaller pieces, less than 3 inches in diameter, unsplit if possible. Wood should age about 6 weeks before burning. If the wood is too dry, it may burn too fast without enough smoke. Too wet, or green, and the fire may die out. If you don't have time to wait for aging, split green wood into thin pieces. Meat can rest on racks during smoking; fish can be hung up, tail down, on home-fabricated wire ''S''-hooks (Diagram 17).

How long to smoke? It varies according to kind of meat and personal taste. Also, smaller hunks of

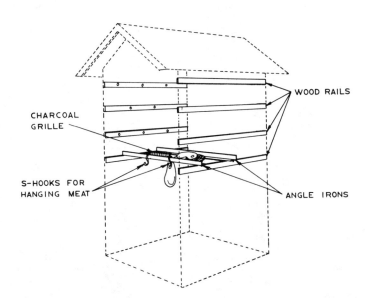

CHARCOAL
GRILLE

WOOD RAILS

S-HOOKS FOR
HANGING MEAT

ANGLE IRONS

Diagram 17. After bolting furring strips to inside-wall anchor bolts, lay angle irons across to fit the width of meat racks. Hang fish with tails down. Paint bucket is converted to a heater with a draft opening at the bottom and a 4-to-3 inch reducer attached to the top vent.

meat require less smoke than larger ones. If you want to *cook* the meat as well as smoke-preserve it, you don't have to be so concerned about separating heat from smoke. Start with a 2-hour smoking period and sample the results. If you want a sharper flavor, add spices to a salt brine for soaking overnight before smoking begins, and smoke the meat longer. Ten hours is maximum smoking time. Meat smoked a minimum of 2 hours will keep at least 3 times as long as unsmoked, refrigerated meat. One smoked meat enthusiast occasionally nibbles from a jar of beef jerky which he claims to have smoked more than 10 years ago. He's also known for his fish stories.

6. SPORTSMAN'S STOVE

Chilly mornings beside the trout stream, frosty nights in the woods, and frigid afternoons on the lake ice have made more *in*doorsmen than *out*doorsmen. But there's an inexpensive way to warm your bones without bundling yourself in costly goose down or pouring precious fuel into a gas-guzzling heater. Our answer is a homemade sportsman's stove. Furnishing the benefits of an inside campfire, it's more powerful than a catalytic heater, and far cheaper to operate than the cooking jets of a propane burner. Once fired up, it can throw heat like a potbelly and fry your eggs at the same time. Because it's vented, you can use it to heat the pickup camper (project 20) and the ice-fishing shack (project 12). It also can deliver smoke to the refrigerator smokehouse (project 18).

We built our model from an empty 5-gallon paint bucket. Our petty cash outlay covered stovepipe fittings and a few dabs of furnace cement. In setting aside the bucket for your stove, don't throw away its lid. Besides covering your fire for a safe heat and proper draft, this lid will be your stove's cooktop.

The only tools required for the project are an electric drill (or hammer and spike), a reciprocating saw with metal-cutting blade (or tinsnips), pliers, a screwdriver, and possibly a rounded file. With these

Paint bucket is converted to a heater with a draft opening at the bottom and a 4- to 3-inch reducer attached to top vent.

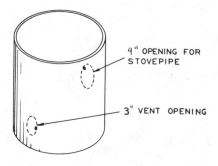

4" OPENING FOR STOVEPIPE

3" VENT OPENING

Diagram 1. Cutting draft openings for the bottom draft and 4-to-3-inch stovepipe reducer near the top. The top cutout may be hinged over the smaller bottom hole to regulate draft.

implements and an hour or so of your time, your finished product should resemble the one in our photograph.

Bill of Materials

5-gallon paint or tar bucket
stovepipe fittings:
3 3" elbows
4-to-3" reducer
3" stovepipe*
sheet metal screws
furnace cement
heavy-gauge wire
2 x 2 block

* Length of pipe will depend on distance from stove opening to outside vent.

Before beginning your metalwork, scour the lid and inside of the bucket. While they dry, use your pliers to bend out the metal lips which secured the lid to the bucket. With a 1/4-inch drill bit or spike, make 2 holes in the bucket: one about 2 inches from the bottom, and the other, across the diameter of the bucket, about 2 inches from the top. These punctures will allow you to insert your saw blade or tinsnips for cutting openings in the bucket. Mark a 4-inch-diameter circle for the top opening, and a 3-inch-diameter circle for the one at the bottom. Your punctures should be on the *inside edge* of the circular markings (Diagram 1), so they won't show after the cuts are made.

Cut out the bottom opening first. This doesn't have to be a perfect incision, but it will be good practice for cutting the top opening. If you stray from your cutting line, make your cutting mistake inside the circle, if possible, because this error can be corrected with a file. When you're pleased with the way the 4-to-3-inch stovepipe reducer fits into the top opening (snug, with minimum air space around the pipe), remove the reducer so you won't dent it while you are finishing the work on the bottom intake draft.

To cover the bottom opening for controlling the intake of the draft, use the 4-inch piece of metal which you cut out for the stovepipe opening. Drill a $1/32$- or $1/16$-inch hole about $1/2$ inch above the bottom opening. Then attach the piece with a sheet metal screw. Make sure the screw is holding it firmly enough for the piece to stay in place as you vary the size of the draft opening.

Next, replace the stovepipe reducer. To attach it permanently, you have at least 3 options: hire a welder to braze it for you, or cut slits in the 4-inch end which can be bent outward against the inside wall of the bucket, or join the collar of the reducer with sheet metal screws. If you choose either of the last 2 methods, seal the joint with furnace cement and let it harden overnight. The third method, by the way, would position most of the 4-inch section of the reducer inside the bucket, so you may want to cut off the excess with tinsnips before sealing the joint with cement.

Line the bottom of the bucket with about 2 inches of sand (not dirt), and your little furnace is ready for test firing. Make this first blaze a small one, to familiarize yourself with the draft control, to "set" the furnace cement properly, and to burn the paint off the outside of the bucket. We've attached a lid handle with heavy-gauge wire and a 2 x 2 block.

Directions for installing your heater vary according to the height of your fishing shack or camper. The smokestack, which can be taken apart between outings, should include 6 basic sections: an elbow from the reducer, enough straight lengths of stovepipe to line up with the bottom of the outside vent opening, another elbow, then a length of pipe through that opening to a third elbow, and enough straight pipe to extend at least a foot above the highest point of the roof (to prevent downdrafts). We favor galvanized pipe for venting this heater, since the stove will be subjected to outdoor elements.

For safety's sake, the section of hot stovepipe that passes through the outside wall opening shouldn't come in contact with wood. A simple way to avoid this is to cut a square out of the wall, then cut a square piece of sheet metal to cover it. Cut a 3-inch opening in the metal to accommodate the stovepipe, and attach this galvanized square to the wall with sheet metal screws.

We'll admit that this little heater, compared with a campfire, may get poor marks for aesthetics; but we give it high marks for efficiency.

7. SNOWSHOES

Snowmobiles have been a boon to thousands of winter sportsmen, but there are situations when it's better to leave these motorized skis behind. Their noise and fumes will spoil a trapline and drive a hunter's quarry well out of range. Sure, a snowmobile can take you into the wintry woods in a hurry, but the only thing remaining when you get there will be the view!

That's why some wilderness areas are closed to powered vehicles. So if you're the kind of naturalist who wants to get around in knee-deep powder without spooking the wildlife—or if you need a way out of the woods when your machine breaks down—consider snowshoes. You don't have to be an Eskimo to own a pair.

We've developed 2 patterns of snowshoes for the do-it-yourselfer, including plans for a permanent, workshop-made set. We'll start with directions for a temporary pair which can be assembled around the campfire. Although this pair is intended for short-term emergency use, you might be interested in making it anyway, to see if you like this method of snow travel before you tool up for our heavy-duty snowshoes.

Our short-life snowshoes are made from saplings about an inch in diameter. We recommend super-

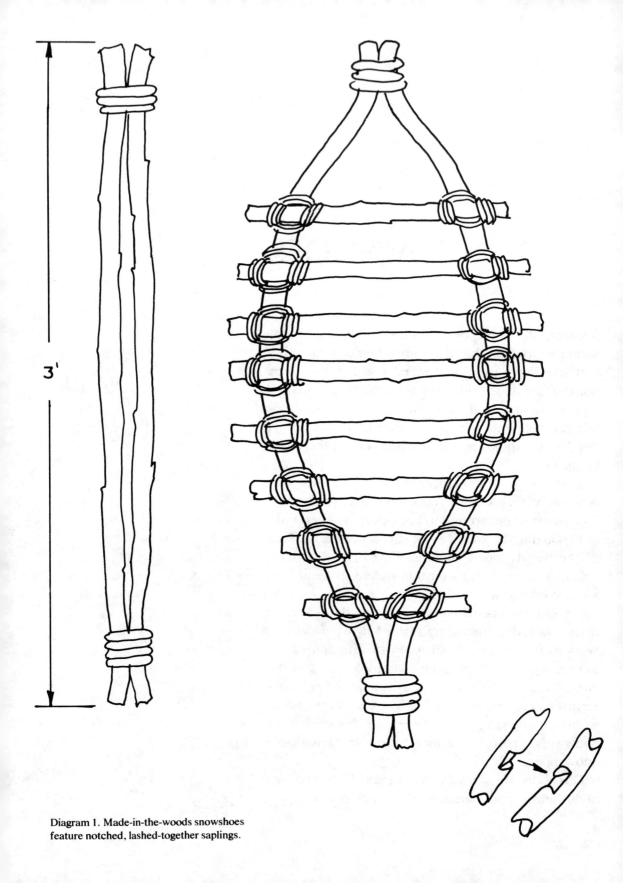

3'

Diagram 1. Made-in-the-woods snowshoes
feature notched, lashed-together saplings.

bendable willow for this work, but alder, aspen, or in a pinch, most other types of "green" wood will do. Cut two 3-foot saplings and lash them together at both ends, using fine wire or fishline. To prevent the lashed joints from slipping, notch the wood before wrapping them tightly with cord. This will be the outside frame. Spread the saplings apart and place your boot inside to get an idea where you'll be setting the tip of your foot. Mark the saplings for cutting flat, inch-long, $1/8$-inch-deep notches. In the workshop, a saw and chisel will do the job faster.

Cut a 1-foot length from another sapling and notch it about $1/2$ inch from each end. These notches should fit those of the long frame like the joints of a log cabin. Lash one end of the shorter piece to a longer one. Spread the longer saplings apart and lash the other side. Without the aid of a third hand, you can accomplish this by propping the frame open with a bent knee or a forked sapling. Reinforce this stress point by lashing saplings above and below it. Preparatory notching isn't necessary for these 2 saplings.

When the 3 saplings are tied on, place your foot into the frame, slip a shorter sapling under your heel, and mark the points where it intersects the outside frame. Again, notch the frame and sapling for a perfect fit, lash the 2 joints, and tie on reinforcement saplings above and below (Diagram 1).

Cut more saplings to span the gaps in the snowshoe and lash them on at intervals 2 inches apart. Wrap a strip of burlap or canvas around the snowshoe, directly beneath where your boot will ride, and sew the ends together with the seam on top. As it goes with other projects, making the second one will be easier. Bind the snowshoes to your feet with the rope-lacing technique described in Diagram 2.

After you've stepped out in this pair, you'll discover the shortcomings of made-in-the-woods snowshoes. As your legs tire, the toe ends will begin

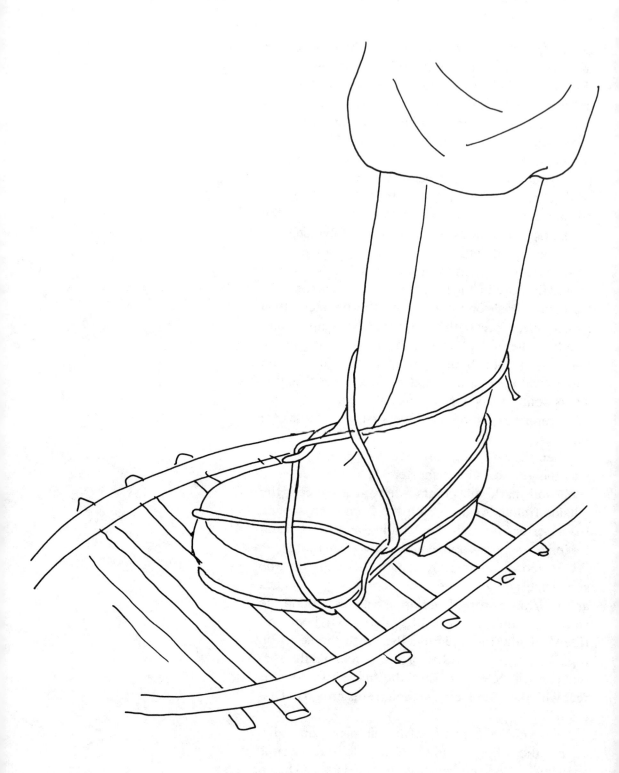

Diagram 2. Over-the-boot lacing technique for snowshoe bindings.

digging into the snow. And while these shoes may get you in and out of the woods more than once, it's a cinch they won't last forever. Saplings are usually strong enough to hold you initially, but the high moisture content that makes them limber also makes them heavy. Worse yet, when they lose their sap, the brittle limbs are good for little more than kindling.

As simple as our metal-frame showshoes may appear, this project probably is the most complex one we offer in this book. The degree of difficulty, however, will depend on whether you can master the art of tying our macrame square knot, and whether you know a friendly electrician who will help you shape the conduit. Besides a $\frac{1}{2}$-inch conduit bender (which we rented for 50 cents from the hardware store that sold us the conduit), you'll be working with the following tools: hammer, center punch, electric drill, brace and bit, crosscut saw, plane, wood rasp, fine sandpaper, screwdriver, adjustable wrench, and possibly a $\frac{3}{4}$-inch rat-tail file.

Bill of Materials

2	10' lengths of $\frac{1}{2}''$ thin-wall conduit	frames
2	$\frac{3}{16}$ x $\frac{3}{4}''$ brass bolts	rear joints
	1$\frac{5}{16}''$ dowel rods or $\frac{1}{2}''$ scrap boards	crossbars
8	$\frac{1}{8}$ x 1$\frac{1}{2}''$ brass screws	
	120' of $\frac{1}{4}$-inch rope	
	(cut in four 30' lengths)	webbing
	Liquid Nails or other waterproof glue	
	waterproof varnish	

Thin-wall or not, this metal piping doesn't bend as easily as you might suppose. Sharp turns and precise angles are impossible without a conduit bender. This electrician's tool, also called a hickey, maintains the conduit's round shape during the bending process. Although you may never have seen one

Crimping conduit in a bench vise.

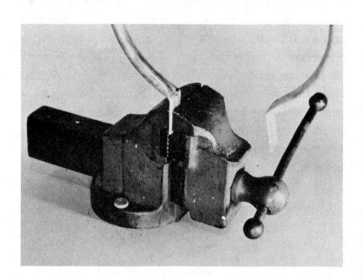

A hickey is used to bend conduit for the tip of the snowshoes.

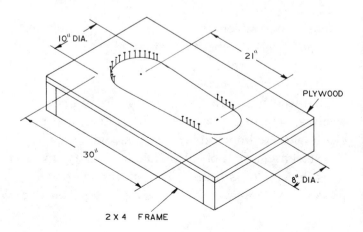

Diagram 3. This "jig" will serve as a guide for bending the snowshoe frame.

10" DIA.

21"

PLYWOOD

30"

8" DIA.

2 X 4   FRAME

before, we'll show you a foolproof method that will help you get professional results with it.

Before trying it out, build a "jig," which is nothing more than a 2 x 4-foot scrap of 2 x 4-framed plywood with spikes to form a pattern for your snowshoe frame (Diagram 3). To get the outline right, draw a 5-inch-diameter circle near the top of the board, measure down 21 inches from its center, and draw a second, 4-inch-diameter circle. Connect the outsides of the circles with 2 straight lines and you've got your oval outline. Drive spikes just above the lines leading to the lower circle. At the top, try to picture the circle as the face of a clock, and put your spikes in an arc from 10 a.m. to 2 p.m.

On one of your 10-foot lengths of conduit, measure 40 inches from one end and place an easy-to-see mark for making what's called a 5-inch radius bend, or one that fits inside the top arc of your jig. We urge you to use a hickey for this, because the tool lets you get a foothold for better leverage and a perfect bend. A 5- or 6-inch V-belt pulley, however, would work almost as well. But don't attempt a freehand bend, because this hairpin curve is certain to crimp the metal.

Set the bent piece in the jig several times during the shaping process to check your work. Go slowly. Mark the 10 o'clock and 2 o'clock spots of your first arc in the metal (6 inches in each side of your 40-inch marker) as bending points for shaping the ends of the conduit to fit inside the spikes leading toward the heel of the oval. Then bend one end of the conduit about 90 degrees to make the curve of the heel and saw off all but about an inch of the excess as it crosses the bottom center of the arc. Do the same with the other end of the conduit. Mark the points where the ends intersect, place each end in a vise, crimp, and bend back 90 degrees. Drill through the crimps and attach them with a $3/16$-inch bolt. Trim the tails about $1/2$ inch below the bolt.

To shape the toe upward (Diagram 4), lay the

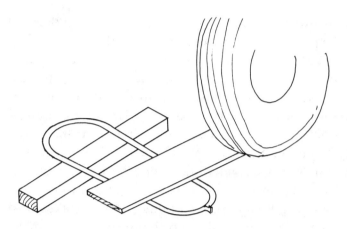

Diagram 4. Scrap lumber and the weight of your car's rear tire will put an upward bend in the toe of the snowshoe frame.

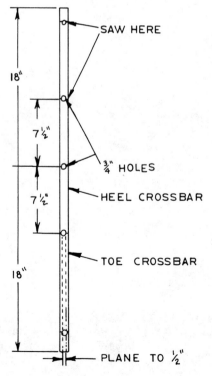

Diagram 5. Making the snowshoe's wood crossbars from 1 5/16-inch dowel rods.

front 6 inches of the frame across a 2 x 4 scrap, place an inch-board scrap across the middle of the frame, parallel with the 2 x 4, and drive over the inch-board with the rear wheel of your car. It works like a charm.

Installing wood crossbars comes next. We recommend placing one of them 7 1/2 inches down from the toe end (measuring *inside* the frame), and the second one 6 1/4 inches up from the heel end. Lay a board straight across the frame at these points to mark the conduit for drilling 1/8-inch holes through the sides. Clamp each side in a vise and strike each mark with a hammer and center punch to steady the drill tip as it starts into the metal.

If you've chosen 1/2-inch wood pieces for your crossbars, you'll need a 7 1/2-inch piece for the heel and a 10 1/2-inch one for the toe. Hollow out each end with a 3/4-inch rat-tail file for a neat fit around the conduit. Drilling an inch deep into the ends of the wood will prevent the wood from cracking when you turn in the screws. Anchor them with a squirt of glue into each hole.

Our crossbars, however, were made from 1 5/16-inch dowel rods, which we drilled and sawed according to Diagram 5, then planed down to 1/2-inch thickness. A 40-inch dowel rod will provide an extra

2 inches on each end, so you'll have enough room to work with a brace and ³/₄-inch bit. Mark for drilling into the center of the dowel, then for 2 more holes on each side, 7¹/₂ and 18 inches from the center. After drilling, cut off the crosspieces by sawing across the center of each ³/₄-inch hole. Plane and rasp ¹³/₃₂ inch off each side of the dowel, and you'll wind up with a ¹/₂-inch-thick piece, ready for drilling and joining to the metal frame (Diagram 6).

Don't worry if the shaped conduit frame is slightly too narrow or too wide where the crossbars are to meet; the wood crossbars will bow it open wider, if necessary, or the screws into the crossbars will draw it together. Sandpaper the wood for a coat of spar varnish or other moisture-resistant wood finish. Allow it to dry at least 24 hours, and apply at least 1 more coat.

While the finish dries, try to learn how to tie macrame knots. The knots we've used aren't as difficult as they may look. This hobby of macrame has become very popular, so if you prefer not to invest the hour or so required to learn the basics, you shouldn't have much trouble finding a woman to do the tying for you. Here are the steps:

1. Double four 30-foot lengths of rope and mount them around the toe curve with larkshead knots, so you're now working with 16 strands of rope (Diagram 7).
2. Tie alternate rows of square knots down to the 10¹/₂-inch crossbar (Diagram 8).
3. Carry the strands around the crossbar (8 strands on each side), and tie four 4-inch rows of square knots.
4. Continue with alternate rows of square knots, tying them a bit tighter and closer as you approach the crossbar below (Diagram 9).
5. Carry the strands under the lower crossbar.
6. Tie off the strands in 8 knots to spread the webbing around the heel area of the frame,

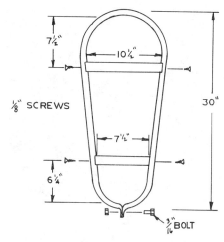

Diagram 6. Attaching crossbars to the snowshoe frame.

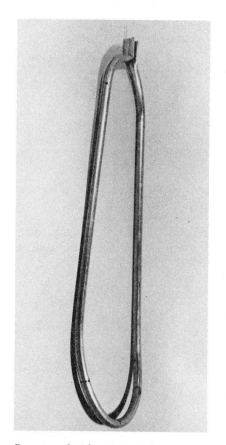

Bent snowshoe frame, ready for bolting at the bottom, then attaching crossbars.

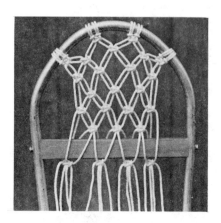

Tying the webbing begins with 4 pairs of larkshead knots at the top, then alternate square knots down to and around the crossbar.

with several wraps around the conduit before tying each knot.

7. Thread excess rope up and down the frame, picking up the edges of the webbing to draw it tightly across the span to the conduit frame, and tie off the ends after several wraps around the conduit.

If you're using nylon rope, as we did, don't make our mistake of tying off the knots so short that they can't be retied when they come loose (which nylon rope knots do). After wrapping the rope ends several times around the frame, tie the knots and fuse them with heat—a match flame touched to each knot until it melts into a black mass.

Our macrame knotting will last for years of trips over powder, but we can't guarantee the webbing will stay taut if subjected to lengthy treks on wet stuff. Even high-priced wood-frame models (which can't be made without elaborate steam-bending facilities) must be relaced more tightly from time to

Diagram 7. Joining rope strands to the toe of the snowshoe frame.

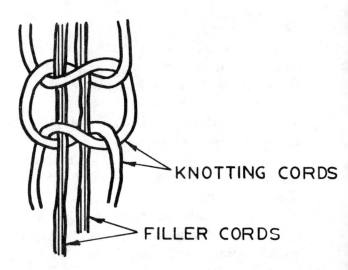

KNOTTING CORDS

FILLER CORDS

Diagram 8. Step 2 of the macrame pattern carries a square knot around a double strand.

SQUARE KNOT

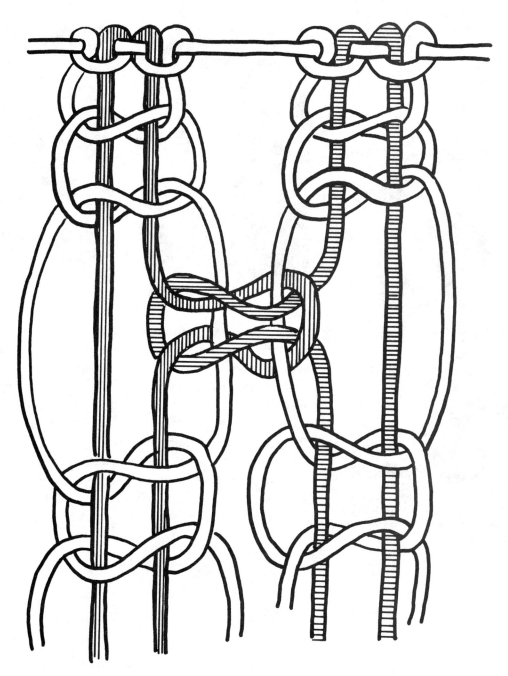

Diagram 9. Crisscross pattern of snowshoe webbing is formed with a crossover of filler cords.

Macrame work continues with 4 rows of square knots, leading to more alternate rows of square knots, which should be tied more closely together on their way down to and under the lower crossbar to the heel of the frame.

Macrame-knotted snowshoe webbing is stretched across the frame with a threading of nylon rope. Knots at the frame edge are fused with the burning tip of a match.

time. Therefore, you may have to weave reinforcement strands across the webbing. These strands may be retied occasionally to take up the sag.

The lacing technique we described earlier may be used to make bindings for these metal-frame snowshoes. Or you may copy one of the commercially available leather harnesses.

We'll admit that we had our doubts about whether our macrame-knotted snowshoes would perform reliably on the snow; but when an Indian trapper offered to buy them from us before their first test, we knew we had a winner!

8. SPORTSMAN'S BACKPACK

When it comes to a backpack, a serious-minded hunter or fisherman tends to outfit himself differently from the fair-weather nature trail hiker. Our kind of sportsman, who goes in for the outdoors in a big way, with maximum comfort, doesn't limit his load of goodies to what he can carry on his back. Over the years of traveling to remote areas, he's accumulated conveniences, such as coolers, lawn chairs, and a portable toilet, that would never fit in a rucksack anyway. His principal load bearer is often a pickup or 4-wheel-drive vehicle that can transport him and his cargo off the highway to his destination, so long hikes don't rob him of valuable time for hunting and fishing. When he straps on a harness, it's usually for short jaunts or portages, rather than for endurance treks in the name of physical fitness. Walking less means he can afford to shoulder a heavier pack, which, in turn, enables a fisherman to transfer the essentials from his base camp to a more productive fishing spot upriver. A hunter also needs extra back-carrying capacity in the event that a good shot adds to the weight he must heft on his return to the buggy.

Weight-carrying capability begins with the pack frame. Heavy-duty models are available in sporting goods stores and catalogs, but they'll cost you

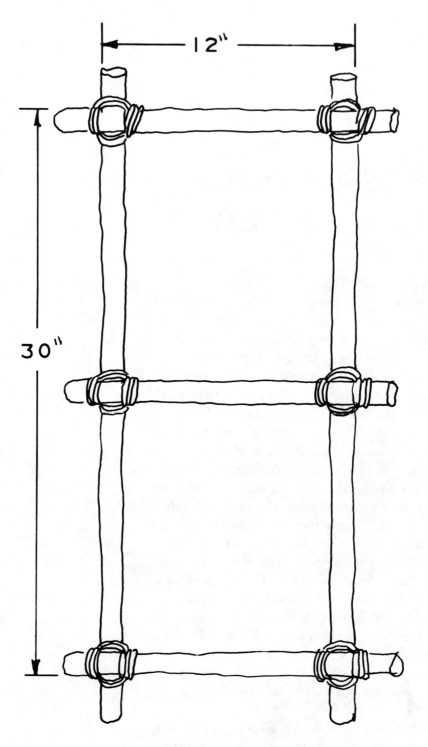

Diagram 1. Made-in-the-woods pack frame of lashed-together saplings.

SQUARE LASHING

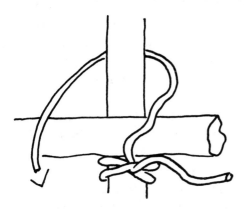

CLOVE HITCH —
TWIST END AROUND
STANDING PART

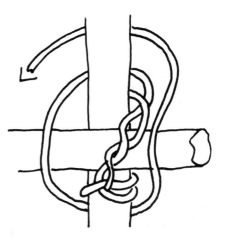

FIRST
WRAPPING

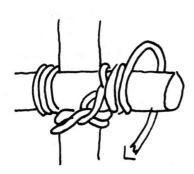

READY FOR
FRAPPING

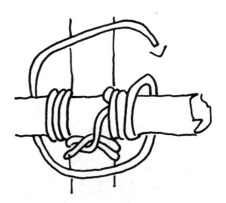

FIRST
FRAPPING

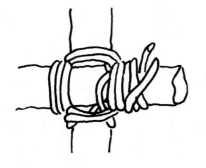

SQUARE
LASHING
COMPLETE

plenty. Before you spend your hard-earned cash on a ready-to-wear frame, we'd like to show you 3 models which you can make much cheaper. After we've told you how to build them, we'll show you how to make a knapsack, and give you some general tips on packing.

Our *bargain basement backpack unit* (Diagram 1) is the simplest of the 3 projects. You can build it for next to nothing. In a sense, it's the most practical pack for a sportsman, because he doesn't have to build it until he really needs it. The frame design, resembling a 3-rung ladder, uses lashed-together saplings which have been notched at the joints, as our snowshoes were in project 7.

Don't use dry branches for this frame, because they're brittle enough to snap under a load. Green wood, on the other hand, will give under weight, and will even bend slightly to the contour of your back. For lashings, use thin wire or heavy fishline. Rope also may be used to bind the joints, but since it's valuable for other projects, string it uncut from one joint to the next. For shoulder strapping, tie rope or canvas strips to the top and bottom joints on each side of the frame.

Our *intermediate-priced frame* can be made from discarded broom and mop handles (Diagram 2). Cut $1/8$-inch-deep notches at the joints with a saw and chisel, and drill $3/16$-inch holes for wing nuts. When not in use, the four 14-inch crossbars and two 36-inch side poles can be threaded with a thin rope, wrapped together, and slung over your shoulder much as a bowman carries his quiver. The frame can be reassembled with 8 bolts and wing nuts from your pocket. We recommend countersinking for flathead bolts, which won't dig into your back.

Our *top-of-the-line model*, made of $1/2$-inch conduit for lighter weight, also features a wide leather belt and arched crossbars to keep the frame off your backbone. We've included a diagonal brace for an 11 x 18-inch shelf at the bottom.

Backpack frame of bent and bolted conduit has a shoulder harness of belts joined at the top with a piece of rope around one of the crossbars. Another belt, strapped across the frame, prevents the curved crossbars from rubbing the back.

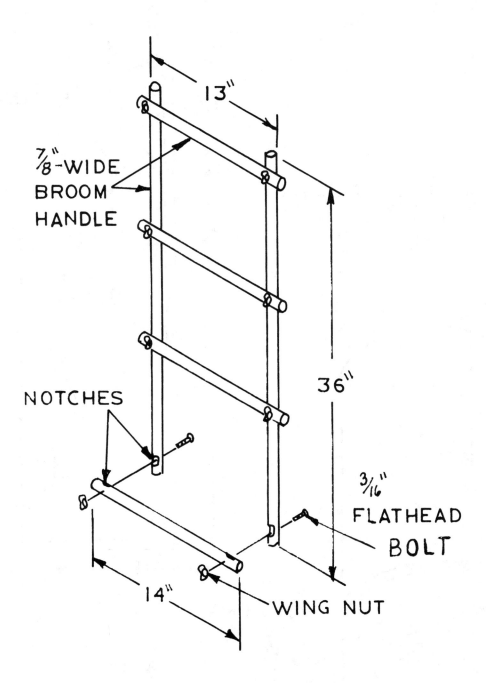

13"

$\frac{7}{8}$"-WIDE
BROOM
HANDLE

36"

NOTCHES

$\frac{3}{16}$"
FLATHEAD
BOLT

14"

WING NUT

Diagram 2. Hardwood broom or mop handles, cut to size, notched, and attached with wing nuts, make a longer-lasting pack frame which can be taken apart when not in use.

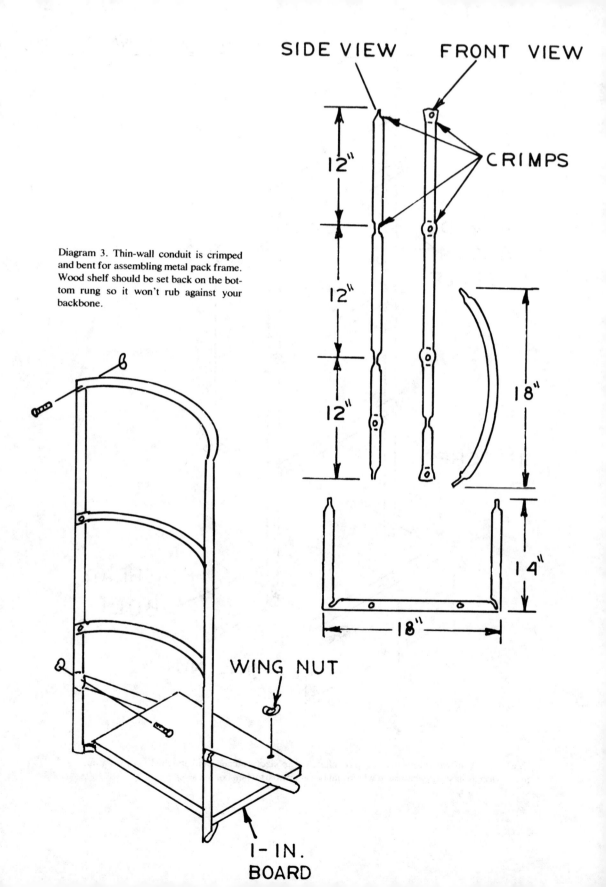

SIDE VIEW   FRONT VIEW

CRIMPS

12"

12"

12"

18"

14"

18"

Diagram 3. Thin-wall conduit is crimped and bent for assembling metal pack frame. Wood shelf should be set back on the bottom rung so it won't rub against your backbone.

WING NUT

1-IN. BOARD

Bill of Materials

$1/2''$ thin-wall conduit (aluminum, if possible):

2	36"	side poles
1	46"	diagonal brace
4	18"	crossbars
1	$1/2$ x 11 x 18" plywood	bottom shelf
3	belts	back rest, shoulder straps
14	$3/16''$ bolts, with nuts	fasteners

When you shop for conduit, don't expect to find pieces in the exact lengths we've specified. Unless your hardware store has a few scrap pieces on hand, you'll probably have to work with 10-foot pieces, which you must cut to length with a hacksaw. Cut the 3-foot side pieces first and place them in a well-anchored vise for crimping and drilling (Diagram 3). Flatten an inch on each end (pounding with a hammer against the vise shaft, if necessary), then put in 2 more inch-long crimps a foot apart. Later, you'll be bolting crossbars to the squeezed-together spots. While each side piece is in the vise, turn the conduit at a 90-degree angle and make another crimp, this one 6 inches from the bottom, slanted upward approximately 30 degrees. Drill $3/16$-inch holes in the center of the crimps.

Now cut four 18-inch pieces of conduit for the crossbars. To bend them without a hickey (conduit bender), lay them across a span of 2 x 4's—2 blocks on each side. Then place a scrap board across the conduit pieces and drive your car over it (Diagram 4). That's right; the weight of the car over the rear tire will put just enough angle in the conduit, without putting a crimp in the bend.

Crimp the ends of each piece with a vise, drill through the crimps, and attach them to the side poles. As you do this crimping, be careful not to turn the metal after making your first crimp, or your drill holes won't line up properly.

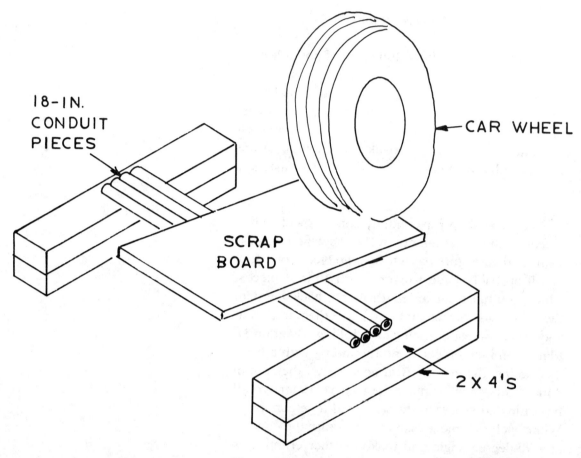

18-IN. CONDUIT PIECES

CAR WHEEL

SCRAP BOARD

2 X 4'S

Diagram 4. One method of bending crossbars for the metal pack frame.

Crimped conduit side pole, ready to be drilled for attaching side poles.

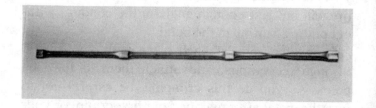

Next, shape a 46-inch length of conduit that will hang diagonally on the frame to support the rear of the shelf. Measure 14 inches in from each end of the conduit and mark these spots for 90-degree bends. Since it doesn't matter if the corners are crimped, this bending may be done in your vise. Flatten each end with 45-degree-angle crimps. Drill $3/16$-inch holes in the 2 end crimps and attach this diagonal piece. Stand the frame straight and mark the cross-bars of the diagonal brace and the bottom of the frame for drilling to attach the shelf. Tighten a wide belt around the frame, just above the bolts holding the diagonal brace, as a back protector. You may want to add rivets or washered bolts to reinforce the loop around the buckle. For appearance sake, the crimped ends of the metal frame can be trimmed with a hacksaw, file, or emery wheel.

As for packing your back buster, the backwoodsman's rule is: *Don't bury it in a backpack if it'll fit in your pocket.* That goes double for often needed items. If you can't put it in your pocket, or wear it on your belt or around your neck, consider carrying a shoulder satchel—or one of your wife's old purses —for odds and ends you'll use more than once a day. Having to dig through a knapsack to get at a camera, a spoon, shotgun shells, or a wad of toilet paper is not only maddening, it's dumb.

Our frame design is adaptable to various pack shapes and sizes. Its crossbar construction enables you to tie down several parcels, from a cigar box to a bedroll to a burlap bag (Diagram 5). These bundles may be covered by a utility tarp—or the tarp itself may serve as your bundle. Spread it out and arrange the pack's contents near one side to match the approximate shape of the rack. Then fold the top and bottom over your pile of gear and wrap the sides around it as if it were a papoose in a blanket. Cinch the pack in the middle, stand it up, and rope it to the rack. We prefer to tie down heavy packs with a

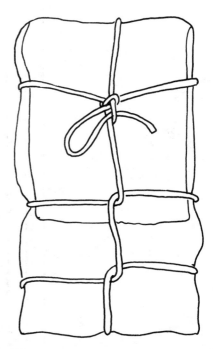

Diagram 5. Express hitch. One of several knots which will secure our strapless pack to the frame.

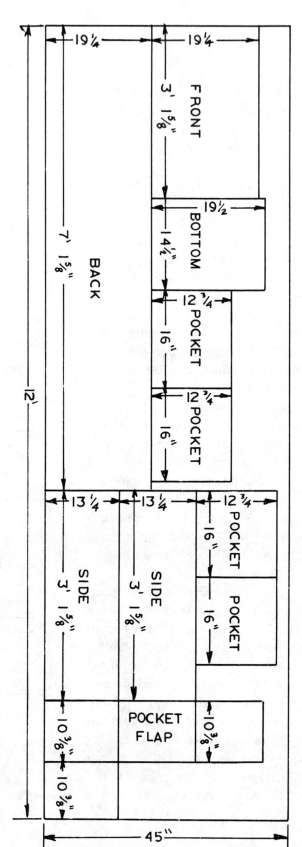

Diagram 6. Cutting pattern for backpack.

separate rope, because sewn-on straps would receive too much strain under the weight.

A home-sewn, compartment-style pack to fit our conduit rack may be the answer for the outdoorsman who's hampered by neck straps or bulging pockets. The question is: Are you as handy with needle and thread as you are with hammer and nails? We suspect you aren't, so we've created an easy pattern (Diagrams 6-22). This means you'll be transferring your do-it-yourself operations out of the workshop and into your living quarters, and you'll be working with 4 yards of 45-inch-wide khaki or lightweight denim, and (here's the kicker) your wife's sewing machine. My wife, who designed this pack to my specifications, assures me that most women can follow this simple, straight-line-sewing pattern.

The project—which may start on the living-room floor if it's the only work surface large enough for cutting out the material—will keep your wife occupied on one of the many weekends you're away from home.

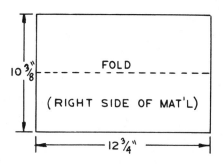

Diagram 7. Make pocket flaps first. Fold each 10 3/8 x 12 3/4-inch piece in half, with the right sides together.

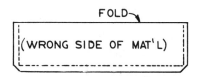

Diagram 8. Sew 5/8-inch seams up the sides of the folded flap and along the bottom, leaving a 4-inch opening so that later you can reach in and turn the flap inside out. Trim about half the excess material around the seam (except for the 4-inch opening), making diagonal cuts across the bottom corner.

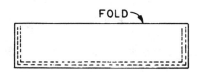

Diagram 9. Turn the flap inside out, press it, and hand-stitch across the 4-inch opening. With the front of the piece facing you, stitch around the sides and bottom, about 1/16-inch in from the edge. This is called a top stitch. Then do another round of top stitching 1/4 inch from the edge.

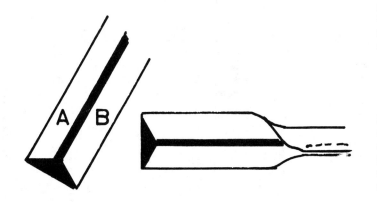

Diagram 10. Make the straps for the pockets, working with the eight 1 3/4 x 8-inch strips. Fold each one over on each side, then fold in the middle and stitch along the open edge. Make 4-inch-long straps the same way, for attaching the buckles.

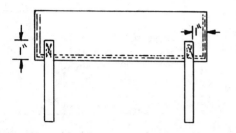

Diagram 11. Sew the 8-inch straps to the underside of the flaps, an inch in from each corner and an inch underneath.

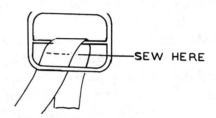

Diagram 12. Fasten buckles to the 4-inch straps.

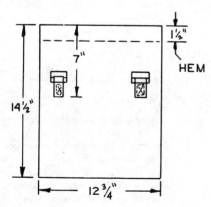

Diagram 13. Hem the pockets, turning under 1 $1/2$-inches of material. Sew buckles to the pockets, 1 $5/8$ inches in from each side, so the straps extend 7 inches down from the fold of the hem.

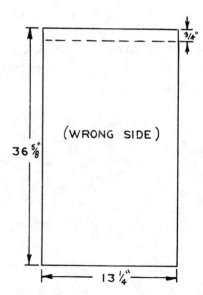

Diagram 14. Hem the sides of the knapsack, turning under the top inch of material.

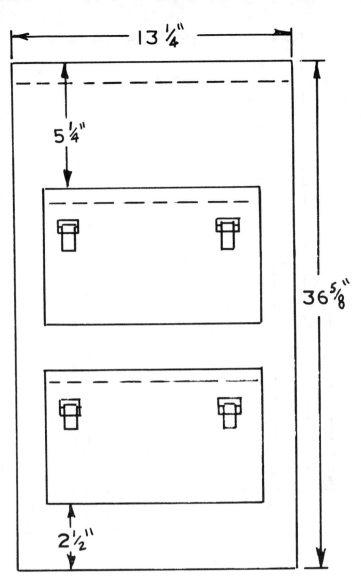

13 ¼"

5 ¼"

36 ⅝"

2 ½"

Diagram 15. Sew the pockets to the side panels. First, fold under ⅝ inch on the sides and bottom, and pin these folded-under pieces to each side. Place the bottom pockets 2 ½ inches up from the bottom edge and sew. Do the same with the top pockets, which should be pinned 5¼ inches down from the top edge.

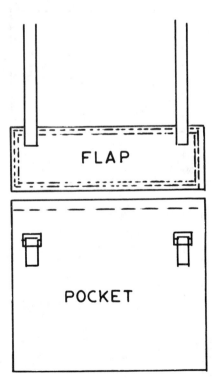

FLAP

POCKET

Diagram 16. Sew the flaps on next. Pin each one upside down with the underside of the flap facing you, so that it meets the top edge of the pocket. Attach the flap with a seam ¹/₁₆ inch from the bottom and another ¹/₄ inch from the edge.

Diagram 17. Working next with the front piece, hem the top, turning down an inch of material. Make the four 28-inch tie-down straps. Sew two 28-inch straps to the bottom of the front piece, attached ⅝ inch up from the bottom.

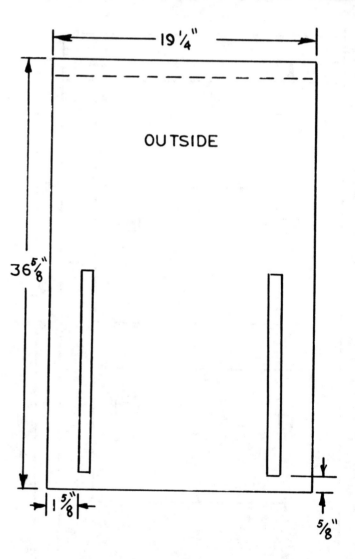

$19\frac{1}{4}"$

OUTSIDE

$36\frac{5}{8}"$

$1\frac{5}{8}"$

$\frac{5}{8}"$

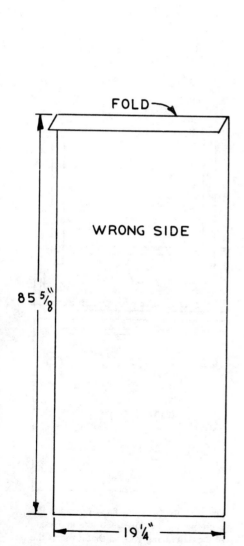

FOLD

WRONG SIDE

$85\frac{5}{8}"$

$19\frac{1}{4}"$

Diagram 18. Now for the piece that rests on your back. Make the flap. Fold over the top inch and press it.

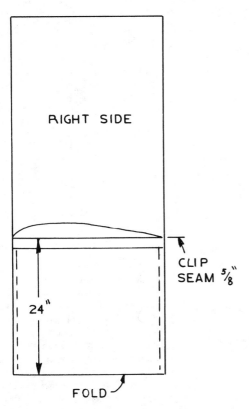

Diagram 19. Flop this back piece and, with the right side facing you, fold down the top 2 feet and stitch a ⅝-inch seam along the side edges. Then, where the 2-foot flap meets the fabric, make ⅝-inch cuts even with the seam on the flap.

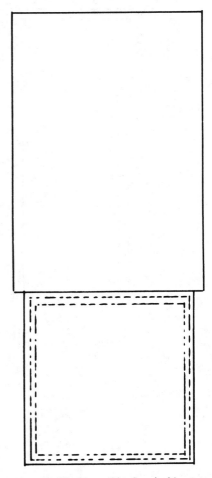

Diagram 20. Turn this flap inside out, press it, and sew on more top stitching.

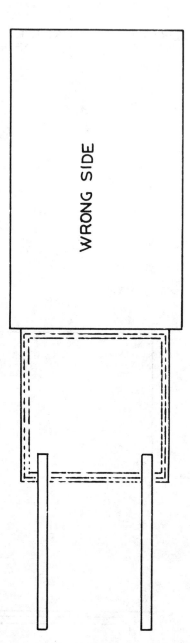

WRONG SIDE

Diagram 21. Flop the back piece again and sew two 28-inch straps to the flap, the way you did with the others.

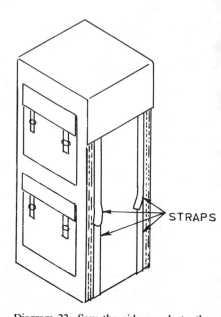

STRAPS

Diagram 22. Sew the side panels to the back and front pieces, using ⁵/₈-inch seams. Turn right side out and make the seams stronger by running over them with double rows of top stitching. (In seamstress lingo, "Don't open seams.") Place the back and one side panel together so the right sides of both pieces are joined, and run a ⁵/₈-inch seam up one edge. Similarly, sew the other side panel to the opposite edge of the back piece, and sew this side piece to the front panel, again with the wrong sides of the fabric facing you. Then sew the opposite side of the front piece to the other side panel. Now you are ready to put in the bottom. Pin the straps out of the way and turn the sack inside out again. Pin the bottom piece to the sides, back, and front panels. These pieces won't fit together perfectly, so you'll have to cheat a bit as you go along each seam, to make sure the pieces line up at the corners. This process is called easing. Again, use ⁵/₈-inch seams. To make them stronger, run reinforcement stitching alongside the first row of thread. Turn the knapsack inside out. Waterproof the pack in a washtub solution of Amway's Drifab water repellent concentrate (or comparable product). After it dries, press it, and it's ready to load.

9. SURVIVAL KIT

Some sportsmen joke about their survival kits. One may say he's got his when he packs a case of beer. Another will check his wallet—either to make sure he's got enough money to buy his way out of a jam, or enough small bills to start a fire. Just as pathetic is the fellow who attains security by bringing along a box of bandages.

The fact is, however, that a responsible sportsman won't go into the woods or cut himself off from the rest of the world without all the items he deems essential. And if he discovers a need for something he's overlooked, he's resourceful enough to get by without it, then thoughtful enough to remember it next time out.

One might think there's a mighty slim chance of disaster striking down a real man of the outdoors. That's true. But it happens, and when it does, it's no laughing matter. I sometimes forget the panic that set in when our 2-man party got lost in unfamiliar terrain, then hobbled by a gashed knee and sprained ankle after a sudden storm forced us back to camp in a hurry. To top off our adversity, we returned to find that the heavy rain had collapsed our tent and soaked everything inside it.

That's when we were thankful for the foresight to stock a few items in our survival kit—namely, the

Stitched-together pockets from an old pair of jeans or overalls, waterproofed and hung over a belt with the openings facing each other, will hold a number of survival kit items within easy reach.

backup compass to replace the damaged one which had steered us astray, the dry matches and paraffin-soaked roll of newspaper that lit our campfire to warm us and start drying our clothes, the first-aid materials for treating our wounds, and the metal flask of peppermint brandy that killed the pain and helped us forget our troubles.

The term "kit" is somewhat of a misnomer, because while we carry some of its contents on our person whenever we're away from the campsite, many of them are best in pockets or on a belt. Items that don't fit there go into a pair of large, waterproof pockets that were cut from an old pair of pants and sewn together like saddlebags to hang from a belt or a crossbar of a backpack, with the pocket flaps facing inward. Some sportsmen wear overalls or many-pocketed vests for extra carrying capacity without the annoyance of dangling doo-dads. Others shoulder a small knapsack for short hikes away from base camp to nearby ponds of hunting stakeouts.

Circumstances and common sense go into stocking a survival kit. You won't include a space age thermal blanket if you're bass fishing in Arkansas, or a bottle of insect repellent if you're snowmobiling in Minnesota. And unless you plan to leave your vehicle behind for several days, there's no need to weigh yourself down with items that can be kept just about as handy in a locked glove compartment, car trunk, or snowmobile utility box. Trailside emergencies a short distance from camp can be tended to in a temporary fashion (a handkerchief dressing of a wound, for instance) until you can provide better attention from your main supply of materials. In other words, don't equip yourself to the hilt against a million-to-one chance of a crippling crisis during your lazy afternoon along a trout stream. On the other hand, don't brave rugged wilderness with only a cigarette lighter and a sandwich. We can't tell you what you're liable to need in either case, but based on the above guidelines and the suggestions that follow, you can build up a survival kit that any backwoodsman would be proud to have.

First-Aid Kit

If you decide to assemble a kit from discount-priced materials, check the inventory of a good commercially available kit for ideas. Even if you buy a kit, you may want to add to it. Besides the basics of iodine and small adhesive bandages, include sterile gauze, a roll of adhesive tape, bandage compresses, and a few pieces of clean cloth 40 inches square that can be folded into larger triangular or cravat bandages for major repairs. Don't forget a pair of scissors. Pack a small plastic bag of Epsom salts to be diluted for soaking aches and infections from hands and feet, a container of baking soda to be diluted (3 tablespoons to a quart of water) for treatment of burns, plus chapstick and salt or salt tablets. Your mini-infirmary is a good place for aspirins and any prescribed medication. A snakebite kit may be a valuable addition to this first-aid package. After you've checked the kit's contents for your next trip, take out a few bandages and aspirins to carry in your wallet.

Gun

Fishermen who prefer the wilder lakes of our backwoods know the importance of holstering a sidearm. Some fellows who fish in bear country routinely strap rifles over their shoulders. Although a fishing rod may provide you with food in the event you are lost or stranded, you can't protect yourself with it, or use it to signal for help. In addition to plastic-encased ammunition and the gun you pack whenever you're away from your vehicle, you may want to keep a spare firearm, such as a shotgun, locked in your car or hidden nearby. After going to the trouble of taking these precautions, you might as well bring along your gun-cleaning and rust-prevention compounds. In subzero weather, remember that lighter fluid or gasoline should be used to re-move these gun-treatment materials, because a cold gun functions best when absolutely dry.

Fishing Gear

Although you may have confidence in your hunting ability to provide food in an emergency, it can't hurt to pocket a handline. A few hooks with it can be converted to spears. Live bait abounds in the wilds—even in winter, when grubs can be hacked out of rotten timber.

Hatchet

A trusty campsite companion, your hatchet doubles as a hammer, and comes in handy to cut pine boughs or blocks of ice for emergency shelter.

Knife

Carry a jacknife in your pocket, or a sheathed one on your hip, or both. The larger blade is worth its weight in extra cutting power, and you'd use it more than your jacknife. Knives will be overworked and abused in some situations, so keep their points and edges in readiness with a small file or whetstone.

Fishline

Have enough on hand to make lashings, snares, and a gill net, to sew tears in your clothing, and to tie loose sleeves and pantlegs against snow or crawling insects.

Cheesecloth or Nylon Mesh

A small bolt of material can be used to make nets and seines, or to protect yourself from biting insects if you've forgotten a pocket-size container of insect repellent.

Wire

Heavy-gauge wire isn't practical to carry in your pocket, but pack a small roll of it in your trunk or under a seat of your 4-wheeler for strong supports and tie-downs. Loop a roll of lightweight wire around your belt for lashings and incidental repairs.

Rope

We believe 1/4-inch nylon rope offers the best all-around combination of light weight, strength, and serviceability. If you *must* cut it, the frayed nylon tips can be fused with a flame, without the need for whipping the ends. We also like the 1/8-inch nylon rope, which we tend to use more often than fishline for lashings and tie-downs. A 100-foot roll of either size deserves a place on your belt.

Fire Starters

Friction fire starters such as the bow and drill, fire thong, and fire plow are all but useless if you haven't practiced using them for several hours. You'll probably get blisters before you get a spark. Flint and steel or a magnifying glass (to concentrate rays from the sun) are more dependable and much less work. A ready flame, however, is much better. You can get one from a cigarette lighter, which also works on the friction principle. Even cheaper fire starters are wooden matches kept dry in a small seltzer bottle or a 20-gauge shotgun shell casing fitted inside a 12-gauge casing. If your tinder isn't bone dry, you can jazz it up by mixing in gunpowder poured from cartridges, oil drained from a crankcase, or gasoline siphoned from a fuel tank. Our trail kit is never without a candle and a few short-life torches made from rolled-up newpaper that's been soaked in paraffin.

Signaling Devices

Aside from your gun and a smoky campfire, a number of store-bought devices, from flashlights to flares to space age thermal blankets, will signal for help. Supplement these with large strips of aluminum foil or improvised flags lashed to bushes,

GROUND-AIR EMERGENCY CODE

Symbol	Meaning	Symbol	Meaning
I	NEED DOCTOR— SERIOUS INJURIES	II	NEED MEDICAL SUPPLIES
X	UNABLE TO PROCEED	F	NEED FOOD AND WATER
«	NEED FIREARMS AND AMMO	K	INDICATE DIRECTION TO PROCEED
→	AM GOING IN THIS DIRECTION	▷	PROBABLY SAFE TO LAND HERE
LL	ALL WELL	L	NEED FUEL AND OIL
□	NEED COMPASS AND MAP	--	NEED SIGNAL LAMP

MAKE LETTER "STROKES" 6 TIMES LONGER THAN WIDE, AS SHOWN

18'   12'   3'

rocks, or trees. Make a signaling reflector by drilling a peephole in the center of a mirror. The drilled hole will enable you to aim the mirror. Memorize some important symbols of the ground-air emergency code (Diagram 1), in case you have to tramp them out in the snow and fill them with brush or boughs.

Sustenance Items

Since your body needs 2 quarts of water a day to remain efficient, consider not 1, but 2 canteens on your belt when you embark on a long trail. Nibble from a length of dried sausage or a bag of jerky or smoked fish (prepared in a smokehouse you can build from directions in project 5). A small bottle of brandy (only for medicinal purposes, of course) will warm you without increasing your heartbeat, we're told.

Orienteering Accessories

A spare compass is a must, because too many horror stories begin with a once reliable compass that's gone bad. Binoculars or a rifle scope should be employed on your first morning out, to sight distant landmarks for a crude map of your area. Add details from time to time. And keep a logbook for dates, inventories, weather conditions, and other jottings. While it's highly doubtful you'll ever have to make such entries, this little notebook can help you document your outdoor exploits for the benefit of nonbelievers back home.

10. TIPS AND TRICKS

If you're not a tidy housekeeper, your workshop or garage would be nearly ankle deep in sawdust by the time you completed all the projects in this book. We exaggerate a bit, but picturing all the sawdust and shavings you'll be spewing out, and wondering how it could be put to good use, led to another chapter for this book. When I asked a few of my back-woodsman friends for their thoughts about recycling sawdust, these "waste-nothing" boys had a few suggestions.

"I keep 'waxies' in it," one said. Yes, these "waxies," "mousies," and other grub-type bait for ice fishing (such as the ones you find in rotting timber and goldenrod stalks) thrive in a sawdust-and-shavings medium. Keep them refrigerated in a rubber-banded cigar box.

"The dry stuff will help start a campfire," said another. Scoop up handfuls from the day's sawing and store them in plastic bags. Scrap trimmings also make good kindling.

A third suggestion: Stockpile sawdust in a trash bag, and carry it with you on fishing and hunting trips. It makes good insulation around wrapped fillets or cuts of game meat which must stay cool on the ride home.

What followed was a valuable bull session on tips and tricks. I've extracted the highlights.

The Versatile Plastic: Trash Bags

Stuff a bag in your pocket before you go out in a boat. When you see rain coming toward you from across the lake, tear a hole in the plastic for breathing and visibility and put the bag over your head. Poke armholes in it to row back to shore.

Trash bags give moisture protection to camping items: your sleeping bag, pillow, blankets, clothing, and food staples such as crackers, cookies, flour, sugar, and salt. One bag will hold an armload of dry wood scraps for kindling logs drenched by a surprise shower while you're away from the campsite.

Another bag may serve as a hamper for soiled clothing.

Ripped bags may be doubled and tied over your shoes as emergency boots, or tucked between your shirts as windbreakers.

On a camping trip, save out one bag for its advertised purpose: a trash bag.

Since you can tie a knot at the top to make this an airtight container, you may save fish heads and entrails in one for digging under the roses or tomatoes. But hold your nose!

Plastic Sandwich Bags and Freezer Bags

These will hold smaller amounts of foodstuffs for your short-duration camping trips, so you don't have to pack large cans. A few spoonfuls of coffee in one, sugar in another, salt, spices, and other items which are used in sprinkled amounts. Label each bag with masking tape or identifying strips of paper inside so you don't confuse sugar with salt.

Wrap eggs individually in little "baggies." In the event of a cracked shell, you can still use the contents.

Before frying fish, dump the ingredients of your breading recipe in a bag and mix them by kneading with your fingers. Drop a fillet in the bag, shake it, and remove the breaded fish for the pan.

Carry a larger bag in your shirt pocket on a hunting drive. If you bag a deer, you'll have a container for the liver and heart.

Tie a small bag over each arrowhead to be sure to keep it dry.

One bag will keep a fresh pair of socks. Put the bag in your pocket. When you need a dry change on the trail, use the bag to store your wet ones until you return to camp.

Plastic Tarp

One 6-ml. (milliliter) tarp has so many applications that you should consider bringing along at least 2 more for extended stays in the woods. For maximum versatility, the tarp should be bordered with grommets. One might come in handy as an emergency tent. Another could be used as a windbreak, easy-to-clean tablecloth (tied underneath), staked-down covering for firewood, backpack protector, water bag, or poncho.

All-Purpose Aluminum Foil

This stuff is so flimsy that it has few permanent uses. But its flimsiness makes it easy to shape for a variety of needs, so carry at least a half roll on your outings.

Wrap 1 or 2 thicknesses around meat or potatoes and shove the wrapped pieces under the coals of your campfire. The foil (a steam cooker) will retain the juices of the food as it cooks—but it doesn't take long, so check the tenderness with a fork.

Wrap cleaned fillets and cuts of meat in a single thickness of foil for your return home. If it was a long trip, open each package and check the condition of its contents before rewrapping in the same foil for freezer storage.

Make emergency pots, pans, and cups from a double thickness of foil. You can form the round shape over the ends of logs of various sizes. After one use over a campfire, allow a foil-cooking utensil to cool down a bit, then add a reinforcing layer of foil inside. Each piece may be reused as long as it retains its shape and doesn't leak.

Don't crinkle once-used pieces of foil into wads for disposal. Smooth them as flat as you can and store them under a weight. Even if they're punctured, they can be combined with other pieces and shaped for some other purpose.

Keep bits of foil in your tackle box and fasten them on or near your hook before you dip it under the ice. Shiny foil also works as an emergency spinner in muddy water. We've also used it as a substitute for pop-tops to catch gullible perch.

Fishline

Your fishing battles seldom use up every bit of your line right down to the core; therefore, most of it rarely, if ever, touches the water. So why replace perfectly good monofilament once a year? Instead, reverse the line on the spool. If you do a lot of casting for game fish, cut off the last 18 inches every 3 or 4 hours, and retie the end knots every hour or so. Stretch that time limit, and the next good strike may be "the big one that got away."

Don't throw out the spool-length fishline you replace. Wind it around your hand and keep the roll together with 3 wraps of masking tape. Squirrel it away in various convenient locations (glove compartment, survival kit, tackle box, pocket) for eventual use.

With a needle and thimble, you can use fishline to mend boots, a tent, tarps, and clothing.

Although a few spots of a fishline may have become too weak to trust a fish on the end of the line, you can use lengths of it in multiple wraps for lashing emergency snowshoes and backpacks made of saplings.

Coffee Cans

No outdoor sportsman in his right mind would allow his wife to throw out a coffee can. With today's inflated prices, saving the cans helps us get more value for the money. The same goes for the plastic lids.

Cut the bottom off a pound-size can, replace it with a plastic lid, fill it with your worms and dirt, then cover the can with another lid. As always happens, the worms will ball up near the bottom by the time you're ready to put the first one on the hook. Instead of digging for them, turn the can upside down and get at them through the bottom "lid." Reverse this procedure from time to time. (For a more ambitious worm collection approach, see project 11.)

With a choice of can sizes, you can keep a variety of foodstuffs under plastic covers for a lengthy stay in the woods: dry beans, oatmeal, flour, and sugar, for example.

The 2-pound can will hold a roll of toilet tissues—or a roll of paper toweling that's sawed off to size. A few outdoor writers have suggested that these items can be inserted in a wire or torn-apart coat hanger for easy-roll convenience—but what happens on a damp morning or a rainy day? You'll agree: "Happiness is a dry roll of toilet paper."

For the Tackle Box

Save burned-out taillight bulbs, or collect them from a service station. Painted with red fingernail polish, they make nice bobbers.

For emergency sinkers, use irregularly shaped pebbles or knifed-open .22 slugs.

An inner-tube strip will help you take the kinks out of monofilament line. Squeeze the rubber over the trouble area and pull the line through.

Empty pillboxes from the pharmacy will help you sort sinkers and hooks.

A small tube of toothpaste (which is also a cleanser) will wash fishy smells off your hands.

Pack the match-striking pieces of used matchbooks in foil and plastic wrap. This is a short-life emery paper that will smooth the rough edges of the guides on your fishing rod.

A common teaspoon makes a good scaler.

Fingernail clippers, besides being good sliver-pickers, do a neat job of snipping fishline.

A discarded hammer handle, used forcefully, will notify catfish, bullheads, and horned pout that you're trying to get them off the hook!

For the Boat

Large chunks of styrofoam (at least 6 x 6 inches) saved from defunct coolers, minnow buckets, and home insulation projects can be used as buoys to mark good spots for fishing. Tie heavy sinkers to the styrofoam chunks.

If you're fishing alone with the motor behind you, put a concrete block and your spare anchor at the other end of the boat for ballast.

Rivets or staples in the gunwale of your boat provide easy reference to legal-size limits for "keepers."

For the Campsite

Nail a large sheet of plywood to 30-inch logs for a kitchen-height table.

Keep at least a handful of dry matches in a fruit jar or seltzer bottle.

A dime-store ("dime"?) clipboard will hold a panfish tail while you attack the scales and body. For extra holding power, cut "teeth" in the holding clip with a triangle file, hacksaw, or bench grinder.

Before you pitch camp, rub bar soap or shaving cream on the bottom and sides of all your pans and skillets, making sure the stuff fills up under your fingernails. Soot and dirt won't penetrate, so cleanup is easy.

Pin a sheet inside your sleeping bag as a liner to reduce the need for frequent laundering. In colder weather, a flannel liner serves the same purpose.

For good-tasting coffee from your campsite supply of surface water (which is often rusty-tasting or otherwise high in mineral content), mix an egg with your coffee grounds, and when the pot comes to a boil, stir in the mixture. Let it brew 4-5 minutes, then allow it to settle for the same amount of time. The egg is such a good clarifying agent that the reheated coffee tastes like fresh-brewed.

Also Worthwhile

If the short wick of your kerosene lantern won't reach the fuel, raise the wick, add water to the bowl, and crank the fiber down to the lighter-weight kerosene which will be floating on top.

Petroleum jelly will clean your shoes, and a lavish application will waterproof your boots.

Minnows will keep longest in cold water. If they're in a tight container, add ice cubes in summer and snow in winter. We're told these cold substances release oxygen as they melt. (For our minnow keeper, see project 17.)

When sand penetrates the gears of your reel, shortening or lard is a good emergency lubricant.

Cut the spiked soles from golf and track shoes. Strapped to your boots, they give you added traction while you fish on the ice.

Cheesecloth or nylon netting is another handy item. You can cover your face with it (and still breathe) when mosquitoes break through your camp defenses. You can catch minnows with this fabric by stretching it between a couple of saplings across a creek bed. Or wrap it around fresh-caught fish and sprinkle it to keep them in good condition on a short drive home. If you can reuse this cloth to cover your head, you're a better man than I am!

FOR THE FISHERMAN

11. WORM BEDS

Ever been caught in a worm shortage? It usually occurs during the hot, dry weather of July and August, when worms burrow deeper for coolness and moisture. Once most of the worms are out of spading range, the price goes up for the few that remain. We've seen tourists who were sucker enough to pay $2 for a dozen scarce night crawlers. But there's a simple way to fight rising costs and ensure a steady supply of wriggling bait: start your own worm farm.

We suggest a small-scale operation to begin with, say, about 1000 worms. If this much worm digging doesn't appeal to you, order your "breeding stock" from one of the classified advertisers in your outdoor magazine. While you're waiting for the worms to arrive, get out your saw, hammer, and nails, and build 2 boxes (Diagram 1) with scrap lumber. These boxes are patterned after low-profile fruit crates, which used to be ideal for worm keeping until cardboard bottoms were introduced. Although our $6^{1}/_{4}$ x $16^{1}/_{2}$ x 18-inch dimensions aren't exactly the same as a fruit crate's, we thought you might welcome an easy project—especially if you're a beginner—that calls for all boards cut to the same length. But feel free to change the measurements and substitute any available scraps you have around.

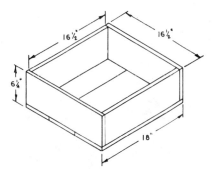

Diagram 1. Starter box for breeding stock of the worm farm.

Bill of Materials

7 1 x 6's, 16 ½" long   bottom, sides
    6d galvanized nails

Next, mix up a moist, fluffed-up batch of rich garden soil, leaves, a cup of cornmeal, and a pound or so of coffee grounds—enough to fill both boxes. Dump about half this mixture in the boxes and put them in a cool spot. Stir the dirt occasionally, because the material may heat up somewhat as it decomposes. When you receive your order of worms, place about half of them in each box, and cover them with the rest of your dirt mixture. Blanket the boxes with wet burlap, tucked in around the edges to keep the worms from crawling out. Water the boxes with a sprinkler at least once a week, and feed the worms every other week by spreading a couple handfuls of coffee grounds, cornmeal, or other healthy garbage down the center of each box.

Build 2 more boxes, because in about 5 or 6 weeks of warm temperatures, the worms will double in number. As your worm population continues to multiply, you should consider building a permanent worm bed (Diagram 2). It must be moleproof (a mole is the worm's worst enemy) as well as birdproof, so the project calls for concrete block construction, plus a slide-off wood top to keep it cool.

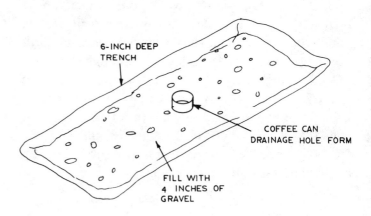

6-INCH DEEP TRENCH

COFFEE CAN DRAINAGE HOLE FORM

FILL WITH 4 INCHES OF GRAVEL

Diagram 2. Drainage bed and form for slab floor of concrete block worm bed.

Besides a saw, hammer, and nails for the carpentry, you'll need the following masonry equipment: shovel, wheelbarrow, hoe, trowel, level, jointer, chalk, and ball of string.

Bill of Materials

24 4" concrete blocks
12 4" corner blocks
 1 bag of portland cement
 1 bag of masonry cement
 1 cu. yd. of foundation-mix gravel
 $\frac{1}{2}$ cu. yd. of sand
 5 1 x 6's, 76" long   cover
 3 1 x 6's, 28" long   cover

After you've selected a level spot for the bed (within reach of your garden hose), dig a 6-inch-deep trench approximately 4 x 8 feet. Pile the sods nearby for use later as part of the worm bedding. Now dump about 4 inches of gravel into the trench and place a coffee can in the center. The can will be the form for the bed's drainage hole.

Following directions in project 5 (concrete block smokehouse), mix wheelbarrow batches of concrete to fill the remaining 2 inches of the trench. Strike it fairly level with a 2 x 4. Measurements and smoothness for the concrete floor and footing aren't critical, since the slab won't be supporting a building, and the floor itself will be covered with dirt. Your main concern is to seal off the worms' escape route.

Allow this concrete base to harden overnight before removing the coffee-can form. Lay 3 courses of 4-inch blocks (Diagram 3), with outside dimensions of 36 x 68 inches, using the procedure described in project 5. Again, there's no need to split hairs when you bubble-check the level of each block. While the mortar joints harden, build a cover of 1 x 6's (or exterior-grade plywood) framed underneath with inch-boards, to provide ventilation while foiling cats

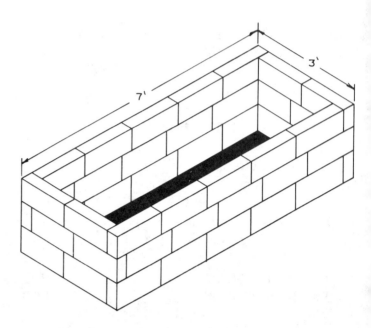

Diagram 3. Three-course pattern for concrete block worm bed. Four-inch-thick blocks are adequate to retain the soil of the bed.

from using the bed as a litter box (Diagram 4). The lid protects against torrential downpours, as well as raids by early birds. Feel free to substitute a junked door or a sheet-metal roofing panel.

The care and feeding of worms in a bed this size isn't much of a problem. For bedding, start with an 8-inch mixture of rich soil (free of commercial fertilizer, insecticide, and herbicide), leaves, coffee grounds, and cornmeal. Let the bedding decompose and cool down before giving your worms a home. Now you may allow the mixture to build up to a height of 18 inches, with regular feedings of table scraps (buried to prevent odor), leaves, lawn clippings, cornmeal, and coffee grounds. A once-a-week watering (not soaking) is adequate.

You should clean out the bed at least once a year, preferably on a hot, sunny day when it needs watering. (But don't water it beforehand, or the bedding will be too mucky to handle.) Remove the cover in the morning, and as the sun heats up the bed, the worms will work their way to the bottom. This will permit you to dig out the top foot or so of bedding to spread around your wife's rosebushes. Loosen the

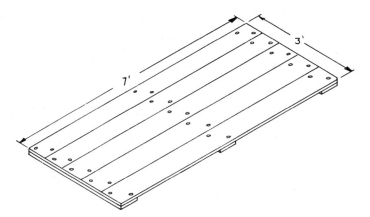

Diagram 4. Cover for the concrete block worm bed can be made from inch-boards.

bottom layer of worm castings with a spading fork and gently hoe the dark mass into a pile in the middle of the bed. Wait ¹/₂-hour for the worms to converge at the center of the pile. Now you can scoop castings from the top of the pile (even better stuff for the garden) without throwing away too much of your live bait. The same method, incidentally, may be used to drive your worms into a writhing mass when you want to divide them into 2 or more beds or boxes.

A bed the size of our concrete model will hold up to 6,000 worms—enough for you and your friends, plus all the kids in the neighborhood. Or you may want to sell your surplus to finance this and other building projects in this book.

12. ICE-FISHING SHACK

There's nothing fancy about our ice-fishing shack; it's not much more than that—a shack that looks like a family-size privy with a picture window. Inside, the holes are in the floor instead. We've added other comforts: a shelf, slots for jigs, coat hooks, a smokestack opening, and a foldout seat. Scaled to slide into the rear of a pickup truck, the shack is made of plywood, to reduce drafts and resist strain at the joints from the shock of being moved around. Also, plywood structures go up faster. Rounded-off runners complete the design.

Before you decide to build a little "home away from home," consider that it may not meet your needs as well as the portable model described in project 13. For one thing, this heavier, wood-frame model isn't recommended for use on less than 4 inches of good, hard ice; so you probably won't dare use it on your first-of-the-season outings. Furthermore, once it's in place and the fish aren't biting, you can't move it across the lake, or to another lake, without a lot of bother.

Still interested? You'll be testing your carpentry skills with a circular saw, saber or keyhole saw, hammer, square, level, stapler, electric drill, adjustable wrench, and stepladder. One more thing: Don't build it inside unless your doorway is big enough to get it out.

This 2-man ice-fishing shack allows plenty of head room, and is mounted on 2 x 6 runners.

Bill of Materials

1	$1/2$ x 42 x 90" A-D exterior-grade plywood	floor
	$1/4$" A-D exterior-grade plywood	
1	48 x 96"	roof
2	42 x 88 x 96"	ends
2	$44^3/4$ x 96"	front
2	$44^3/4$ x 88"	rear
4	2 x 6's, 24" long	runners
4	2 x 4's, 39" long	joists
3	2 x 4's, 42" long	joists
	2 x 2's:	
1	61"	"X" floor brace
2	$28^1/2$"	"X" floor brace
2	38"	end shoes
5	39"	rafters
2	88"	rear corner studs
2	96"	front corner studs
1	89"	end stud, center
4	86"	front, rear shoes, plates
5	85"	rear studs
4	93"	front studs
2	$26^1/2$"*	window framing
2	40"*	window framing
1	38"	door framing
1	78"	door framing
1	$11^1/2$"	door framing

window
door latch
heavy-duty hinges
wing screws
Liquid Nails or other waterproof glue
8d galvanized nails
6d galvanized nails
$1/2$" roofing nails
$1/4$" staples
tar paper
rolled roofing
roofing tar
roofing nails
2 eyebolts

* Length will depend on size of window.

Our 2-man shack has the usual 4 fishing holes, which let you jig for panfish while other lines are out for walleye or northern. For the more ambitious ones who like to keep an eye on tip-ups over the outside ice, we've added plans for a window (a standard, 28-inch-wide model, installed sideways) that can be removed if you're worried about breaking it in transit. We picked a large window for 2 reasons: (1) it was available, and (2) along with the 8-foot ceiling, it helps us 6-footers avoid feelings of claustrophobia. You may wish to substitute smaller Plexiglas windows, which can be attached with screws between the studs.

The floor of this house is actually a fishing platform mounted on runners. However, we felt that long 2 x 6 runners down each side of the house would make it too heavy, so we cut four 2-foot ones from one board, rounded the bottom corners, and nailed them flush to the corners of a 42 x 90-inch sheet of $1/2$-inch plywood. Two 39-inch 2 x 4's fit across the span between the runners at each end, and three 42-inch 2 x 4's serve as joists across the center. We've joined the 2 x 6's and 2 x 4's with an "X" brace of 2 x 2's (two $28^{1}/_{2}$-inch pieces and a 61-incher, cut on an angle at both ends) to reinforce the floor. Whether you choose full-length 2 x 6 runners or our lighter-weight platform support (Diagram 1), attach the 2 x 4's first. Since this floor isn't quite 8 feet long, the 7 joists are spaced about 15 inches on center. Apply glue to all framing boards before nailing them on. Remember to provide a $1^{1}/_{2}$-inch gap for the runners on each end of the shorter 2 x 4's. Mark nailing rows across the top of the sheet to make sure all your nails find a home. Your fishing holes should be located on the side of the floor that will be at the rear of the shack, away from in-and-out traffic. After the framing is in place, turn the floor upside down and paint it.

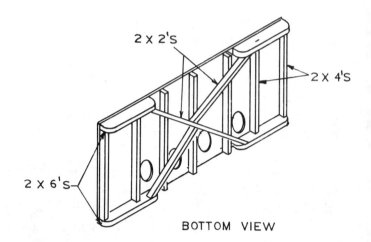

2 X 2'S

2 X 4'S

2 X 6'S

BOTTOM VIEW

Diagram 1. Floor framing of the ice-fishing shack includes rounded-off runners and an "X" brace.

Allow the paint to dry, and yourself time to think through the next stage—assembling the framing for the walls and roof. Proceed cautiously, because if the plywood panels don't meet later, it will probably be caused by a mistake here. Note from Diagram 2 that the "shoe" (bottom 2 x 2) of each section isn't nailed flush with the edge of the plywood floor; it's set in exactly ¼-inch to allow for the plywood walls. So don't pick up another board until you've drawn a ¼-inch border around the floor as a guide for the outside edge of the 2 x 2 shoes. Another reminder: If you're using ripped-apart 2 x 4's for framing, keep in mind that one side of these boards will be slightly wider than the other, so they should be lined up uniformly. Of course, the floor should rest on a level surface (shimmed if necessary) while you attach the framing. Here again, we're using glue and nails.

Assemble the far-end framing (opposite the doorway) first. To get the right angle cut on the 2 x 2 studs, or "stringers," measure down 5/32 inch from the top and draw a diagonal line to the other corner

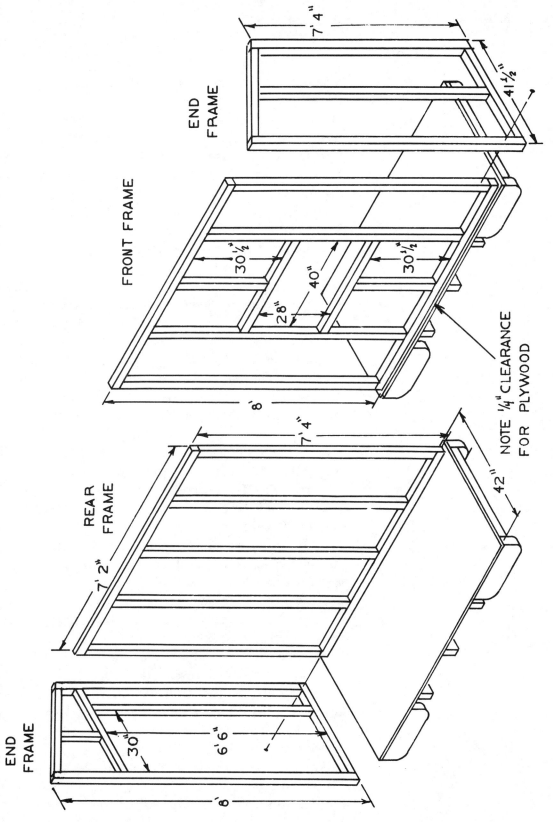

Diagram 2. Framing for the walls of the ice-fishing shack should take your own window dimensions into account.

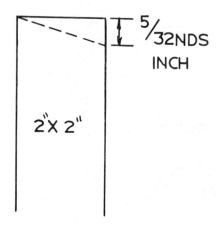

Diagram 3. Cutting angle for end studs, to provide for a pitch in the roof of the fishing shack.

(Diagram 3). Use inch-boards to brace this section in level position, then build the doorway end, which must provide for a 30 x 66-inch doorway. This means you must run a 66-inch stud up to a 38-inch header, and join this to the rafter with an 11½-inch stringer. Brace this piece temporarily and check its position with the bubble of your level.

Your front and rear frames should fit between the first 2, but it's wiser, we think, to assemble them on the spot than to nail them together and lift them into position. Start with the rear, joining the end panels with a "plate" (on top) and a shoe on the bottom. Between continuing level checks, secure the joints with studs at each corner, then nail three more studs across the center.

Attach the front the same way, joining the plate and shoe, nailing studs into each corner, and repeatedly checking with your level. The position of your center stringers will depend on the framing required for your window.

Space 5 more rafters across the span for your roof, and the framing is finished.

To give this frame more stability while you fit panels around the doorway and window openings, attach plywood to the other 2 sides first. A helper is valuable here, because the panels must be held in position while you tack them on temporarily to mark for cuts with your saw blade. The 2 front panels must join at the center stud, so you'll have to trim the plywood on each end (6½ inches, by our measurement), to fit them flush with the corners of the framing. The far-end panel, marked for an angle cut on top and a 6-inch trim on the short side, should overlap each side of its frame by ¼ inch to cover the edges of the front and rear panels.

The doorway panel, besides being penciled for roof-pitch angle and side trimming, also must be marked for a doorway cut. You'll have to step inside to mark this along the framing. After removing this panel, move the cutting mark for the top of the doorway another ¹/₂ inch up, so the exposed 2 x 2 header will also serve as a door guard. Nail on this piece, then go through the same motions (leveling, fitting, tacking, marking, and cutting) for the 2 front panels, which require facing cutouts for the window.

The roof, consisting of a full 4 x 8-foot plywood panel, allows for a 3-inch overhang on all sides. Once it's nailed in place, protect it with tar paper and rolled roofing.

Hinge the door, screw on a door latch, insert the window, then eyebolts for a tow rope, and the shack is ready for its first turn on the ice. The sportsman's stove in project 19 is ideal for this little structure. To vent it, cut out a 5-inch square and screw on a 6-inch-square piece of galvanized sheet metal that includes a 3-inch hole for the stovepipe. In selecting a spot for coat hooks or shelving, stay away from areas directly above the fishing holes. Of course, you shouldn't hang your jacket or other clothing too close to the stove.

A simple fold-up chair or bench (if the ones in project 14 don't appeal to you) can be made from scrap plywood or inch-boards attached to 2 x 2 framing. Measure up 18 inches from the floor (under the window) and nail a 2 x 2 between the studs. Support this crossing piece with 3 vertical 2 x 2's, which should extend 15 inches down to the shoe, and hinge it to the seat platform. Cut 2 short lengths of chain or rope and thread it through holes drilled in the chair and studs above. This contraption (Diagram 4) can be locked into a swung-up position with hook-and-eye sets.

A jig-holding accessory (Diagram 5) is even easier to make: Drill shallow holes in a shoe between 2 of the studs, then nail a scrap board across them.

Finally, don't count on being able to use this shack when the ice begins to soften near the end of the ice-fishing season—unless you're prepared to salvage your house from the deep. On a popular

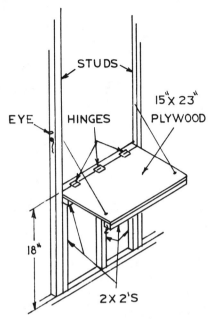

Diagram 4. Swing-up fishing chair mounts to the front framing of the fishing shack.

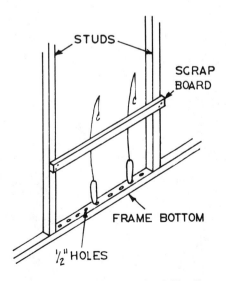

Diagram 5. Simple holder for fishing jigs inside the shack.

lake here in the north country, an early thaw surprised hundreds of fishermen, who discovered one morning that their shacks had drowned overnight. These guys got an even bigger surprise when they were ticketed and fined for polluting the lake!

13. PORTABLE ICE-FISHING SHACK

Discovering the advantages of a portable ice-fishing shack was a highlight of our trip to bob for lake trout off Madeline Island in Lake Superior. Our plywood fishing house, left behind on a pond-sized lake back home, would have been impractical up there; ice cover on this largest of the Great Lakes may not be dependable from one day to the next. On the afternoon we arrived, a coast guard helicopter rescued a fishing party who had floated away when the current broke off a 1/2-mile-wide chunk of ice. That scare story impressed on us an important rule of Lake Superior ice fishing: *Don't take anything out there that can't be brought back off the ice the same day.* Besides, there was no way we could have hauled a heavy shack 2 miles across 4-inch-thick ice to our destination.

So when a friend offered to loan us his custom-made portable fish house, we took him up on it. And when we returned it to him with our thanks, we borrowed something else: his pattern.

Basically, this portable shack is a wood- and aluminum-frame tent of collapsible canvas, with options for foldaway ski mounting. You can tow it by hand or snowmobile, and once you've got it on the ice, you can set it up in minutes. This project fea-

Portable ice-fishing shack sets up or folds down in minutes. Outside paint markings line up with fishing holes inside.

Portable shack folds up for cartop or pick-up-bed hauling.

tures thin ($\frac{1}{4}$-inch) plywood, reinforced with trim boards, for lighter-weight construction. Screwed-together, glued joints provide shock resistance and protection from moisture damage.

Building it requires these tools: circular saw or crosscut handsaw, electric drill, pencil compass, keyhole or saber saw, hacksaw, hammer, rasp, screwdriver, staple gun, paint brush, scissors, and sewing needle.

Bill of Materials

1	$\frac{1}{2}$ x 48 x 96" marine plywood	floor
1	$\frac{1}{4}$ x 48 x 82" marine plywood	front
1	$\frac{1}{4}$ x 48 x 80" marine plywood	rear
1	1 x 6, 48" long	rear hinge plates
1	1 x 4, 48" long	rear hinge plates
2	1 x 4's, 48" long	front hinge plates
2	1 x 4's, 94$\frac{1}{2}$" long	bottom sideboards
2	$\frac{3}{8}$" aluminum stripping (or hanger iron), 16' long	canvas fasteners

2 ³/₈" aluminum stripping
   (or hanger iron), 94" long   canvas fasteners
   canvas, 96 x 194"   wall, roof fabric
   2" trim boards:
2 64¹/₂"   front reinforcement
2 66¹/₂"   rear reinforcement
2 44"   headers
3 48"   doorway framing
2 6 x 9" Plexiglas sheets   front windows
2 12 x 12" Plexiglas sheets   rear windows
2 telescoping tent poles   canvas roof frame
4 2 x 4 blocks, 4" long   pole inserts
2 thumb screws   pole locks
   rope   tie-downs
   metal snap
   ¹/₈ x 1" flathead brass screws
6 heavy-duty brass hinges,
   with screws   front, rear joints
   6d galvanized nails
   ¹/₄" staples
   Liquid Nails or other waterproof glue
   nylon thread
2 large brass drawer handles, with bolts
1 drawer pull
2 spring hinges
4 medium-size eyebolts
   Optional for ski mounting:
   flathead brass screws
   medium-size brass hinges, with screws
   hook-and-eye sets

Step one is to cut fishing holes in the ¹/₂-inch sheet of plywood. With a compass or pan bottom, mark four 10-inch circles, each centered 11 inches from one long edge of the sheet. The edges of your circles, in other words, will be 6 inches from the edge of the plywood. On this near edge of the plywood, make 4 pencil marks in line with the center of each circle (Diagram 1). Later, you will be painting these marks to serve as guides for augering fishing holes

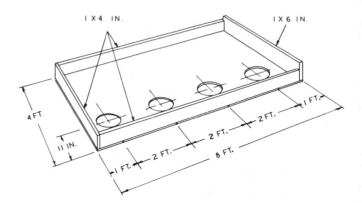

Diagram 1. Cutting fishing holes in the floor of the shack.

outside the shack. To make your circular openings in the floor, drill a $\frac{1}{2}$-inch hole on the inside edge of each circle, so you can insert the blade of a saber saw or keyhole saw.

Next, attach sideboards and hinge plates to the floor. Flop the sheet, apply Liquid Nails or other waterproof glue to a long edge of a 4-foot 1 x 4, raise the front end of the plywood sheet, and position it on the glued edge of the board. Pound in a few 6d nails to draw the plywood tightly into the glue. Do the same with the 1 x 6 board on the rear, then the $94\frac{1}{2}$-inch 1 x 4's on the sides (which also must be glued and tacked at the ends). While the glue sets with the floor upside down, drill $\frac{1}{16}$-inch holes (2 or 3 inches apart) around the edge of the sheet and into the glued corner joints. Then countersink the holes for flathead screws. Diagram 1 also shows this assembly.

After cutting out the front and rear plywood panels (Diagram 2), use a rasp to round off the peak and top corners of these $\frac{1}{4}$-inch sheets so there will be no pointed edges to tear the canvas. Then, from the bottom of the front sheet, cut out a 30 x 60-inch center doorway opening and set this cutout door aside for hinging later.

Now you must attach hinge plates and 2-inch framing/reinforcement boards to the inside of the front and rear plywood sheets. To hold up the alu-

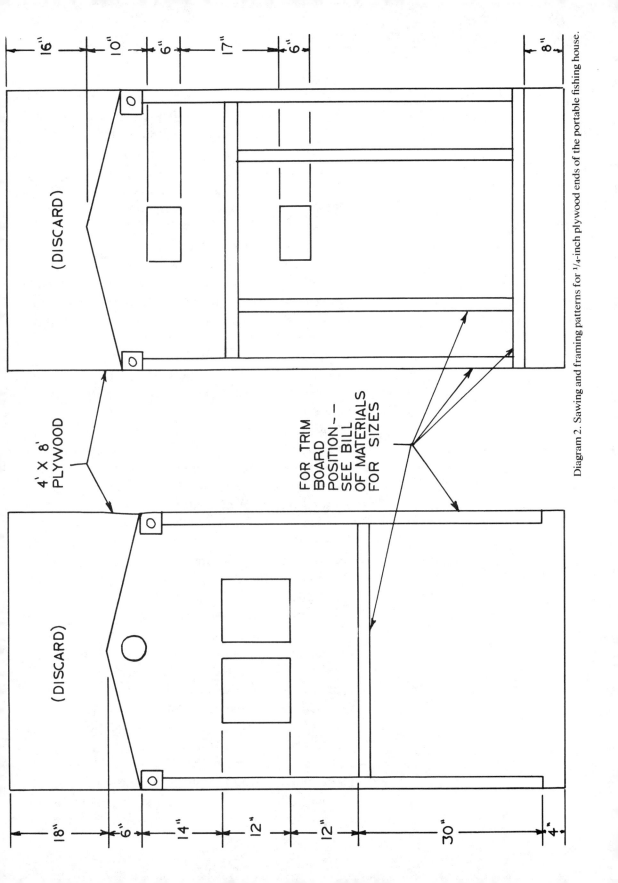

Diagram 2. Sawing and framing patterns for 1/4-inch plywood ends of the portable fishing house.

minum tent poles from front to rear corners, we're using 2 x 4 blocks with $3/4$-inch insert holes. Secure these blocks with screws. But don't try to be a superman with your screwdriver; drill holes for the screws before you turn them in. You'll note that framing diagrams suggest cutouts for window and vent openings. Exact measurements for your own openings may vary.

Once the $1/4$-inch plywood sheets are hinged into position (from the inside), they should be propped up to complete the structural work of the project. To do this, insert one set of aluminum poles and telescope them until the sheets stand straight. Mark the poles at the center joint for drilling a thumbscrew hole in the "female" pole. The screw will hold up the plywood panels while you install the other telescoping crossbar and lock it open with another thumbscrew.

Covering the house with canvas will be the most time-consuming part of the project. When ours was built (in 1961), our tent-and-awning supplier didn't stock canvas in the width we required. So we bought 2 narrower pieces and sewed them together with heavy nylon thread. The 96 x 194-inch dimensions we've specified allow for folding under the edges of the canvas before it's stapled to the wood. You'll need help with this 4-handed job: the canvas must be stretched to reach from front to back, and over the top to the other side of the floor (Diagram 3). To make it easier on you and your helper, loosen the thumbscrews and let the tent poles telescope inward a foot or so. With the screws tightened again, the plywood sheets will be tilted toward each other, allowing some play in the canvas. The staples will hold the canvas edges in place while you attach stripping over the hems, using brass screws 2 inches apart. The house in our photographs used a combination of scrap trim boards and fabric strips—whatever was handy. But if you must buy material for this purpose, we recommend galvanized hanger

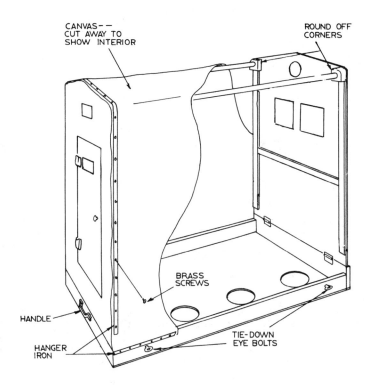

CANVAS— —
CUT AWAY TO
SHOW INTERIOR

ROUND OFF
CORNERS

BRASS
SCREWS

HANDLE

HANGER
IRON

TIE-DOWN
EYE BOLTS

Diagram 3. Canvas-covered portable shack is ready for fishing. To collapse it for hauling, fold down the front panel, then the rear panel over it, and tie down the folded sections.

iron, which is sold in strips already perforated for your screws. The stripping should go all the way across the bottom sideboards. However, the stripping up the sides and over the top should start 4 inches up on the front corner, and 6 inches up on the rear. This gap at the bottom corners will permit the hinges to operate properly. Hacksaw off the excess stripping.

Spring-type hinges replaced conventional ones on the door of this portable shack. This feature eliminates the need for door latches, and it closes the door behind the fisherman who's in a hurry to check a tip-up flag on the outside ice. A drawer pull serves as a doorknob. Carrying handles are bolted into the 1-inch bottom boards on each end. Insert 2 eyebolts in each sideboard, just below the canvas on the outside, for attaching ropes that tie down the folded

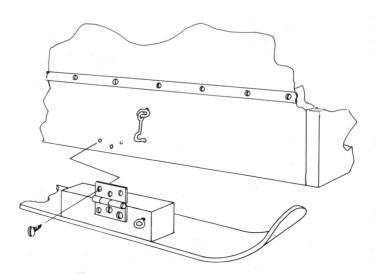

Diagram 4. Optional ski runners for the portable fishing shack can be hinged to swing out during hauling or fishing.

panels, and the other for securing the unit on a cartop carrier. To load the shack onto this type of carrier, lift the front and rest it on the sidebar, then swing the rear around and slide the thing forward.

Ski runners are optional with this portable shack; it skims over the ice and snow without them, but we'll concede that skis would make for a smoother run and less wear on the bottom of the floor. If this option appeals to you, remember that the skis must be hinged to swing out from under the shack before you step inside. Six-inch 2 x 2's may be used as hinge plates for each ski section (Diagram 4). Secure them to the top of the ski with glue and flathead brass screws turned in from below, but drill holes and countersink them first. Hook-and-eye sets will lock the skis up for fishing or cartop hauling.

Our plan can be modified into a 1-man model, simply by shortening its length by 4 feet. This calls for a 4 x 4-foot floor, 46½-inch sideboards, and a 50 x 194-inch piece of canvas.

After you've towed this little beauty out on the ice and erected it, bring in your heater and fire it up. Then go outside and drill holes in line with the paint marks on the sideboard. Gently push the shack over the holes. The place will be plenty warm by the time you're back inside.

If a 1-man model is more of a project than you want to tackle for only a few ice-fishing sessions, Diagram 5 shows a windbreaker you can fashion from a canvas tarp and pieces of conduit, using a hacksaw and electric drill, and possibly a needle and thread.

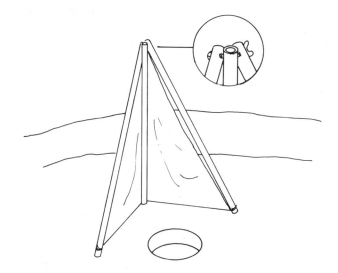

Diagram 5. Ice-fishing windbreak made from canvas tied to a tripod of conduit poles joined with a bolt and wing nut.

Bill of Materials

1 6 x 6' canvas triangle
2 $^1/_2$" conduit poles, 6' long
1 $^1/_2$" conduit pole, 5' long
1 $^3/_{16}$ x $2^1/_2$" bolt, with wing nut
  nylon thread

This triangular windbreak is designed to protect a fisherman seated on the chair we described in project 14. A rectangular canvas tarp may be adapted for this windbreak by folding it into a triangular shape, and cutting conduit to fit the dimensions. Drill a $^3/_{16}$-inch hole through the top of the poles and bolt them together to form the tripod support.

If you decide to cut out a triangular piece of canvas, make your cut from corner to corner so the grommets on each side edge can be used for tie strings. Then fold over $^1/_4$ inch along the bottom edge and sew a hem to prevent fraying. If the canvas has no grommets, you may tie strings to the tip of each corner, or sew on tie straps which we describe for the pockets of our backpack in project 8.

14. FISHERMAN'S CHAIR

Here's a fishing aid that sounds like it belongs in the "What Will They Think of Next?" category. However, the fisherman's chair we're touting offers several advantages to the panfish angler who has settled on a productive spot under the ice or along the shore. First, it sure beats standing. Second, it's sturdier than a collapsible campstool or lawn chair. Third, and most important, it has a handy but hidden compartment for your fish. Simply unhook the fish and drop it through a slot under the seat onto a screened bottom or into a plastic ice-cream bucket of water that fits inside. When you're through fishing, raise the hinged seat to get at your fish—but until then, no curious passerby can see how well you're doing. The slot, by the way, also serves as a carrying handle.

We got this idea from a shallow-lake ice fisherman, who designed it to protect his territory from being "punched out"—a common complaint. "When other guys see you're catching fish," he explained, "they went to punch holes right next to yours. After all that pounding and commotion, the fish stop biting."

Yes, this chair helps bring out the fisherman's devious personality. He can stuff his catch in the secret hold, then lie about his luck. And let's face it:

Flip-up seat of our fisherman's chair provides for easy retrieval of fish. We've included a jig and ice skimmer in the accessory pocket, to suggest the chair's suitability for ice fishing.

when you've found a good hole, the last thing you want is a competing angler on your elbow—or a game warden over your shoulder—leering at the fish on your string.

With some scrap lumber and an hour or so of carpentry, using hammer, saw, vise, saber or key-hole saw, electric drill, and screwdriver, you can put together a seat-of-the-pants fishing companion that will help you keep your luck to yourself.

Bill of Materials

$3/4''$ A-D exterior-grade plywood:

1	8 x 12½"	seat
2	2 x 12½"	seat
2	10 x 14 x 15¾	front, rear
2	10 x 10½ x 12½"	sides

$1/4''$ A-D exterior-grade plywood:

1	10 x 12 x 14"	pocket
1	3 x 14"	bottom trim
2	¾ x 13"	bottom trim
1	¾ x 12½"	bottom trim
4	2 x 2's, 18" long	legs
	chicken wire or mesh, 14 x 14"	
2	medium brass hinges, with screws	
16	$3/16$ x 2" brass screws	
4	⅛ x ¾" brass screws	
	6d galvanized nails	

This little construction is designed to help use up plywood scraps from other projects in this book. You may elect to substitute inch-boards. Quarter-inch plywood is sufficient as a wall for the side pocket, because this piece won't be supporting your weight. We also recommend ¼-inch plywood for stripping underneath, because thicker plywood tends to break up when sawed into narrower pieces.

Although this is one of our least expensive, least time-consuming projects, faulty measurements of

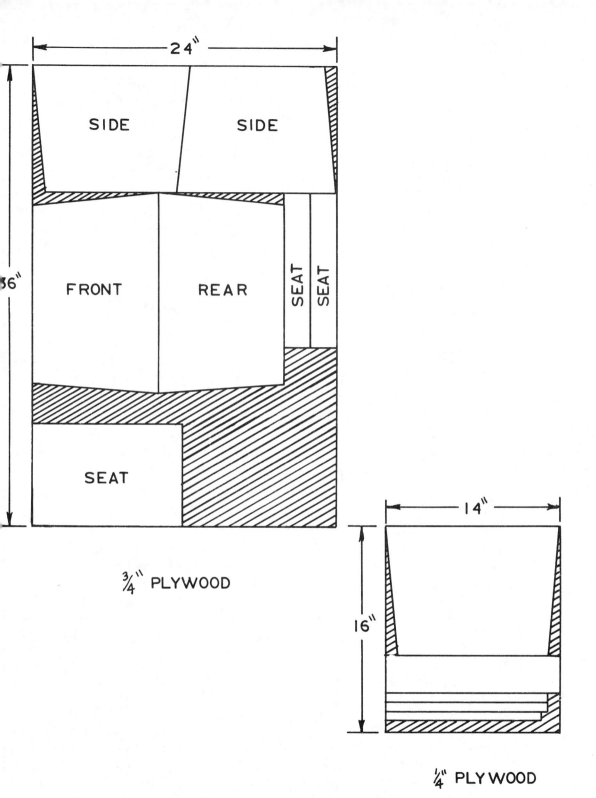

24"

SIDE   SIDE

36"

FRONT   REAR   SEAT SEAT

SEAT

¾" PLYWOOD

14"

16"

¼" PLYWOOD

Diagram 1. Cutting pattern for plywood pieces of fisherman's chair.

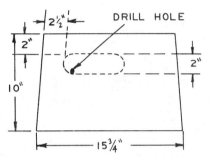

Diagram 2. Cutting the oval opening for inserting fish into the chair bottom.

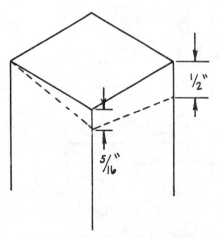

Diagram 3. How to cut the chair legs' complex angle without a radial-arm saw.

inefficient sawing can cost you money and man-hours. That's why an experienced woodworker draws a cutting diagram before plugging in his saw (Diagram 1). If you're a novice, chances are that this simple chair is one of the first building ideas you'll attempt from this book; so lay out a cutting pattern (based on our bill of materials) for minimum waste of plywood. As a double check against error, you may want to cut pieces of cardboard or newspaper to size and arrange them on the plywood. Remember to provide for the width of your saw blade in making your cuts, and to saw on the waste side of your pencil marks.

Place the front panel in a vise and cut out the slot that will serve as your carrying handle and fish storage slot (Diagram 2). This is done by drilling a 1/2-inch hole *inside* your penciled oval line, as a start for your keyhole saw.

Our chair has slanted legs for added stability. Making the correct-pitch cut on these legs is a simple matter with a radial-arm saw blade which can be tilted for a 7 1/2-degree compound angle cut. This is somewhat trickier with a handsaw, however, because your angle cut must be made from one corner to the opposite corner (Diagram 3). If you're working with a planed 2 x 2, measure down 1/4 inch on the right-hand edge and draw a line up to the left-hand corner. Then turn the 2 x 2 to the adjoining side, mark the right-hand corner 1/2 inch from the end, and draw a line from this point to the 1/4-inch mark. Often, however, the so-called 2 x 2's you buy from a lumber mill are really ripped-apart 2 x 4's. Since the ripped edge isn't planed, one side of the board is about 1/4 inch wider than the other. In that case, measure down 5/16 inch for your first pencil mark on the wide side of the board, then 1/2 inch to the other. A slight mistake in your cutting angle on one end of a 2 x 2 isn't disastrous, because the messed-up end can serve as the top of the leg, where the angle is less critical.

The legs also make up the corner framing for the chair's plywood panels, so drill and countersink $^3/_{16}$-inch holes to screw on to the $^3/_4$-inch side pieces, flush with the side and top of the legs. The front and rear panels extend $1^7/_8$ inches to form the sides of the chair's accessory pocket. Make sure the holes you drill into adjoining sides don't line up exactly, or your screws will meet inside the 2 x 2's. Your partly built chair should stand solidly on a level floor. If it wobbles a bit, you have 2 options: either adjust the height or angle of the troublesome leg by drilling new holes (at least $^1/_2$ inch from the original ones), or merely put up with it; the ice- or riverbank you fish from won't be perfectly level, anyway.

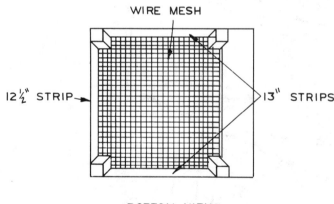

WIRE MESH

12 $^1/_2$" STRIP

13" STRIPS

BOTTOM VIEW

Diagram 4. Wire mesh or chicken wire may be used for the bottom of the chair.

Now, drill $^1/_8$-inch holes for screwing on the $^1/_4$-inch panel for the side pocket, turn the chair upside down, make $1^1/_2$-inch corner cuts on your wire mesh, and staple it to the bottom edge of the panels (Diagram 4). Nail the panel to the pocket and the $^1/_4$-inch strips to enclose the bottom edges of the chair.

Back on top, screw on the 2-inch plywood strips —one flush with the inside wall of the pocket, and

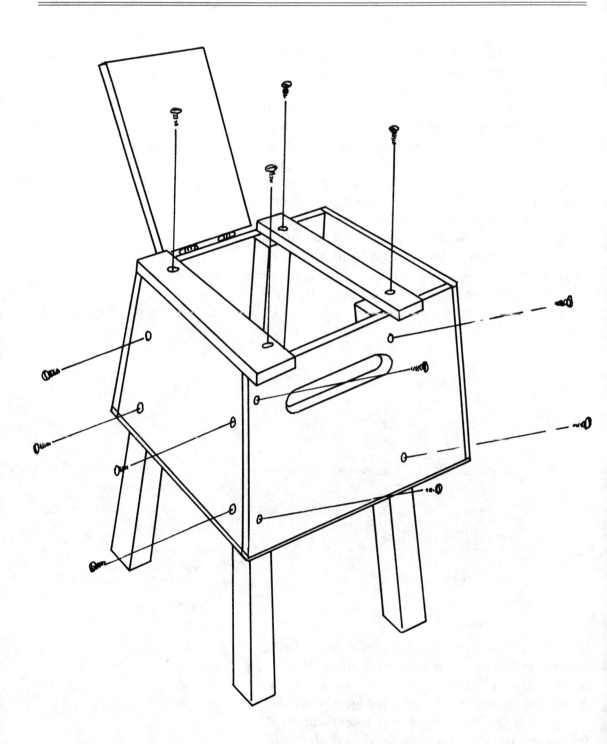

Diagram 5. Assembling panels and stripping of the fisherman's chair.

the other flush with the opposite side. Then hinge the top flap between them (Diagram 5).

An easier-to-build chair, designed primarily for ice fishing, is fashioned from a crate that once held quart-sized soda pop bottles. The front opening also allows you to keep your panfish under the seat, and to store your jigs and ice skimmer as you travel over the ice.

Bill of Materials

$3/4''$ A-D exterior-grade plywood:

2	11 x 12$^{1}/_{2}''$	top, bottom
3	11 x 16''	rear, sides
1	2 x 11''	front reinforcement
2	1 x 6's, 12'' long	front
2	$^{1}/_{8}$ x $^{5}/_{8}''$ brass screws	belt fasteners
	6d galvanized nails	
	eye screw	
	small chain	
	old belt	

This ice-fishing chair was made from a soda pop case. We show you how to adapt a design with scrap lumber.

15. ANCHORS

This book includes a few small projects intended to use up lumber scraps from bigger jobs. But what can you do with pieces of concrete that are left over from masonry work?

Make anchors. A few cents' worth of form-hardened concrete (which would be wasted otherwise) will secure your boat as well as a manufactured weight that sells for $10 or more. No fisherman should venture out in a boat without at least 1 spare anchor. It will come in handy when the rope tears loose from the other one, it may serve as ballast for the front of the boat when you're fishing alone, and it will give you an added tie-down when you want to stay put over a good spot in choppy water. Other anchors can be used to weight down the minnow trap (project 16) or the "live" boxes (project 18).

We're offering 3 basic designs: the plastic bottle, the milk carton block, and our old favorite, the tractor disc.

Although a sand-filled plastic bottle makes a good emergency anchor, it can't be expected to last an entire fishing season, because the handle which holds the tie rope, plus the rounded edges of the plastic, will become brittle and crack or wear out with age. To improve the life of this bottle model, fill it with concrete instead. Water down the con-

Three money-saving anchor ideas: a concrete-filled plastic bottle, a smaller weight of concrete hardened in a milk carton, and a tractor disc.

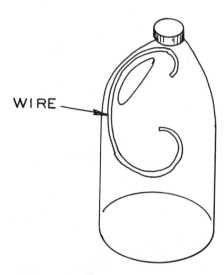

WIRE

Diagram 1. Before pouring concrete into the plastic bottle, reinforce the handle with heavy-gauge wire.

crete mixture so it's soupy enough to pour through a funnel into the cap opening. Before it hardens, insert a length of heavy wire through the handle as reinforcement for the concrete (Diagram 1).

A milk carton serves as the form for our second concrete model. Cut off the top of the carton, fill it with concrete, and insert a 1/4-inch eyebolt (with a nut and wide washer at the bottom) into the hardening mass.

A 1/2 x 12-inch eyebolt is also an integral part of our tractor disc style, made from an old disc harrow, which you've probably seen rusting along fence rows or farm implement junkyards during your travels through the country. The sharp metal edge of this anchor really digs into the lake bottom for a sure hold. Tighten a nut against an oversize washer on each side of the square opening in the center of the disc. To add weight to the disc, you may pour molten lead into the concave side of the disc, or merely bolt on a second disc, as we did.

We've sold surplus concrete anchors for $2 each to defray building expenses; and, cheapskates that we are, we've packaged the heavy things in gaily colored wrapping as "what is it?" joke gifts for some of our sportsman friends.

16. MINNOW TRAP

Tired of paying a dollar a dozen—or more—for bait-shop minnows? Or finding most of them floating belly up by the time you get them out to the lake?

These are good reasons for making your own minnow trap. It will cost you less than a week's supply of store-bought minnows, and its fresh-caught fingerlings will keep longer. Also, it will save you gas money by making trips to town for more bait unnecessary. And it's easy to operate: Merely lower it into the water along the shore before you pitch camp, and by next morning, it should contain a day's worth of bait.

Bill of Materials

¼″ galvanized wire mesh:		
1	24 x 51″ rectangle	holding cylinder
1	16″-diameter circle	end
1	5″ square	door
1	16 x 32″ semicircle	trapping cone
	¼″ staples	
	fence staple	
2	½ x 2 x 24″ scrap boards	spine
	heavy-gauge wire	
	fine wire	
	scrap rubber	
	cord or chain	anchor rope
	⅛″ brass nuts and bolts	

Minnow traps can be made in various sizes, with single or double cones.

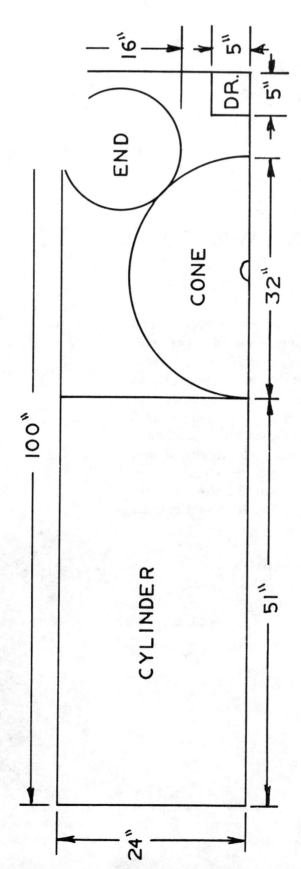

Diagram 1. Cutting pattern for 1/4-inch wire-mesh sections of minnow trap.

Needlenose pliers, tinsnips, hammer, electric drill, and staple gun will aid you with this trap construction. Use the tinsnips to cut the 1/4-inch mesh into 4 pieces: a 24 x 51-inch rectangle for the cylinder, a 16-inch-diameter circle for the end, and a 16 x 32-inch semicircle to be shaped for the trap cone (Diagram 1).

Shape the cylinder first by rolling it and joining the ends with a seam of thin wire. Place one of the 24-inch scrap boards inside the cylinder along the seam and join it with a staple on each end. Then run a scrap 2 x 4 through the cylinder underneath the 1/2-inch "spine." The 2 x 4, rested across a couple of sawhorses, will hold the cylinder while you drive home the rest of the staples and drill holes for bolting the wood to another 24-inch piece on the outside of the cylinder. Pound a fence staple into the top board of the spine, 4 inches from the rear of the cylinder.

Next, form the cone. Cut a 1 x 2-inch semicircle from the bottom of the 16 x 32-inch semicircle, and join the corners. A simple wire hook (shown in project 18) will help you with the wire work. After you thread the 2 sides of the base together, your finished cone will be 16 inches in diameter, reducing to a small minnow entry hole at the tip. With this tip pointed into the cylinder, thread the 16-inch-diameter mouth to the rim. Diagram 2 shows the assembly.

If you attach the 16-inch end to the rear of the cylinder with a threading of lightweight cord, you can use this end piece as a flap for getting at your catch of minnows. Or you can attach it permanently with more wire, then cut a 4-inch-square opening in the side of the cylinder and cover it with a 5-inch-square flap hinged with wire. Secure the flap with a homemade hook of heavy-gauge wire that's hitched to the fence staple with a thick rubber band (cut from a discarded inner tube.)

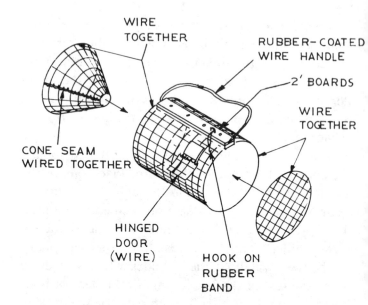

WIRE
TOGETHER

RUBBER-COATED
WIRE HANDLE

2' BOARDS

WIRE
TOGETHER

CONE SEAM
WIRED TOGETHER

HINGED
DOOR
(WIRE)

HOOK ON
RUBBER
BAND

Diagram 2. Assembling the minnow trap.

Feel free to deviate from our design with a longer or shorter double-cone model. In that case, one of the trap cones can be hinged with wire for an access door, or a hinged flap opening can be installed somewhere in the middle of the cylinder wall. To figure the size of the piece to be cut for your cones, measure the diameter of the cylinder and double it to get the radius of the semicircle. Check your computations by making a mock-up cone from cardboard or newspaper, to make sure you won't be wasting wire mesh because of cutting error.

Tie on heavy-gauge wire for a carrying handle, and a rope or chain for an anchor, and the trap is ready for its first trial dip in the water. This unit may serve as a "live" box for keeping minnows on weekend fishing trips. Other minnow keeper plans are covered in projects 17 and 18.

17. MINNOW KEEPER

Sportsmen have devised scores of contraptions for keeping their minnows alive, but our handiness award goes, posthumously, to the one who invented the bathtub. The guy *had* to be a fisherman, because his invention makes such a dandy minnow keeper. It's deep and spacious, providing plenty of room for minnows to seek their own comfort zones. Its light color allows the fisherman to eyeball his inventory easily. And it comes with a built-in drainage system to receive a steady stream of fresh water.

If you want to convert a discarded bathtub to a minnow aquarium, and you have a shady spot for it (which is not served by city water which could kill the fingerlings), your first step is to find the tub. Dumps or junkyards are likely places to begin looking. Another possibility is your local plumber, who frequently tears out old bath fixtures to make room for new ones.

Set the tub in permanent shade near the house or summer cabin. The distance from here to your outside faucet will determine the length of garden hose you'll need to supply water. Other items needed to complete the installation will depend on the way your tub is equipped. The rubber stopper is a must. If the faucet fixture is intact, put a wrench to the fittings on the other side of the tub and loosen them

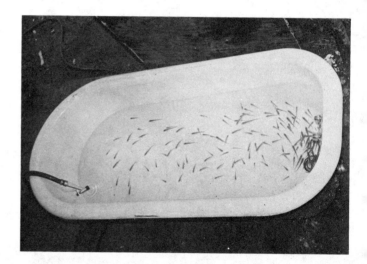

Discarded bathtub makes a dandy minnow keeper.

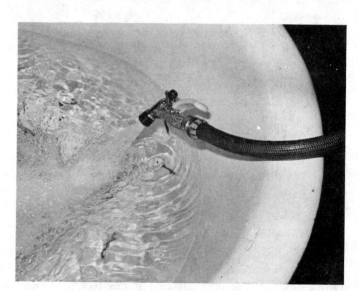

Pistol-grip hose nozzle delivers a pressurized spray into our bathtub minnow keeper. Water runoff returns to a nearby lake.

just enough to insert a piece of ¼-inch mesh under the base of the fixture. With the mesh in place to prevent the little fishies from swimming out the overflow hole, tighten the fittings.

A pistol-grip nozzle on the end of the hose will deliver a pressurized spray into the tub, away from the drain for better circulation. Also, make sure the stopper is secure in the bottom drain. As a precaution against mischievous children pulling this plug, remove the stopper's wire ring.

Bill of Materials

discarded bathtub
pistol-grip hose nozzle
$1/4''$ wire mesh scrap
old door or plywood sheet   cover

This makeshift tank will hold dozens of minnows for a month or more, it you care for them properly. Fresh, cold water is essential for their survival, so provide it at regular intervals during the day. Feeding them isn't necessary, because they can subsist by cannibalizing the weaker ones among them, and by pecking away at insects that land in the water. Keep the water clean of leaves and other debris, and about twice a month transfer your bait to minnow buckets while you scrub algae and mineral deposits from the walls and floor of the tub (but don't use soap or detergent). Also, remember to drain the tub before freezing weather sets in.

Most important, cover this minnow keeper nightly with a sheet of plywood or a discarded door. If you forget, some raccoon will use the tub as a feeding trough!

18.   "LIVE" BOXES

There are fisherman among us who've never seen a "live" box. But for those of us who've stumbled onto one, it's hard to resist the urge to look inside. There's something intriguing about them, tucked away in the high reeds at the edge of a lake, or under a thick clump of bushes that overhangs a creek. You never know what you'll find when you open the lid. One may contain minnows, while another may contain a near-record-size fish that the owner hasn't finished bragging about. Still another may be holding a catch of out-of-season bass, to be collected for cleaning after nightfall.

Far be it from us to advise you to build a "live" box that will help you violate fishing laws. As far as we're concerned, its 2 main functions—holding minnows and keeping game fish in good condition until you're ready to clean them—are justification enough to build one. We'll cover 3 of the many homemade designs.

The first, your basic box for panfish and larger sizes, is built of wood with a hammer and saw. It may be chained to a tree along the shoreline, or weighted down with an anchor or a bottom lining of rocks. In nailing it together, allow about 1/2 inch between boards, to provide for expansion and water circulation. The 3-foot-square box in Diagram 1

Our "live" box, made of galvanized mesh and a frame of brass curtain rods, is large enough to keep bragging-size fish until you're ready to clean them.

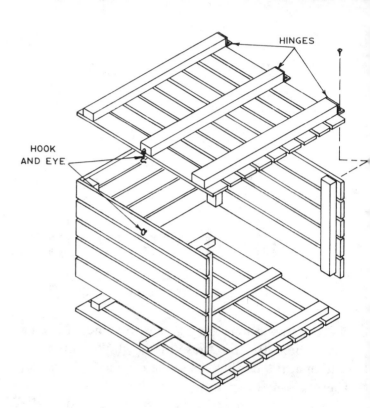

Diagram 1. We've cut away one side of our wood "live" box to show its assembly. The box can be weighted down with rocks.

uses 4-inch lumber (actually 3½-inch planed). However, feel free to vary the measurements of your boards according to whatever scrap lumber you have on hand.

Bill of Materials

4 2 x 4's, 19¼" long	corner framing
3 2 x 4's, 36" long	lid framing
19 1 x 4's, 36" long	cover, side boards
20 1 x 4's, 34½" long	end, bottom boards
2 2 x 4's, 31½" long	bottom framing
3 medium brass hinges, with screws	lid fasteners
hook-and-eye set	lid fasteners
8d galvanized nails	
6d galvanized nails	

Build the 2 ends first. Each one takes five 34¹/₂-inch 1 x 4's, nailed to the narrow side of two 19¹/₄-inch 2 x 4's. Your 1 x 4's should be spread apart slightly for a box height of 20 inches. The 2 x 4's should be flush with the top, leaving a ³/₄-inch gap at the bottom, or an opening that's the exact thickness of the 1-inch boards. Join the sides with 36-inch 1 x 4's. To assure a precise fit, nail the first 2 boards flush with the top, 2 more 36-inch boards flush with the bottom 1 x 4's, then finish nailing in between. Flop the box and build the bottom, which is a simple arrangement of nine 34¹/₂-inch 1 x 4's framed with another 34¹/₂-inch 1 x 4 in the middle and two 31¹/₂-inch 2 x 4's on the sides. In laying out the boards for nailing, the 1 x 4's should be spaced to cover a span of 34¹/₂ inches, providing a 1¹/₂-inch overhang (or the thickness of 2 boards) at both ends of the 2 x 4's. This will assure that the bottom section will settle neatly into the bottom opening for nailing. The only problem you could run into here would result from thickness of the inch-boards, which may vary from ³/₄-inch to ⁷/₈-inch. If your lumber measures ⁷/₈ inch thick, you may have to alter board lengths by ¹/₄ inch to get perfect fits—if perfection is your goal.

The lid of this "live" box consists of nine 36-inch 1 x 4's that are spread apart slightly to fit the framing of three 36-inch 2 x 4's or 2 x 2's on top. Hinge it to the rear of the box, close the lid, and attach a hook-and-eye set.

Our *all-metal "live" box* is lighter, longer-lasting, and more easily hidden from nosy anglers. It's made from ¹/₄-inch mesh that's also suitable for keeping minnows. This material is commonly sold off a 2-foot roll in most hardware stores. Also, you may want to reinforce it with metal rods along the corners (ours are an assortment of lawn-chair parts and curtain rods). The only tools required are tinsnips, hacksaw, needlenose pliers, electric drill, and homemade "crochet hook."

A homemade crochet hook will help thread wire through the seams of the metal "live" box.

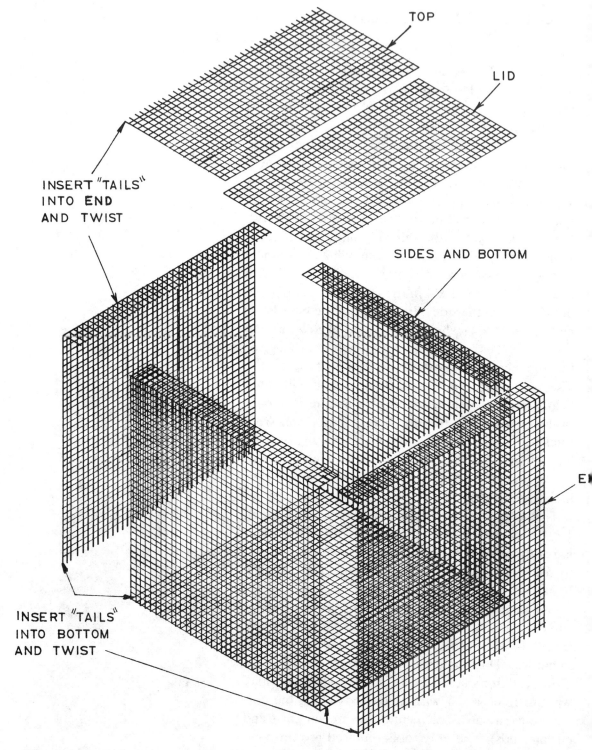

TOP

LID

INSERT "TAILS"
INTO **END**
AND TWIST

SIDES AND BOTTOM

E⟩

INSERT "TAILS"
INTO BOTTOM
AND TWIST

Diagram 2. Assembling the wire-mesh "live" box. Enough "tails" will hold seams in place for threading with fine wire.

Bill of Materials

$\frac{1}{4}''$ wire mesh, 2' wide:

1	76"	bottom, sides
2	26¼"	ends
2	12"	top, lid

reinforcement rod or brass curtain rods
heavy-gauge galvanized wire
light-gauge galvanized wire

From your roll of wire mesh, cut a piece exactly 76 inches long. This piece should be cut smooth on both ends with tinsnips. Use a scrap 2 x 4 block to bend this long piece, forming the 24-inch bottom, 24-inch sides, and 2-inch upper ledges.

The side pieces, cut smooth on only one edge, should be bent at the top to provide corresponding 2-inch ledges. The ¼-inch "tails" should be twisted around the wire edge of the bottom section to hold the edges together temporarily while you join them more securely with fine wire (Diagram 2). A few twists of wire also will help keep the seams lined up during the threading process. A simple hook of heavy-gauge wire will speed up the work of fishing wire back and forth through the ¼-inch holes.

Don't attach the top yet, because it will only be in your way when you wire on the reinforcement rods (Diagram 3). For strength, we're recommending 1 vertical rod inside each corner, 1 across each side on top and bottom, and 1 more across the top at the center. The 4 vertical rods should be exactly 24 inches high. To figure the length of the other rods, double the width of the rod you're using and subtract that measurement from 24 inches. If yours are ⅜-inch rods, for instance, the correct length would be 23¼ inches. But it's wiser in this case to cut each piece to fit as you go along, because the mesh tends to bow out.

Stand up one 24-inch rod in each corner and join the rod-reinforced seam with a threading of light-

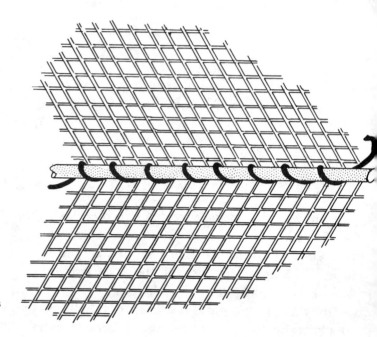

Diagram 3. Attaching reinforcement rods to corner seams of the "live" box.

gauge wire. When the 4 corners are completed, wire 4 rods on the bottom, from corner to corner. Wire the 2-inch ledges together, then lay one of the wire-mesh pieces of the top section at the rear of the wire box. Wire this piece, also, to the ledges on the rear and both sides. Tie 2 more rods inside the top edges, from front to back, and another one across the center, so that the top piece is attached to rods on all 4 sides. One more rod should be wired across the top front. The lid is another 12-inch piece of mesh with rods wired to all 4 sides. Drill a hole in the center of each long rod, and hold it in position with a twist of wire while threading it in place. Construct the hinges, locking hook, and carrying handle from heavy gauge wire.

Our third design is *merely a carrier* for the frogs, turtles, and lizards your son may collect while you're busy with the *serious* fishing. Built of wood scraps and nylon screening or wire mesh, it features a slide-out top which can be opened partway so the creatures have less chance to jump out during

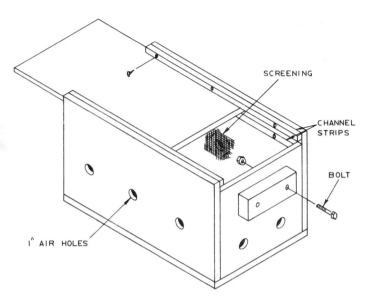

Diagram 4. "Live" box for your kids' lizards and frogs—or in a pinch, for your minnows. Slide-away top prevents creatures from jumping free.

"show and tell" time. This pattern calls for ³/₄-inch plywood and inch-board remnants, but you may use whatever stray pieces you have available. In building it, you'll be working with a saw, hammer, electric drill or brace and bit, stapler, screwdriver, and —if the sliding door doesn't operate smoothly— plane or wood rasp.

Before nailing the box together, drill the circulation holes, staple on the inside patches of screening, and screw in the slide-out top's guiding strips (Diagram 4). Use a ¹/₈-inch drill bit before inserting any of the screws, or you're certain to crack the strips of wood.

Bill of Materials

³/₄" plywood:
3 13¹/₂ x 16"   bottom, sides
2 12 x 12"   front, rear
1 12 x 16"   sliding top
   inch-board scraps:
4 16" strips   top channel

2	2 x 4"	handles
12	1$^1/_8$" screws	channel strip fasteners
4	$^1/_4$ x 1$^3/_4$" bolts	handle fasteners
	6d nails	
	screening or wire mesh scraps	

19. FISH-CLEANING CENTER

Anglers may have their disagreements about surest-fire lures and sportiest fish, but there's one thing they agree on: they'd much rather be catching fish than cleaning them—a messy job which no cleanliness-minded woman would allow to be performed inside her house. But we've found an item there that lets us take the slimy newspapers and sticky scales outside the house where they belong. An ordinary bathroom sink (yep, that's right), flanked with counter tops and hooked up to running water, can be transformed into an efficient work area which we call our fish-cleaning center.

When we borrowed the idea from a resort dockboy who fillets thousands of fish for summer tourists, we were tempted to buy a new fixture for the project. However, we were fortunate enough to locate a suitable one, complete with faucet fittings, at the town dump. If you're not so lucky, contact a plumber; next time he replaces a sink, he may let you have the old one for the hauling. From there, it's a job for saw, hammer, screwdriver, electric drill, and adjustable wrench.

Fish-cleaning center consists of a sink mounted between 2 table tops. Faucet is attached to a garden hose.

Bill of Materials

left-hand table:
3	2 x 8's, 48" long	tabletop
4	2 x 4's, 39" long	legs
2	4 x 4's, 45" long	base
3	2 x 4's, 22" long	top frame
2	2 x 2's, 21³/₄" long	diagonal braces
1	1 x 6, 23¹/₄" long	side guard
1	1 x 6, 48" long	rear guard

right-hand table:
3	1 x 8's, 20" long	tabletop
4	2 x 4's, 34¹/₂" long	legs
2	4 x 4's, 45¹/₂" long	sink, table frame
2	2 x 4's, 20" long	sink support
1	1 x 4, 42" long	cross brace
4	2 x 4 scraps	
	section of garden hose (female end)	
	¹/₂" hose clamp	
4	¹/₄ x 4" bolts	
	16d spikes	
	8d nails	
	screw hook	

Our setup is designed for working from left to right—scaling and cleaning on the left, rinsing in the center, and soaking fillets in a dishpan on the right. The framework for the sink and counter tops, which must support the weight of a heavy plumbing fixture while standing up to a summer-long pounding of weather, should be constructed of heavy lumber. And because the sink and double-counter arrangement is an unwieldy thing to lug in and out of storage as a 1-piece unit, ours is built as a 2-piece sectional. Though this outdoor furniture may not win a *Better Homes and Gardens* award for appearance, it's fairly representative of a backwoodsman's building philosophy: *If you can save money by using materials on hand, then looks aren't important.* Common sense should tell you that sanded-smooth board edges and a lacquered finish would be wasted on fish-cleaning counters which are bound to take a lot of abuse. Enough said.

The left-hand counter is little more than a small, well-anchored picnic table which stands at a comfortable 33-inch work height, with side and rear guards of inch-boards to prevent your fish from flopping away from you and sliding off the table. This counter top is considerably heavier than the right-hand one, because it covers a wider span; and it's broader-based, because we often use it as a seat while cleaning our limit of panfish. A screw hook holds the utility pail underneath. Our model was put together with heavy cross members off an old telephone pole (again, whatever's handy) and some unplaned lumber that was milled from home-grown timber, so we're adapting the plan to let you work with planed boards.

The 4-foot-long tabletop is an assembly of three 48-inch 2 x 8's and three 22½-inch 2 x 4's. The outside 2 x 4's, set in 1½ inches from each edge, must be mortised on 1 end to provide room for joining the inside legs of the table. Since the legs are 2 x 4's to be joined at an angle, saw a 1½ x 3⅞-inch notch on the end of the board which will be hammered to the rear of the tabletop (Diagram 1).

To join the legs, measure down 15½ inches from the top of the 39-inch 2 x 4's and drill ¼-inch holes for the bolts. Bolt each pair of legs together and open up the legs in scissors fashion until the outside corners of the top portion are 23¼ inches apart (or the width of your table). Lay a yardstick across from corner to corner and mark the pieces for angle cuts. Then—without moving the legs—mark the bottom portion in the same manner (Diagram 2).

After your other pair of table legs is drilled, bolted, and sawed, spike the 2 sets in place (Diagram 3). You may wish to use lag screws or bolts and washers to connect the mortised joints.

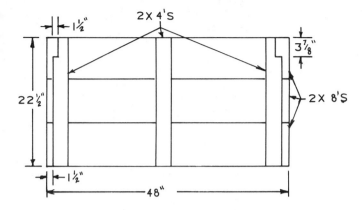

Diagram 1. Framing the left-hand cleaning table. Note mortising for legs.

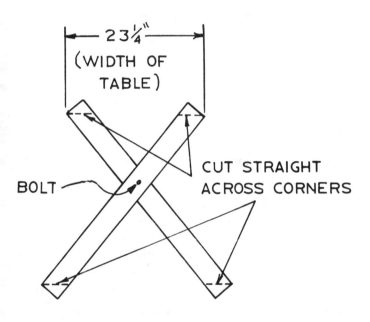

Diagram 2. Marking the angle cut for left-hand table legs.

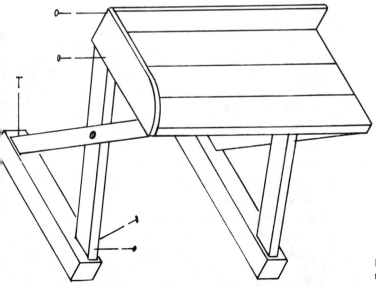

Diagram 3. Joining the table legs to table-top and base of 4 x 4's.

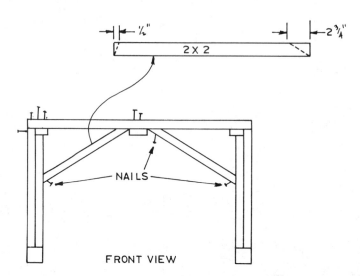

Diagram 4. Bracing the left-hand table with 2 x 2's.

FRONT VIEW

Attach the diagonal 2 x 2's underneath. Each brace requires angle cuts on both ends so it can be nailed to an inside leg, just above the bolt, and to the underside of the table (Diagram 4).

The beauty of this project, unlike most others, is that if you don't have time to finish it at this point, you've still got a serviceable product to show for your efforts: a compact picnic table. But should you decide to get on with the thing, nail on the 1 x 6 rear and side guards (Diagram 3) and proceed with the second section.

The right-hand section is designed to support the sink and to provide a small counter (built of 1 x 8's) for cleaned fillets. Therefore, it needn't be wider than the framework required for the sink. You'll notice from the photograph above and from Diagram 5 that the legs under the right-hand counter are joined at a closer angle. We did this in order to keep both counters on the same level. Your measurements for this side of the project may vary slightly, according to the dimensions of the bathroom fixture you have available (though a 16-inch-wide bowl is standard). However, your basic construction would follow Diagram 5. The two 20-inch 2 x 4's that sup-

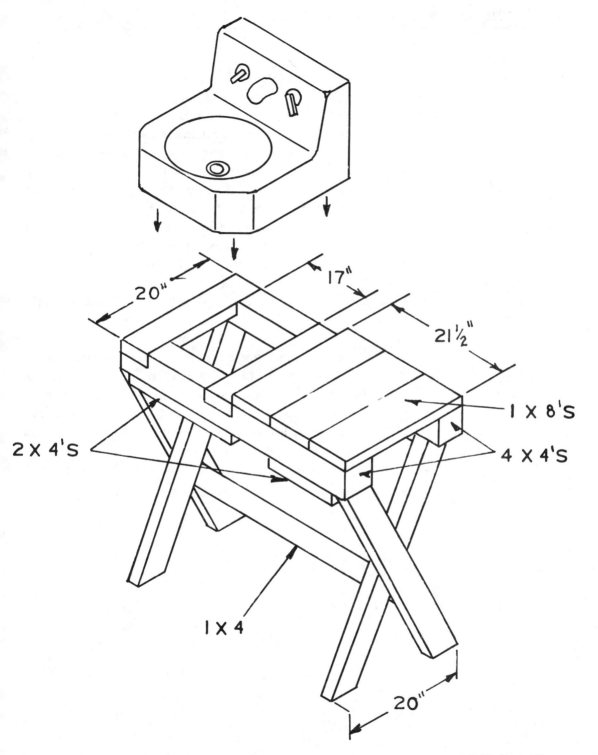

Diagram 5. Mounting the sink on the assembled right-hand table.

port the sink will fit into $1^1/_2$ x $3^1/_2$-inch mortise cuts in the 4 x 4 framing of your tabletop. Measure down $17^1/_2$ inches from the top of the 2 x 4 table legs to mark for drilling bolt holes, and cut the top and bottom angles the way you cut the legs of the left-hand table. Nail the tops of the legs into 2 x 4 scraps that have been spiked into the bottom of the 4 x 4's. Since diagonal braces might get in the way of the sink drain, we suggest a 1 x 4 or 2 x 2 nailed to the rear of the inside legs. There'll be plenty of room to hang a dishpan from a nail in back.

Since this is an outside job, there's no need to call in a plumber for the sink hookup. If the faucet fittings are intact, use a hose clamp to connect the cold-water pipe to the female end of a short piece of garden hose, and connect this to the hose from your outside water tap. If the faucet fittings are missing, you can supply water on demand from a pistol-grip hose nozzle shown in project 17. Dig a trench under the sink drain to channel water away from your feet while your're rinsing off your fish.

Build this one, and your wife will love you for it!

WAYS TO
GET THERE

20. PICKUP CAMPER TOP

Weekend sportsmen who travel great distances to the best hunting and fishing spots often encounter "no vacancy" signs when they arrive—or the prospect of having to set up camp in the dark. Such inconveniences make it difficult to unwind after a hard week at the office. That's one reason why pickup camper tops are so popular. These little mobile homes have their selling points. While they're providing storage space for your gear, they're also protecting the pickup bed from the elements. More important, they offer instant, on-location lodging to the weary traveler who wants to sack out as early as possible for a head start on Saturday's adventure. The weekend living accommodations of a pickup camper are cheaper in the long run than motel rooms, and can be readied for occupancy more quickly than you can pitch a tent. Advantages, sure. But have you priced one lately?

When *we* did, we decided to devote one of our outdoor weekends to a light construction project. We built the shell for less than it would have cost us for 2 nights at a resort cabin. What's more, we finished the job in less time than we normally spend making and breaking camp. Anxious to try it, we took this no-frills camper on several outings before deciding on refinements. Based on this field testing,

Our inexpensive plywood camper has seen 5 years of service on backwoods trails.

we developed a plan that features optional windows and a smokestack opening to vent the sportsman's stove described in project 6. For extra comfort, a ³/₄-size mattress slides between the wheel wells.

To build it, you need the following tools: electric drill, hammer, screwdriver, pliers, adjustable wrench, caulking gun, tinsnips, and because you'll be making a lot of plywood cuts, a circular saw and a saber or keyhole saw. A crosscut handsaw may be used to cut out the rear flap opening. Also, you'll be using 2 sawhorses.

As with other pickup-mounted items in this book, you should check and double-check the measurements of your pickup bed before cutting boards or plywood sheets. Our camper plans are designed to fit over a pickup bed that's 71⁵/₈ inches wide and 8 feet long.

Bill of Materials

¹/₂″ A-D exterior-grade plywood:

2	23³/₄ x 96″	sides
2	24¹/₄ x 71⁵₈″	front, rear
2	48 x 71⁵/₈″	top

2 x 2's:

2	67⁵/₈″	front, rear beams
8	20³/₄″	studs
4	46¹/₄″	side plates
2	96″	side rails
1	48″	flap handle/guard
1	2 x 4, 71⁵/₈″ long	front rail
1	2 x 4, 70⁵/₈″ long	center beam

2 tubes of Liquid Nails or other waterproof glue

  6d galvanized nails

3 heavy-duty brass hinges

4	9 x 25″ Plexiglas sheets (optional)	windows
6	³/₁₆ x ³/₄″ brass bolts, with washers	hinge fasteners
2	window locks, with ³/₄″ flathead brass bolts	flap fasteners
42	¹/₈ x ¹/₂″ roundhead brass screws (optional)	window fasteners
14	¹/₈ x ⁷/₈″ roundhead brass bolts (optional)	rear window fasteners
2	6″-square pieces of galvanized sheet metal	stovepipe opening
	¹/₈″ sheet metal screws	
4	³/₈ x 2″ bolts, with washers	camper fasteners

Planed 2 x 2's (actually measuring 1¹/₂ x 1¹/₂ inches) are used in this design. But as we've warned you elsewhere in this book, some lumber mills sell ripped-apart 2 x 4's as 2 x 2's. These boards, unplaned on one side, will measure 1¹/₂ inches on one side, but 1⁵/₈ to 1³/₄ inches on the other. A variation of ¹/₈ to ¹/₄ inch in board width may result in a botched-up project—unless you allow for this in modifying your own plans or positioning the 2 x 2's uniformly.

Well, time's a-wastin'. Slide one of your plywood sheets out of your pickup bed and mark it for a lengthwise cut (Diagram 1). Your cutting line, almost down the center of the sheet, should measure 23³/₄ inches from one edge (for a side panel) and

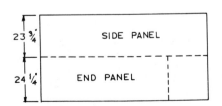

Diagram 1. Cutting pattern from a 4 x 8-foot sheet of plywood.

24^1/$_4$ inches from the other edge (for a front panel). A second sheet of plywood, cut the same way, will yield the second side panel and the rear piece. On these cuts, saw directly on the pencil line rather than on either side of it. Because the plywood-cutting blade of your circular saw will take about a ^{1}/$_8$-inch bite out of the wood, the 2 pieces won't measure exactly 23^3/$_4$ and 24^1/$_4$ inches wide (probably ^{1}/$_{16}$-inch less), but the ^{1}/$_2$-inch difference in width between the side and end panels will assure a draft-free fit at the roof. Set the end pieces aside for later.

If you want side windows, now's the time to mark and saw the openings. We're using Plexiglas to cover the openings, although you may want to insert something fancier—or do without openings. But before you check out what your recreation vehicle dealer has for sale, shop several building materials suppliers for a possible good buy on display-size storm windows. For us, however, Plexiglas panels from an abandoned store's display case offered the cheapest way out. Our plans call for 8 x 24-inch cutouts, to be covered with screwed-in Plexiglas pieces measuring 9 x 25 inches. After marking each window opening, drill a ^{1}/$_2$-inch hole inside one corner of the rectangle. With the opening started, cut the rest of it with your saber or keyhole saw. Do the same on the other side panel.

Now load your caulking gun with Liquid Nails to apply a generous coating of glue to the 2 x 2 framing as you nail it on. Your 6d galvanized nails will draw the 2 x 2's against the plywood for a good seal. Nail the 8-foot 2 x 2's first, flush with the bottom and ends of each panel. Then nail two 46^1/$_4$-inch 2 x 2's along the top edge of each sheet, flush with each end, leaving a 3^1/$_2$-inch gap for a 2 x 4 beam that will join the 2 roof panels and help support the roof. Finish the side framing (Diagram 2) by nailing the four 20^3/$_4$-inch studs—one on each end and 2 for center supports, which are especially important if you've decided on a window opening. Nails should

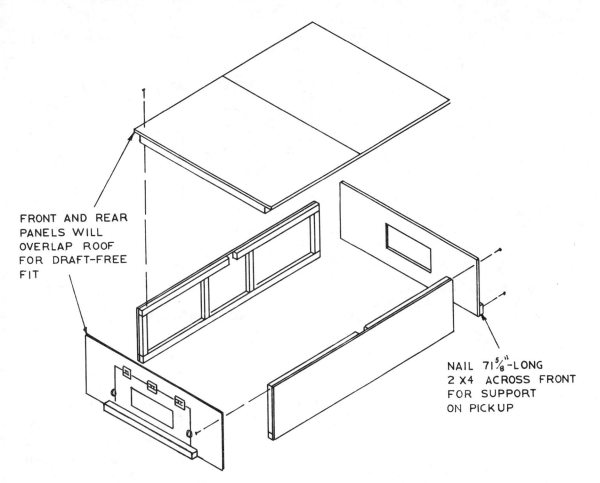

FRONT AND REAR
PANELS WILL
OVERLAP ROOF
FOR DRAFT-FREE
FIT

NAIL 71$\frac{5}{8}$"-LONG
2 X4 ACROSS FRONT
FOR SUPPORT
ON PICKUP

Diagram 2. Framing and assembling the camper top. Cutouts for side windows are optional.

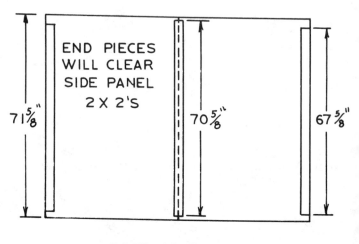

END PIECES
WILL CLEAR
SIDE PANEL
2 X 2'S

$71\frac{5}{8}''$ $70\frac{5}{8}''$ $67\frac{5}{8}''$

Diagram 3. Roof assembly provides for space to attach side panels underneath the roofing sheets.

ROOF ASSEMBLY

be about 2 inches apart, but the rule for this type of framing work is to nail it temporarily in place, and make sure everything fits, before nailing it on completely—otherwise, you may be working more with the claw of the hammer than with its head. Don't puzzle too long, though, or your glue will set.

Your next step is to saw and assemble plywood panels and 2-inch framing for the roof section (Diagram 3). Go ahead and cut two 71⁵/₈-inch lengths from fresh sheets of plywood. Don't worry about the waste, because you can use large leftover pieces for other projects in this book. Nail 67⁵/₈-inch 2 x 2 flush with a long edge of each roofing sheet, allowing a 2-inch overhang of plywood at each end of the 2 x 2. Now join the other long edges with a 70⁵/₈-inch 2 x 4 beam, allowing a ¹/₂-inch overhang of plywood at each end, so the plywood side panels will fit underneath, flush with the edge of the top sheet (Diagram 2).

If there's a time to start cussing (and with most projects, there is), you may be approaching it when you begin to join the roof to the sides. The problem is keeping the loose assembly from crashing apart every time you try to set the first nail. It helps to have a willing assistant (preferably one with asbestos ears) propping the roof while you nail the other side temporarily into the top 2 x 2's. To do the job by yourself, stand a side panel in position against a wall, and place one side of the roof assembly into position on it. Momentarily leave the other side resting on the ground. Then brush glue on top of the 2 x 2 frame of the second panel and place it into position next to the lower roof edge. After making sure hammer and nails are within reach, lift the roof and slip the panel edges into place. Maintain a slight pressure against the assembly toward the wall as you nail the roof to the side panel, and the assembly will remain solid. Turn the camper top and repeat the procedure for the other side.

At this point, your nearly finished canopy will be a little wobbly, so postpone your coffee break until after you've taken steps to correct that condition— namely, joining the front and rear panels. From one of the 24^1/$_4$-inch-wide sheets of plywood you set aside earlier, cut a piece 71^5/$_8$ inches long (Diagram 1). Now mark and cut out a window opening that lines up with the rear window of the cab. Ours is 8 x 24 inches. Nail a 71^5/$_8$-inch 2 x 4 to the bottom of this front panel, flush with the edge and both ends of the sheet, but *on the outside* (Diagram 2), because this board will rest on the front edge of the bed.

For the rear panel, saw a 71^5/$_8$-inch length off the other 24^1/$_4$-inch strip of plywood, and cut out another window opening in line with that of the front panel (so you'll be able to see out the back with your inside rearview mirror). You have several options for the rear window and flap opening. If you choose an extra-large window, for example, the entire rear panel may be hinged at the top and secured at the bottom corners with window locks or hook-and-eye sets. In that case, the inside of the plywood that borders the opening should be reinforced with 2 x 2's or inch-boards. Specially made camper windows are sold by RV dealers; the aluminum-framed models feature lock-open arms that can be bolted to your 2 x 2 framing. Nice, but costly. We decided against a picture window view out the rear, because we'd seen too many rear panes cracked, scratched, or shattered by backing into limbs, or simply by the repeated pounding of opening and closing the flap. Since a smaller pane is less expensive to replace, we settled on a smaller access flap and window opening. Also, we believe the remaining plywood that surrounds our smaller flap gives greater stability. To duplicate ours (which has an 8 x 24-inch window opening), measure in 16 inches from each side of the panel and mark 2 vertical cutting lines that run 21 inches up from the bottom. Your horizontal cut, then, is 3 inches from the top of the panel. To make that one, let your circular saw blade dig into the cutting line (somewhere in the middle) and finish the cut with a saber saw or handsaw; remember, a circular saw won't do a neat job at the corners.

Next, nail a 48-inch 2 x 2 to the *outside* of the flap, along the bottom edge. This board will serve as a crude handle, and will prevent the flap from swinging inward and straining the 3 heavy-duty brass hinges. We're recommending bolts for attaching this flap, as well as the rear windowpane and window locks, because constant use would tear screws out of the plywood. Also, use washers to protect the wood during the bolting process.

The remaining windows may be fastened with screws spaced about 4 inches apart. First, drill 1/8-inch holes about 1/4 inch from the edge of the Plexiglas pieces.

By ruling out shelving in the close quarters of this camper, you could profit from one of our mistakes. After we put in the removable, adjustable type, we learned we couldn't use them unless the truck rested on fairly level ground. Later on, we ruined a transistor radio which we had forgotten to take off a shelf before driving down a bumpy trail.

If you're planning to heat the camper occasionally with our sportsman's stove (project 6), cut a 5-inch-square hole in the upper rear of a side panel. Mark the cut, drill a 1/2-inch hole inside one of the corners, and saw out the opening with your saber or keyhole saw. Next, cut a 3-inch circle in the center of a 6-inch-square piece of 28-gauge galvanized metal, and fasten it with sheet metal screws through 1/16-inch holes drilled along the edge of the sheet. This piece should be attached to the outside of the side panel, and another one may be attached inside with a small bolt, so the stovepipe hole will be covered when the heater isn't in use.

Mounting your finished camper is a 2-man job. Lift it up and slide it onto the ridges of the pickup body. Ask your helper to steady the camper while you climb inside and drill four 3/8" holes—two through each of the bottom rails on the side panels, and then through the metal ridges of the truck. Slip a washer up next to the head of each bolt (to protect the wood) before inserting it. Once you've mounted the thing and tightened the bolts, you know that dismounting it (for better-visibility driving between weekend outings) is as simple as unscrewing 4 bolts and sliding the camper top over the side. Ten minutes, at most.

Windows notwithstanding, you'll find that the camper top will restrict your rear vision. For that reason, we recommend the big, Hollywood (sometimes called West Coast) mirrors for each side of your pickup truck. For extra vision, attach fish-eye mirrors to the lower outside corners of the Hollywoods.

Our son, who helped build our camper top, much prefers our weekend voyager to the family car. At least it keeps him off the streets.

21. PICKUP CARGO CARRIER

One of the first things the owner of a new pickup truck discovers is its lack of trunk space. For all its television stunt ruggedness, weekend practicality, and *macho* maneuverability, this 4-wheeled sportsman's friend isn't much of a luggage carrier during inclement weather. So in our list of truck improvements, a storage compartment rated a higher priority than a CB radio.

If you've checked out side-access pickup utility boxes, chock full of slots, trays, and other compartments, you've probably decided that these slimline boxes are better suited to a construction site plumber than a weekend outdoorsman. In lieu of trunk space, what's needed here is a wide-mouth pickup box with enough room to lay in your prized fishing rod or shotgun, and plenty of space left for tent, sleeping bags, tackle boxes, suitcases, pots and pans, and other gear.

The box we built has enough room (nearly 20 cubic feet) for all these things, so there's no need for a woman's cram-minded help in packing it. The carrier rests without bolts on the side ridges of the truck box, between cab and tire wells, with clearance underneath to prevent damage when it rains while the parked truck is pointed down an incline.

Pickup cargo carrier, offering nearly 20 cubic feet of storage space, features a slanted, lipped lid and 2 x 2 side supports to keep the box off the truck bed.

One man can lift the lid from the side, or slide out the entire carrier when more hauling space is required, or when an outing requires the camper top we've described in project 20. Our design features ³/₄-inch plywood for sturdiness and heavy-load capability, and includes a slanted, lipped cover to shed driving rains.

The building project calls for circular saw, electric drill, sawhorses, "C" clamps, hammer, carpenter's square, screwdriver, block plane or rasp, and caulking gun. We'll warn you again, however, that pickup bed measurements may vary, so check your distances from the front ridge of the bed to the wheel wells, and from side to side. Our carrier was built to provide maximum cargo space in a 35 x 65 ⅝-inch opening, without impairing rearview visibility. Our 64¼-inch-wide box allows just enough play for easy removal.

Bill of Materials

³/₄" A-D exterior-grade plywood:

1	37 x 67"	lid
1	32³/₄ x 62³/₄"	bottom
1	17 x 64¼"	front
1	18½ x 64¼"	rear
2	17 x 18½ x 32³/₄"	sides

1-inch framing boards:

2	1½ x 66"	front, rear lid lips
2	1½ x 34½"	side lips
1	2 x 64¼"	front hinge plate
1	4 x 64¼"	rear hinge plate
2	1 x 62³/₄"	bottom furring strips
2	1 x 31¼"	bottom furring strips

2 x 2's:

2	16³/₄"	rear corner braces
2	15¼"	front corner braces
2	32³/₄"	supports

Liquid Nails or other waterproof glue
6d galvanized nails

6 ¹/₄ x 2¹/₂″ bolts, with washers
3 heavy-duty "T" hinges
2 hasps
   ¹/₈ x 1¹/₈″ screws

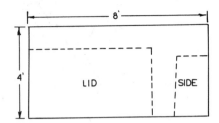

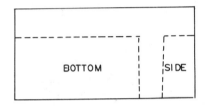

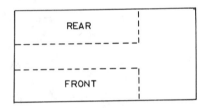

Diagram 1. Cutting pattern for plywood panels of pickup cargo carrier.

In cutting the sheets of plywood, keep in mind that this ³/₄-inch exterior grade is expensive stuff, so a few dumb mistakes here could double your building cost. Therefore, double-check your pencil markings before you start making sawdust. Diagram 1 provides a cutting pattern. Note that by turning the side pieces horizontally, both can be cut from the same piece of plywood used for the bottom, thereby leaving a larger usable piece on the "lid" sheet. But that requires sawing the bottom of a side piece by hand, which can result in a slight wobble in the finished box. We decided to choose a guaranteed cut, and more scrap.

After your sawing, you might as well trim the top angles at the top of the 2 inside-corner 2 x 2's attached to the rear panel (which will allow the lid to close properly later). Mark each 2 x 2 exactly ¹/₁₆ inch from the end and, on the same side of the board, draw a diagonal pencil line to the other corner. This trimming may be too fine a cut for your saw blade, so use a block plane or wood rasp. You have 2 other options here: either saw this angle when you cut the 2 x 2's from a longer board, or forget the angle cut entirely, sawing the 2 x 2's slightly shorter to leave gaps at the top of the box.

Now, glue the corner braces to the inside of the front and rear panels, flush with the top, leaving a ³/₄-inch gap at each end and a 1¹/₂-inch overhang of plywood at the bottom. To get that ³/₄-inch gap exact, simply use a scrap piece of ³/₄-inch plywood as a spacer. This gluing can be done without "C" clamps. Brush the adhesive on one side of the 2 x 2, lower the plywood panel onto it (with the outside of the sheet facing you), and pound in 6d nails about 2 inches apart.

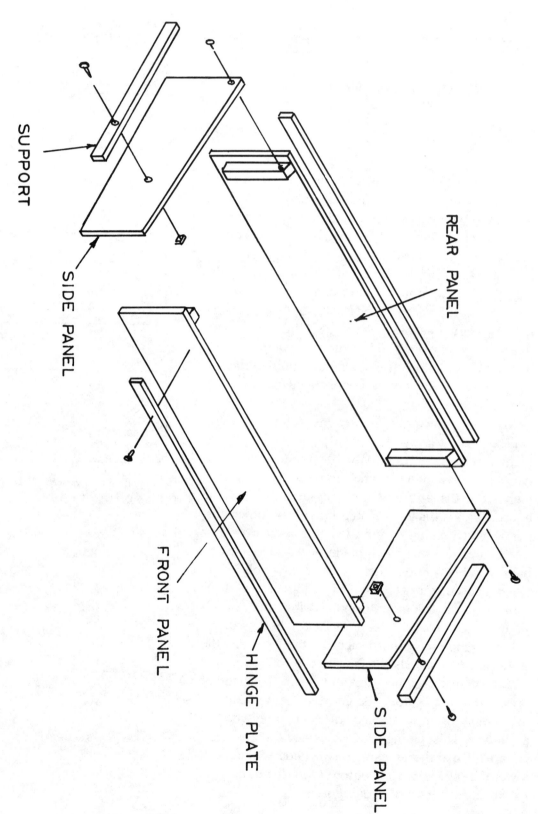

SUPPORT

SIDE PANEL

REAR PANEL

FRONT PANEL

HINGE PLATE

SIDE PANEL

Diagram 2. Assembling the 4 sides of the cargo carrier.

It will be easier to attach your outside hinge plates to the front and rear pieces now than to try hammering them on after the box is assembled. Measure down 1½ inches from the top of each panel and draw a line across. This will be your positioning guide for the top of each inch-board.

The 2 x 2 side supports also should be fastened in advance. Measure up 13½ inches from the bottom of each side piece and draw a line across as a positioning mark for the bottom of each 2 x 2. Drill three ¼-inch holes for bolts, but before inserting them, apply a coat of glue to the inside edge of the 2 x 2. Flop each side panel and drive in a row of 6d nails, 3 inches apart, before the glue sets.

The 4 sides are ready for assembly. Stand up the rear panel on a level floor and apply glue to one of the plywood edges, as well as the side of the 2 x 2. Now stand up 1 side piece and tack it in position at top and bottom before driving in a row of nails, 3 inches apart, into each side of the 2 x 2 joint. A third row of nails, about ¼ inch from the edge of the rear panel, will help seal the plywood ends more tightly. These joined panels should stand by themselves while you join the other side piece, then the front panel (Diagram 2).

Turn the half-finished box upside down. If all your measurements are right, the 32¾ x 62¾-inch plywood sheet will nestle neatly on the butts of the 2 x 2's, with an inch of space between the bottom of the sheet and the bottom edge of the walls, to provide for furring strips (Diagram 3). If the bottom won't go into place, it's possible that the 4 sides of the box are resting slightly out of square. Correct this by lining up one corner with your carpenter's square, and try again. If it still won't fit, perhaps the front or rear sheets of plywood are bowed slightly inward. Spread them with a board scrap underneath for another try at the fitting. As a last resort, plane or rasp the bottom sheet. Another problem can arise as a result of cutting the sheet a shade too short or

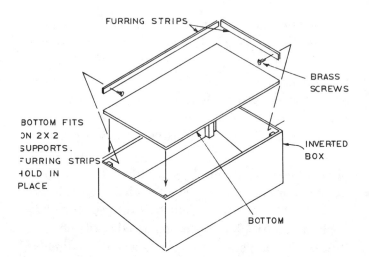

FURRING STRIPS

BRASS
SCREWS

BOTTOM FITS
ON 2 X 2
SUPPORTS.
FURRING STRIPS
HOLD IN
PLACE

INVERTED
BOX

BOTTOM

Diagram 3. Joining and reinforcing the bottom of the cargo carrier—a gluing process.

narrow (which happens to all of us). This error may not be too serious, in this project, because you will be attaching furring strips to support the bottom panel on all 4 sides. Even if you've cut the sheet an inch or 2 short, you may choose to attach wider furring strips (including another bracing board across the center) rather than scrap such a large sheet of plywood. Our design allows you to use 2 x 4 furring strips, if necessary, because the finished carrier won't rest on the bed of the pickup anyway. But let's hope for the best!

Glue the furring strips in place (Diagram 3). We don't suggest that you rush out and buy the half bushel or so of extra "C" clamps to secure all 4 furring strips at once. A portable vise, a pair of vise grips, and wired-together pliers will help hold the side strips, and across the shorter span from front to rear you may use scrap boards as temporary struts. Drill holes *from the inside* for brass screws, 3 inches apart. Here, you have the option of countersinking for flathead screws, or, because your work won't show, using roundheads.

To prevent the bottom sheet from rattling when you bounce along a scrubboard road with an empty carrier, you should secure it to the sides of the box.

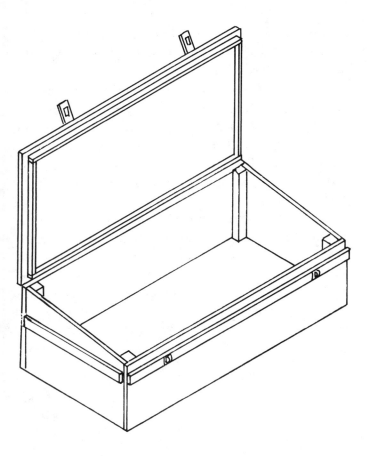

Diagram 4. Lid of the pickup cargo carrier, including a protective lip for weathertightness, is attached at the rear with "T" hinges and secured with hasps.

To do this (while the box is still upside down), measure 1³/₈ inches from the bottom and draw a line around the box, parallel with the edge. This is a nailing guide for your 6d nails, spaced 2 or 3 inches apart. The trick is to pound them in straight, so they don't poke through the plywood sheet.

Putting a protective lip around the bottom edge of the lid (Diagram 4) means still more glue and nails, plus a good deal of "C" clamping. If you didn't have enough clamps for the furring strips, you won't have enough for this step, either; so you'll have to fasten one 1¹/₂-inch strip at a time, and wait a few hours for the glue to harden before transferring your clamps and makeshift holders to another side. Put off the nailing until the glue on all strips has had at least 24 hours to dry. Your parallel-line pencil mark for 6d nails should be $7/8$ inch from the edge of the top sheet.

The rear lip also serves as a plate for hinging the lid to the box. The hinges should allow the cover to rest open more than 90 degrees against the back of the cab while you're loading and unloading cargo. As an optional finishing touch before painting, you may want to bolt a 1 x 2 scrap board inside as a swing-up prop.

Our pickup storage box also has been put to occasional use as a dog carrier. We provided air circulation by laying a board across the front of the open box, from side to side, and tying the front hasps with thin rope or wire. (Another plan for a dog crate can be found in project 3.)

22. SNOWMOBILE CARRIER

Is there any outdoor recreation that compares with hunting and fishing for gear-conscious enthusiasts? We think snowmobiling comes close. Once bitten by this bug, the owner of a new machine wastes little time accessorizing himself for greater enjoyment of the sport. First it's the helmet, then the suit, then perhaps the biggest accessory of all—a second snowmobile for the little woman or youngster who wants to tag along. "Two-snowmobile families" are common here in the north woods, because this activity thrives on the company of others to share the fun, and we've never met a snow rider who prefers the back seat to the driver's seat.

This second machine may settle the question of "Who rides in back?" but it often raises another one: "How do we haul it?" Our pickup truck furnished a dandy bed for carting a snowmobile, but the narrower width between wheel wells wouldn't accommodate 2 of them.

The answer, we decided, was *not* to buy a tilt-bed trailer, complete with special hitch, tires, and taillights to maintain. To be frank, a family that sinks money into that second machine may not have enough leftover loot for fancy wheels to tow it. We believe our solution is not only more economical,

Room for 2 snowmobiles is provided by our pickup carrier, which mounts over the wheel wells. A cleated plywood access ramp is attached to the lowered tailgate with strap iron hooks. Wider-track machines may be mounted side by side in opposite directions.

but safer and more trouble-free than pulling a trailer load of expensive machines.

We built a platform above the wheel wells of our pickup, where there's ample room for side-by-side machines. A cleated ramp works in combination with a slanted approach deck, allowing snowmobiles to be loaded directly from the road, rather than from a high snowbank. After driving the machines onto the platform, we can raise its hinged approach deck and slide the ramp underneath for storage. And the 2 snowmobilers who use this carrier can easily remove it to make room for other pickup-mounted units (described in projects 20 and 21), during other recreation seasons.

With circular saw or crosscut handsaw, level, square, hammer, screwdriver, and electric drill, you can build a carrier similar to ours in less than a day.

Bill of Materials

2	2 x 12's, 96" long*	platform supports
18	1 x 6's, 63" long	deck boards
1	2 x 4, 84" long	platform reinforcement
2	2 x 4's, 40" long	platform reinforcement
3	2 x 2's, 45³/₄" long	struts
1	³/₄ x 48 x 96"	ramp
7	1 x 2's, 12" long	ramp cleats
2	2 x 2's, 96" long	ramp side rails
2	1 x 4's, 26" long	approach deck framing
1	2 x 4, 48" long	approach deck reinforcement
2	2 x 4's, 22" long	approach deck reinforcement
2	heavy-duty hinges, with bolts	
2	strap iron hooks	
4	³/₁₆ x 1" stove bolts	

*2 x 10's or even 2 x 8's may be adequate.

Before buying lumber or cutting any of it to size, don't assume that all pickup beds have the same dimensions. A friend of ours made this mistake when he tried to copy our pattern, and discovered too late that our platform wouldn't fit in his pickup.

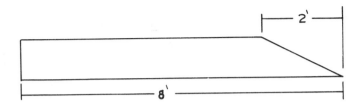

Diagram 1. Sawing 2 x 12 support for the slanted approach deck.

So to avoid wood wasting and return trips to the lumberyard, take careful measurements of your truck bed. To make sure of a snug fit and a square platform as the project goes along, you may want to build part of the thing right in the pickup.

As you've noticed from the photograph, the deck of our carrier consists of a platform and slanted approach ramp. To get a satisfactory angle for this slant, measure down 2 feet from one end of each 2 x 12 and draw a diagonal line to the corner on the opposite edge of the board.

After sawing the corners off both boards (Diagram 1), set the 2 x 12's in the pickup bed and line them up squarely against the wheel wells. As a double check on your measurements, try to close the tailgate; if you can't, you'll have to trim each board on the butt end.

With the 2 x 12's held squarely in place, tack a 1 x 6 across the bed to join the butt ends, and another 1 x 6 across the other end of the level platform section, 1 inch ahead of your angle cut to provide for hinge action. (Our decking boards were sawed to length from 6-foot lumber; but we didn't cut them to fit until we were ready to nail the first one to the 2 x 12's.) While the first 2 boards are nailed temporarily, lay on more 1 x 6's to fill the platform span. The reason for this, as we've explained with other projects, is to make certain the boards will fit the space neatly before you begin nailing them on permanently. If there's a gap too narrow for another board, you have several options, such as trimming a board or substituting a wider or narrower one. How-

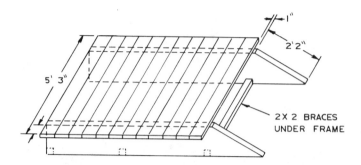

Diagram 2. Assembling the deck of the snowmobile carrier.

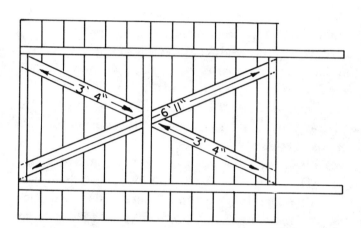

Diagram 3. An "X" brace of 2 x 4's on the underside of the deck will help it support the weight of 2 machines.

ever, since draining melted snow is a desirable feature for a snowmobile platform, it's perfectly all right to spread the boards out a bit, leaving uniform spaces in the decking. When you're satisfied with the lineup, check it with your level and mark a nailing row across the platform boards above each 2 x 12. Finish hammering the platform together and lift it out of the pickup bed for trimming the sides (if necessary) and underpinning work (Diagram 2).

An "X" reinforcement of 2 x 4's on the underside of the platform will enable it to support the weight of 2 snowmobiles with little or no sag. Tack on these 2 x 4's by nailing from the bottom, then set the

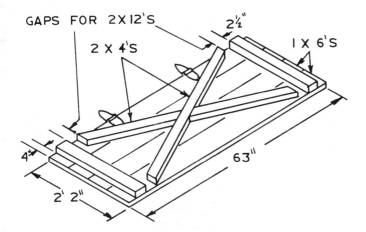

GAPS FOR 2X12'S

2 X 4'S

2½"

1 X 6'S

4"

63"

2' 2"

Diagram 4. Optional hinged approach deck for the snowmobile carrier, showing underside framing of 2 x 4's.

platform rightside up on sawhorses, mark a corresponding X-shaped nailing row, and nail from the top (Diagram 3). To prevent an eventual toe-in of the 2 x 12's, brace them across the bottom with three 2 x 2's.

The ramp section of the deck is next. You may decide to build it without a swing-up feature. In that case, nail the 1 x 6's down the slant, with drain spaces between boards (or trimming a board if necessary), and add support with an "X" reinforcement of 2 x 4's. But we think you'll appreciate the convenience of a hinged ramp for access to more storage space. If so, the deck boards for the hinged ramp for access to more storage space. If so, the deck boards for the hinged ramp shouldn't be nailed to the 2 x 12's, but to 2 x 4 framing—2 boards on each side and 3 more that make up the "X" brace. Be certain to leave space for this ramp to close over the 2 x 12's below. Heavy-duty strap hinges will secure the hinged deck to the platform (Diagram 4).

As for the 8-foot ramp up to the truck bed, don't plunge into building it until you take accurate width measurements of the snowmobiles you'll be hauling. The ramp must be wide enough for the ski runners. Nail on 2 x 2 side rails and 1 x 2's for cleats.

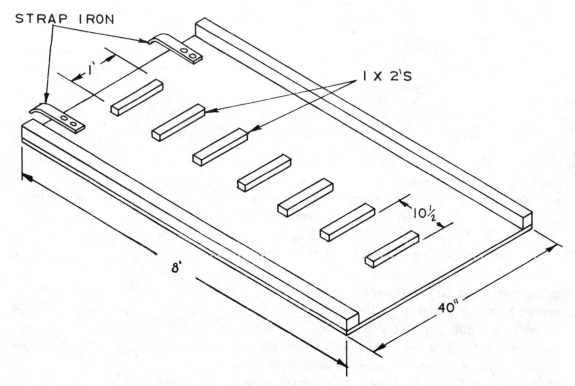

STRAP IRON

1'

1 X 2'S

$10\frac{1}{2}$

8'

40"

Diagram 5. Cleated plywood ramp to the snowmobile carrier can be hooked to the edge of a fully lowered pickup tailgate.

Centering these cleats isn't critical, except for appearance. The ramp is ready for loading when you've bolted on strap iron hooks and attached them to the lowered tailgate (Diagram 5).

INDEX

(Boldface numbers refer to illustrations)

THE COMPLETE ILLUSTRATED STORY

ISBN 0 78580 715 2

Executive Editor: Lorraine Dickey
Design: Vicky Harvey, Tony Truscott
Picture Research: Sharon Hutton
Editor: Lol Henderson, Ian Cranna
Production: Sarah Schuman

Printed in Italy

THE COMPLETE ILLUSTRATED STORY

Terry Burrows

CHARTWELL
BOOKS, INC.

CONTENTS

INTRODUCTION

Saturday, July 6th, 1957 is not a date that would evoke strong memories for many people. In Liverpool it was probably much the same as any other mid-summer day. The school term would have broken up until the end of August, so the city and the suburbs would have been littered with bored teenagers looking for adventure or mischief. They might have been hanging about in coffee bars feeding the juke box. They certainly wouldn't have been listening to the radio – all they would have heard was the dull drone of light orchestral music and middle-aged crooners. It would have been just like any other day.

John Lennon, a 17-year-old art student, had found one way around the boredom. It was rock and roll. His skiffle group, the Quarry Men, played wherever and whenever they could find an audience. Today, though, he failed to notice that someone in the typically small crowd was watching his performance more intently than anyone else. After the show, John's friend Ivan Vaughan told him there was someone he wanted John to meet. Paul McCartney stepped forward. Saturday, July 6th, 1957 was indeed a historic date in the annals of popular music.

The mid-1950s had seen the start of a revolution imported from across the Atlantic that would forever divide generations: the cult of youth. With rock and roll, the first teenagers were born. To Lennon and McCartney, and a million others, Elvis Presley had come to save the world from

7

INTRODUCTION

The Beatles - more than just a pop group

terminal mediocrity, and given their lives a new meaning. But with a new decade now about to start, things seemed to be drifting backwards. Elvis had been drafted and was now a shadow of his former self. Buddy Holly was dead. Sure, there were new stars, but these were just a new generation of clean-cut, all-American crooners – or worse still, feeble British imitations. It was beginning to look as if those ageing wishful thinkers who had doubted rock and roll's longevity might have been right – perhaps it was just a fad. However, it was too late for Lennon and McCartney; they'd caught the fever and there would be no going back.

When the Beatles' debut single, "Love Me Do", gently crept into the British top twenty near the end of 1962, most people thought they were a new group – an overnight sensation. Few knew about the years they had devoted to learning their craft, just hoping to be taken seriously in Liverpool. Few outside of their home town knew of the seven-hour performances in seedy nightclubs on Hamburg's Reeperbahn, which had turned them into highly polished performers. And nobody knew that popular culture was about to be blown apart, and that almost everything the Beatles would do over the next seven years, not only their music, but their clothes, their haircuts, their behaviour, their album sleeves, their attitudes would define an era.

Think of the key events of the decade, from John F. Kennedy's assassination to Neil Armstrong setting foot on the moon. Now start filling in the holes: "Beatlemania"; the Beatles on Ed Sullivan, preparing to conquer America; the Royal Variety Show; the MBEs; the "more popular than Jesus" controversy; "Yellow Submarine"; "Sgt Pepper"; "All you need is Love" on the first world-wide satellite link; the Maharishi; the "bed-

ins"; the drug busts... the list seems endless. Right up to their miserable demise in 1970, the fortunes and activities of the Beatles mirrored the path of a generation and a decade. For many people – and some who were not yet born – the 1960s were such special years because they were touched by the genius of the Beatles.

The influence the Beatles had on the course of popular music was, of course, profound – indeed it is incalculable. That influence has continued to make its presence felt in the gap left by their parting. Almost every major songwriter of the past 20 years cites Lennon and McCartney as a source of inspiration. Producers point to the collaboration between the Beatles and George Martin as benchmarks in the use of the recording studio. Some have gone a whole lot further. Each successive generation seems to produce its own faux Beatles – from the Electric Light Orchestra in the 1970s to Oasis, one of the most popular bands of the 1990s.

Living in an age where the old divisions of high and low culture have largely been demolished, it comes as no surprise to see the Beatles afforded as much respect as the greatest composers or jazz musicians. What is surprising is how much they have become a part of our lives. Although over a quarter of a century has passed since they made their final recordings, the Beatles remain the most famous pop group in the world.

TERRY BURROWS

FROM LIVERPOOL TO HAMBURG AND BACK AGAIN

First they were the Quarry Men, then the Silver Beetles. As the Beatles, John, Paul, George, Pete and Stu struggled to establish themselves in their home town. It was a three-month stint in Hamburg that turned them into seasoned professionals ready to take on the world.

The city of Liverpool, the principal port in the north-west of England, and one of Europe's traditional seafaring gateways to America, was not the safest place to be living in the early days of the Second World War. The city's naval shipyards and miles of commercial dock land along the river Mersey made it a particularly attractive target to the *Luftwaffe* who were regularly terrorizing mainland Britain. The October 9th, 1940 saw a particularly fierce spate of night raids, but this was the last thing on the mind of the young Julia Lennon as she lay in Liverpool's Oxford Street Maternity Home. With bombs falling around the hospital, Julia gave birth to a boy. She decided to name him John. His second name, in honour of Britain's heroic wartime leader, was Winston.

Julia was one of five daughters. Her father worked for the Glasgow and Liverpool Salvage Company – the numerous shipwrecks along the Mersey had kept him and his colleagues busy ever since the air raids had first started. Julia was the wild one of the family. Two years earlier, while wandering on Sefton Park, she had met a merchant seaman named Freddy Lennon. They quickly became an item, although seemingly more interested in having a laugh than enjoying any serious commitment to one another. Nonetheless, on an impulse, and much to her family's dismay, Julia announced that they were to marry. It was not to be the closest of partnerships – Freddy worked on the great

passenger liners that travelled between Liverpool and New York and they were apart more often than not. Freddy was berthed in New York when war broke out. Wanting to avoid participation at all costs he jumped ship. He was eventually interned at Ellis Island, and ended up serving a sentence for desertion at a British military prison in North Africa. Julia herself would later admit that her decision to marry Freddy was one of the least serious of her life. While Freddy returned to Liverpool for a few brief visits in 1940 – long enough to "put her in the family way" as she put it – he pretty well disappeared from her life after that.

The war brought hardship to everyone, but it was an especially difficult time for a young mother. Julia was not only unhappy but unsettled. She longed for the carefree times she had before the war, and before she became tied down with John. While Julia was not a poor mother, much of the burden of child care fell on the rest of her family. It quickly became apparent that her sister Mimi was forming an especially close relationship with John. Far from causing any jealousy, it came as a relief to Julia. As the war came to an end, life in Liverpool began to get back to normality.

Julia was still young and attractive and there was soon a new man in her life. Working at a café in Penny Lane, she met John Dykins and decided that she would live with him. Julia would not be taking John with her either. An extremely satisfactory solution was worked out – John would be adopted by the childless Mimi and her husband George Smith. He would go with them to live at *Mendips*, a semi-detached house in Menlove Avenue, Woolton. A stark contrast to the Newcastle Road address where John had spent his first few years, Woolton was a pleasant middle-class suburb three miles outside

Liverpool – Europe's gateway to the Atlantic

Mendips – 251 Menlove Avenue, Woolton

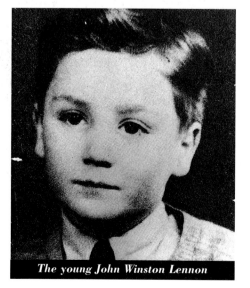

The young John Winston Lennon

Liverpool's city centre. George Smith was a well-respected man who owned the local farm and dairy. Julia knew that her son would be well looked after.

From birth, John Lennon's artistic leanings made themselves known to the world. He was a very bright child who had easily learned to read by the age of four. "Aunt Mimi" sent him off to school at Dovedale Primary, near Penny Lane. One of John's earliest passions was for reading, especially Richmal Crompton's *Just William* books – a series that described the misadventures of an uncontrollable 11-year-old. He soon developed an interest in writing and drawing his own books and comics. He also began to develop a taste for the kind of petty mischief that would get him into trouble time and time again in the future.

When he was 12, John was sent up to Quarry Bank Grammar, a school with a fine record of academic achievement. He started out as one the school's brightest hopes, but with his friend Pete Shotton always close at hand, John began a startling academic decline. As Shotton says, "We started in our first year at the top and gradually sank together into the sub-basement."

John Lennon became more and more of a troublemaker. Mimi, by now a widow,

Mimi Smith – "Aunt Mimi" – the most influential figure in John's childhood

began to dread the periodic phone calls from the school secretary detailing John's latest misdemeanours. The Quarry Bank punishment book records the diversity of the boys' criminal activity: "insolence", "throwing a blackboard duster out of the window", "gambling on the school field", "failing to report to a school office"... the list was endless. Admittedly these "crimes" didn't amount to anything too serious, but it was clear that, by his early teens, John Lennon had already carved out a reputation as a fledgling rebel.

Whilst John worshipped Aunt Mimi, Julia had always remained in close contact with John, visiting him most weeks. As he grew older he began to see more and more of her, often cutting out classes to do so. He thought of Julia more as an older sister than his mother. What's more, she told them the kind of things that he wanted to hear, like not to worry about homework or what they might do in the future. This was a singular contrast to Aunt Mimi, who was something of a disciplinarian.

MEET THE QUARRY MEN...

In mid-Fifties England there was no such thing as a teenager. When you reached the age of sixteen you were deemed to be an adult and would start dressing much the same way as your parents. That was until the Teddy Boys started to appear. These young rebels would wear outlandish draped jackets, frilled shirts and skin-tight "drainpipe" trousers. The hair was something else entirely. In a post-war era where the crew-cut was still the norm for any respectable young man, the "Teds" stuck out a mile with their greased locks and quiffs flopping down over the forehead. They also had their own music. Rock and roll, the new American fad, was gradually beginning to take off in England's cities. In 1955, their anthem, 'Rock Around The Clock', had turned an ageing country singer called Bill Haley into the first manifestation of youth rebellion. When Elvis Presley emerged the following year society began to change – things would never be the same again. Teenagers understood it; everyone else was baffled.

John Lennon was by now well ensconced in the rock and roll lifestyle. He would take every opportunity to beg Aunt Mimi or Julia to buy him the clothes. Mimi held out the longest saying, "Those drainpipe trousers and drape jackets are no kind of dress for a Quarry Bank boy." Her arguments were in vain. At this time, rock and roll was still very much an American phenomenon. As John Lennon remembered, "There was no such thing as an English record... the first one that was anything near it was 'Move It' by Cliff Richard. Before that there was nothing." A pivotal moment in British rock history came when Tony "Lonnie" Donegan, a banjo player in a well-known "trad jazz" group, formed a small skiffle band and recorded an American folk song called 'Rock Island Line'. The group's principal instrument was an acoustic guitar, but the

Ken Brown, guitarist in the Quarry Men

The Lonnie Donegan Skiffle Group

rhythm was provided by playing a wash-board with a thimble – the washboard was still used by many people at this time to scrub their clothes. 'Rock Island Line' topped the record charts, and suddenly skiffle groups began to spring up all over the country.

John became obsessed. He had to have a guitar – that was all there was to it. Eventually Mimi succumbed to the pressure. One Saturday morning, she checked her purse, put on her coat, and took John down to Hessey's music shop in the middle of Liverpool. Mimi paid £17 for a steel-strung Spanish guitar. From that moment John Lennon was a lost cause in terms of conventionality. Mimi had still to be con-

vinced, however, and told him, "The gui-tar's all very well, John, but you'll never make a living out of it."

Mustering all the enthusiasm that they'd failed to put into their school work, Lennon and Shotton, Quarry Bank's resi-dent teenage rebels, decided to form their own skiffle group. They called themselves the Quarry Men. John would sing and play the guitar and Pete would play the wash-board. They were joined by a growing number of enthusiasts: Nigel Whalley and Ivan Vaughan, who shared duties on the tea-chest bass; Rod Davis, whose parents had just bought him a banjo; guitarist Eric Griffiths and drummer Colin Hanton. The Quarry Men performed Lonnie Donegan's

songs, as well as American rock and roll hits like Carl Perkins' 'Blue Suede Shoes'. The Quarry Men began to get engagements at school dances and youth clubs, but were rarely received with any great enthusiasm. For the moment, the Quarry Men were completely without ambition – at least half of them were only doing it for a laugh. However, although there were differing views on the direction they should take, there was no disputing that John Lennon was the boss.

John's school work had now deteriorat-ed to the point where he was unlikely to pass any exams at all – if he even both-ered turning up to take them. In the mean time, a new young headmaster had arrived at Quarry Bank. He realized that the only subject Lennon enjoyed was art – even if he always failed his exams – and used his connections to arrange a place for John at the local art school.

"This Is Paul. This Is John."

The Quarry Men kept stumbling along, mostly fired by John's enthusiasm. Somehow they were invited to play at St Peter's Parish annual church fete in Woolton. They would have to perform on the back of a lorry in the parade and then afterwards on stage at the fete. The event was to take place on July 6th, 1957. Nobody could have predicted the significance of this date. Ivan Vaughan, no longer playing with the Quarry Men, came to the fete, bringing along a school friend from the Liverpool Institute. He was especially keen for John to meet his friend – he felt sure that they had a lot in common, and would hit it off. That friend was Paul McCartney. As the Quarry Men played their set, Paul watched intently from the side of the stage.

James Paul McCartney was born in Liverpool's Walton General Hospital on June 18th, 1942. His father Jim, like many "Scousers", had an Irish background. He worked during the day on the Liverpool Cotton Exchange in Chapel Street, before the war forced its closure. At night, however, he turned to his first love – music. Jim was a self-taught pianist who led the Jim Mac Jazz Band, making an extra few shillings playing at social clubs and works dances. Whilst Jim McCartney had a reputation as a diligent and skillful salesman, he was also by all accounts something of ladies' man. Having successfully escaped the responsibility of marriage and a family throughout his twenties and thirties, he seemed destined for a life of bachelorhood. Then he met Mary Mohin. They married in 1941, a few months before Jim's 40th birthday.

Paul was seemingly graced from birth with charm that would get him out of all manner of childhood scrapes. Performing well at primary school, Paul easily passed

his "Eleven Plus" examinations, winning a place at the City's most prestigious grammar school, The Liverpool Institute. Paul was an innocuous enough pupil, always helpful and quietly studious. He held his own in the school's A-stream, finding that most school work came to him quite easily. In subjects that he didn't care for he could still usually muster enough effort to achieve a low-grade pass.

In 1955, when Paul was still only 13, his mother fell ill. After experiencing pains in her chest she was diagnosed as having breast cancer. By the time she was taken into hospital for exploratory surgery, the cancer had already spread too far and the proposed mastectomy operation could not be performed. Mary died shortly after-

wards. Devastated by her death, Jim took over the arduous task of looking after the family finances – Mary's wages as a health worker had always been relied upon to keep their heads above water – and rearing Paul and Michael, his two teenage sons.

With a musician for a father, the McCartney household had always been filled with music. Like many homes before the arrival of television, the piano was the centre-piece around which the family would congregate for communal sing-songs. But the McCartneys were now distinctly out of tune with one another. Like John Lennon, Paul had heard Lonnie Donegan and wanted a guitar. While Jim McCartney did display an interest in the

Jim McCartney encouraged Paul's musical development

new rock and roll music, he was more concerned that his family should not have a Teddy-Boy in their number.

Eventually, without too much persuasion, Jim relented. One night he came home from work carrying a sunburst-coloured guitar and set about teaching Paul some basic chords. However, he was surprised to see the difficulty with which Paul squeezed the fingers of his left hand into position on the fret board. Paul struggled for a while before giving up – it seemed that he just didn't have it. That is, until the day that Paul discovered that by holding the guitar in the other hand the whole process was that much simpler. It seems that whilst he was right handed in everything else, for some unfathomable reason playing the guitar right-handed felt completely wrong. After restringing the guitar, Paul set about learning the chords again. This time there was no turning back. All his waking hours were devoted the instrument and the promising start to an academic career was cut short by the six-stringed beast.

John and Paul's first meeting started out as a cool affair. A few diffident "Hi's" were tossed about until Paul revealed a winning secret. As Pete Shotton says, "He actually knew how to tune a guitar." Lennon's attitude softened further when Paul revealed that he knew the words to quite a few rock and roll songs "all the way through". John had recently taken to making up his own lyrics, although this was primarily because he could never remember other people's all the way through. The meeting ended with Paul playing a brief set of Little Richard's songs with John carefully studying the chord shapes Paul was playing.

Having Paul McCartney on the scene posed John Lennon quite a dilemma. Until then, the Quarry Men had been an extension of his school gangs – there was a strong crossover of personnel between the two. In both areas, John was the undisputed leader. Paul would be a major asset to the Men, but he was also clearly a far better musician than any of them. He also possessed a cocky arrogance and Lennon realized that he wouldn't be able to boss

him around like the others. Nonetheless, within a few weeks John made up his mind – he sent Pete Shotton out on a mission to tell Paul that he wanted him in the band.

Lennon and Shotton, Quarry Bank's troublesome duo, gradually became less and less inseparable. Eventually, after John smashed the washboard over his head, Pete retired from the music business! It was now John and Paul who began to spend more and more time together. While two more different personalities were hard to imagine – John, rebellious with his dry cutting wit, and Paul, ambitious, hard-working with a desire to please everyone – their shared love of music and guitars brought them close together. The other Quarry Men were less convinced. They found McCartney bossy and big-headed. He always seemed to know best, telling the musicians how to play their own instruments.

Little by little, the Quarry Men became more proficient, until they were offered a gig at a well-known jazz club in Mathew Street. The club had reluctantly begun to allow skiffle music, but didn't permit rock and roll. The gig seemed to be going well when John was handed a note from the audience. "John thought it was a request," remembers drummer Colin Hanton, "but it was from the management, saying 'Cut out the bloody rock'." Little did they know that it wouldn't be the last time they played at this particular club – The Cavern.

THE FAB THREE

1957 would be a difficult year for the Quarry Men. John Lennon was now at art school, but fared no better than he had at Quarry Bank. In fact, in many ways things were worse – instead of the "street" credibility that school rebels often have among their peers, he was now surrounded by jazz-loving art students, who despised the Teddy Boy in their midst. Frankly, he was miserable: "When I was at art school they'd only allow jazz to be played, so we had to con them into letting us have it [rock and roll] on the record player by

calling it 'blues'." Matters deteriorated badly when, following a visit to Mimi's house, his mother Julia was knocked over and killed by a car. John was devastated – Julia had been totally indulgent of his moods and attitudes. He saw her as a carefree spirit – someone who would approve of anything he did without question. Now she was gone. The shared experience of losing a mother brought Lennon and McCartney closer together.

In the meantime, the other Quarry Men were in the throes of school exams or sorting out careers for themselves. Whilst Paul's school work had slipped badly, his father still hoped that he would do well enough to get into the sixth-form and finally go to college to train as a teacher. Paul, although he had other plans himself, went along with the idea for the time being.

The duo threw themselves more and more into making the Quarry Men work. Skiffle had been a short-lived fad. Rock and roll was the real thing. All the best Liverpool skiffle bands were changing their names – The Gerry Marsden Skiffle Group became Gerry and the Pacemakers, The Alan Caldwell Skiffle Group became Rory Storm and the Raving Texans. The drive, as ever, was coming from America. In Britain, the music being served up was a never-ending stream of crooners or limp, second-rate rockers like Tommy Steele and Marty Wilde. Those who were hip knew the real names – Bill Haley, Fats Domino, Little Richard and needless to say, the greatest of them all, Elvis. But there was also something new going on. Rising stars like Eddie Cochran and Buddy Holly were not only brilliant performers, they also wrote their own songs. So it was that Paul McCartney and John Lennon set to the task of creating new material. They became extremely competitive, writing songs as if their lives depended on it, each one trying to outdo the other.

At around the same time, Paul started to strike up an uneasy friendship with another pupil at the Liverpool Institute. George Harrison was 18 months younger than Paul, and was in the year below him. He was also a keen guitarist and they soon started to rehearse in George's bedroom.

George was born on February, 25th 1943. His father Harry had originally been a steward on a passenger ship, but lost his job during the Depression. He now worked for Liverpool Corporation as a bus conductor. George's mother Louise had worked in greengrocer's shop before starting a family. Compared to John or Paul, George's Liverpool upbringing was a much earthier affair.

George attended Dovedale primary school at the same time as John Lennon, although he was two years younger. As age differences to primary school children often seem vastly exaggerated, they were pretty well unaware of one other. George,

like Paul, won a place to the Liverpool Institute, but his school career was destined to go nowhere and at a great speed. George quickly developed a hatred for all kinds of formal teaching. Unlike Lennon, he didn't cause trouble or make a nuisance of himself. He rebelled quietly, simply refusing to take part in school life. By the age of 13 he had found solace in the guitar and skiffle music. He borrowed the money from his mother to buy a good guitar – one with a cutaway at the top of the body. He paid off the debt by taking a Saturday morning delivery round at his local butcher's shop. This was all George cared about.

Paul suggested that the Quarry Men

admit George to their ranks. Everyone in the band hated the idea. For a start he was only 14. Even so, Paul introduced him to the band one night. More interested by his flashy cutaway guitar than anything else, the others listened. John was impressed, but George was still only 14!

Undeterred, George became one of the band's most faithful followers. He would invariably turn up at their gigs, always with his guitar in hand. From time to time, if John was feeling generous, he would let him take the odd solo. George, however, had an important trick up his sleeve – he told John that it would be fine for the band to rehearse at his house at weekends. This

The Fab Three – all they needed was a drummer

is how George gradually eased himself into the Quarry Men.

THE SILVER BEETLES

The Quarry Men, now down to a core of Lennon, McCartney and Harrison, began playing in various combinations under names like the Rainbows or Johnny and the Moondogs. At around the same time, John had finally met another art student whom he could bear to be with. Stuart Sutcliffe was a brilliant young artist, destined for great success – everyone from his fellow students to the tutors was agreed on that. Sutcliffe was also an outcast from the other students. He would wear skin tight jeans and brightly coloured shirts, but he was in no way a Teddy Boy. In fact, to many of the other students he was worse than Lennon, he was just plain weird.

Stu and John quickly became close friends. He taught John about art movements, creating an interest and enthusiasm that none of his tutors had ever managed. Although Stuart Sutcliffe had never played an instrument or showed any signs of musical ability, Lennon wanted him in the band. Stu was interested, but had no money for equipment. The answer came when Sutcliffe exhibited a painting at a John Moores Exhibition at the city's prestigious Walker Art Gallery. John Moores, one of Liverpool's greatest patrons, was so impressed with the painting that he bought it for himself. Stu received the hefty sum of £65. His proud parents thought the money would keep him in expensive art materials for the rest of his course. Their pride turned to dismay as Stu went straight out to Hessy's music shop and bought a Hofner "President" bass guitar.

Rock and roll really took off in Liverpool in 1960 when Larry Parnes, Britain's major pop impresario, brought US rockers Eddie Cochran and Gene Vincent to play at the Liverpool Empire. The show was a sell-out success. Local promoter Allan Williams had the idea of bringing the stars back to Liverpool this time supporting them with local talent. Mr "Parnes Shillings and Pence" agreed to the idea.

Liverpool's 6000-seater boxing stadium would be the venue. Cochran and Vincent would be supported by Rory Storm and the Hurricanes, easily the city's most popular rock and roll combo. The Hurricanes, well respected by the likes of Lennon and McCartney, had quickly progressed beyond their skiffle origins and now featured a tight rocking rhythm section. The band's drummer was a mournful-looking young man with rings on every finger. His name was Richard Starkey, but everyone called him Ringo.

The concert was all set to be a sell-out

when the news began to filter through of a road accident. Eddie Cochran and Gene Vincent had been returning to London from an engagement in Bristol. Vincent was seriously injured – Cochran was dead. Allan Williams had already invested considerable sums of money in the show. Rather than cancelling, he decided to recruit more local bands and make it a showcase for Liverpool's rock and roll talent. The Quarry Men thought this might be their chance and approached Williams. He was unimpressed. The band who would eventually change the face of pop music

Stuart Sutcliffe – a talented young artist

Liverpool's top rocker, Rory Storm, takes tea with his mum, Vi Caldwell

Richard Starkey – Ringo to his mates – with his mother Elsie and step-father Harry Graves

was not even deemed good enough to be considered for the bill. In the event, the show was a sell-out success that helped to establish Liverpool as the focal point of British rock and roll outside London.

All was not lost for the band: Allan Williams started to become an important figure. He gave them the occasional gig at the tiny Jacaranda club, where his office was based. Williams also found them a drummer, 36-year-old Tommy Moore. Tommy, apart from being nearly twice their age, didn't fit in with the band at all, but he was a good musician, and their lack of a permanent drummer was something of an embarrassment to them. Perhaps one of Williams' best pieces of advice was to come up with a suitable name – something like Buddy Holly's band, the Crickets. Stu

Sutcliffe laughingly suggested that they be called the Beetles. John, unable to let an opportunity for a pun pass him by, changed the spelling to "Beatles". Williams and everyone else at the Jacaranda agreed that this was a terrible name. They became the Silver Beetles.

Larry Parnes, ever on the look out for a new way to make or save money, came up with a brilliantly original idea. He began to sign up solo artists, re-christen them with suitably rock and roll names, and tour them around the country accompanied by cheap backing musicians. Impressed with the talent that Allan Williams had presented to him, he decided to hold auditions in Liverpool to find a backing group for his latest teenage sensation, Billy Fury. Ronald Wycherley had formerly been a

Liverpool tug-boat worker, but after Parnes renamed him Billy Fury he became a massive success. Fury was not only Liverpool's first rock star, but also one of Britain's few credible rock and rollers. Consequently, Liverpool's top bands turned out for the audition. The Silver Beetles, gazing around the hall at the opposition, felt out of their class. Although Fury was reported to have liked them the best, they didn't get the job – that went to Cass and the Cassanovas. Parnes, though, was impressed enough to offer them another job. The Silver Beetles would tour Scotland backing one of his new signings, Johnny Gentle.

The tour was only supposed to last for two weeks. But for Tommy Moore it seemed to go on forever. On only the second night Tommy was injured when

Pete Best completes the line-up

Johnny Gentle, the worse for wear from the alcohol he invariably used to soothe his stage fright, reversed their van into a parked car. Tommy was in the back of the van, and the entire drum kit fell on top of him. He was rushed off to the local hospital but managed to limp through the rest of the tour under heavy sedation. When the Silver Beetles returned to Liverpool he announced his retirement from the music business.

Around this time, the summer of 1960, the band started to make occasional recordings. These were low-fidelity affairs performed in Paul McCartney's home, recorded on a borrowed reel-to-reel tape machine. Three recently unearthed tracks appear on the 1995 *Anthology 1* album. The first track is a cover of the Ray Charles hit 'Hallelujah I Love Her So'. 'You'll Be Mine' is the most interesting of the trio as it is the earliest recording of a Lennon and McCartney joint composition. The track, featuring Paul on lead vocals, clearly shows the influence of black American doo-wop groups like the Platters and the Inkspots. The final track 'Cayenne' is a Shadows-like guitar instrumental written by Paul. These tracks are the only known recordings to feature Stuart Sutcliffe. While the recordings bubble with a crude energy there is barely a hint of what would come later.

GERMANY CALLING...

As a result of the Johnny Gentle tour, the Silver Beetles could at least now be considered a little more seriously. What's more, Allan Williams had told them that he'd be prepared to get them more engagements when they found a new drummer. Williams was at this time enjoying some new-found success overseas. He had sent off two of his artists to play residencies at the Kaiserkeller club in Hamburg. From the accounts he was receiving from the club's owner, Bruno Koschmider, his bands Derry and the Seniors and solo singer Tony Sheridan were going down a storm. Koschmider was so happy with this new arrangement that he decided to hire a third

Hamburg – the Beatles' first great adventure

band to play at another one of his joints – the Indra club. The request posed a problem for Williams. He wanted to send his top band, Rory Storm and the Hurricanes, but they were already playing a lucrative summer season at a Butlins holiday camp in Skegness. Reluctantly Williams offered Koschmider the Silver Beetles – or the Beatles, as they now insisted on calling themselves

The band didn't even need to be asked. All that had to be sorted was the logistics of easing out of their existing responsibilities. The matter was no problem for John and Paul. John was already set to abandon his disastrous art school course, and Paul had just finished his "A" level examina-

tions and so had effectively left school. George, who had finished school at the age of 15 with virtually no qualifications at all, had been taken on by a local company as an apprentice electrician. Oddly, whilst at 17 he was the youngest member of the band, his family had no qualms about him giving up his job to play in a rock and roll group in Germany: if that was what he wanted then it was fine by them. Things were more difficult for Stu. The talented artist with a great career ahead of him was about to engage in post-graduate studies at the art school. At first he decided that it was too much to give up – everyone knew he was a useless musician anyway. John quickly persuaded him otherwise. Stu's

tutors were disappointed, but his reputation was such that the college reluctantly agreed to keep his place open for him.

One problem still remained: there was no drummer. The solution came from an unexpected source. The Casbah club, in the basement of a 14-room house in Hayman's Green, had been a popular haunt for the band over the years – they had played, rehearsed and hung out there on numerous occasions. The club's owner, Mona Best, had a son who often played the drums with the bands that rehearsed and played in the club. Pete Best was a brilliant pupil and athlete from the Liverpool Collegiate Grammar School, who happened to find himself at a loose end. Like Paul,

Vi Caldwell reads a card from Hamburg. Paul had dated her daughter Iris.

Beatles to Hamburg himself in his battered old Austin minibus. He generously advanced them £15 so that they could buy themselves a set of matching black crew-neck sweaters from Marks and Spencer. They took few possessions – their instruments and a small suitcase each. The only luxury was a tin of home-made scones thoughtfully provided by George's mum.

Planning for the tour had been pretty well non-existent, which meant the Beatles lacked the necessary permits to work in Germany. Williams gave them the same advice that he offered to all his travelling bands – if questioned at Customs claim to be visiting students.

Hamburg, a port on the north coast of Germany, appeared to share many similarities to Liverpool. The reality came as a shock to the band. Fifteen years after the war had ended, their home city was still full of debris and bomb sites. Hamburg, on the other hand, had felt the full effect of the German *Wirtschaftswunder* – the great economic recovery. To a group of poor working class kids from Liverpool it was an education – everywhere they looked there seemed to be fashion shops and coffee bars. It was all too civilised. Until they arrived at the Kaiserkeller club to meet Bruno Koschmider, that is. The Kaiserkeller was sited in the middle of Hamburg's notorious Reeperbahn, an area filled with bright lights, loud music and brothels. It was a favoured haunt for sailors whose ships docked at the port. A short way around the corner they were taken to the Indra club. Their view of Hamburg as the most civilised place on earth vanished the moment they were shown their living quarters. Over the road from the Indra, Herr Koschmider owned a cinema. Home for the next two months would be a single room inside the cinema with the constant drone of German film dialogue audible well into the early hours of the morning.

The first gigs were a complete disaster. The band huddled together on a tiny stage and played their set of rock and roll standards before audiences of a dozen or less. Unlike the Kaiserkeller, the Indra had no reputation for live music. The Beatles

he had just completed his "A" levels and so had left school. What's more, his band, the Black Jacks, had just broken up. Without a single rehearsal, Paul McCartney offered Pete Best the job of a two-month stint in Hamburg. It was settled

– Pete Best took up the vacant drum stool.

The Johnny Gentle fiasco had been their first real adventure away from their homes and families. But two months in a foreign land was a different matter altogether. Allan Williams offered to drive the

clearly hated it. After continually being goaded by Williams and Koschmider to at least look as if they were enjoying themselves, John took to leaping about maniacally during the show – no mean feat on such a small stage. As George remembers: "There was this little guy who used to come around and say 'Mach Schau! Mach Schau!' [Put on a show], so John used to dance around like a gorilla and the rest of us used to knock our heads together." Little by little, these displays began to attract the interest of clubbers at the raunchier Kaiserkeller. The Beatles quickly turned into a tight little rock and roll band. Howie Casey of Derry and the Seniors, now well established in the city, was astonished at their improvement – at the Billy Fury auditions they had seemed to be embarrassed to be there, but within a few months, "something had happened to them. They'd turned into a good stomping band."

The workload was heavy. Sets often lasted over four hours and they would invariably play more than one set a day. Predominantly however, it was a time of four young lads growing up into young men. They quickly discovered an appetite for the beer that seemed to flow freely around them the whole time. Not to mention the women – frequently working prostitutes – that were very happy to hang out with a group of young innocents. The Beatles were also continually tired – they worked hard and getting a good night's sleep at the cinema was impossible. They were introduced to the ideal remedy – Preludin tablets. "Prellies" were slimming tablets that suppressed the appetite and boosted activity. It was, in effect, amphetamine or speed. John's memory of these times was vivid: "When the waiters would see the musicians falling over with tiredness or with drink, they'd give you the pill... then you'd be talking, you'd sober up and you could start working almost endlessly until the pill wore off – then you'd take another pill."

Their performances on stage, John's especially, became increasingly manic – a favourite being his impersonation of the crippled rock and roller Gene Vincent. During this first month, the Beatles honed their stage act and grew in confidence. Even though they lived in appalling conditions and had little free time to them-

George Harrison and Rory Storm in Hamburg

selves, Lennon and McCartney continually strove to improve their songwriting skills, often slipping the results into the live set.

LEAVING THE INDRA

Relief from the Indra came from an unexpected source. Ever since the club had opened it had been the subject of noise complaints from a neighbour. One day the police finally decided to take action and the club was closed down. Bruno decided to move the Beatles to the Kaiserkeller. By this time, Derry and the Seniors had returned to England to be replaced by Williams' top band Rory Storm and the Hurricanes. They had been used to rather better living conditions than those on offer, and complained constantly – especially their drummer Richard Starkey, who was now known to everybody as Ringo Starr. The fierce rivalry that had initially existed between the two bands rapidly disappeared in the coming weeks as they began to create their own little Liverpool in the north of Germany.

A significant accident of pop history came in October 1960. Lou Walters, the Hurricanes' bass player, decided that he wanted to have a shot at being a singer. He found a studio in Hamburg where one-off records could be cut. John, Paul and George agreed to back him. On the day of the recording Ringo Starr came along. The five played a couple of popular standards – 'Fever' and 'Summertime'. It was the first time the "Fab Four" played together.

Stu Sutcliffe, with an altogether more serious attitude to life than the others, had begun to drift away from the band. He spent more and more time with his new found artist friends Klaus Voorman and Astrid Kirchherr, a couple who played active roles in the local avant-garde art scene. Stu introduced the couple to the rest of the Beatles, and they began to spend time together. Astrid felt that the band's stage appearance was too haphazard and that they needed a clearer image. She began to make clothes and design a "look" for the band – the first one she came up with was the classic "mop-top"

hair style that within a few years would be worn by any self-respecting pop fan. Klaus began to take artfully posed black and white photographs of the Beatles, who were flattered at this kind of attention – it was all a long way from the Jacaranda club. Within a short time, Stu and Astrid became inseparable.

Towards the end of the two-month stay, the Beatles were becoming a useful attraction to the Kaiserkeller. They were offered a job playing at the much larger Top Ten club – a new venue operated by one of Bruno Koschmider's bitterest rivals. Under veiled threats from their former employer, the band moved in above the Top Ten club, intending to return to the cinema for their meagre possessions the following day.

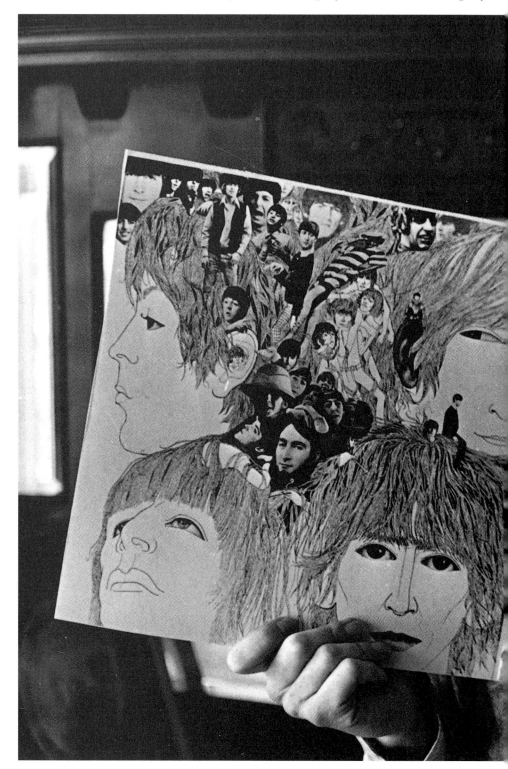

There then followed several days of disaster. Firstly, the police made a routine inspection of the club and demanded to check their passports. They discovered that as George was under 18 he was too young to be in nightclub after midnight. He was packed off back to Liverpool immediately. The others thought it would be best to carry on for a few days at the Top Ten, with John gamely attempting George's solos. The following night, Paul and Pete decided to return to the cinema to pick up their belongings. With virtually no lights working in the place, Paul struck a match to see where he was going and inadvertently started a small fire. Although it caused very little damage, Koschmider, still seething at what he saw as betrayal by the Beatles, informed the police. Paul and Pete were traced to the Top Ten club and arrested. Koschmider agreed to drop the charges, but the hapless pair would have to be deported. There was nothing left for the remaining two to do. Stu reluctantly took a flight back to England paid for by Astrid. John jumped on a train, wondering what was going to happen next.

Klaus Voorman, artist and musician

27

THEY CALLED IT "MERSEYBEAT"

THE BEATLES RETURNED TO LIVERPOOL WITH AN UNCERTAIN FUTURE BUT SOON FOUND, TO THEIR SURPRISE, THAT THEIR NEW REPUTATION HAD BEATEN THEM ACROSS THE NORTH SEA. OVER THE COMING YEAR THEY WOULD BECOME HEROES IN THEIR HOME TOWN AND BEGIN TO MAKE AN IMPRESSION ON THE REST OF BRITAIN.

The Beatles had gone to Hamburg as four innocent(ish) young lads with high hopes of fun and adventure. They returned dejected with no clear idea of what to do next. In fact, the five of them were back in Liverpool for almost a month before they even met up again. When they did they contacted Allan Williams to find out what had been going on in their absence. To their surprise, they found a burgeoning beat scene that had developed its own style and sound. To their greater surprise, they discovered that their reputation had spread back to Liverpool via the other Mersey bands who had done stints in Hamburg. Their first gig in Liverpool was at Mona Best's Casbah club. This time, instead of the apathy they had previously encountered, their powerful sound and performance transfixed the audience. The Beatles had left Liverpool as a bunch of enthusiastic also-rans and returned as one of the city's hottest acts.

Things were changing by the day. Ray McFall, the owner of the Cavern jazz club, had noticed the popularity of the new beat groups, and had started to introduce them

The Beatles make an early appearance at the Cavern

at lunch time sessions in his club. Mona Best had managed to persuade McFall to give the Beatles another shot. The Cavern was an underground network that was made up of three tunnels. The first one was the entrance to the club, the second was the main club area, and the furthest was the dance floor. In its three-year history, the Cavern had played host to some of the country's top jazz musicians.

At the end of January 1961, the new-look Beatles started playing at the Cavern. They were offered a block booking for which they were paid 25 shillings (£1.25) per day. For this they would have to play two 45-minute stints each day – something of a short order for a band more used to the four-hour, amphetamine-fuelled sets they'd worked through in Hamburg.

The Beatles live were now positively electric. Like many bands who had come up through the social club entertainment circuit, their set consisted predominantly of covers of American rock and roll and rhythm and blues: songs that had drifted across the Atlantic with the merchant seaman. Stage favourites included Carl Perkins's 'Matchbox' or Chan Romero's 'Hippy Hippy Shake', often the climax of their set. However, these numbers were usually interspersed with popular standards from the stage shows of the Forties and Fifties, such as 'Til There Was You' from the show *Music Man*.

The band quickly became a big live attraction. It was at the Cavern that they first began to experience the screaming teenage girls that would soon come to dominate their lives, and provide a poignant snapshot of a whole era.

Things seemed to be going well for the band, but Stu Sutcliffe was beginning to feel more and more of an outsider. For one thing, he missed being with Astrid. He was also well aware that he was the weak link in a good band. On the verge of quitting music, Stu tried to return to art school, only to find that his tutor's offer of re-admission was no longer open to him. There was also his difficult relationship with Paul McCartney. Whilst Stu's playing had improved, Paul was openly beginning to tire of his limitations – he wanted to

take over bass. John still insisted on having Stu in the band – he thought he was important for their image. In retrospect, Paul regrets some of his behaviour towards Stu: "It created a few rifts in the band. Looking back perhaps I could have dealt with him more sensitively, but then who's

sensitive at that age? Certainly not me!"

However, one thing that none of them had quite realized was that while he was quietly and efficiently doing his job at the back of the stage, it was Pete Best who more often than not was the target of female adulation.

Outside the Cavern

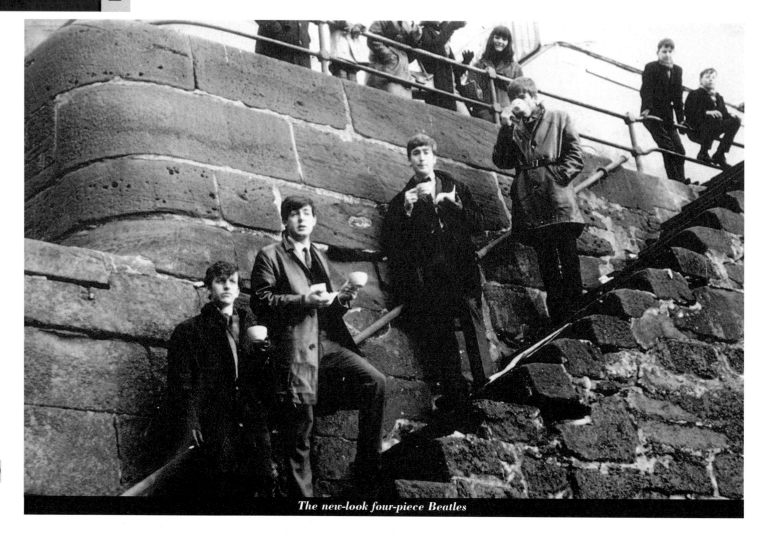

The new-look four-piece Beatles

In April 1961, the band were again offered the chance to go back out to Hamburg. This time, playing at the Top Ten club they would be earning twice as much as before – £40 each per week. This wage was considerably more than any of them could have expected doing unskilled work back home in Liverpool. What's more, the accommodation was almost civilised. They would have to work harder, though – the sets would start at seven in the evening and they would alternate with Tony Sheridan until three in the morning.

EXIT STU

Stu was beside himself to be back with Astrid, but he was becoming increasingly unenthusiastic about the Beatles. Predictably, Stu's way out of the mess came from Astrid. She encouraged him to enrol as a student at the Hamburg State Art College. This was a particularly attractive prospect as Eduardo Paolozzi, one of Stu's idols, had been appointed to run a series of master classes at the college. Paolozzi was highly impressed by the work he was shown, and not only admitted him to the course but managed to get him a state bursary. From that point, Stu gradually began to step back from the band. He never formally left the Beatles – Paul just gradually played the bass more and more often until one day he played bass all the time.

Germany, like most other European countries, was slow to get to grips with this new rock and roll phenomenon. Of course, everywhere an American influence could be found there was a potential rock scene, but this rarely occurred outside the transatlantic ports like Hamburg, or the areas surrounding the numerous US Air Force bases that had sprung up after the war. German rock and roll bands existed, but they were rarely more than imitators of a culture that seemed totally alien. In fact, when in the late Sixties Germany found its own modern voice they frequently came out of the avant-garde classical scene. (Can and Kraftwerk, probably Germany's most influential rock exports, were either students or ardent followers of controversial modern classical composer Karlheinz Stockhausen.) Clearly, Germany was coming from somewhere else. In the early Sixties a well-known orchestral band leader became a prominent producer. Bert Kaempfert was trying to create German rock and roll. To him this entailed playing popular songs of the past two decades over a rock and roll rhythm. Coming across Tony Sheridan and the Beatles playing at the Top Ten, Kaempfert asked them to make a record.

The two songs he chose were unlikely in the extreme. 'My Bonnie Lies Over The Ocean' was an age-old Scottish folk song, rarely heard in the UK outside primary school singing lessons. Kaempfert surpassed himself with the choice of flip side – 'When the Saints Go Marching In' had been a staple of trad jazz groups for as long as jazz had existed. The band, renamed the Beat Brothers for the project, were given a dull, vaguely Chuck Berry-style arrangement to play and Tony Sheridan did the vocal duties. At the session, John Lennon persuaded Kaempfert to listen to some of the songs he had been writing with Paul McCartney. Kaempfert didn't much care for the songs, but he could hear that they were a good, tight band, and let them record a couple of tracks for possible release. Kaempfert let them play one of the terrible fillers from their set list, an old show tune 'Ain't She Sweet'. They also recorded George's Shadows rip-off, jokingly entitled 'Cry for a Shadow'. In spite of what the Beatles thought about the sessions, 'My Bonnie' hit the German Top 10 and turned Tony Sheridan into a minor star. The Beatles made no money from this record – for their efforts they had each been given a one-off session payment of 300 marks (about £25) – but the experience of recording was a valuable one.

"RIGHT THEN BRIAN, MANAGE US."

Back in Liverpool, it seemed that the beat revolution was everywhere. There was even a Liverpool music paper – *Mersey Beat*. Started by Bill Harry, a young art student and music enthusiast, *Mersey Beat* would become an influential magazine that would play a significant role in the Beatles early successes. Harry had known John Lennon from art school and remembered his fondness for drawing witty and scurrilous cartoons. For the first issue of *Mersey Beat* he asked John to write an amusing story of how the Beatles started. Lennon's article, "A Short Diversion on the Dubious Origins of the Beatles" was very reminiscent of his comic heroes, The Goons. *The Goon Show* was a surreal

and absurd popular radio show of the time that featured the comic talents of Peter Sellers, Spike Milligan and Harry Secombe. John's article, and others like it, helped to distinguish the Beatles from the fierce competition that they now faced from other local groups.

One of *Mersey Beat*'s first advertising customers was the NEMS electrical shop – then Liverpool's best-stocked record shop – "The Finest Record Selection in the North" as its adverts proclaimed. The shop was one of a chain run by the Epsteins, a wealthy and prominent Jewish family. The record department had been built up in a

short space of time by the owner's son Brian, a 27-year-old former RADA student. In spite of his age and former occupation, Brian Epstein appeared as the absolute epitome of conservatism. Always smartly dressed in well-cut tailor-made suits, many of his customers, if asked, would have put his age at closer to 40.

Epstein took great pride in being able to obtain any out-of-stock records his customers wanted. It was to his surprise that one week a succession of teenagers came in asking for the Beatles' recording of 'My Bonnie'. No matter how many record company availability lists he scanned he could

Brian Epstein, the Beatles' guiding light

Merseybeat's supporting cast: Billy J. Kramer and the Dakotas, Cilla Black, Brian Epstein, Tommy Quickly and the Fourmost

find no mention of its existence. He felt compelled to find out more about this mysterious group. Who were they? Where were they from? His curiosity was further aroused when a customer told him that they were a local band who were currently playing at the Cavern, just a few hundred metres away.

Brian Epstein paid a visit to the Cavern one lunchtime when the Beatles were doing two short sets. He was quite taken aback by what he saw. "This was quite a new world really for me. I was amazed by this dank atmosphere... they [the Beatles] were somewhat ill-clad and the presentation left a little to be desired. Amongst this, however, something tremendous came over. I was really just struck by their music, the beat and their sense of humour on stage. Even afterwards, when I met them, I was struck again by their personal charm. It was there it all started."

In the early Sixties, homosexuality was far from commonly accepted – it was still an illegal act and an unspeakable subject. In a tough, industrial city like Liverpool, admitting to it could be life-threatening. Epstein had been a practising homosexual for many years and was forced to lead a secret double-life. The sight of four young men in tight black leather clothes sweating away on the tiny Cavern stage might have been one that excited him. But it was the effect that the Beatles were having on the lunchtime crowds – of both sexes – which attracted the businessman in him.

Epstein made several more visits. The Beatles began to notice this curious-looking man with a suit and briefcase in the audience. Eventually, in November 1961, Brian Epstein finally arranged to meet the Beatles after one of their now frequent lunch time Cavern performances. He offered the band his services as a manager. After Paul had satisfied himself that Epstein would play no role in their music, they agreed.

For the last few months of 1961 had not been eventful for the Beatles. They seemed to be in a rut. As far as the Mersey Beat bands were concerned, the Beatles were now at the top of the pile. Yet outside the area, even in Manchester – Liverpool's

LITHERLAND TOWN HALL

EVERY THURSDAY

THE MAGNIFICENT

BEATLES !!

JOHN, PAUL, GEORGE AND PETE

ALWAYS A

LIVELY **T**IME **H**ERE
LITHERLAND **T**OWN **H**ALL

YOUR THURSDAY DANCE DATE
If it's Thursday, it must be Litherland!

big brother – they were virtually unknown. Brian Epstein knew that the only way of breaking the Beatles was to get them to the attention of the big London record companies. Getting his band an audition was not going to be a difficult job. As the manager of NEMS, one of the biggest record stockists in the north, no label would want to risk upsetting him unnecessarily. As far as Epstein was concerned, all he had to do was get the labels to hear the band – their music would do the talking.

The first label Epstein tried was Decca – one of the most powerful of Britain's record companies. The audition would take place at their London studio at 165 Broadhurst Gardens, in West Hampstead. The band arrived promptly, having been driven down by Neil Aspinall, one of John's Liverpool friends. It was the first day of January 1962.

At this time, the recording process, even in the most sophisticated of studios, was thoroughly crude by today's standards. Overdubbing or multitracking were quite rare – the province of maverick experimental producers like Joe Meek. The Beatles simply plugged in their instruments and Decca's A&R ("artist and

repertoire") man Mike Smith asked them to play. He and a studio engineer set the levels and then the tape recorder was switched on. In the space of a few hours the Beatles had laid down 15 tracks. Many of these have surfaced on bootleg recordings over the years, but five of them found their first official release in December 1995 on the *Anthology 1* album.

Listening to these tracks, one of the things that shines through is the humour and versatility of the band. This was certainly one of Brian Epstein's intended selling points – after all, beat music was still thought of as a fad, but one out of which a new generation of popular family entertainers would hopefully emerge. They were also clearly a band used to playing together. Whilst none of the Beatles could have ever been described as virtuoso musicians, in his short time as a bass guitarist, Paul McCartney was clearly turning into a player of considerable substance. Nonetheless, renditions of Leiber and Stoller's 'Three Cool Cats' and 'Searchin'', as well as a jokey, swinging version of the show tune 'The Sheikh of Arabie', sung by George with the occasional "Not 'arf" interjected by John and Paul, still provide few clues as to what might happen over the next few years.

The Beatles were not happy with their performance, but Mike Smith, Decca's man on the spot, thought it would be enough to a secure a deal. Things changed when Smith contacted his boss Dick Rowe. At the same time, Decca had auditioned another group – Brian Poole and the Tremeloes, from Dagenham in Essex. Smith was told that a choice would have to be made between the two bands. Rowe didn't really mind which band it was. The decision went against the Beatles solely because the Tremeloes were based near London, where Decca thought it would be easier to deal with them. Whilst The Tremeloes went on to have their moments of glory – a handful of easy-listening pop hits, one or two hitting the top of the charts – the decision has become a legendary one. In one of pop music's most celebrated errors of judgement, Dick Rowe informed Brian Epstein that he didn't want the band

because "they sounded too much like the Shadows", but even that was irrelevant since "groups with guitars are on the way out". A few years later John and Paul would remember this incident – Paul: "He must be kicking himself now"; John: "I hope he kicks himself to death."

"DON'T WORRY BRIAN, WE'LL HAVE TO SIGN TO EMBASSY"

Brian Epstein's response to Decca's rebuff was an audacious one. He was furious. Such was the faith he held in the Beatles that he contacted Decca's head office demanding an explanation. None was forthcoming. Even in the depths of despondency, John was still unable to resist a wise-crack. "Don't worry Brian," he would say in his driest deadpan Scouse accent, "we'll have to sign to Embassy." The Embassy label was owned exclusively by the Woolworth's chain – their releases were cheap cover versions by anonymous session musicians and they cost less than half the price of normal records.

Epstein's next step, at the suggestion of Decca's Dick Rowe, was to approach an independent producer, hire studio time and try to sell a finished product. Although this is a common enough way of doing business nowadays, in the early 1960s it was almost unknown. Dick Rowe suggested that he try Tony Meehan, the former drummer with The Shadows, who was setting up as independent record producer. Epstein arranged a meeting, but it went badly. Meehan turned up extremely late, and it quickly became clear that he felt that dealing with the Beatles was somehow beneath him and a waste of his time. It was a worthwhile attempt, but Epstein again returned to more traditional selling techniques.

Brian turned his attention to moulding the Beatles into his own idea of what a pop group should be. He tried to instil a new discipline in the band. They may have been Mersey Beat's top band, but they also had a reputation for unreliability that worried the serious promoters. Brian produced

The new-look Beatles after the Epstein make-over

a series of typed memoranda to each member of the band detailing the new regime. Punctuality was in, shouting at mates in the audience was out. Working to an agreed set list with no deviations was in, belching into the microphone – a great favourite with John Lennon – was out.

Most important though, the black leather outfits that they had taken to wearing, under the influence of Stu and Astrid in Hamburg, had to go. Black leather had too many connotations with troublemakers. Brian took them down to Beno Dorn, a local bespoke tailor and had them measured up for a set of matching brushed-tweed grey lounge suits with narrow velvet collars. John still managed to have his say: "My little rebellion was to have my tie loose with the top button of my shirt undone, but Paul would always come up to me and put it straight." Paul was always the ambitious one – if they had to wear these dreadful suits to make it, then that would be fine by him. After all, they

hadn't exactly set the world alight doing their own thing.

In March of 1962, Brian booked the Beatles to open a major new venue in Hamburg, the Star Club. The band were clearly moving up in the world now – instead of being huddled in the back of an old van driving through England and Holland to the North of Germany, they took a flight from Manchester's Ringway airport. They were looking forward to seeing some of their old mates, not least Stu and Astrid. In spite of Stu's having been forced out of the band, he and John had remained close friends, writing to each other frequently. They arrived in Hamburg to terrible news. Stu was dead. He had recently suffered a spate of increasingly serious headaches. The reason cited on his death certificate was "cerebral paralysis due to bleeding into the right ventricle of the brain." The band were devastated – Pete and George cried continually. Only John, trying his hardest to keep his tough

Scouser image, refused to crack, but everybody close to the band knew that it was he who had taken it by far the worst.

While the Beatles were doing their thing in Hamburg, Brian was busy in London trying to get them a deal. He had now tried hawking their Decca demo to every reasonably sized label he could find. Having hit on the idea of having a demonstration disc to play to prospective labels, Brian went to the HMV store in London's Oxford Street. Here it was possible to have one-off records cut from a master tape. Brian's arrival at the HMV shop kicked off a sequence of good fortune. It started when the engineer who processed the record took an immediate liking to the sound of the band. He suggested that Brian take it to EMI's publishing wing, which was based in the same building. That same day, Brian visited EMI's head of publishing, Sid Coleman. He listened to the record, and liked what he heard. He immediately agreed to publish two of the songs – the

Brian Epstein with George Martin and future Epstein proteges, Gerry and the Pacemakers

Lennon and McCartney compositions 'Love of the Loved' and 'Hello Little Girl'. This was a major breakthrough. Epstein expressed his gratitude but patiently explained that while he would be more than happy to sign a publishing deal, he was really after a recording contract for the Beatles. Coleman said he knew exactly the man to talk to. He picked up the phone and called his friend George Martin, then head of A&R for Parlophone, one of the smaller subsidiaries of the vast EMI empire. Although Martin was out of the office, his secretary Judy Lockhart-Smith made an appointment for Brian Epstein for the following week.

George Martin was unusual among A&R men in the pop field. There was little trace of the "Tin Pan Alley" mentality in his approach to finding new artists and material. George Martin had come from a grounding in classical music, having studied piano and oboe at London's Guildhall School of Music. On graduating, he had joined the BBC's music library, but soon grew bored and took a job at EMI. By the time he was thirty he was running EMI's Parlophone label, which had enjoyed a few successes with comedy or novelty recordings. One of Martin's earliest hits as a producer was recording the Peter Sellers hit comedy album, *Songs for Swinging Sellers*.

Martin had reluctantly begun looking for talent among the countless newly formed beat groups. This was clearly where the money was being made, at least for the time being. So it was with no great expectations that Martin listened politely to the demonstration record brought to him by this softly spoken, besuited Liverpool man. Indeed, there was nothing revelatory to be heard. He was most impressed by George's guitar work and Paul's vocals, but on this evidence they seemed to have little that was vastly different to many other good beat groups. He was, however sufficiently interested to offer them an audition. As he said, "I thought to myself: 'There might *just* be something there'."

The first EMI recordings are the subject of some conjecture. Popular opinion seems to be that the session was set up as

an audition for the Beatles, as they had done for Decca six months earlier. However, there seems to be evidence that Martin was prepared to offer the band a conditional contract before he ever met them in person, and that hopefully their first session would produce a debut single.

June 6th, 1962, was the agreed date of the recording session. It was their first visit to EMI's Abbey Road studios, a large detached house in the middle of St John's Wood, an up-market area of north London. The recording would take place at Studio 3, the smallest suite in the complex. Again, they concentrated on their usual mix of standards and their own material. When Brian had sent them a telegram in Hamburg telling them about the EMI session, they had immediately got to work writing new material. The new songs were clearly a lot stronger than their previous efforts, showing a newly found confidence. The two surviving songs from the session are the Coasters' hit 'Besame Mucho' sung with great charm by Paul. The other was a new composition, 'Love Me Do'.

PROBLEMS WITH THE DRUMMER

Again, George Martin liked what he heard, but just didn't find it exciting enough. The standards were all too corny, and the self-penned material was really not commercial enough. Something he was certain of though, was that Pete Best was not a good enough drummer to use on recordings. He told Brian Epstein that if the Beatles made a record he would insist on using Andy White, his own session drummer. Martin mulled over the matter for a further month before committing Parlophone to a minimum by offering the Beatles a one-year contract. Epstein had finally done it. After all the rejections of the past months, the Beatles now had a recording contract with EMI, even though they had been turned down by two other EMI labels, HMV and Columbia.

What to do about Pete became an immediate problem. When the other members found out George Martin's views, Paul and George were keen to sack him just to

get the matter out of the way. Rumours were circulating around Liverpool, but the unsuspecting Pete still refused to believe them, and life carried on as normal. Little did he know that his lunchtime gig at The Cavern on Wednesday, August 15th was going to be his last as the Beatles' drummer.

The following day, Pete was called to Brian Epstein's office and given the news, "Pete, the boys want you out of the group. They don't think you're a good enough drummer." Pete was overcome: he had spent the past eighteen months playing with them and felt he was one of a group of mates. Not once had anyone complained to him about his playing and now none of them had the good grace to tell it to his face. The band were due to play at Chester's Riverpark Ballroom that night. In spite of his feelings, Pete agreed to fulfil his obligations for that show. During the afternoon he grew angrier and changed his mind – he didn't turn up and his stool was filled for the night by Johnny Hutchinson of the Big Three. The Beatles have mostly remained tight-lipped over the whole affair, although recently George commented: "Historically it may look like we did something nasty to Pete... and it may have been that we could have done it better."

Pete Best continued to try and develop a musical career, but he is now remembered as the Beatle who nearly made it. The following years were severely testing: being ejected from the band was bad enough, but he then had to witness the flood of reports detailing their huge success. For many, Pete Best is simply the unluckiest man in the history of pop music – the clearest possible example of how little consolation there is in the word "nearly".

The Beatles' camp was still turbulent. Throughout the Pete Best sacking, one voice had been uncharacteristically quiet. John Lennon had other things on his mind. To his horror, his long-standing girlfriend Cynthia had announced that she was pregnant. In spite of his mother's earlier example, the notion of having a child outside wedlock was too much, even for Lennon the rebel. John did "the decent

The first signs of Beatlemania appear at the Cavern

thing". The day after Pete Best's sacking, John and Cynthia were married at Mount Pleasant registry office, the same place where 24 years earlier Freddy Lennon and Julia had been married.

Once again, the "Fab Three" were without a drummer. Top of their recruitment list was Ringo Starr. Ringo had begun to lose interest in a musical career. He had left Rory Storm to return to Liverpool where he did little for the first part of 1962. In desperation, Rory persuaded him to rejoin the band for yet another thrilling summer season in Skegness. He had nothing better to do, so off he went. It was John who phoned Ringo at Butlins holiday camp to ask him to join the band. The only preconditions were that Ringo had to shave off his beard, and brush his Teddy Boy hairstyle forward, in keeping with the others. His credentials clearly made him the only man for the job. As John recalled, "Ringo was a professional drummer who sang and performed with one of the top groups in Liverpool before we even had a drummer." Paul was also impressed: "Ringo Starr had a beard and was grown up, he was also known to have a Zephyr Zodiac!"

Ringo Starr made his debut as a fully fledged Beatle on Saturday August 18th, 1962 at the Hulme Hall, Port Sunlight, near Birkenhead. The event was the local horticultural society's annual dance!

Back in Liverpool, an unlikely crisis was brewing. *Mersey Beat* had broken the news of Pete's sacking. This had brought an outcry from his female fans. They mounted all-night vigils outside his house, and picketed the Cavern. When the cameras from the TV show *Know the North* visited the Cavern to film the Beatles a week after Pete's sacking, the closing chords of 'Some Other Guy' are clearly punctuated not only by the usual cheering and screaming, but also by a lone voice crying out "We want Pete!"

Brian Epstein was thoroughly bemused by all the fuss. It was common knowledge among his close gay friends that it was not the pretty-boy Pete Best, nor the fresh-faced looks of George Harrison or Paul McCartney that attracted him to the band. It was the rough and ready John Lennon, whose sharp tongue and acid humour were often targeted at what Lennon would later call the "Queer Jew."

Ringo, Rory and the Hurricanes take Butlins by storm

"GENTLEMEN, YOU HAVE JUST MADE YOUR FIRST NUMBER ONE"

The sessions to produce the first Beatles single were to take place on September 6th and 11th, 1962. George Martin had decided that the best approach from the start would be to use their original compositions. He selected two tracks 'P.S. I Love You' and 'Love Me Do'. Nobody had told George Martin that Pete Best had been sacked. When the Beatles arrived they were introduced to Andy White, their drummer for the day. He had already been hired so there was no way that Martin would not use him. This time the recordings were to take place in Abbey Road's number 2 studio. This placed the Beatles

The Beatles make an early trip to London

in hitherto unknown professional surroundings. The band would lay down a backing track with no vocals or lead parts played – these would be overdubbed afterwards. It was all highly sophisticated to the band.

During the second session the following week, George allowed Ringo to play on the recordings, and he was pleasantly surprised by what he heard. Whilst Ringo was not up to the standard of his session drummer, he was clearly a major improvement on Pete Best – and he did have his own quirky style, especially his use of the tom-toms. Eventually, they came up with two different versions of 'Love Me Do', the song that was clearly going to be the "A" side of the single. The version with Andy White playing was released three weeks later on October 4th: Ringo's version would eventually surface on their first album. Ringo recalls the distress he felt at the time: "It was devastating…we did the single, which Andy plays on, then we did the album which I play on. So he wasn't doing anything so great that I couldn't do it." George Martin jokes, "Ringo to this day bears those scars. He'll say to me 'You didn't let me play, did you?'"

Outside Liverpool, the Beatles were still largely unknown. As the first week passed after the record's release, nothing much seemed to happen. It was played on Radio Luxembourg, but that was about all. Brian Epstein, knowing the numbers required to get a record into the charts, knew there was only one thing for it – through NEMS he bought 10,000 copies from Parlophone. Whilst the record caused a sensation in Liverpool and went straight to the top of the *Mersey Beat* charts, the vast majority of them gathered dust in the NEMS storeroom. Finally, the single made a showing in the national *New Musical Express* chart at number 27. By the middle of December it peaked at number 17.

It was a modest beginning, but it did bring the Beatles to a national audience for the first time. Following this success, George Martin offered the band a five-year contract, which Epstein gratefully accepted. However, for the publishing side, Epstein decide not to renew his contract

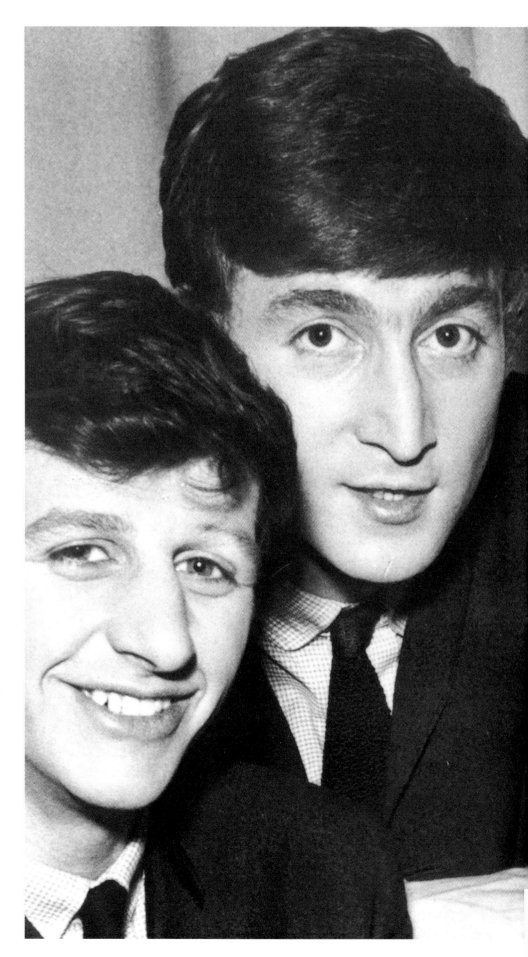

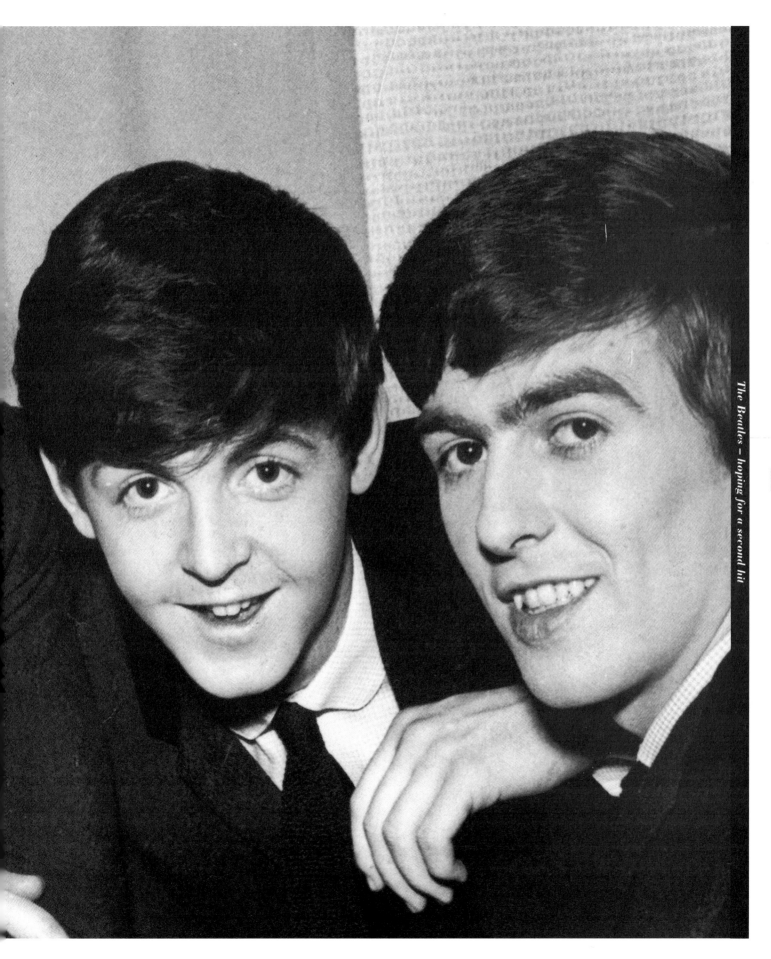

The Beatles — hoping for a second hit

The Beatles, including new boy Ringo, rehearse for fame

with EMI. Instead he started looking at other possibilities. One that he found very appealing was a new publishing company set up by a former ballad singer, Dick James.

At the end of November it was decided that the Beatles would record their second single. For this release, both Brian Epstein and George Martin favoured a song brought to them by Dick James. 'How Do You Do It?' was a new composition by Mitch Murray, one of James' house composers. Everyone was convinced that this would be the song to take them to the top of the charts. Not for the first time, they reckoned without the obstinacy of a band that had ideas of their own. The Beatles wanted to persevere with their own material, especially a gutsy new number, 'Please Please Me', that showed off the band's vocal harmony skills to the full. During the recording, George Martin new instinctively that it was going to be a hit on a massive scale. At the end of the session he pressed the studio intercom button to speak to the band. "Gentlemen," he announced, "you have just made your first number one."

Dick James, having recovered sufficiently from the rejection of 'How Do You Do It?', was so impressed by the new single that he immediately offered them a deal. Consequently, Northern Songs was formed as a part of Dick James Music to administer exclusively Lennon and McCartney's songs. James went straight to work, and within an hour had arranged a TV appearance for the Beatles to perform the single on the Saturday night pop show *Thank Your Lucky Stars*. Further exposure would follow on the pop show that reviewed new releases, *Juke Box Jury*. Both would coincide with the release of the new single in January 1963.

In an attempt to garner even more exposure for the band, Brian Epstein pulled off what he hoped would be a coup for the boys. He managed to find the home telephone number of the country's largest tour promoter, Arthur Howes. He made all of his usual claims that the Beatles would be the biggest thing music had ever seen. Howes had been in the business too long to believe anyone's ears other than his

own. He agreed to put the band on the bill for one night only, at the Embassy, a theatre venue in the small East Anglian town of Peterborough. Although the Beatles were due to play that night at the Cavern, manager Ray McFall generously let them off for the night.

At the Embassy, they were one of a number of supporting artists for Frank Ifield, an Australian singer whose hit records such as 'She Taught Me To Yodel' and 'I Remember You' were popular with middle-of-the road audiences. To understand the nature of the event, and the way in which pop music was perceived by the British entertainment industry, one has to look at some of the other artists on the bill – Tommy Wallis and Beryl were a "xylophone duo", The Lana Sisters, an old-fashioned harmony vocal group, and a second rate comic named Joe Black, who also compered the show. It was a mismatch of classic proportions. Number after number was greeted by the East Anglians with negligible response, even their national hit 'Love Me Do'. In his review of the concert, local newspaper reporter Lyndon Whittaker had strong words for the band.

"The 'Exciting Beatles' rock group quite frankly failed to excite me. The drummer apparently thought that his job was to lead, not to provide rhythm. He made far too much noise and in their final number 'Twist and Shout' it sounded as though everyone was trying to make more noise than the others."

Yes, it was the cry of "Turn it down!" that youngsters would have to endure for at least the next twenty years. Mr Whittaker was, however, magnanimous enough to say that he found 'Love Me Do' "tolerable"!

One might imagine that the Beatles would have been able to laugh this off. Instead, the collective ego of band was taken down a peg or two. Surprisingly, they found an unusual ally in Arthur Howes, who realized their unsuitability for this type of bill, but could envisage a time when he might want to use them again.

After years of struggling, they seemed to have made great progress in the space of a few months. It was all too easy to forget that they still had a contractual

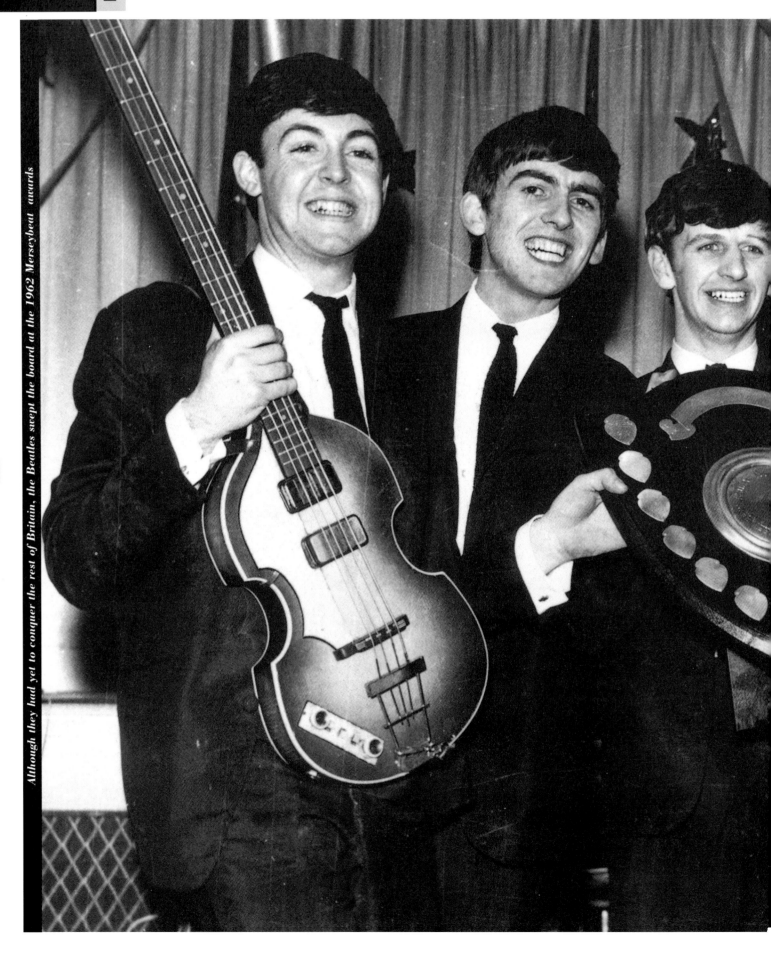

THEY CALLED IT "MERSEYBEAT"

Although they had yet to conquer the rest of Britain, the Beatles swept the board at the 1962 Merseybeat awards

obligation, dating from the previous summer, to play another stint at the Star Club in Hamburg. Suddenly, that part of their lives no longer held any appeal. They'd done that, and had moved on. They'd had a Top 20 hit in Britain, but now they had to go back to Hamburg. It was all the more frustrating because they felt that this two-week stint was keeping them out of the British public eye. To make matters worse, they were not even the stars of the show, they were supporting Johnny and the Hurricanes, an American instrumental band, who, although well-known, were by now four years past their big hits like 'Red River Rock' and 'Beatnik Fly'.

The Beatles acquitted themselves barely adequately. Their playing was, by their own admission, less than perfect. This is quite plain from the recordings of their final Hamburg gigs that were issued, against the wishes of the band, in 1977. By the time they played their final gig in Hamburg, on New Year's Eve of 1962, they had played something like 800 hours on stage in those few Reeperbahn clubs. The experience had turned them from a band with little hope of getting even a minor record deal, into (when they felt inclined) one of the tightest and exciting rock groups in the country.

1962 had been an extraordinary year. *Mersey Beat* voted them the best band for the second year running, but as someone said at the time "They would, wouldn't they?". Perhaps of more value was that in their annual poll, readers of the national *New Musical Express* voted them fifth best British vocal group.

Right now though, they were stuck in Hamburg. They were bored. They were tired. It was Christmas and they were away from their families and friends. They couldn't wait to get away from the place.

BEATLEMANIA

ALTHOUGH THEIR DEBUT SINGLE HAD CREPT INTO THE TOP 20, IT HAD HARDLY SHAKEN THE FOUNDATIONS

OF THE MUSIC SCENE. THAT WOULD SOON CHANGE. THE COMING YEAR WOULD SEE THE BEATLES UNDERTAKE

A PUNISHING SCHEDULE THAT WOULD SEE THEM BECOME THE MOST POPULAR ENTERTAINERS IN BRITAIN.

The Beatles flew back into Britain on the second day of 1963. But there was no time to rest – a five-day excursion north of the border in Scotland had already been arranged, starting the following day. Excitement was in the air. The new single, 'Please Please Me', was due for release any day and they all had high hopes for a major success. After all, George Martin, their producer, had more or less guaranteed it.

Despite this optimism, the tour started disastrously. That winter was one of the worst in living memory, and, as usual, Scotland had been much more seriously affected than the rest of the country. The first gig on the tour was in the Highland town of Keith – one of the stops on their ill-fated Johnny Gentle tour two years earlier. However, the weather worsened during the day and snowdrifts made many of the roads impossible to pass. Their plane was forced to land at Aberdeen instead of Edinburgh, and when they arrived they were told that the show had been cancelled. The four remaining dates went ahead successfully, if uneventfully. The Beatles were biding their time.

January 11th was the big day. 'Please, Please Me' hit record shops throughout the nation. Brian Epstein and Northern Songs publisher Dick James put a combined effort into publicising the new release. As good as his word, prompted by his friend Dick James, TV producer Philip Jones gave the Beatles a slot on his Saturday night pop show *Thank Your Lucky Stars*.

The show was made by the Birmingham-based, independent ABC television company, but it was broadcast throughout Britain's commercial television network. *Thank Your Lucky Stars* was one of the most influential music shows of its time. This was because, firstly, it was geared towards a teenage audience, and secondly because new releases were played and judged by a panel of listeners. One of these critics, a teenage girl known simply as Janice, had built up quite a cult following of her own – new releases that met with her approval were marked with the

A valuable autographed copy of the Beatles' first album, 'Please Please Me'

George Harrison and John Lennon were early exponents of the Rickenbacker guitar sound

highest score possible, five. Delivered in the thickest Midlands accent possible, "Oi'll give it foive" became a popular teenage catch phrase.

The show was usually recorded a week in advance. On Sunday, January 12th, the Beatles turned up to the ATV studios in Aston, in Birmingham, to mime their new single in front of a wild teenage audience. The following Wednesday they delivered a similarly mimed performance for Granada TV's *People and Places* programme. The next day they were booked for two live performances on their home territory – a Cavern session at lunch time, and then down the road to Birkenhead's Majestic Ballroom later that evening. The Majestic gig had sold out well in advance, leaving 500 disappointed fans trying to get in on the night.

At this time pop groups were often viewed by disapproving adults as "long-haired layabouts" and the phrase "they should get a proper job" could often be heard. Yet anybody who looked at the Beatles' day-to-day activities with the non-stop round of concerts and promotions would need little convincing that here were four young men as hard-working and driven with ambition for success as you'd find in any "proper" career.

The frenzied promotion continued apace. Positive reviews of 'Please Please Me' began to emerge. *New Musical Express* praised it as "full of vigour and vitality", and BBC radio's Brian Matthew – an influential figure in his day – rated them as the best thing he'd heard since the Shadows. However, none of this could compete with the impact that television brought. The biggest kick of all came when *Thank Your Lucky Stars* was broadcast the following Saturday, January 19th. Although they were effectively bottom of the bill the

Beatles were a sensation. It was here that most of Great Britain first experienced the Beatles.

The band presented an image that set them clearly apart from other groups of the time – the "mop-top" fringes and the buttoned-up suits. Most of all, the Beatles refused to appear mean and moody like so many other rock and rollers – instead they bounced around the television screen with beaming grins. This didn't look like a choreographed act, it looked as if they were four lads having a damn good laugh. And it was infectious, too!

The music was also different. Their driving energy and use of high-pitched falsetto vocals set them apart from the competition. It was a technique that they had taken from the dramatic – almost operatic – singles that Roy Orbison had recorded a few years earlier. 'Please Please Me' was the first public outing for

BEATLEMANIA

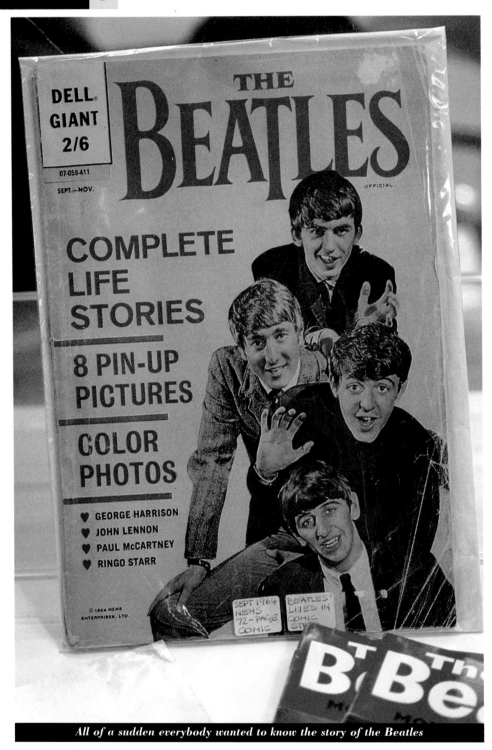

All of a sudden everybody wanted to know the story of the Beatles

Howes, the promoter who had presided over their Frank Ifield fiasco just before Christmas. This time they were to open a six-act bill that starred the singer Helen Shapiro. In 1961, as a 14-year-old schoolgirl, Shapiro had burst onto the British pop scene with 'Walking Back to Happiness', but barely two years later her career was already on the wane. This tour, it was hoped, would re-establish her as one of Britain's top female vocalists. The first leg of the tour was, by all accounts, fairly uneventful. The most amusing incident was when a contingent of bored post-gig musicians (the Beatles, Kenny Lynch and young Helen, herself) were ejected from a golf club in Carlisle. The reason seems to have been that the Beatles were wearing leather jackets! The story was reported in the national press, although the Beatles were not mentioned by name.

On February 10th, the Beatles travelled down to London for another recording session with George Martin. Quite pleased at their growing success, Martin still thought they were capable of a good deal better. The aim of the session was to record a debut album that captured the energy of their live set – an aim that many performers have tried to achieve, usually with little success. One thing the recordings certainly captured was spontaneity. They started work at Studio 2, Abbey Road at ten in the morning and carried on until eleven at night, stopping only briefly for lunch and dinner.

The recordings were produced by George Martin with his engineer Norman "Hurricane" Smith. In the space of barely 13 hours they recorded a staggering 79 takes of 14 songs. Eight of them were Lennon-McCartney originals and the other six were covers from their stage show. Over the next month Martin would decide which takes they would use to go on the album.

Nowadays it would be hard to imagine a major recording artist producing an LP in a single day – indeed, it's more common for albums to be drawn out over a period of several months! For the Beatles, the process was a simple one, they plugged in and played. It was nearly all recorded live,

what would soon become one of the hallmarks of the early Beatles sound. It was clear from their TV performance that shifting the dynamic in this way had an obvious impact on their teenage audience – it made them scream more loudly! Roy Orbison was one of John Lennon's early heroes. He only discovered how influential he had been to the development of the Beatles when he worked with George

Harrison in the Traveling Wilburys, just before his death in 1988.

HITTING THE TOP

At the beginning of February, with 'Please Please Me' about to make its entry in the Top 10, the Beatles embarked on their first national tour. They were booked by Arthur

The Beatles on **Thank Your Lucky Stars**

with a minimum of vocal and instrumental overdubs. The next day they went straight back to their live work – a schedule that now saw them performing in different venues throughout the country pretty well every day of the week.

On March 2nd, George Martin's prediction was fulfilled. After hovering in the Top10 for a few weeks, 'Please Please Me' went to the top of the charts. Again, timing proved to be problematic for the Beatles. A month or so earlier, Arthur Howes had signed them to another one of his showcase tours, this time playing support to a pair of American singers, Tommy Roe and Chris Montez. It quickly became evident from the reaction of the audience that it was the Beatles whom they had come to see. Howes rapidly changed the billing, and ensured that the Beatles ended every

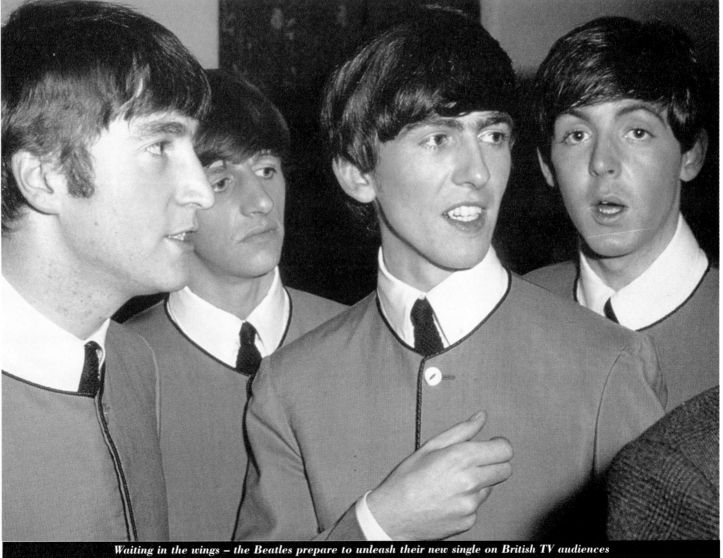
Waiting in the wings – the Beatles prepare to unleash their new single on British TV audiences

George Martin, the man who refined the Beatles' sound

show by burning through the number that was now the climax of their set – The Isley Brothers' 'Twist and Shout'.

Somehow they managed to fit another day's recording into their heavy schedule. Once again, they travelled down to Abbey Road to record some new material for a possible single. The previous week, while on the second leg of the Helen Shapiro tour, they had written a new song that they had hoped she would record. It should be remembered that in the Fifties and Sixties, the notion of a "career pop star" was seen by most as an absurd idea. Many in the industry thought that rock and roll was just a fad and within a few years we would all be listening to crooners and balladeers as we did in the good old days. At the height of their fame, even John Lennon stated that he didn't necessarily expect the Beatles to last long, and he thought that he and Paul would ultimately pursue a professional songwriting partnership. Ironically, since they had signed the publishing contract that created Northern Songs, Lennon and McCartney had spent more time writing separately, but often helping the other one with ideas. Nonetheless, regardless of whoever was actually responsible for a song, they were always registered as joint-compositions.

The song that John and Paul wrote for Shapiro was 'From Me To You'. At a recording session on March 5th, they performed 13 takes of both this number and an older composition, 'Thank You Little Girl'. As a footnote to this session, with some remaining studio time they quickly rushed through a couple of takes of 'The One After 909' and 'What Goes On'. Neither of these songs saw the light of day at the time, but new versions appeared on later albums.

With 'Please Please Me' now a smash, the Beatles were becoming big news. The national newspapers, which rarely reported on teenage interests, began to travel to Liverpool to interview the band. One such interviewer was Maureen Cleave of the *London Evening Standard*. She was the first journalist to give the band a wider, more considered coverage. In her interview she was struck by the mischievous,

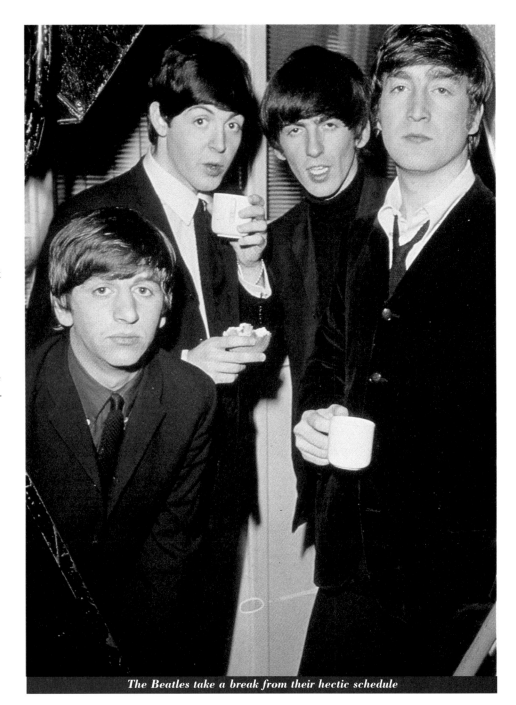

The Beatles take a break from their hectic schedule

sharp wit of these four bright young lads; John Lennon in particular. She could see how infectious their enthusiasm was. She was, perhaps, the first journalist to capture the essence of the Beatles interacting as mates, something that became such a feature their debut film, *A Hard Day's Night*. It was now more than six years since John Lennon's had dreamed of making the Quarry Men a success. Now, at last, people were sitting up and taking notice, even if the public did think that the Beatles were an overnight success.

As their first number one began its inevitable fall from the top of the charts, Parlophone released the Beatles' debut album on March 22nd. To cash in on the success of the single, the album was titled *Please Please Me;* after all, George Martin wasn't so sure that they wouldn't go the way of so many one- or two-hit wonders. He need not have worried – the momentum was building fast and it didn't look like slowing down for a minute. The album came straight into the LP charts at number nine.

PLEASE PLEASE ME

LABEL:	PARLOPHONE PCS 3042
CD RE-ISSUES:	(UK) CDP 746 435 2; (US) C2-46435-2
PRODUCER:	GEORGE MARTIN
RELEASE DATE:	MARCH 22ND, 1963

SIDE ONE

I SAW HER STANDING THERE
(McCartney/Lennon)
(2:50)

This Chuck Berry-influenced song had been a part of the Beatles' live set for some time. It was written in 1961 by Paul McCartney – back then he had called it 'Seventeen'. Later, John Lennon came up with some additional lyrics. Paul apparently wrote the song about a girl named Iris Caldwell, whom he had dated back in Liverpool. Iris was the seventeen-year-old sister of Rory Storm. Paul sings the lead part, but John provides backing vocals in the chorus.

MISERY
(McCartney/Lennon)
(1:46)

John wrote 'Misery' back stage at a gig in Stoke-on-Trent. He originally intended it to be for Helen Shapiro, but she never recorded it. Instead it was given to Kenny Lynch, a black British singer – unusual at that time – who also appeared with the Beatles as a part of the Helen Shapiro tour package. Lynch's version of 'Misery' is noteworthy as the first cover of a Lennon and McCartney song. John and Paul share the lead vocals.

ANNA (GO TO HIM)
(Alexander)
(2:52)

American r&b singer Arthur Alexander had recorded this song himself in 1962, but without any chart success. John, in particular, liked the song and sang lead.

CHAINS
(Goffin/King)
(2:23)

Husband and wife songwriting team Gerry Goffin and Carole King were among the most successful songwriters in the world in the early Sixties. Carole King herself enjoyed a highly successful musical career, which peaked with her album 'Tapestry', one of the biggest sellers of the Seventies. 'Chains' had been a Top 5 hit in America for the Cookies. The Beatles' version features George on lead vocals for the first time.

BOYS
(Dixon/Farrell)
(2:22)

Although he would eventually enjoy a good few hits in his own right, Ringo Starr will never be remembered as one of pop music's greatest singers. Here he drones his way through another song which shows the Beatles' love of American r&b, Luther Dixon and Wes Farrell's 'Boys' (originally a Shirelles "B" side). This song was popular with many of the Liverpool bands; Ringo had originally sung it with Rory Storm and the Hurricanes.

ASK ME WHY
(McCartney/Lennon)
(2:22)

John sings this rather tame little ditty which first appeared on the flip side of 'Please Please Me'.

PLEASE PLEASE ME
(McCartney/Lennon)
(1:58)

The single that put them on top of the charts. Everything about it works – the harmonica-led introduction, unusual vocal harmonies, "galloping" guitar chords that link the verse sections, and the falsetto chorus. John wrote 'Please Please Me' at Aunt Mimi's house after hearing Roy Orbison singing 'Only the Lonely'.

SIDE TWO

LOVE ME DO
(McCartney/Lennon)
(2:18)

The band's first hit. Paul wrote the song one when skipping school and John contributed the middle eight. The version that appears on the album is not the same as the single, which features George Martin's (uncredited) session drummer Andy White. Ringo plays on this cut.

P.S. I LOVE YOU
(McCartney/Lennon)
(1:59)

The flip side of 'Love Me Do'. Paul is mainly responsible for this song, which he sings, backed by George and John. Again, Andy White plays drums on this version.

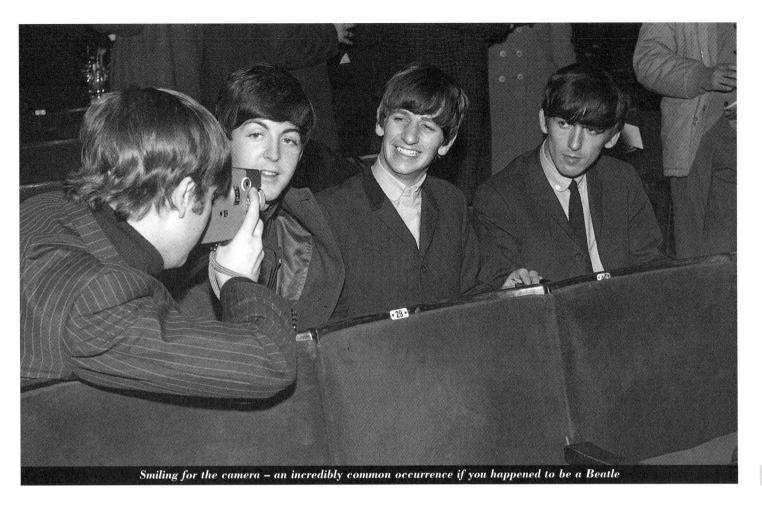

Smiling for the camera – an incredibly common occurrence if you happened to be a Beatle

BABY IT'S YOU

(David/Williams/Bacharach)
(2:36)

John sings lead on another song originally recorded by the Shirelles – this one had been a big US hit in 1961. It was one of Burt Bacharach's early successes – the Bacharach/David songwriting partnership went on to become one of the most important in modern music.

DO YOU WANT TO KNOW A SECRET

(McCartney/Lennon)
(1:54)

John wrote this song for George to sing. He claimed the idea came from watching a Walt Disney film, either *Cinderella* or *Fantasia* – he couldn't remember which. In fact, it's more likely to have been *Snow White*, in which the heroine sings 'I'm Wishing' – the two songs have very similar first lines. 'Do You Want To Know A

Secret' was recorded by another of Brian Epstein's artists, Billy J. Kramer. It went to the top of the British charts in May 1963.

A TASTE OF HONEY

(Scott/Marlow)
(1:59)

One of Paul McCartney's favourite show tunes, 'A Taste of Honey' was written by Ric Marlow and Bobby Scott for the play of the same name. Martin Denny, a somewhat peculiar arranger of light orchestral music, scored a minor hit with the song in 1962.

THERE'S A PLACE

(McCartney/Lennon)
(1:47)

Written by John, 'There's a Place' is an early example the introversion and the desire to escape that would crop up time after time in his lyrics. Although not easy to detect, the song was also evidently an

attempt to create a Motown type of sound. Around the beginning of 1963, American soul music was beginning to take off in Europe and such Motown artists as Smokey Robinson and Marvin Gaye were among the Beatles' favourites.

TWIST AND SHOUT

(Medley/Russell)
(2:31)

Another of the most important American black groups of the time was the Isley Brothers. 'Twist and Shout', written by Bert Berns under an alias, had been the Beatles' live show-stopper since they first heard the song. John gives a ferocious vocal performance, all the more impressive considering this was recorded at the end of a 13-hour session, when his voice had almost gone. Somewhat ironically, a few months later the song was a great success for Brian Poole and the Tremeloes – the very band whom Decca had signed in preference to the Beatles.

THE MERSEY INVASION

The national success of the Beatles was about more than just a group of guys who got lucky. Very soon the big London record labels realised that there had been a serious music scene going on in the North of England about which they had little knowledge. Brian Epstein more than anyone else, helped to put Merseybeat on the map. By the middle of 1963, Epstein's NEMS Enterprises had a roster that in retrospect reads like an A-Z of early Sixties British pop music. He signed up the best that Liverpool could produce and, setting up a new head office in London, used the success of the Beatles to get his new acts recording contracts. More often than not, Epstein's bands found fame with Lennon and McCartney compositions.

Liverpool's other big success story of the time was Gerry and the Pacemakers – still considered as Liverpool's number two band, even though they had managed to score a number one single a few weeks before the Beatles. They also achieved another feat that the Beatles couldn't match: that of having their first three singles go to number one, starting with Mitch Murray's 'How Do You Do It?" – the song that the Beatles had turned down! This feat would not be emulated until the Eighties – by another Liverpool band, Frankie Goes To Hollywood.

Among the other Mersey bands to experience a taste of success were Billy J. Kramer and the Dakotas, and the Fourmost, both of whom enjoyed a number of Lennon and McCartney hits. The Searchers also enjoyed a lengthy career mostly playing unknown American hits:

Billy J. Kramer and the Dakotas

Almost a Who's Who of Merseybeat: the Beatles, Gerry and the Pacemakers, and B

"Sugar and Spice", "Sweets for my Sweet" and "Needles and Pins" all managed high chart placings.

There were others in Liverpool who were affected by this turn around in fortune – the Beatles' families. Aunt Mimi was completely bewildered by it all. John's wife Cynthia was living at *Mendips* along with their baby son Julian. But life was far from normal – teenage girls kept a continuous vigil outside the house, hoping for an increasingly rare appearance from a Beatle. It was the same for the other families. Elsie Gleave, Ringo's mother, couldn't believe how much money her son now seemed to have. In fact, she wasn't so sure that Ringo's business was entirely legal.

The Beatles themselves also had to adjust to the way people they had known now treated them. For Ringo this even extended to his family: "I was at my auntie's and we were having a cup of tea one night – it may have been after one of the shows… someone knocked into the coffee table and some of my tea spilled into the saucer. Suddenly it was 'He can't have that now' and they took it away and gave me a clean saucer. That would never have happened before! I thought, hmm, things are changing!"

On April 12th, Parlophone released the third Beatles single, 'From Me to You'. Unlike its predecessor, critics were not overly impressed – it was seen as a copy of 'Please Please Me', and slightly less interesting. It was a little slower, but the ingredients were much the same. To the Beatles though, it was seen as a good progression. As Paul McCartney says, "We were always just trying to improve on what we and other people we heard were doing… It was nice when we got that minor chord in the middle of 'From Me to you'. It was something we hadn't done before."

In spite of any critical misgivings, the wheels were now well and truly in motion. Sunday, April 21st saw the Beatles play their biggest gig yet. It was to a crowd of 10,000 people at the *New Musical Express* poll winners show, at the Empire Pool, Wembley. The major attraction was Cliff Richard and the Shadows – the Beatles were second on the bill. A week later 'From Me to You' went to number one. The single sold over half-a-million copies and scored the band their first silver disc.

After a frenzied year, the Beatles needed a break. As John would later say of the period, "We had to do an album in 12 hours and a new single every three months. We'd be writing new songs literally in the hotel or in the van." Brian decided that

er and the Dakotas. Brian Epstein, who managed all three bands, is sixth from the right

With 'From Me to You' at the top of the charts, the Beatles seem unstoppable

The bigger the success, the bigger the stage

they should all have two weeks off. Paul, George and Ringo took their girlfriends off to Tenerife for 11 days. Meanwhile, Brian and John flew off to Spain, leaving Cynthia to look after Julian with Aunt Mimi. Over the years, John's holiday with Brian has prompted all kinds of speculation – even a television drama – as to the true nature of their relationship. Needless to say there was never any response from either party.

MORE OF THE SAME

Refreshed after their break, the Beatles came back to a pleasant surprise; in their absence their album had gone to the number one spot. It was looking as if it would be one of the year's top sellers. What's more, they were about to embark on a third national tour. This time it was with Roy Orbison – one of their great heroes. The Beatles and Gerry and the Pacemakers were to be second and third on the bill. However the inevitable happened – the audience reaction betrayed the real stars of the show. Quickly, and with a sense of unease given the awe with which they held Roy Orbison, the Beatles became top of the bill.

Radio shows, TV appearances and all kinds of offers arrived day after day, yet the Beatles were still performing live four or five times a week. After a show in Newcastle on June 26th, John and Paul decided to get together in their hotel room to see if they could write their next single. They were beginning to feel the pressure: there had been two number one hits in succession and anything less this time would be a disaster for the band. As they talked and fiddled with their acoustic guitars, John made a suggestion that instead of writing about "me and you" they try something about a third person. Paul, again stressing the band's desire to keep moving forward remembers, "We hit on the idea of doing a reported conversation, 'She told me what to say, she said she loves you', giving it a dimension that was different to what we'd done before."

The song they came up with was 'She Loves You'. Five days later they went back to Abbey Road to record the song. Everyone who heard the rough mixes was convinced that it would become a classic. It had all the features that had made the Beatles so popular, plus the additional "yeah, yeah, yeah" chorus – now seen as one of the most famous hooklines in the history of pop music.

The single was released on Friday, August 23rd. A gentle ballad entitled 'I'll Get You', another Lennon and McCartney

In 1963, Liverpool's "Big Two" could do nothing wrong

It was during these sessions that George Martin began to realise that there was more to the Beatles than the four charismatic lads that he had first worked with. The band themselves were becoming more at ease in the studio, and started to take a keen interest in how to use the studio more effectively. John in particular was keen to understand the new recording techniques, he quickly grew fond of double-tracking the lead vocal: recording the vocal twice and keeping both versions in the mix to fill out the sound of the voice. He used the technique so much that George Martin had to plead with him to stop on some tracks. Also, the Beatles' own songs were gaining in confidence and complexity, and their sources of inspiration were continually widening.

BEATLEMANIA IS BORN

An indication of the way pop music was viewed by the "serious" media of the day can be seen in the first documentary that featured the Beatles, filmed at the end of August 1963. BBC producer Don Haworth wanted to make a film about the Merseybeat phenomenon, but rather than shooting a film full of Liverpool bands, he chose to view the whole thing from a sociological perspective. The 30-minute documentary featured the Beatles and other Mersey acts playing and talking, interlocking with an attempt to give the viewer a feel for life in Liverpool.

When the resulting *Merseybeat* was broadcast at the end of October, it was a success with the public – as one would expect any programme that featured the top group of the moment. It was also a major success with the critics. In many ways it was the first time that the serious media had been prepared to concede that pop music was not just for poorly educated, working class teenagers. Don Haworth's film would also play a small but significant role in the Beatles' imminent invasion of America. *Merseybeat* is now looked on as an important document in the history of British pop music, and clips from the film continue to be shown.

composition, was featured on the flip side. 'She Loves You' went straight to number one, selling half-a-million copies within the first two weeks. It also had an unusually long chart life for a single, staying at the top for a month, dropping back into the top three for the next two months, and then going back up to the top again. By the end of November, 'She Loves You' had sold over a million copies. It would be Britain's biggest selling single of the Sixties. In fact, only two singles have out-sold it since, the Band Aid single 'Do They Know It's Christmas?' in 1984 and Paul McCartney's own 'Mull of Kintyre' in 1977.

Earlier in August, with their first album still at the top of the charts, the Beatles took some time out of their busy schedule to record some new material for a second album. Again, Abbey Road's Studio 2 was the home for the sessions. This time instead of rushing through they were given a little longer – three days!

October 1963 saw the Beatles embark on their first European tour – seven dates in Sweden. Although not well known as a hotbed of rock and roll, Sweden was the Beatles' first major overseas conquest; they had achieved a cult reputation in the north of Germany, but without ever hitting the big time.

The tour began with a broadcast on Swedish national radio. The seven dates that followed produced the audience mayhem that would forever be associated with the Beatles: screaming teenage girls. Alongside them in the crowd would be their boyfriends, sporting the immediately recognizable haircut thought up by Astrid Kirchherr – amusingly referred to by the Swedish press as the "Hamlet" style!

Although the Beatles were beginning to get used to the teenage girls, their return to Britain came as something of a shock. As their plane taxied down the runway at London's Heathrow Airport the sound of the jet engines faded to the sound of hundreds of screaming Beatle fans. The scenes of madness made headline news in the

national press, which helped to perpetuate the feeling that Beatle hysteria was running out of control.

The Beatles couldn't keep out of the headlines now. On Monday, November 4th, they played what was then for many entertainers the truest indication that they had reached the top of their profession – the Royal Command Performance. This was an annual British "showbiz" tradition where a cast of top variety artists – singers, comedians, magicians, acrobats – performed before members of the British Royal family. The show was broadcast on a Sunday night and always received among the highest annual TV audience figures – so much so that, with a spirit of gentlemanly fair play that characterised the early days of British television, the two major networks took it in turns to broadcast the show.

The Beatles caused a sensation in many ways. Although clearly nervous, their cheeky humour won

John Lennon, the joker in the pack

Sweden is the first European country to take the Beatles to its heart

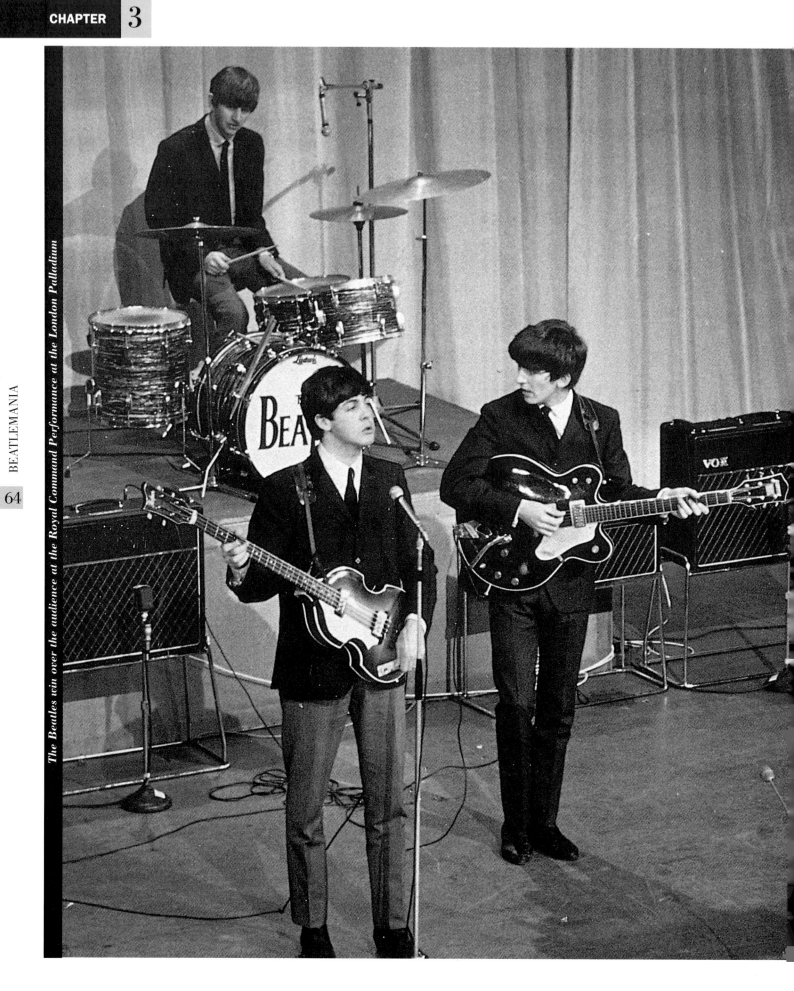

The Beatles win over the audience at the Royal Command Performance at the London Palladium

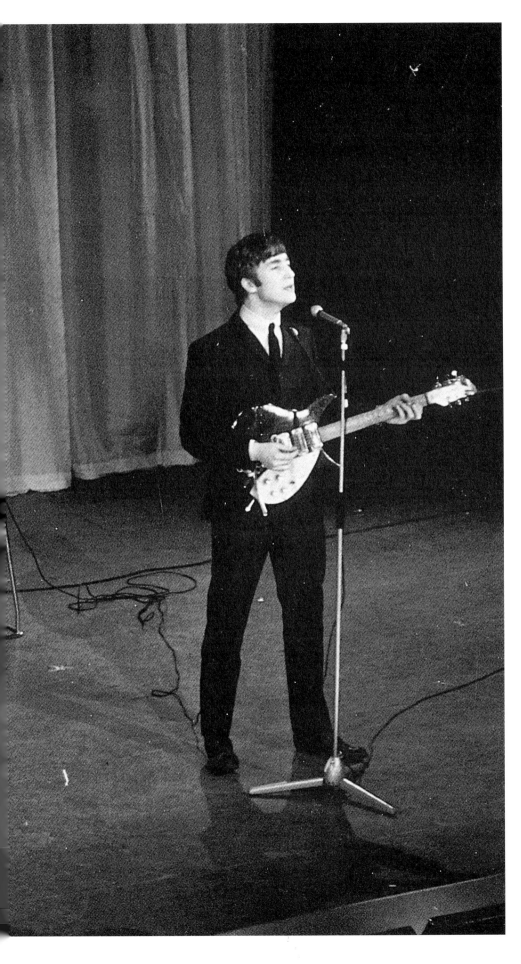

over the starchy, conservative, dinner-jacketed audience. Before playing their final number – the usual 'Twist and Shout' – John made his now legendary request for audience participation: "Will people in the cheap seats clap your hands? All the rest of you, if you'll just rattle your jewellery!" The quip was outrageous in such an environment of utter deference, and yet its delivery came across as innocent cheek. But it could have been very different. Before the show John had joked with Brian that if the audience were being too subdued he would "just tell 'em to rattle their fuckin' jewellery".

The newspapers couldn't get enough of the Beatles. They reported that both the Queen Mother and Princess Margaret – the two "Royals" at the show – had visibly enjoyed the performance which was described in a headline by the *Daily Express* – "Beatles Rock The Royals". When she met them after the show, the Queen Mother asked them where they were performing next. When she was told they were playing in Slough, Her Majesty mischievously replied, "Oh, that's near us." The *Daily Mirror*, reporting on the scenes of mayhem outside The Prince Of Wales Theatre, could find only one world to describe this new phenomenon: "Beatlemania".

DOMINATING BRITAIN

The final two months of 1963 saw an unprecedented level of interest in a group of entertainers. Fleet Street endowed them with front page after front page. The *Sunday Times*, in examining the apparent effect the Beatles had on young girls were the first to start drawing sexual parallels. One psychologist, writing for the Sunday scandal-sheet the *News Of The World*, pronounced that the screams of young girls were subconscious preparations for motherhood! The Beatles were even spoken of in Parliament – a place whose members would ordinarily have little interest in, or knowledge of, popular culture. Finally, in spite of all Brian's attempts to cover it up, the news broke that John was married with

A teenage girl, overcome with emotion, is lifted out of the audience. Such scenes would soon become commonplace at concerts by the Beatles

a son. However, nobody seemed that bothered about it. It was just another interesting fact in an ongoing saga.

On November 22nd, 1963 the Beatles debut album was finally dislodged from the top of the album charts. But only by their follow-up album, *With the Beatles*. There had never been such anticipation for a pop LP. An album had usually been viewed as a collection of songs released on the back of a successful single; the term "album", in fact, comes from the days of the "78" when a number of records were packaged in one collection. Advance orders of a quarter of a million copies of *With the Beatles* confirmed the band's hold on Britain.

At this time, there were no rules attached to the various British music charts – they merely reflected units sold. *With the Beatles* entered the LP charts at the number one spot, but it also sold so many copies that it briefly came into the singles chart at number 15. The Beatles' first two albums went on to set a record that no other artist has come anywhere near: 50 consecutive weeks at the number one spot – 29 for *Please Please Me* and 21 for *With the Beatles*.

With the Beatles was a pioneering album in many ways. The music was notably more sophisticated than its predecessor, and it showed how much the band were growing in confidence. Its presentation also set it apart from other albums. Sleeve design for pop records had always tended to be a rather pedestrian affair. It was only American jazz albums, released by labels such as Verve and Blue Note, that seemed to make any connection between music and art: pop artist Andy Warhol was responsible for many fine jazz album covers in the late Fifties. For the jacket of *With the Beatles*, Brian Epstein hired one of Britain's top fashion photographers, Robert Freeman, who produced four moody black and white portraits, each one half in shadow. The photographs were arranged artfully on each quarter of the jacket. It was very similar to some of the things that Klaus Voorman had done in Hamburg three years earlier.

A week after *With the Beatles* had begun its reign at the top, a new single was

The Beatles are forced to take increasingly desperate measures to outwit hysterical fans

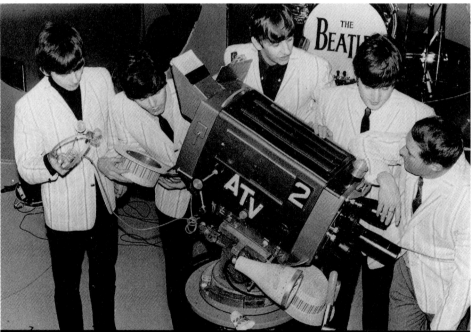

Hitting the mainstream with an appearance alongside comedians Morcambe and Wise

unleashed. Unusual in that it was not featured on the new album, 'I Want to Hold Your Hand' had advance orders of over one million copies in the UK. Naturally it went straight to the top of the charts. John and Paul had written the song a few months earlier in the basement of a house in London's exclusive Harley Street. It was actress Jane Asher's family home, and she was Paul's new girlfriend. 'I Want to Hold Your Hand' would later become the biggest-selling single in the world by a British artist, with sales estimated to be in excess of 15 million copies.

By the end of 1963 the Beatles had overwhelmed the British pop scene and media in way that had never happened before and is unlikely to occur ever again. But it was still only Britain and a few European cousins. Brian Epstein knew that the biggest battle in his game-plan was still to come. The Beatles had yet to conquer America.

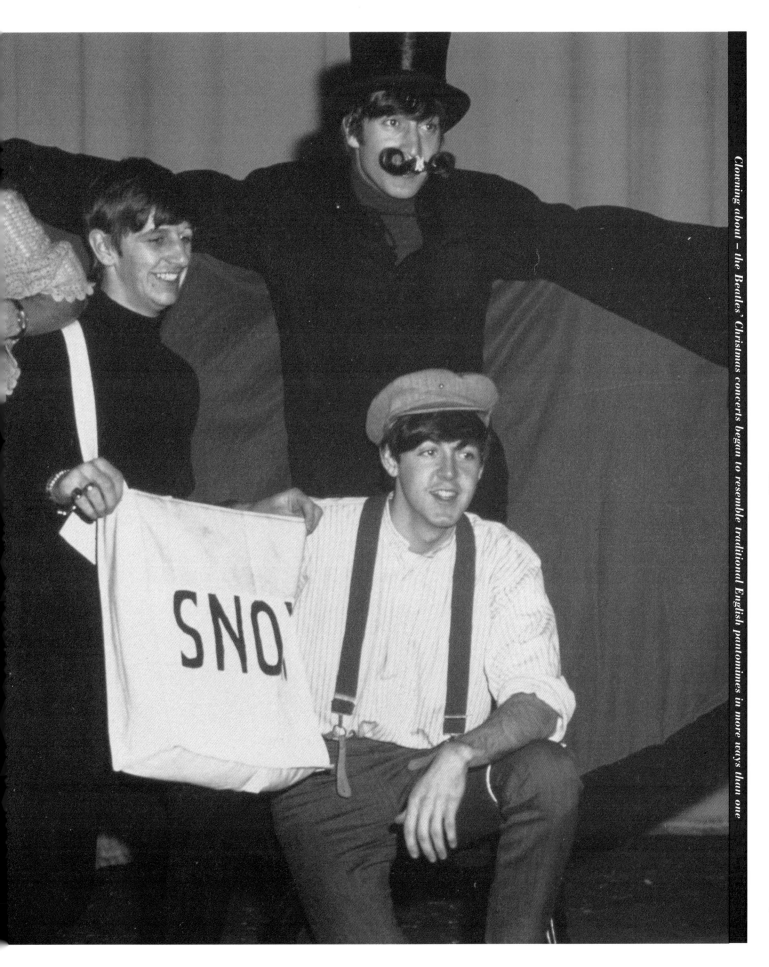

Clowning about – the Beatles' Christmas concerts began to resemble traditional English pantomimes in more ways than one

WITH THE BEATLES

LABEL:	PARLOPHONE PCS 3045
CD RE-ISSUES:	(UK) CDP 746 436 2; (US) C2-46436-2
PRODUCER:	GEORGE MARTIN
RELEASE DATE:	NOVEMBER 22ND, 1963

SIDE ONE

IT WON'T BE LONG
(Lennon/McCartney)
(2:09)

Written and sung by John, 'It Won't Be Long' was intended as the follow-up to 'She Loves You' but was rejected because it wasn't strong enough. In the context of the album, however, the song makes a thoughtful opener.

ALL I'VE GOT TO DO
(Lennon/McCartney)
(1:59)

Another song written wholly by John. He later said that it was an attempt to produce something that sounded like Smokey Robinson.

ALL MY LOVING
(Lennon/McCartney)
(2:04)

One of the most famous of the Beatles early hits, 'All My Loving' was written and sung by Paul. It started life as a poem. As Paul says, "It was the first song I wrote where I had the words before the music."

DON'T BOTHER ME
(George Harrison)
(2:24)

Although George had been responsible for the odd guitar instrumental, 'Don't Bother Me' was the first song he completed. It was put together in a hotel room in Bournemouth in August, where the Beatles were playing six concerts.

LITTLE CHILD
(Lennon/McCartney)
(1:43)

A joint composition that features Paul on piano and John on harmonica, with shared vocals. 'Little Child' seems to have been another song written primarily to give away to another artist.

TILL THERE WAS YOU
(Wilson)
(2:10)

Another show tune, this time written by Meredith Wilson for the show *Music Man*. Paul sings and plays bass, George and John play acoustic guitars and Ringo joins in on the bongos. This is an unusually spartan arrangement for a beat group.

PLEASE MISTER POSTMAN
(Holland/Bateman/Gordy)
(2:30)

John's vocal is double-tracked on this version of the Marvelettes' 1960 US million-selling debut single. The song was written by the Motown team of Brian Holland, Robert Bateman and owner Berry Gordy.

ROLL OVER BEETHOVEN
(Berry)
(2:42)

Chuck Berry was one of rock and roll's pioneers. He not only coined many of pop's best-known guitar licks, but was a genuinely original lyricist. He was perhaps the first person to capture the spirit of teenage life in an intelligent or amusing way; ironic perhaps in that Berry himself was well into his thirties when he found fame. His classic 'Roll Over Beethoven' dates back to 1956, and had been in the Beatles' set before they even set foot in Hamburg. On the recorded version, George takes the double-tracked vocal.

HOLD ME TIGHT
(Lennon/McCartney)
(2:28)

One of Paul's efforts that he regarded as a "work song" – something knocked out for someone else to sing. It was a left-over from the first album, although newly recorded here. John was by all accounts not keen on this song. One could easily imagine it being sung by popular girl groups of the time, such as the Shirelles or the Chiffons, whose hits they had covered so often.

YOU REALLY GOT A HOLD ON ME
(Robinson)
(2:58)

22-year-old William "Smokey" Robinson was already a massive star in the US, with his group the Miracles, although they were relatively unknown in Europe. John and George share the lead vocal on 'You Really Got a Hold on Me', their second million-seller. John's early patronage of Smokey Robinson helped to pave the way for his many UK hits throughout the Sixties and Seventies.

I WANNA BE YOUR MAN
(Lennon/McCartney)
(1:56)

More closely associated with the Rolling Stones, cited throughout the Sixties as the Beatles' bitter rivals, although in truth they were good friends. The Stones' manager Andrew Oldham ran into John and Paul and asked if they had any new material that the Stones could use for a new single. They went into a studio where the Stones were rehearsing and played them a half-finished version of the song. The band liked it so Lennon and McCartney disappeared to finish it off, emerging a few minutes later with the last verse and middle eight! Whilst it was a Top 20 hit for the Rolling Stones, the Beatles chose to let Ringo loose on their cut of 'I Wanna Be Your Man'.

DEVIL IN HER HEART
(Drapkin)
(2:22)

George takes the lead vocal again on this track, again a cover of a song by a relatively obscure US girl-group, the Donays. Ringo plays the maracas.

NOT A SECOND TIME
(Lennon/McCartney)
(2:03)

Written by John, who double-tracks the vocals, 'Not a Second Time' is another soul-influenced number. This led to William Mann, the music critic of *The Times*, writing an article entitled "What Songs the Beatles Sang". He compares the track to Gustav Mahler's *Song of the Earth*, saying: "One gets the impression that they think simultaneously of harmony and melody, so firmly are the major tonic sevenths and ninths built into their tunes." He continues in this vein, going on to discuss the Aeolian cadence at the end of the song. John thought Aeolian cadences sounded "like exotic birds".

MONEY (THAT'S WHAT I WANT)
(Bradford/Gordy)
(2:46)

'Money' was originally recorded by Barrett Strong, and was Motown's first ever number one hit. John sings the album's closing number and George Martin plays the piano.

Meet-and-greet sessions – all part of the job

TAKING AMERICA

In 1956, the hysteria throughout America that had surrounded the rise of Elvis Presley had been unprecedented. Eight years later, on February 7th, 1964, a Boeing 707 touched down on American soil. The reception waiting to greet the Beatles eclipsed even the King himself.

Everyone knew that America had invented rock and roll. There was Elvis, Chuck Berry, Eddie Cochran, Buddy Holly – the list was endless. They had created every trend of the past ten years: they'd even invented the teenager. So why would America care about an English pop group? That was the question the Beatles were asking themselves at the beginning of 1964.

One might have thought that a contract with a major international record company like EMI would have immediately opened doors abroad. Especially as Parlophone's owners EMI already owned the powerful American label Capitol. George Martin, as head of A&R for Parlophone, was also responsible for licensing his label's work overseas. He sent a copy of 'Please Please Me' to his opposite number at Capitol Records. The response was not a positive one. Martin continued to cast around, eventually finding a small independent label in Chicago, Vee Jay Records, who

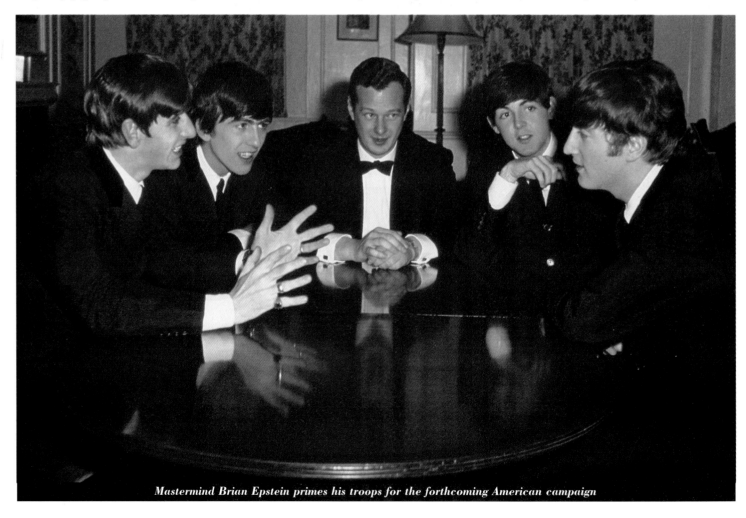

Mastermind Brian Epstein primes his troops for the forthcoming American campaign

Meeting Ed Sullivan, the man who introduced the Beatles to America

released the single. Although enthusiastic, Vee Jay lacked the resources for heavy promotion and consequently the single bombed. Martin went through the same process for the next two singles. 'From Me to You' stalled at number 116, and after switching to the Swan label of New York, 'She Loves You' suffered a similar fate. Vee Jay also released their own version of the *Please Please Me* album, although excluding the title track. It went out as *Introducing the Beatles* with a sub-title "England's Number One Vocal Group". England's number one they might have been, but nobody in America seemed remotely interested.

Things began to move when Brian Epstein made his first visit to New York, ostensibly to sign Billy J. Kramer to the famous Liberty label, home of Eddie Cochran's greatest recordings. When

Epstein called in on Brown Meggs, Capitol Records' Director of Eastern operations, he brought with him the demo of 'I Want to Hold Your Hand' that John and Paul had recorded in Jane Asher's basement. After much deliberation, and given the band's domination of their own country, Capitol finally agreed to give the Beatles a try.

However, the ammunition for Brian's onslaught came from a less expected source. Ed Sullivan had a nationwide television show that had launched many a celebrity into the national limelight; not least Elvis Presley himself. While Capitol seemed unaware of the pandemonium that surrounded the Beatles in Europe, Sullivan had experienced it first hand. Following a trip to Europe, his flight from London's Heathrow Airport had been delayed by the Beatles' heroic return from Sweden. Always on the lookout for new talent, Sullivan was

impressed with the impact they had on their fans and could see nothing to stop it being repeated across the Atlantic. He made Brian Epstein a provisional offer to book them on two of his shows in February 1964. The fee agreed was $3000, which, unknown to Brian, was a paltry figure even for a new artist.

Brian returned to the UK at the end of 1963 to find that Beatlemania was still in full swing. Critical acclaim was also beginning to erupt. The Beatles won five 1963 Ivor Novello awards, the most prestigious accolade that the British music business could give. John and Paul won four of the awards as composers, and in a special fifth award, the Beatles, Brian Epstein and George Martin were acclaimed for their "special services to British music".

Nobody could argue that it was Brian Epstein who "made" the Beatles, but it

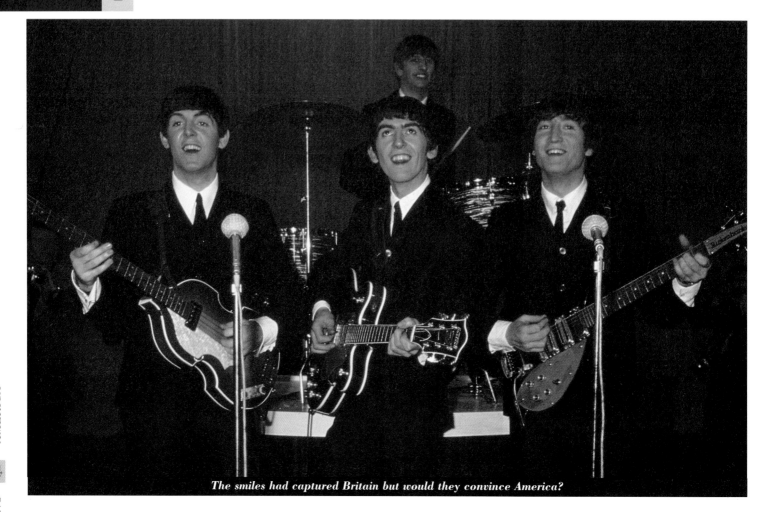

The smiles had captured Britain but would they convince America?

was gradually becoming clear that although things worked well while he was in control, he was beginning to lose his grasp. Quite simply, the whole Beatles phenomenon was becoming bigger than anyone could have dreamed. Scrupulously fair in his dealings with everyone, Brian's inexperience in the world of big business would soon begin to let him down. He found that he had less and less time to deal with the minutiae of the band's affairs – the things he did so well – and relied on others who were less capable to take care of things on his behalf.

This failing was no more evident than in a series of appalling decisions regarding the Beatles' merchandising arrangements. As a by-product of Beatlemania, all manner of Beatles ephemera began to appear – "mop-top" wigs, Beatle jackets, Cuban-heeled boots, aprons, bedspreads, miniature plastic Beatle guitars, the list was endless. To begin with, Epstein had personally vetted

all products, but this soon became impractical and he handed the task to his lawyer David Jacobs.

Today, pop stars are frequently marketed as a complete package – a new album launch by stars such as Michael Jackson or Madonna is likely to be accompanied by videos, T-shirts, books, dolls, stationery, crockery, computer games and CD-ROMs. In the Sixties, pop stars were considered to be too short-lived to think seriously about merchandising. David Jacobs knew little about the manufacturing business and looked elsewhere for help.

He found it in the form of Nicky Byrne, a well-bred London socialite who frequented the fashionable Chelsea set. Byrne and some friends set up a new company called Seltaeb (Beatles spelled backwards) to administer merchandising exclusively. When discussing the precise percentage split between NEMs and Seltaeb, Byrne plucked a figure of 90% out of the air. To his amazement, Jacobs agreed. NEMS

would only get 10% of the merchandising royalties. At the stroke of a pen a small fortune was signed away.

NEWS FROM THE OTHER SIDE

1964 kicked off with an assault on Paris. France was one of the few European countries that had yet to yield to rock and roll on a grand scale. The Beatles arrived in France in a blaze of publicity, but for once the great hype machine failed. Firstly there was, and to some extent remains, resistance to songs not sung in French.

Secondly, and more surprising to the Beatles, they were met by a predominantly male audience who were less interested in Lennon and McCartney's romantic compositions than in straight down-the-line rock and roll. What's more, the gigs were plagued by technical difficulties – George's Vox AC30 amplifier was cutting out with such regularity that he began to

French rock fans go wild but not everyone seems impressed

suspect that it was being sabotaged. To make matters worse, the all-important French press were less than convinced. While the Beatles would later enjoy success in France, the hysteria never came close to the heights it achieved in Britain and America.

In the midst of this minor setback, on January 16th, completely out of the blue, Brian Epstein received a telegram from Capitol Records in New York. 'I Want to Hold Your Hand' had been making steady progress in the lower reaches of the *Billboard* charts, but this week it had shot up from number 43 to number one!

The activity surrounding the single was remarkable, especially for the large, diverse American market, which was fragmented to such an extent that an artist could be a star on the east coast and barely known on the west coast. Stories of

The Beatles take time out to meet some of the Parisian locals

On a good night, the Beatles were one of the best live acts around

Despite their tough start, the Beatles eventually won over the French

information was circulated to radio stations throughout America. Along with open-ended interviews, where radio stations received tapes of the Beatles' stock answers to questions recorded in England – the local DJ would simply re-record the questions in his or her own voice giving the impression of an exclusive interview.

Events leading up to the band's first appearance on the *Ed Sullivan Show* were fast-moving. The show received over 50,000 applications for the 728 available tickets. Despite this encouraging start, few

extraordinary happenings began to emerge. Radio station WWDC in Washington had obtained a British copy of the single and after a few plays had been besieged by listeners wanting to know more. Similar stories were reported in Chicago and St Louis. Capitol, bemused by the advance interest in what they saw as a reluctant

low-profile release, seized the opportunity and launched a major publicity campaign. The Beatles were due to arrive in America at the beginning of February and Capitol made sure that people knew it.

To begin with there was a massive "The Beatles Are Coming" poster and windscreen-sticker campaign. Promotional were prepared to predict that America would succumb to the Beatles in the same way as Britain had. Nicky Byrne, who had astutely set up a merchandising office in New York, could see the way things were going. He wanted the band to arrive in a magnificent blaze of publicity, but felt that Capitol were still not doing enough.

Unable to contact Brian Epstein, Byrne planned his own campaign. He had thousands of T-shirts printed and took out adverts on two prominent New York radio stations. His offer was a generous one: any teenagers who went to the newly named John F. Kennedy airport to greet the Beatles would receive a free T-shirt and a dollar bill.

All of this was unknown to the entourage on board Pan-Am flight 101 that was leaving London's Heathrow Airport. The Boeing 707 arrived at JFK at 1:20 pm on Friday, February 7th. The sight awaiting the Beatles made the scenes of UK Beatlemania seem tame. It was truly frightening. As they began to climb down the steps from the plane, they were greeted by 5000 screaming teenagers. The noise was enough to drown out the noise of jets from other parts of the airport. As they made their way into the arrivals terminal, a 100-man police cordon held back the surging mass. They were led through the Customs point to an immediate press conference with a 200-strong contingent of New York's media.

Clearly dazed but excited by the commotion surrounding them, the Beatles fielded every question – from the most intelligent to most inane – with all the

77

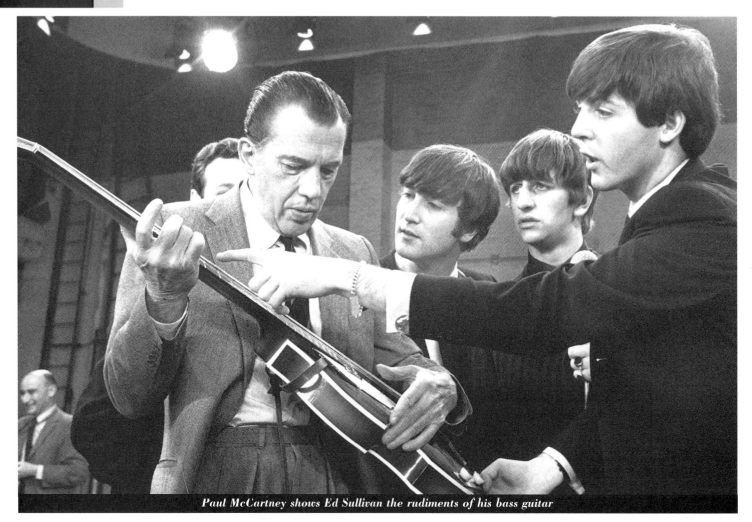

Paul McCartney shows Ed Sullivan the rudiments of his bass guitar

sharp, knockabout "laddish" humour they could muster. When asked if they would be having a haircut while they were in America, John answered, "We had one yesterday." Every one-liner was met with laughter or applause by the gathered media. The Beatles had won their first big battle.

Outside the airport, four chauffeur-driven Cadillac limousines waited to spirit them away to their temporary home, the Plaza hotel, on New York's famed Central Park. The Beatles had been booked into the hotel a month earlier as a group of "London businessmen". When the hotel owners discovered who these "business-men" were, they were not pleased. The Beatles were the absolute antithesis of the clientele to whom the hotel usually catered and the owners tried hard to have the band moved to a different hotel. They were unsuccessful, however, and the Beatles settled into their suites – the entire 12th

It's beginning to look as if teenage Beatle fans are the same the world over

floor of the hotel had been given over to the entourage.

The scenes of hysteria at the airport were reported with a similar tone. It was the top national story of the day. Not since war hero General MacArthur had returned from Korea had there been such a huge public welcome. Within the first few days the Beatles received nearly 100 sacks of mail from all over America: Brian Epstein had to set up a small administration department in another hotel to deal with the correspondence.

Two days after their arrival, with George Harrison suffering from a severe throat condition, the Beatles made their first ever performance on American soil. The venue was Studio 50 – The Ed Sullivan Theatre on New York's West 53rd Street. Sunday, February 9th was the day

when the Beatles conquered America.

After a day of rehearsing, and recording material for a later broadcast, the *Ed Sullivan Show* began at 8:00 pm. It opened with a dramatic announcement from the host himself:

"Yesterday and today our theatre has been jammed with newspapers and hundreds of photographers from all over the nation. These veterans agree with me that this city never has witnessed the excitement created by these four youngsters from Liverpool who call themselves the Beatles.... Ladies and gentlemen, THE BEATLES!"

A scream erupted from the studio audience. Paul gave a count-in. "1, 2, 3, 4, 5" and the band launched into 'All My Loving', quickly followed by 'Til There Was You' and 'She Loves You'. Later in the

hour-long programme, they performed 'I Saw Her Standing There' and their number one hit 'I Want to Hold Your Hand'. As a helpful introduction to the band – as if any was really needed – during their second song, the cameras presented an individual close-up to each of the Beatles, showing his name. John's introduction bore an additional line of information: "Sorry girls, he's married."

The Beatles were visibly thrilled by their reception, but the experience was capped when, after their first three songs, Ed Sullivan announced that they had just received a telegram from Elvis Presley and Colonel Tom Parker wishing them success on their first visit to America.

This legendary show made television history immediately. The Nielsen ratings system estimated that the *Ed Sullivan*

During the course of one evening, America falls to the Beatles

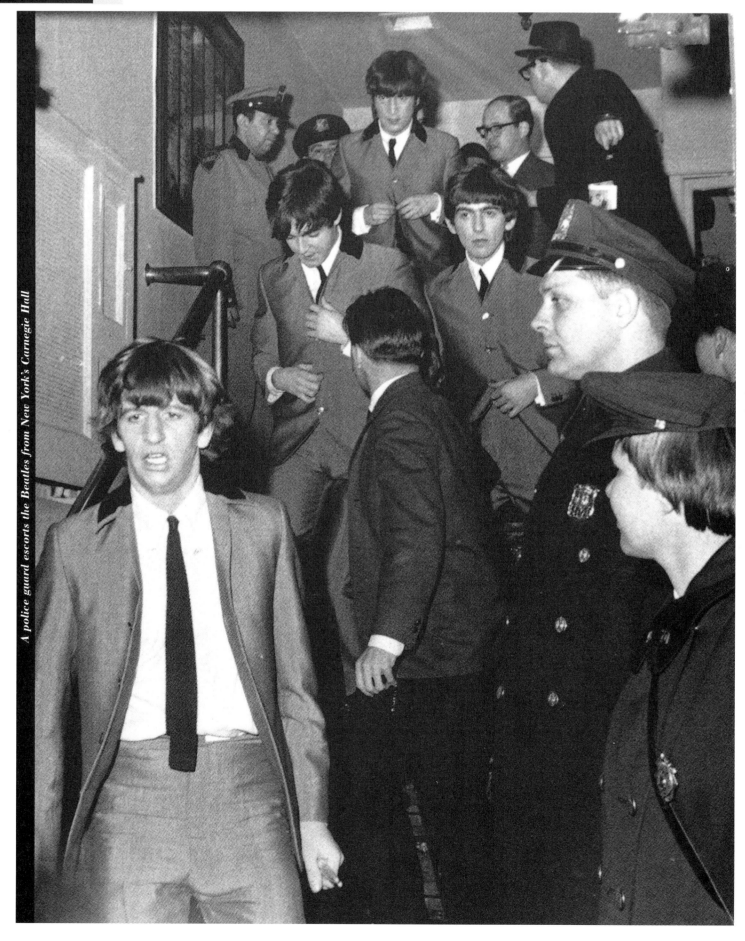

A police guard escorts the Beatles from New York's Carnegie Hall

Show had been watched by 73 million people in 24 million households. In other words, more than 60% of all American TV viewers – the world's largest TV audience – had tuned in to watch the Beatles play. George Harrison later said: "Afterwards they told us that there was no reported crime. Even the criminals had a rest for ten minutes while we were on."

Within a week the Beatles had played high-profile concerts at Washington's Coliseum and New York's prestigious Carnegie Hall. It was as if they could do no wrong: during February 1964 America became besotted with the Beatles. It stayed that way: long after the band's acrimonious split, and during the fledgling solo careers that followed, it was America more than anywhere else that remained true to the "Fab Four".

When the Beatles left the US at the end of the month they left a continent with an insatiable appetite. The earlier Vee Jay and Swan singles that previously couldn't be given away, were suddenly repromoted and found themselves firing up the charts. This culminated, on April 4th 1964, in the total surrender of the *Billboard* chart. With the top two positions in the album charts, Beatles singles could be found at numbers 1, 2, 3, 4, 5, 31, 41, 46, 58, 65, 68 and 79.

The same would soon be true the world over. In Australia the Beatles took the top six chart positions. It goes without saying that no artist in the history of popular music has ever come anywhere near this level of domination. It is difficult to imagine how it could ever happen again.

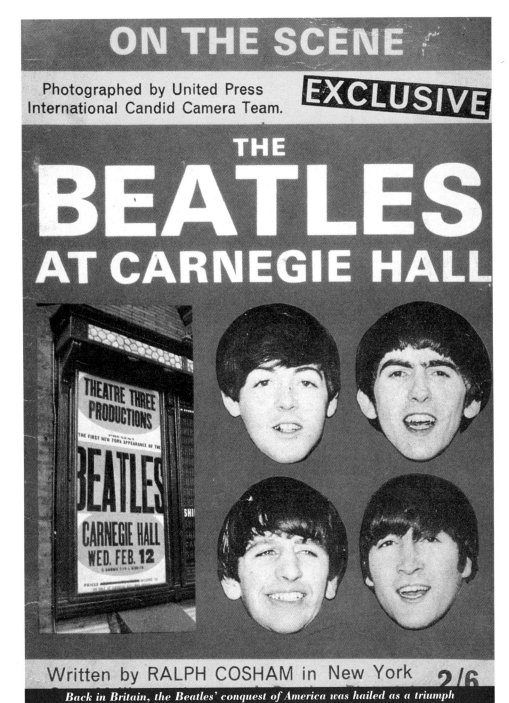

Back in Britain, the Beatles' conquest of America was hailed as a triumph

THE SILVER SCREEN

As ever, Brian Epstein was busy preparing the next phase of his masterplan. But once again, his inexperience with big business would almost undermine his success. While in America, Nicky Byrne had made almost $100,000 in merchandising. When he presented Brian with a cheque for the NEMS share, which had been agreed at 10%, Brian was pleasantly surprised then wanted to know how much he had to pay Nicky Byrne! It was a similar story when

the Beatles made their first feature film. Brian went into negotiations with United Artists with a firm threshold figure of 7.5% of the royalties – he would under no circumstances accept anything less. United Artists, meanwhile, had been expecting, and prepared, to pay up to 25%. In addition, he signed a deal that committed the Beatles to three films and allowed the rights to revert back to the producer, Walter Shenson, after 15 years. Although Epstein's lawyer David Jacobs

eventually renegotiated the fee, it was more evidence that things were getting out of control. Joe Orton, one of Britain's top playwrights of the Sixties – probably best known for his brutal murder in August 1967 at the hands of his lover Kenneth Halliwell – also had doubts about Epstein. He had been commissioned to create a script for a Beatles film, but felt that Epstein was not equipped to judge its merits. A Beatles fan himself, Orton states in his diaries that it is "extraordinary that

TAKING AMERICA

The Washington DC Coliseum had never witnessed such hysteria until the Beatles arrived

someone like Epstein has absolutely no idea how valuable a property the Beatles are". It seemed that Epstein was playing out of his league: he was unable to comprehend the financial potential of his protégés, and was too closely involved with their development to appreciate their growing cultural significance.

During March and April 1964 Beatlemania had developed a momentum that no longer needed to be stoked continuously by a heavy performing schedule. This period was devoted to making a feature film. Exploitation spin-offs had long been a staple part of the pop diet. Often not especially lucrative to the stars involved, they were nonetheless popular because as much as anything else, the lure of big-screen immortality was too great for the pop star ego to resist.

The working title for the film had originally been *Beatlemania* but this was later dropped in favour of one of Ringo's Liverpool phrases: *A Hard Day's Night*.

Richard Lester was the director given the task of converting the group humour onto the big screen. Lester was a good choice; his best known work up to that point had been *The Running, Jumping and Standing Still Film* featuring John's radio heroes, the Goons. The script was to be written by Alun Owen, who had a reputation based on a number of highly acclaimed gritty Liverpool-based television dramas. It was felt that his knowledge of the Beatles' home city would give a more authentic feel to their dialogue. The producers sensibly avoided placing too much pressure on the band themselves. After all, they had reached the pinnacle of their profession as musicians, not actors. In fact, nobody had the slightest idea how well they would stand up.

The storyline would be a simple one: the Beatles would play themselves in a series of set-pieces that could easily have come straight from incidents in their own hectic lives. The press release for the film

John and Paul chat to fans in Florida

The Beatles drop in on Muhammad Ali, then still known as Cassius Clay

issued by United Artists captured the tone:

"Once upon a time there were four happy Liverpool lads, John, Paul, George and Ringo and they played their music all over the country. Now, when they'd finish playing in one place they'd run to the nearest railway station and go on to a new place to play some more of their music, usually pursued by hundreds of young ladies…."

A Hard Day's Night shows the Beatles in their familiar wisecracking press-conference mode, but extended throughout an entire film. The Beatles were so convincing that many thought that the film really was the Beatles just playing around

and making it up as they went along. This was a myth that producer Walter Shenson was keen to dispel: "I don't think enough credit has been given to Alun Owen's script… actually the film was very tightly scripted and not improvised at all." Owen eventually received an Oscar nomination for his work on the film.

There were, however, a few aspects of *A Hard Day's Night* that bothered the band. Years later, John Lennon would recall: "We were a bit infuriated by the glibness and shiftiness of the dialogue and we were always trying to get it more realistic, but they [Lester and Owen] wouldn't have it. It ended up OK, though."

The Beatles themselves were a revelation. Bolstered by a sturdy British cast that included Wilfrid Brambell (BBC television's old man Steptoe) and Shakespearean actor Victor Spinetti, there were few signs of the stilted or wooden performances that marred so many similar projects: almost all the Elvis Presley films since his discharge from the US Army, for example.

All four Beatles played their parts with great confidence, especially Ringo whose performance was singled out by a number of critics. During a lengthy scene where he "escapes" from the band and walks beside a canal on his own, he delivers a performance of engaging pathos. Although to this day Ringo claims to know the real reason that the scene was so successful: "That came about because I came to work straight from a nightclub and I was hungover to say the least. Why I look so cold and dejected is because I felt like shit! There's no acting going on – I just felt so bad."

When the film was released in August, the critics were generally in favour. In a review that would have no doubt pleased at least one member of the band, Leonard Mosly in the *Daily Express* said, "There's been nothing like it since the Goons on the radio and the Marx Brothers in the Thirties." Patrick Gibbs in the *Daily Telegraph* called them "engagingly provocative and wonderfully photogenic." New York's *Village Voice* called the film "The 'Citizen Kane' of jukebox movies." Finally, again proving their ability to traverse traditional lines of taste with the greatest of ease, the *Monthly Film Bulletin* – one of the more serious cinema magazines – describes the "freshness which overcomes its neo *nouvelle vague* air."

A Hard Day's Night proved to be a great success internationally, earning $14 million on its first release. There were a number of foreign-language versions that went out under alternative titles. In Germany, where the Beatles had enjoyed two hits sung in translation 'Komm, Gib Mir Deine Hand' and 'Sie Liebt Dich' (bizarrely, also hits the US!), the film was issued as *Yeah Yeah Yeah – Die Beatles*. Italians saw the film as *Tutti Per Uno* (All for One) and the French as *Quatre Garçons dans le Vent* (Four Boys in the Wind).

Naturally, a film starring the Beatles playing themselves had to have a brand new set of songs. Before the cameras started to roll, they recorded three days' worth of new material with George Martin at Abbey Road, much of which they had written during the marginally successful visit to France. In addition, as the film's musical director, George Martin also recorded a number of instrumental takes on the same songs.

A Hard Day's Night was also the first Beatles album to be made up entirely of original Beatles compositions. At this time,

perhaps a hangover from the Quarry Men days, John Lennon was still seen as the dominant force in the band. Of the eight Lennon/McCartney compositions used in the film, John was largely responsible for seven of them.

Presentation of the Beatles' soundtrack albums always differed between Britain and America. In the UK, the songs from the film appeared in sequence on the first side of the record – the other side featured new material that was recorded in June,

after the film had been completed. Some of this material found its way onto the many EPs (four-track "extended play" singles with picture sleeves) that were also released at the time.

In America, *A Hard Day's Night* was treated purely as a soundtrack album and contained only the songs featured in the film. To pad the album out to a respectable length, some of George Martin's incidental music – often orchestral versions of the same songs – was inserted.

If Elvis could do it, why not the Beatles?

85

TAKING AMERICA

Ringo with co-star Wilfrid Brambell, famed for his long-running television role as Albert Steptoe

Director Richard Lester prepares the Beatles for a take

AUSTIN REED

*The premier of **A Hard Day's Night** caused as much mayhem as a concert*

A HARD DAY'S NIGHT

LABEL:	PARLOPHONE PCS 3058
CD RE-ISSUES:	(UK) CD 746 437 2; (US) C2-46437-2
PRODUCER:	GEORGE MARTIN
RELEASE DATE:	AUGUST 10TH, 1964

SIDE ONE

A HARD DAY'S NIGHT
(Lennon/McCartney)
(2:28)

From the distinctive chime of the Rickenbacker guitar in the opening chord, 'A Hard Day's Night' illustrates a continuing maturity in Lennon and McCartney's compositions. The song opened and closed the film, and was released as a single a month before the album. With advance orders of over half-a-million it became the Beatles' third consecutive single to enter the charts at number one. John wrote the song for his son Julian, who was about to celebrate his first birthday. *The Goon Show* star Peter Sellers also enjoyed a Top 20 hit with a comedy version of the song in 1965. His take was delivered music-free in the style of a Shakespearean monologue. Pianist Ramsey Lewis also scraped into the lower reaches of the Top 30 a year later with a jazz version.

I SHOULD HAVE KNOWN BETTER
(Lennon/McCartney)
(2:41)

John wrote, sang double-tracked vocals and played harmonica on this track. 'I Should Have Known Better' also features George playing a Rickenbacker 12-string guitar – he was largely responsible for the popularity of the instrument which was later taken up by American bands like the Byrds.

IF I FELL
(Lennon/McCartney)
(2:16)

In the film, there deliberately being no romantic interest for any of the Beatles, John sings this gentle love song to Ringo! The scene had to be shot a number of times as the band regularly broke down in fits of laughter.

I'M HAPPY JUST TO DANCE WITH YOU
(Lennon/McCartney)
(1:57)

Another of John's songs, although this time given to George to sing to allow him "a piece of the action".

AND I LOVE HER
(Lennon/McCartney)
(2:27)

It was generally assumed, although later denied, that Paul McCartney wrote 'And I Love Her' for his new girlfriend, actress Jane Asher. The recording is a completely acoustic one, with Ringo playing percussion. Unusually, given that it is an album track, this song is one of the most covered of all Beatles songs, with around 400 versions recorded.

TELL ME WHY
(Lennon/McCartney)
(2:06)

A throwaway up-tempo number written by John, again, with an American girl-group in mind. It was used during the concert sequence of the film.

CAN'T BUY ME LOVE
(Lennon/McCartney)
(2:10)

Primarily Paul's number, this was a late addition to the film. 'Can't Buy Me Love' was recorded in Paris, although George decided to overdub a 12-string Rickenbacker lead guitar part in London – the original solo is still audible in background. The track had already been released as a single in March, to the highest ever advance sales – over two million in the US and one million in the UK. Inevitably the single entered the charts at number one.

SIDE TWO

ANY TIME AT ALL
(Lennon/McCartney)
(2:09)

John Lennon has said that this track was a recycled version of 'It Won't Be Long' from their last album. He sings the lead, with Paul and George performing the backing vocal duties.

The Fab Four with Wilfrid Brambell, who plays Paul's grandfather in the film

I'LL CRY INSTEAD
(Lennon/McCartney)
(1:43)

John originally wrote 'I'll Cry Instead' for the film, but director Richard Lester felt it was unsuitable for the scene he had in mind – a sequence involving a fire escape. 'Can't Buy Me Love' was used instead.

THINGS WE SAID TODAY
(Lennon/McCartney)
(2:34)

The flip side of the 'A Hard Day's Night' single, this was another of Paul's supposed love songs to Jane Asher. He wrote it on a yacht in the Caribbean during May, when all four Beatles took a month-long break after filming had ended.

WHEN I GET HOME
(Lennon/McCartney)
(2:15)

When John Lennon was asked what song he wished he could have written, his immediate reply was Marvin Gaye's 12-bar 'Can I Get a Witness'. 'When I Get Home' was John's attempt to write a similar style of song.

YOU CAN'T DO THAT
(Lennon/McCartney)
(2:32)

The flip side of 'Can't Buy Me Love' was recorded in Paris at the same time. John wrote the song and played lead on his new Rickenbacker guitar, while George played a 12-string guitar.

I'LL BE BACK
(Lennon/McCartney)
(2:20)

Written by John after Del Shannon's 'Runaway'. Shannon, who had enjoyed a spectacular career in the US, took a cover version of 'From Me To You' into the lower end of the American Top 100 charts before the Beatles ever managed to get there.

NOWHERE TO RUN

Having conquered America, the Beatles returned from their month off ready to take on the rest of the world. After a brief spell in Holland and Scandinavia, they flew out to the Far East and Australia. The scenes that greeted them were by now becoming familiar. On their flight from Hong Kong to Sydney, they made an unscheduled refuelling stop at Darwin in the north of Australia. Even at 2 o'clock in the morning a crowd of 400 fans suddenly came out of nowhere to greet the Beatles. The first part of the world tour was marred by illness. Ringo had developed tonsilitis before they came out, and rather than cancel the tour Brian Epstein decided to use a stand-in. Through George Martin, he hired an experienced young session drummer, Jimmy Nichol, until Ringo could be flown out to join the tour. With virtually no rehearsal, Nichol quickly learned what was necessary and during the week or so he played with the most famous pop group in the world; few who came to see them realised there was anything wrong.

On their return to the UK, the Beatles spent a few days at Abbey Road laying down tracks for yet another new album before jetting off for a second US tour. This time their reception was, if it were possible, even more hysterical. At San Francisco airport, they were carried from the airport in what can only be described as protective iron crate. This time, they would be playing all over the country. For the event they hired a private Lockheed Electra jet plane to get them from city to city.

It was at this time that it began to sink in that they were experiencing something totally unique; something that nobody outside of the band would be able to comprehend. They had lost control of their lives and turned into a gigantic money-making machine. Paul McCartney, as "the ambitious one", found this easier to handle but for John Lennon the desire to escape began to grow. Being a part of a band made things easier to deal with. As George said, "I always felt sorry for Elvis because he was on his own – nobody else knew what it felt like to be Elvis, but it was different for us – the four of us shared the experience."

In the eyes of their fans, they were now more than a successful group of musicians – they were hyper-human! George Martin recalls some of the pressures they were under: "Wherever they went there were hordes of people trying to get hold of them... in some places they'd wheel in paraplegics who were brought in to touch them – it was like Jesus, almost." Derek Taylor, the band's young press officer was horrified: "The situation just became nightmarish."

George Harrison remembers feeling like a prisoner at the time: "The only place we ever had any peace was when we got back to the suite, and went to the bathroom!"

The Beatles stayed in America for just over a month: they played 32 dates in 34 days in 24 cities, created havoc and then came home. With barely time to slot in overdubs for the new album and record a

The Beatles "down under" in Adelaide

Striking a more serious pose for the cameras in Sydney

The Beatles second tour of America creates an even bigger stir

At every performance the music is drowned out by the screams of teenage girls

new "A" side, their incredible workload continued with another major British tour.

CHANGING TIMES

The new album, entitled *Beatles for Sale*, largely reflected the chaotic lifestyle in which the four now found themselves. In a short space of time they had all become fabulously rich. Wealthy enough to buy a country mansion, and wealthy enough to allow their parents to retire in luxury – with the exception of Ringo's mother Elsie, who steadfastly refused to leave her family home in Liverpool.

But the constant pressure of life on the road began to take its toll on the music. *Beatles for Sale* was a rather disappointing effort that harked back to their old days at the Cavern. Rather than coming up with a complete set of new material, they filled

20,000 American teenagers turn out to see the Beatles in Atlantic City, New Jersey

AMERICA

TAKING

they were the most popular entertainers on the face of the planet, they were happy to acknowledge that there were a lot of other interesting things going on. As George recalls, "We had Dylan's album and we played it over and over again – it gave us a real buzz." Paul was even more enthusiastic: "He was our idol."

It is not hard to understand Dylan's appeal to such craftsmanlike songwriters as Lennon and McCartney. The sparse acoustic backing allowed the lyrics to do the talking. Until now the Beatles had concerned themselves with developing their music. The lesson that they, and countless others, learned from Bob Dylan was that it was possible to say something more than just the blindingly obvious or emotionally trite in the context of a pop song.

Beatles for Sale (or *Beatles '65* as it was known in the US), came out in December 1964, only four months after their previous album. In spite of being generally regarded as a less substantial piece of work, the album shot straight to the number one position, both in Great Britain and America – in each case replacing *A Hard Day's Night* at the top. In total, the album sold nearly six million copies throughout the world.

1964 ended with the Beatles having conquered the world. Apart from the success of *Beatles for Sale*, a new single, 'I Feel Fine' – regarded by many as their best so far – was perched at the top of just about every chart in existence. As groundbreaking as ever, the single opens with guitar feedback before the familiar riff is played. This is reckoned to be the first example of feedback – soon a part of every guitarist's armoury – to appear on vinyl.

The year had also taken its toll on the band. Photographs from their run of Christmas shows at London's Hammersmith Odeon show them looking fatigued: John scarcely trying to mask his exhaustion and even the ever-friendly Paul finding it hard to raise a smile. They'd achieved greater success than any other artists in history, so where else was there to go now? One thing was certain, it was not a year that they would or could, go through again.

holes using old rock and roll songs that they had been playing for years.

However, one new development could be heard in some of the group's new songs. While they were in America, the New York folk scene had thrown up the "protest" song. The most prominent of these new folk singers was the young Robert Zimmerman, or Bob Dylan as he called himself. His albums *Bob Dylan* and

Freewheelin' and such songs as 'The Times They Are A-Changin'' became anthems for a disaffected American youth. While on tour, the Beatles met Bob Dylan – it was then that they were reputed to have first smoked marijuana. The whole band fell under the spell of Dylan's music.

Perhaps one of the Beatles greatest strengths was their open-mindedness to new influences. In spite of the fact that

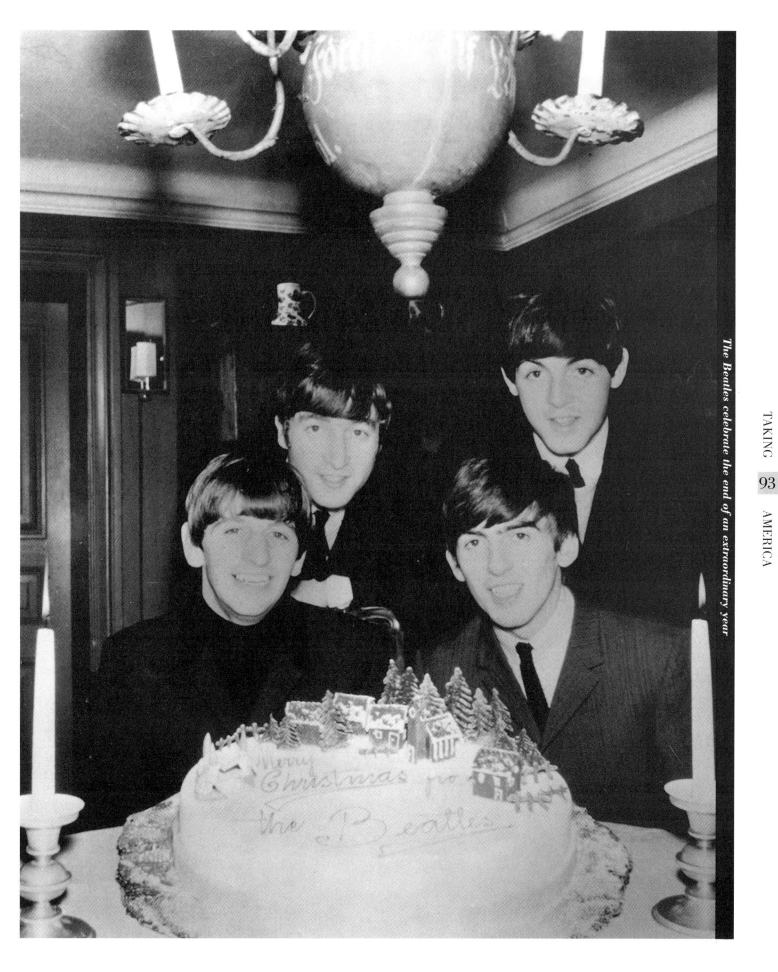

The Beatles celebrate the end of an extraordinary year

Beatles for Sale

LABEL:	PARLOPHONE PCS 3062
CD RE-ISSUES:	(UK) CDP 746 438 2; (US) C2-46438-2
PRODUCER:	GEORGE MARTIN
RELEASE DATE:	DECEMBER 4TH, 1964

SIDE ONE

NO REPLY
(Lennon/McCartney)
(2:13)

Lennon's 'No Reply' is based on a late Fifties American hit called 'Silhouettes' by the Rays. Along with 'Eight Days a Week', it was considered as a possible new single, until John came up with 'I Feel Fine'. Northern Songs publisher Dick James regarded it as Lennon's best song to date.

I'M A LOSER
(Lennon/McCartney)
(2:26)

John wrote and sang this Dylan-influenced number. John has also claimed that this was the first of his songs to be influenced by the BBC interviewer Kenneth Allsop. Earlier in the year Lennon published *In His Own Write*, a best-selling book of his drawings, poems and nonsense verse – much the same kind of thing that he had been doing for years. Allsop encouraged Lennon to write more songs based on his own experiences and feelings. 'I'm A Loser' is perhaps the first of Lennon's many future attempts at self-exploration.

BABY'S IN BLACK
(Lennon/McCartney)
(2:03)

Written by John and Paul, 'Baby's in Black' was the first song they had sat down to write together since 'I Want to Hold Your Hand'.

ROCK AND ROLL MUSIC
(Berry)
(2:28)

One of Chuck Berry's best-loved songs, and a genuine classic, 'Rock and Roll Music' had been on their set list since their first days in Hamburg.

I'LL FOLLOW THE SUN
(Lennon/McCartney)
(1:47)

Written by Paul in 1959 after the death of his hero Buddy Holly. Holly had a major impact on the Beatles, being one of only a few pop stars to write their own material. In the Seventies, McCartney bought the publishing rights to all Buddy Holly's songs. Ironically, McCartney does not own the rights to his own Beatles songs – they were bought in the Eighties by megastar Michael Jackson.

MR MOONLIGHT
(Jackson)
(2:37)

Written by Roy Lee Jackson, the song was originally recorded in 1962 by Dr Feelgood and the Interns. Although it was not a hit, several of the Merseybeat bands did their own versions. On the Beatles' version, John takes the lead vocal, Paul plays a Hammond organ and George plays an African drum.

KANSAS CITY
(Leiber/Stoller)
(2:35)

Although only credited as 'Kansas City' on the LP sleeve, it is in fact a medley that segues to Little Richard's 'Hey, Hey, Hey'. Paul sings the lead vocal, with John and George joining in at the end.

SIDE TWO

EIGHT DAYS A WEEK
(Lennon/McCartney)
(2:42)

Written predominantly by Paul after one of Ringo's descriptions of the Beatles' workload at the time. John and Paul share the lead vocals.

WORDS OF LOVE
(Holly)
(2:01)

John and Paul share the vocal on one of Buddy Holly's early singles, which flopped when it was originally released in 1957. Instead of playing the drums, Ringo taps out a rhythm on a packing case.

HONEY DON'T

(Perkins)
(2:55)

Carl Perkins was one of rock and roll's pioneers, who is perhaps best remembered for writing 'Blue Suede Shoes'. Ringo takes the lead vocal here in his own inimitable style.

EVERY LITTLE THING

(Lennon/McCartney)
(2:00)

Written by Paul with some help from John. 'Every Little Thing' is a love song dedicated to Jane Asher. John and Paul share the lead vocal.

I DON'T WANT TO SPOIL THE PARTY

(Lennon/McCartney)
(2:33)

John wrote the song and sings the lead vocal. It was written at a time when John was beginning to find it increasingly difficult to retain the loveable chirpy Beatle image when meeting people from the music industry.

WHAT YOU'RE DOING

(Lennon/McCartney)
(2:28)

'What You're Doing' takes a novel approach to group singing – the band shouts out the first word of each verse while Paul goes on to finish the line. It shows an attention to detail that would become an increasingly important element of subsequent recordings.

EVERYBODY'S TRYING TO BE MY BABY

(Perkins)
(2:23)

Another Carl Perkins song, this time sung by George Harrison. All three of the Perkins songs covered by the Beatles ('Matchbox' originally appeared only on the 'Long Tall Sally' EP) were lifted from Perkins' 1958 Sun album *Teen Beat*.

ADDITIONAL NOTES:

• AMERICA *Beatles for Sale* was issued in America as *Beatles '65*. American albums of the time were usually shorter than their British counterparts, and the track listing differs. Side one features only the first five tracks, while side two comprises 'Honey Don't', 'I'll Be Back' (an out-take from the film), 'She's a Woman' (flip side of the new single), 'I Feel Fine' and 'Everybody's Trying To Be My Baby'. Of the unused tracks, 'Eight Days a Week' was a million-selling single in 1965, and the others found their way onto the US-only *Beatles VI* album released six months later.
• An additional track, 'Leave My Kitten Alone' (a British beat group favourite written by Fifties American r&b performer Little Willie John), was also recorded for the album but never mixed. It appeared on many bootlegs over the years before finding a first official release in 1995 on *Anthology 1*.

The Beatles have a drink with film star Jayne Mansfield

FROM POP TO ART

THE BEATLES WERE BY NOW THE MOST POPULAR ENTERTAINERS IN THE WORLD. YET BENEATH THE SUCCESS THERE LURKED A STRONG DESIRE TO DEVELOP AS ARTISTS. IT REMAINED TO BE SEEN IF THE PRESSURES OF GLOBAL BEATLEMANIA WOULD ACCOMMODATE SUCH A CHANGE.

If 1964 was the year in which the Beatles took on the whole world, 1965 was to be their year of transition. Although they were still fantastically popular, the Beatlemania phenomenon was beginning to show signs of running out of steam. Nonetheless, the Beatles themselves were still under extreme pressure to consolidate their remarkable success. For 1965, Brian Epstein's game plan would include another tour of the US, a second feature film and more performances in Britain and Europe. But while the great wheels of the NEMS empire were grinding relentlessly onwards, the four young men

Taking to the slopes of Obertauern during the filming of Help!

at the sharp end were beginning to have other ideas. For one thing, they were finding live performances harder and harder to take seriously. They had once prided themselves on being an extremely tight, accomplished group of musicians. Nowadays all they could hear when they played was the incessant screaming of teenage girls. Nobody, it seemed, came to actually listen to them any more. While they made light of it publicly – John would say, "If they want to pay their money to come and scream at us, that's fine by me" – privately they were beginning to feel that it was all rather futile.

They began to take less and less interest in live music; performances became increasingly mechanical and by their own admission, their standard of musicianship was beginning to fall. They had already found to their amusement that any one of the band – even Ringo – could stop playing for a few seconds without anybody noticing. John, who had always jokingly told the screaming fans to "Shaddup!" no longer bothered – he was more inclined to yell obscenities at the audience away from the microphone.

Privately, without telling Brian, they all agreed that some major changes were needed. Principally they wanted to cut

Brian Epstein – the band were beginning to grumble behind his back...

down on the amount of time devoted to touring. Instead, they would throw all of their energies into songwriting and mastering the recording process. If 1964 marked

...but Paul's not saying a word

the Beatles as the most potent commercial force in music history, then 1965 sowed the seeds of a transformation that would make the Beatles among the greatest artists in the history of popular music.

January kicked off exactly as the last year had finished. Like the great British tradition, pantomime season, which carries on well into the new year, so "Another Beatles Christmas Show", at London's Hammersmith Odeon, ran on well past the middle of January.

The following month the Beatles attempted to resume their normal family lives – as if such a thing were possible. John, George and Ringo returned to their various newly acquired Surrey estates to sort out personal matters and write new material for the soundtrack of their new film. It was as yet untitled, but, according to producer Walter Shenson, it would be "...a holiday picture filmed in two totally contrasting holiday resorts... from calypso to yodel with a lot of yeah yeah thrown in."

John quickly settled into *Kenwood*, his mansion home, with Cynthia and

The newly engaged Ringo and Maureen

Julian. Although still the most controversial and provocative Beatle, John was a homeboy at heart, one who liked nothing more than lounging on a sofa watching television, reading books and magazines, or listening to records. Cynthia, who had been woefully neglected throughout her husband's rise to fame, began to take heart at the amount of time he was spending with her and Julian.

John's appearance had altered more dramatically than any of the others: he suddenly put on weight and his face developed a puffy roundness. Cynthia was happy to interpret this as contentment as night after night, when Julian had been put to bed, the pair would sit around smoking marijuana and listening to Bob Dylan records.

Paul McCartney seemed happy to play the role of social climber. He was frequently to be seen with Jane Asher in tow – or tagging along with her, to be more accurate. Jane's background couldn't have been more different from Paul's. The Asher family lived in London's fashionable Wimpole Street. Jane's father was a well-respected doctor who was a consultant in mental disorders at Central Middlesex Hospital. Her mother was a professor at the Guildhall School of Music and Drama

who had, coincidentally, taught the oboe to George Martin.

While Paul had grown up in the "children-are-seen-and-not-heard" working class tradition, Jane had been more accustomed to after-dinner discussions on cultural matters or new developments in the field of psychiatry. This was a new world for Paul, and it was one he was desperate to experience. Rather than buy his own property, as the others had done, he moved into a vacant room at the top of the Ashers' home.

Jane seemed like the perfect girlfriend for the perfect Beatle. She was beautiful, intelligent and most of all, discreet. Their romance was a highly public one and they would be continually hounded by the press to "name the day". For the moment they kept silent, for there was a problem on the horizon. Jane, while barely 20 years old, had already established herself as a fine young actress, with a number of high-profile roles to her credit. In Paul's self-improvement programme, there seemed to be one part of his background that couldn't be turned around so easily – his view of a wife's role. If Jane was to be his wife she would have to abandon her blossoming career. Right now that was the last thing in the world she wanted. It was a problem that they would never manage to resolve.

In the eyes of the world the "lesser" Beatles, George and Ringo found themselves under much less public scrutiny. They were allowed to go about their relationships with a little more ease. George had become smitten with a young model named Patti Boyd whom he had met on the set of *A Hard Day's Night* the previous year. They could be seen hanging out together out at London's most fashionable clubs. Later on in the year Patti moved into *Kinfauns*, George's massive luxury bungalow set in a wooded National Trust estate in Esher, Surrey – the heart of England's "stockbroker belt".

Brian Epstein had initially gone to great lengths to present the Beatles as four young, fun-loving and most important of all, unattached young lads. Like many a star-maker before him, he felt that an important tactic was to promote the fantasy

that any teenage fan, no matter how humble, might just be the one to tie their chosen Beatle down. When the Beatles started to "go public" with their women, the treatment meted out by the fans to the Beatle-girls produced some fascinating outcomes.

Cynthia Lennon was now well-established. She had won her man before he had become sought-after and had already started a family, so she was accepted by the fans as a part of the Beatle package. Jane and to lesser extent Patti also proved relatively popular because, as actress and model respectively, they were typical aspirational figures for teenage girls. And they were exactly the kind of girlfriends that everyone would wish and expect of the "Fab Four".

However, young Maureen Cox, just 18, was dealt a much poorer hand. She had been Ringo's girlfriend since he spotted her waiting to see the Beatles at the Cavern. For a long time their relationship had been a long-distance one. Even though he, like the others, was now based in London, she remained in Liverpool where she worked as a hairdresser. Perhaps it was because she was just a regular local girl and, while attractive, not in the same glamour league as Jane and Patti, that she felt the full venom of Liverpool's teenage girls.

Many of these girls, while proud of the Beatles' international success, were angry that the band had now abandoned their home town. Perhaps, though, it was her station that caused the most problems: quite simply, Maureen Cox had showed that a teenage fan's fantasy could come true. In many ways this made her the most envied of all the Beatles' women.

"WON'T YOU PLEASE HELP ME?"

On Monday, February 15th, 1965, the Beatles moved back into what was fast-becoming their second home – Abbey Road's Studio 2. With budgets gradually growing commensurate with their popularity, they were given a whole week to come

Fans at Heathrow to see their heroes off

up with a soundtrack album for their new film. This would also hopefully include a couple of hit singles. After that they would have to spend the majority of the next three months back in front of the cameras.

A Hard Day's Night had proved to be more successful – both commercially and artistically – than anyone could have hoped. It had been shot in black and white

at a very reasonable cost of a half a million dollars. Even on its first release it yielded $14 million dollars in profit. Subsequent income from television, video and even a CD-ROM have continued to make it a highly profitable movie. Spurred on by this success, United Artists agreed to producer Walter Shenson's new budget request of $1.5 million. This time the film would be shot using the new Eastmancolor process.

When the cameras first rolled, on location in the Caribbean paradise of Nassau in the Bahamas, the film was still provisionally being referred to as *Beatles Two*, although Ringo's wittily surreal suggestion – *Eight Arms to Hold You* – was also used for a time. In the end they settled for *Help!*, after one of the songs that John had written for the soundtrack and which was under serious consideration for the next single.

Help! was to be an altogether less satisfying experience than its predecessor. Richard Lester was again at the helm, helping to retain the madcap absurdism

that made *A Hard Day's Night* so appealing but this time the story was written by Marc Behm. Unlike previous writer Alun Owen, the highly rated Behm produced a script which, while funny in its own right, failed to capture the essence of the Beatles dry, laconic, in-joke humour. This is perhaps the film's greatest failing, along with the fact that this time the story wasn't about life as a successful pop group, but about the Beatles in a comic adventure.

The story revolves around a mythical Indian religious cult discovering that a sacred ring has gone missing. We quickly discover that it now belongs to Ringo, having been sent to him by a mysterious fan. The problem for poor old Ringo is that it seems to be impossible to remove the ring from his finger. The Beatles are pursued for the rest of the film by members of the cult – played by such well-respected British actors and comedians as Leo McKern, Warren Mitchell, Roy Kinnear, Victor Spinetti and *Cambridge Footlights* star Eleanor Bron – who want the ring returned to its rightful owners.

Help! was shot in a variety of point-lessly exotic locations – from the Bahamas they moved on to Obertauern in the snow-capped Austrian mountains. The overall air of the film was more chaotic than their previous attempt, making the plot, such as it was, difficult to follow in places: the internal logic that director Lester clearly understood was not always apparent. In places *Help!* came close to a parody of a James Bond film, but the superficial comparisons dredged up by the film critics were, as before, the Goons and the Marx Brothers. The Beatles, aided no doubt by the constant use of marijuana on the set, did loosen up noticeably and all gave adequate performances. However, as both the victim and hero of the film, Ringo again stands out as the most naturally capable actor.

On its release at the end of July, *Help!* was another major commercial success – the biggest-grossing British film of 1965 in fact. However, the critics were less enthu-siastic. Although most reviews were fairly ambivalent, the *Daily Worker* made a more negative plea: "Save me… from the

In spite of tight filming schedules, Paul and John find time to explore the Bahamas

Ringo dons his uniform and joins the band

Not quite Sgt Pepper's Lonely Hearts Club Band!

unhinged, unbridled lunacy that has no roots, no meaning, no sequence, no consequence, no let-up, no pause!"

The Beatles themselves hated *Help!*. In later years John simply called it "crap... it was just bullshit because it had nothing to do with the Beatles". Closer to the time he was a little more charitable, but only a little: "*Help!* was a drag because we didn't know what was happening... we were on pot by then, so the best stuff is on the cutting-room floor, with us breaking up and falling about all over the place."

With typical Lennon sarcasm, when asked by a reporter if we could "look forward" to any more Beatle movies, he replied stoically, "Well, there'll be many more but I don't know whether you can look forward to them or not."

With one more film to make to fulfil their contract with Walter Shenson and United Artists, Brian Epstein attempted to find a suitable writer. Sadly, they missed an opportunity to use the work of one of the great cult figures of the mid-Sixties. It was late in the next year that an approach was made to a young playwright named Joe Orton. He had just made his name in London's West End with *Loot*, a scurrilously funny black comedy that had shocked the establishment with an attitude towards death, crime, and bisexuality that was outrageous at the time. In the space of a few hectic years between 1965 and 1967, the prolific Orton, who was unashamedly homosexual, became the darling of London's theatre set. He embraced the prevailing wind of "Swinging London" as much as anyone, before meeting a violent death at the hands of his embittered lover, the struggling actor Kenneth Halliwell.

Orton was eventually commissioned to write a script for the third Beatles film. After discussions with Walter Shenson, he met the Beatles in person. Although one would have imagined a certain empathy in both background and attitude with John Lennon, Orton's diaries, published in 1986, reveal that it was Paul with whom he had most direct contact. The project, much to Orton's annoyance, never got off the ground. This was as much a result of the Beatles' reluctance to go through the

On the set of **A Hard Day's Night**

movie process again as to any problems with the material. The script – *Up Against It* – was eventually published long after Orton's death.

Help! was to be the Beatles last foray into the world of acting, as a group at least. They would eventually go on to make their own television film, the much-criticised *Magical Mystery Tour*. Furthermore, they overcame United Artists' contractual requirements by allowing themselves to be filmed rehearsing, the result being *Let It Be*, the fly-on-the-wall documentary made in 1969.

While the hysteria of 1964 was slowly beginning to calm, the popularity of their music showed little signs of abatement. April saw the release of the first fruits of their last trip to Abbey Road – John's 'Ticket to Ride', a single that would have a big impact on their peers. 'Ticket to Ride' revolves around an instantly memorable riff, played on a Rickenbacker guitar,

which introduces the song and carries on into the verse. Throughout the verse the riff plays over a driving beat and single-note throbbing bass line. John later referred to it as "one of the earliest heavy metal records ever made". The Kinks' guitarist Dave Davies may well have had something to say about that – brother Ray's 'You Really Got Me' having hit the charts the summer before – but it was an early milestone in pop's gradual transformation into "rock". 'Ticket to Ride' was released in April 1965 and went to number one on both sides of the Atlantic. It achieved global sales of nearly three million copies.

After the filming of *Help!* had ended, the Beatles returned to the studio to record some more songs for the second side of the soundtrack album, and which didn't feature in the film. On Monday, June 14th, Paul McCartney started the recording of a song on which he'd been working for some

time. The tune had been conceived earlier in the year at the Ashers' home. Waking up early one morning he immediately sat down at the piano he'd had installed in his bedroom and composed the chord structure. Without lyrics, but to get a feel for a main melody, he began to sing a random selection of words – "Scrambled eggs, oh you've got such lovely legs." By the time of the recording, the song had become 'Yesterday'. Although it was not released as a single in Britain at that time, it has become one the Beatles' most famous songs. It is also one of the most recorded songs of the past 40 years.

The recording of 'Yesterday' was also ground-breaking. George Martin decided that such a beautiful song should be arranged as delicately as possible. Instead of using a band arrangement, he hired a string quartet to accompany Paul and a solo acoustic guitar. This was a revolutionary approach to the arrangement of pop

FROM POP   TO ART

John displays a hidden talent for flamenco dancing – an unexpected treat for the waiting fans

Paul shakes hands with Princess Margaret at the London Palladium

music. Just as it is impossible to estimate the impact the Beatles made on the path of popular music, it is also impossible to underestimate George Martin's influence on the development of the Beatles.

Although few would doubt that the Beatles would still have gone on to enjoy some kind of success had Martin not signed them to Parlophone, it was the way in which he nurtured their blossoming talents that played such a major part in the creation of their greatest music.

One prime reason for this success was simply mutual respect: right from the beginning, Martin strove to create the feeling that they were all working together for a "greater good". Martin could easily have simply told the Beatles what he wanted to do – he was after all, in a position a great power. But he allowed them to explore and learn for themselves, only stepping in when he thought he could achieve the things that they wanted.

For this editorial intelligence alone George Martin is considered by many as pop's premier producer. However, as the Beatles' music became increasingly

ambitious, his role in the group became greater and greater. It was he who taught the Beatles the importance of arrangement; added his superior piano skills to many of their records; used his formal music school training to arrange and conduct orchestras; and taught the Beatles (and the rest of the world) how the recording studio could be treated almost as an instrument in its own right.

Perhaps most significantly though, Martin in his quietly authoritative way was able to control the potential excesses of the era. No matter how openly rebellious or controversial the band became in public or to one another, they always treated George Martin with reverence. Martin, for his part, seemed happy just to be working in the background – while he now owns London's Air Studios, one of the world's top recording complexes, during his time recording the Beatles he was merely a salaried member of staff at EMI.

He was also vitally important to the band in that he was able to see the success of the Beatles for what it was. He knew that the four cheeky, lively and slightly

nervous boys who had turned up for an audition three years ago, had not suddenly transformed themselves into gods. To him they were a talented group of musicians who were very, very popular indeed. But that was all they were. The Beatles were by now surrounded by people continually feeding their egos. They needed someone in the camp who could keep their feet firmly on their ground. George Martin fulfilled this role admirably.

Within the space of two weeks from the end of July, *Help!*, the single, the album and the film were all unleashed on the public. All three went straight to the top of their respective charts. The onslaught started on July 23rd when the single arrived, with advance orders of 300,000 in Britain alone. It went on to sell over two million copies world-wide.

The soundtrack album was similarly successful, selling in roughly the same quantities. Over the years since, the album has sold many more copies, a new "wave" occurring, as with all the other Beatle albums, when the CD version was issued for the first time in the Eighties.

HELP!

LABEL:	PARLOPHONE PCS 3071
CD RE-ISSUES:	(UK) CDP 746 439 2; (US) C2-46439-2
PRODUCER:	GEORGE MARTIN
RELEASE DATE:	AUGUST 6TH, 1965

SIDE ONE

HELP!

(Lennon/McCartney)
(2:16)

One of John Lennon's personal favourites, it was originally written as a slow, Dylanesque acoustic number and he later regretted that the song had been "Beatlefied". 'Help!' features some of his most deeply personal lyrics, reflecting his increasing dissatisfaction with himself and his life: "It was real… it was me singing 'Help!' and I meant it… I needed the help." He also added, "I don't like the recording much; we did it too fast trying to be commercial."

THE NIGHT BEFORE

(Lennon/McCartney)
(2:30)

Written by Paul, the song is performed in the film with the band surrounded by tanks and soldiers on Salisbury Plain. John plays the electric piano. The *Help!* album showed that the imbalance between Lennon and McCartney as songwriters was showing signs of levelling out.

YOU'VE GOT TO HIDE YOUR LOVE AWAY

(Lennon/McCartney)
(2:06)

The clearest manifestation of the power that Bob Dylan's music had over John Lennon at this time. The song was written, played and sung by John with session men brought in to provide the flutes. 'You've Got To Hide Your Love Away' is another very personal song, of which he later said: "When I was a teenager I used to write poetry, but was always trying to hide my real feelings… instead of projecting myself into a situation I would just try to express what I felt about myself… I think it was Dylan that helped me realize that."

I NEED YOU

(Harrison)
(2:25)

Written by George – his second writing contribution to the Beatles – 'I Need You' shows a developing confidence, but that his songwriting still lacked the sophistication of the other two writers in the band.

ANOTHER GIRL

(Lennon/McCartney)
(2:02)

Paul wrote and sang 'Another Girl'. Paul was always considered to be the natural musician of the band. Here, keen to display his fast-growing talents, he also plays lead guitar. John and George provide backing vocals.

YOU'RE GOING TO LOSE THAT GIRL

(Lennon/McCartney)
(2:14)

John makes a threat that if "you" continue to mistreat your girlfriend he's ready to make a move on her himself. Better watch out.

TICKET TO RIDE

(Lennon/McCartney)
(3:03)

Already a million-selling single by the time *Help!* was shown, John wrote the song and rated it among his personal favourites. Paul takes the lead guitar again.

SIDE TWO

ACT NATURALLY

(Morrison/Russell)
(2:27)

A Beatles album wouldn't have been the same without Ringo stepping out from behind his kit to take the microphone for one song. 'Act Naturally' was a novelty country and western hit for Buck Owens in America. It tells the story of how easy it is to be a sad movie star because "all you have to do is act naturally".

IT'S ONLY LOVE

(Lennon/McCartney)
(1:53)

At a time when his lyrical ideas were becoming increasingly sophisticated, John

Lennon also showed how he could turn out clichéd rhyming couplets as easily as any Tin Pan Alley hack. Later he would admit: "I was always ashamed of that because of the abominable lyrics." Oddly, a cover of 'It's Only Love', recorded by Gary US Bonds, scraped into the nether regions of the charts as recently as 1981.

YOU LIKE ME TOO MUCH

(Harrison)
(2:33)

One of nine demos originally handed to Richard Lester for the film, 'You Like Me Too Much' was eventually recorded for side two. When George published his autobiography *I Me Mine* in 1980, he made no mention of either of his contributions to *Help!*. This may be because while he would, within a few years, be a more than competent composer in his own right, the tracks presented here show him feeling his way, still well and truly under the shadow of his two senior colleagues.

TELL ME WHAT YOU SEE

(Lennon/McCartney)
(2:34)

One of Paul's lazier efforts, 'Tell Me What You See was also rejected from the *Help!* soundtrack.

I'VE JUST SEEN A FACE

(Lennon/ McCartney)
(2:02)

Paul had been playing this tune on the piano for some time back in Liverpool. His Aunt Gin was so taken with the melody that it became known as 'Auntie Gin's Theme'.

YESTERDAY

(Lennon McCartney)
(2:02)

One of the most famous songs in pop history. Within ten years 'Yesterday' had been recorded by 1186 other artists. The figure is now probably approaching 2000.

DIZZY MISS LIZZY

(Williams)
(2:51)

When in doubt, the Beatles would always return to their origins. 'Dizzy Miss Lizzy' was another rock and roll classic that they had been performing since the Kaiserkeller days in Hamburg. The Beatles performed several songs by its American author, Larry Williams, whose principal success came in 1958 with the million-seller 'Bony Moronie.

Additional Notes:

• On the British pressing of *Help!* only the songs on the first side can actually be heard in the film. The American pressing features only these six song,s interspersed with orchestral versions or some of musical director Ken Thorne's incidental compositions.
• 'I've Just Seen a Face' and 'It's Only Love' appear on the US version of the later *Rubber Soul* album.
• 'Yesterday' and 'Act Naturally' appear on the US-only compilation album, *Yesterday and Today* (see page 112).

If one goes, they all go!

JOINING THE ESTABLISHMENT

A month before *Help!* was released, the Beatles found themselves at the centre of an unexpected controversy. Since October 1964, the prevailing political wind in Great Britain had undergone a radical change in direction. After 13 years under the rule of the Conservative Party, a dynamic and (relatively speaking) young former academic called Harold Wilson captured the imagination of the country's voters, confidently describing an expanding Britain "forged in the white heat of technological revolution".

The Labour Party under Wilson was especially popular with young voters, and, unlike any politician before him, he was keen to embrace popular culture. Although Wilson had been educated at Oxford, become a don at an unusually early age, and shown himself to be similarly capable in the field of politics, he was keen to play up his northern working-class roots. What better way of showing his belief in a young dynamic Britain than to acknowledge its highest profile export of recent years?

On June 12th, the Queen's Official birthday, came the announcement of those names who would be "honoured" this year. Traditionally this list was personally drawn up by the Prime Minister and sanctioned as a formality by Her Majesty. It typically consisted of military men, politicians, civil servants and businessmen. This year's list had four names the likes of whom had never been seen on such a list. Each one of the Beatles was to receive the MBE – becoming a Member of the Order of the British Empire.

The popular press were beside themselves – headlines like "She Loves Them, Yeah! Yeah! Yeah!" reflecting the popular triumph. There were some who were less than happy about a group of pop musicians being honoured in such a way. Former Canadian MP Hector Dupuis was one of many who returned their hard-won awards, complaining that "The British House of Royalty has put me on the same level as a bunch of vulgar numskulls". One outraged naval hero, Colonel Frederick Wagg, returned 12 medals, resigned from the Labour Party and cancelled a large contribution to party funds. Ex-RAF squadron leader Paul Pearson returned his MBE "…because it had become debased". At the same time there were establishment figures, such as Lord Netherthorpe, who were happy to join in the debate on the side of the Beatles: "They thoroughly deserve the award," he declared.

Two reactions from the Beatles' camp speak volumes for the increasing polarization of the band's creative axis.

John Lennon was as blunt as ever: "I thought you had to drive tanks and win wars to get an MBE." But he became irritated when the protesters began returning their medals. As far as he was concerned, army officers were given the award for killing people: "We got ours for entertaining. On balance I'd say we deserve ours more." In the Seventies he was more direct: "Taking the MBE was a sell-out for me. Before you get an MBE the Palace writes to you to ask if you're going to accept it, because you're not supposed to reject it publicly… He [Brian Epstein] and a few other people persuaded me that it was in our interests to take it… but I'm glad, really, that I did accept it because it meant that four years later I could use it to make a gesture." (In 1969 he returned the medal as, among other things, a protest at Britain's involvement in "the Nigeria-Biafra thing".)

Paul McCartney's feelings were clearly a little different: "I think it's marvellous. What does this make my dad?"

One person, however, was especially unhappy. Many thought that there should have been five medals awarded. As George Harrison put it when asked to comment on Hector Dupuis' protest: "If Dupuis doesn't want the medal he had better give it to us. Then we can give it to our manager Brian Epstein. MBE really stands for 'Mr Brian Epstein'." Brian became depressed about what he saw as a snub, putting it down to the fact that he was Jewish and (now fairly openly) a homosexual.

The investiture took place at Buckingham Palace on October 26th. Outside Buckingham Palace, 4000 screaming fans were held back by a heavy police cordon. Their chant (which seems rather quaint in these altogether more cynical times) was "Long Live The Queen! Long Live The Beatles!" The event also gave rise to another of the great Beatles myths. In 1970 a French magazine,

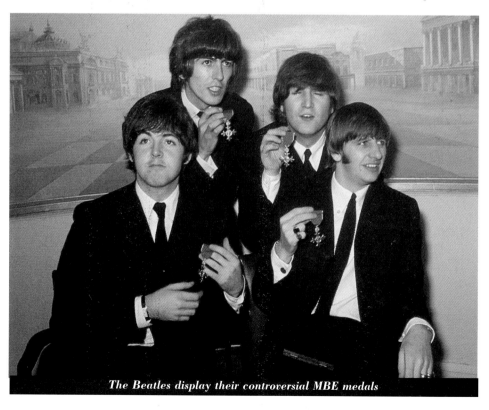

The Beatles display their controversial MBE medals

Was he stoned at the Palace?

L'Express, interviewed John Lennon who claimed that the Beatles had all smoked marijuana in the toilets of Buckingham Palace before the ceremony. This would seem to be simply John making mischief – the others continue to strenuously deny that it ever took place.

During the ceremony, and at the press conference afterwards, the Beatles kept up their quirky humour. When the Queen asked Paul how long they'd been together, Ringo chipped in "Forty years". Outside, waving their silver crosses in front of the assembled press Paul told them that the Queen was, "...lovely, great. She was very friendly. She was like a mum to us," and that Buckingham Palace was a "keen pad".

THE ACID HOUSE

One evening, during the same period, George and Patti invited John and Cynthia to a dinner party given by a friend. John would later refer to him as a "middle-class London swinger". After enjoying dinner they all retired to the drawing room. There, waiting for them were four small sugar lumps arranged in a line on the mantelpiece. Coffee was served, and their host dropped a lump of sugar into each of their cups. After they had drunk the coffee he advised them not to leave.

Pandemonium ensued. Everyone panicked. Nothing in the world could keep them in the house. They quickly escaped and underwent an unusual trawl of London's nightspots. Cynthia remembers: "The room seemed to get bigger and big-

ger. Our host seemed to turn into a demon. We got away somehow in George's Mini, but he came after us in a taxi. It was like having the devil follow us in a taxi." John also remembered the journey: "We were going about ten miles an hour but it seemed like a thousand, and Patti was saying let's jump out and play football." They finally made it back to George's house, but strange things were still happening. By now, John was enjoying the experience: "God, it was terrifying, but it was fantastic. I did some drawings at the time... of four faces saying 'We all agree with you'... George's house seemed to be like a big submarine, and I was driving it."

They had been given their first acid trip. Acid, or lysergic acid diethylamide (LSD), its full pharmaceutical name, was the latest drug to hit London. A powerful hallucinogen, LSD had been developed in the Fifties and had been widely used on mental patients. However, it had been quietly growing in popularity as a leisure drug with such American intellectuals as the outspoken Harvard teacher Dr Timothy Leary. Within two years, use of LSD would become widespread in alternative circles – the impact it had on the culture of the latter half of the Sixties is quite incalculable.

During the following year, John and George became heavily involved with the drug, although it was John who found it the most profound experience. His songwriting contributions to the Beatles over the coming two years have the word "acid" written over them in very large and brightly coloured letters. It was much later when Paul and Ringo attempted the drug. Paul was particularly negative: "I don't recommend it. It can open a few doors but it's not any answer. You get the answers yourself." Later, John recalled Paul's reactions: "I think LSD profoundly shocked him, and Ringo. I think maybe they regret it."

BACK TO AMERICA

Only days after the premiere of *Help!* the Beatles hit America for a third time. While their departures and arrivals were now cre-

ating slightly less havoc than before, the tour ahead proved that they were still capable of record-breaking feats. After an obligatory recording for Ed Sullivan, Sunday, August 15th saw their momentous concert at the William A. Shea Municipal Stadium, home of the Mets baseball team in New York City.

As the concert and surrounding events were being turned into a television film, it was planned to make the Beatles' entrance as dramatic as possible. The original idea was to have the band flown into the stadium by helicopter, however this was rejected by the NYC authorities who feared it was potentially too dangerous. Instead, the group left their hotel in a limousine and drove to a helipad along the Hudson river. From here they flew onto the roof of the World's Fair building – only a few hundred metres from the stadium – to complete their journey in an armoured truck. At 16 minutes past nine, to the deafening screams of over 55,000 fans, the Beatles sprinted through the players tunnel, climbed the steps onto the stage, plugged in their guitars, and launched into the opening riff of 'Twist and Shout'.

As it was the first concert on the tour, the Beatles were swept along by the magnificent spectacle and gave a performance of startling energy. Luckily, this concert was captured on film. *The Beatles At Shea Stadium* was produced by Ed Sullivan's own company in conjunction with Brian Epstein's NEMS, and a new company – Subafilms – owned by Epstein and the Beatles. It captures not only the Beatles giving fine performances of their greatest hits, most of which they had more than enough of, but the very essence of Beatlemania: the fan hysteria; the expressions on the faces of the teenage girls veering between extreme pleasure and extreme pain; the sheer disbelief that they were in the same place as their idols.

The Shea Stadium concert represented the absolute pinnacle of the Beatles as public performers. The crowd of 55,600 fans was at that time the largest ever assembled for a pop concert, the box office receipts – $304,000 – were the highest of

The Beatles at New York's Shea Stadium – then the biggest ever pop concert

all time, as was the Beatles' own share of the takings – $160,000. From that point on there was only one possible way to go: downwards.

The rest of the tour lacked the sparkle of the opening triumph – the band quickly lost interest. What's more, they had actively begun to hate being on tour. They were now so famous that it didn't matter where they went, the routine was identical: airport; police convoy; hotel room; police convoy; stadium; police convoy; hotel room; police convoy; airport. It was just so boring. It was with some relief that on September 1st, the day after their final US date of the tour in San Francisco, they returned home to a six-week break.

In fact the break was to be less relaxing for Lennon and McCartney. They were still contractually obliged to record a new album before the end of the year. Now less inclined to write new material on tour, and wanting more time to produce higher quality work, they found themselves having to write 12 new numbers for the new album. With such pressure, it seems rather surprising that the resulting album, *Rubber Soul,* was such a strong one.

Whatever, it was certainly their transitional album. As George Martin said, "It was the first album to present a new, growing Beatles to the world." Everything about it was just that little bit better than its predecessor. There was also an exploration of new sounds – George's growing love affair with all things Indian, the first uses of tape manipulation (in the form of George Martin's double-speed piano) – that would play such a prominent role in their later recordings.

However, it was still John that seemed to be making the most interesting moves. Compositions like 'Norwegian Wood (This Bird Has Flown)' showed that, still infatuated with Bob Dylan, his lyrics were becoming more personal, even confessional. Similarly 'Nowhere Man' with its rich vocal harmonies and sophisticated arrangement, seems to be a declaration of his lack of direction and faith in himself, and the boredom with which he was beginning to view his life.

It was Paul who conceived the album's title – it was a humorous reference to white artists trying to play soul music. His role was now clearly that of an expert

tunesmith, but his lyrics sometimes failed to stand up to too much scrutiny. Take, for example, the middle-of-the-road ballad 'Michelle', where Paul's song seems structured around a declaration of love to a French girl simply so that he can sing a verse in French.

The sleeve was also a major departure. Along with the psychedelic swirls that make up the album's title, the band, photographed through a "fish-eye" lens, are no longer the four "mop tops" of old, but four reflective (perhaps even stoned) long-haired young men. Finally, as almost everybody in the civilized world recognized these four faces as easily as any film star or head of state, there didn't even seem to be any need to mention that it was an album by the Beatles.

On December 3rd, the Beatles celebrated two new releases. Not only was *Rubber Soul* presented to the world, but

also a new single – John's 'Day Tripper' backed with Paul's 'We Can Work It Out'. This was a particularly bold move by Parlophone in that both sides of the single were given equal status – it was a double "A" side. More unusually, however, the two songs were not featured on the album. As was by now traditional, the single went straight to the number one spot – and stayed there until the new year. It was similarly successful across the Atlantic, and sold around three million copies throughout the world.

Rubber Soul was the first Beatles album to be given a serious critical thumbs-up. The public, of course, still needed very little convincing. In Britain, *Rubber Soul* became their fifth consecutive album to enter the charts at number one, where, like the single, it stayed for well into the new year. In America it broke all records selling 1.2 million copies within nine days.

A year on, the American fans are as enthusiastic as ever

The Beatles begin to tire of the endless rounds of press conferences

RUBBER SOUL

LABEL:	PARLOPHONE PCS 3075
CD RE-ISSUES:	(UK) CDP 746440 2; (US) C2-46440-2
PRODUCER:	GEORGE MARTIN
RELEASE DATE:	DECEMBER 3RD, 1965

SIDE ONE

DRIVE MY CAR
(Lennon/McCartney)
(2:25)

This was one of John and Paul's increasingly rare joint efforts. In an amusing reversal of regular roles, the lyric tells the story of the possible favours that might result if the man in the song becomes "her" chauffeur. The chorus also features the famous "Beep-beep, beep-beep, yeah" backing vocals that have accompanied many a radio traffic broadcast ever since.

NORWEGIAN WOOD
(Lennon/McCartney)
(2:01)

'Norwegian Wood' was, by John's own admission, an attempt to confess that he had been unfaithful to Cynthia without actually telling her directly. John was not happy in his marriage and was known to have taken advantage of the numerous groupies and hangers-on that inevitably follow a band of the Beatles' stature.

The track is also notable for being the first use of the Indian sitar on a pop record. George had become interested in the instrument when one was used as a prop during the filming of *Help!*.

YOU WON'T SEE ME
(Lennon/McCartney)
(3:18)

Paul seemingly writing about a crisis in his relationship with Jane Asher, which was beginning to look decidedly shaky. Paul plays piano and long-term friend and road manager Mal Evans plays the Hammond organ.

NOWHERE MAN
(Lennon/McCartney)
(2:40)

In John's own words, "I was just sitting, trying to think of a song. And I thought of myself sitting there, doing nothing, and getting nowhere... sitting in this nowhere land." This was a departure in that up to that point every Beatles song had, to some extent, been about love.

THINK FOR YOURSELF
(Harrison)
(2:14)

George's best composition to date, featuring an unusual fuzz bass line courtesy of Paul.

THE WORD
(Lennon/McCartney)
(2:39)

In his song 'The Word', John marks the beginning of the love-and-peace era. By now, the influence of LSD was beginning to permeate John's work. This time, as it would so often in the future, it resulted in a calling for universal love and peace. He later described the song as the Beatles' first "message" song.

MICHELLE
(Lennon/McCartney)
(2:40)

Following the most startling song on the album, Paul's 'Michelle' comes across as a pretty, if rather trite, love song. For the French lyrics he contacted Ivan Vaughan – the school friend responsible for introducing him to John Lennon. Ivan was now married to a French language teacher. She provided him with *"sont les mots qui vont tres bien ensemble"*, a translation of the previous line, "these are words that go together [very] well".

'Michelle' is probably the most famous song on the album – versions by the Sandpipers and British duo David and Jonathan all had chart success. David and Jonathan were really Roger Cook and

Roger Greenaway, who would become two of Britain's most prolific and successful songwriters of the early Seventies.

SIDE TWO

WHAT GOES ON

(Lennon/McCartney/Starkey)
(2:43)

Ringo's first compositional credit: "I used to wish that I could write songs like the others – and I've tried, but I just can't." He later admitted that his input to the track was "about five words". Ringo also takes the lead vocal.

GIRL

(Lennon/McCartney)
(2:26)

At one time John said, "This was about a dream girl." Later however, he somewhat ironically stated he "was trying to say something about Christianity". This was a subject that was concerning him a lot at the time – as the world would dramatically discover in 1966. As an additional joke, the backing vocals feature Paul and George repeating the word "tit".

I'M LOOKING THROUGH YOU

(Lennon/McCartney)
(2:21)

With Jane Asher refusing to sacrifice her career to be the good little Beatle-wife, Paul was placed in a dilemma that was having an obvious affect on his lyric writing. In this bitter attack on a woman who seems to have changed, he threatens that his love can disappear as easily as it arrived. Better watch out.

IN MY LIFE

(Lennon/McCartney)
(2:22)

In John's view, 'In My Life' was the Beatles' "first real major piece of work". One of John's most poignant sets of lyrics started life as a free-form poem that looked back nostalgically on some of the landmarks he remembered as a child, all of which were gradually disappearing or changing beyond his recognition. After losing the specific references 'In My Life' becomes a lament to the inevitable losses and changes that are outside our control. The source of the tune remains something of a controversy – John maintained that he wrote it with a little help from Paul; Paul recalls having written the whole tune.

WAIT

(Lennon/McCartney)
(2:10)

Jointly written by John and Paul, 'Wait' was recorded for *Help!* but not used. It was only resurrected for *Rubber Soul* because they were a song short.

IF I NEEDED SOMEONE

(Harrison)
(2:18)

Along with Bob Dylan, the Byrds – an American band that had taken electric guitars to folk music – were another growing influence on the Beatles. George's 'If I Needed Someone' was inspired by two Byrds' numbers – 'She Don't Care about Time' and 'The Bells of Rhymney'. The Hollies became the first band to cover one of George's songs when they took 'If I Needed Someone' into the Top 30. George's response to such an honour was a public declaration that he didn't much like their version!

RUN FOR YOUR LIFE

(Lennon/McCartney)
(2:16)

"I always hated 'Run For Your Life'," John said about the album's closing track. He openly acknowledged that he lifted two lines from Arthur Gunther's 'Baby Let's Play House', an early hit for Elvis Presley during his time recording for the Sun label in the mid-Fifties.

Additional Notes:

• Each side of the American version of *Rubber Soul* opens with a track from *Help!* – 'I've Just Seen a Face' and 'It's Only Love'". 'Drive My Car', 'Nowhere Man', 'What Goes On' and 'If I Needed Someone' do not appear on the album.

JESUS, THE BUTCHERS AND THE PRESIDENT'S WIFE

1966 WAS THE YEAR THAT THE BEATLES MOVED ON. THEY HAD COME AS CLOSE TO DOMINATING THE WORLD OF ENTERTAINMENT AS ANY POP GROUP COULD, BUT NOW THEIR INTERESTS LAY ELSEWHERE. THEIR NEW ALBUM *REVOLVER* SAW THE BEATLES SETTING A NEW BENCHMARK FOR POP ARTISTRY.

For the first three months of 1966 it was all quiet on the Beatle front. In fact it was not until May that they actually played live again – by far their longest break since the days of the Quarry Men. The Beatles stepped back into their (relatively) ordinary lives.

On April 6th they once again congregated at Abbey Road to begin work on album number seven. This time they worked solidly in the studio for almost three months – an unheard of extravagance in those days. Magazines and newspapers speculated on what they could be up to. And well they might.

If the Beatles were beginning to enjoy this new lifestyle, June 1966 would soon jolt them back into reality with three nightmare months. It all began started well enough. The first fruits of the Beatles' epic studio stay were issued. Paul's 'Paperback Writer' was released as a single. Again moving away from the standard love themes, Paul writes a song that is, in effect, a letter written from a would-be author to a potential publisher.

Things started to go wrong at the end of the month when their American label, Capitol, had planned to issue a compilation album, *Yesterday and Today*. This would contain album tracks that were not used on the US pressings of *Help!*, *Rubber Soul* and their newly completed masterpiece *Revolver*. All their US albums up to this point had been scaled down versions of their British counterparts, leaving spare tracks to make up new money-spinning albums. On the early albums it had been seen as a sign of the American desire to maximize profit, or simply greed, depending on your viewpoint. However, *Revolver* and to a lesser extent *Rubber Soul* were more of a self-contained package. By chopping them up in this way, Capitol – in the eyes of the Beatles at least – was

George and Patti take their vows in a Registry Office in Epsom

Preparing for an uneventful tour of the Far East – or at least that's what they thought...

acting as an uninvited artistic editor. This American tradition was now beginning to irk the band, but they were powerless to act; *Yesterday and Today* just seemed like another American rip-off album. They had no idea of the chaos that was ensuing at Capitol headquarters.

Yesterday and Today was planned to appear in a sleeve created at the Beatles' request by British photographer Robert Whitaker. The scene depicted the "Fab Four" with huge grins on their faces but wearing white butcher's smocks covered in slabs of raw meat and mutilated dolls. Capitol's production and promotion process went ahead as planned, but the week before the album's release, Capitol was inundated with complaints about the offensive nature of this photograph. After an emergency meeting Capitol decided that it should be withdrawn. Label staff spent the week prior to release replacing

the sleeve with a less offensive picture of the band standing around a large suitcase.

In the majority of cases, the original sleeves were simply destroyed, but in some cases this did not happen. American record sleeves of the time differed from their European counterparts in that they were not made from printed card, but printed paper glued onto a cardboard sleeve. As a result, some chose simply to stick the new picture over the top of the old one. Years later, people discovered that if they were very lucky they could find the original sleeve by peeling away the top layer. This opened up a whole new industry, with serious collectors debating the most appropriate ways of removing the outer layer without damaging the original. Original copies of the "Butcher" sleeve can now change hands for up to $4000.

The Beatles were completely baffled by the controversy, although there was specu-

lation that they shot the photograph as a protest at the way in which Capitol had "butchered" their albums. This was not true. The photograph had already been used extensively in the British press to promote 'Paperback Writer' with no apparent reaction at all. It is appropriately ironic that, despite taking the American number one spot, *Yesterday and Today* has the unique honour of being the only Beatles record to make a loss – the repackaging fiasco was said to have cost Capitol an additional $200,000.

THE PHILIPPINES ADVENTURE

July looked as if would be a fairly uneventful month. Once again, under duress from Brian Epstein, the Beatles were to go out on the road. Following a few nondescript dates in Europe they flew on

JESUS, THE BUTCHERS   AND THE PRESIDENT'S WIFE

The 1966 Beatles were no longer the tight musical unit of the days in the Cavern

to play their first ever dates in Japan. Their arrival in Tokyo created chaos. Leaving the plane at Hanseda Airport they were greeted by 1500 fans – to the Beatles it was now an unwelcome déjà vu. The Japanese authorities were not used to this kind of behaviour from their young people, and the police were, to say the least, heavy handed in controlling the crowds.

The Beatles had been used to police protection, but nothing like this. Wherever they went they would be surrounded by numerous police guards. A total of 35,000 security men were employed throughout their three-day stay. During each of their shows at the Nippon Budokan – already a controversial choice of venue as it was deemed by many to be sacred – the audience of 10,000 had to contend with 3000 policemen! Throughout their stay in Japan, the Beatles were "imprisoned" in their suite at the Tokyo Hilton. Armed police guards stood by every possible entrance. The Beatles managed to break out to view Tokyo for themselves but were quickly rounded up and returned to the hotel. When John Lennon managed to go walkabout early one morning the police threatened to withdraw their services completely. This mayhem was only a dress rehearsal for what was about to happen.

On Sunday 3rd July, the Beatles flew on to play two shows at a football stadium in Manila, the capital city of the Philippine islands. The local newspapers had helped to create an air of anticipation with stories of how President Marcos and his family were to be guests of honour at the concerts, and how the Beatles had been invited to visit Mrs Imelda Marcos at Malacañang Palace the following morning. The only problem was that nobody had mentioned this to the Beatles.

The morning after their concerts, a palace official came to pick them up, only to be told by Brian Epstein that they were all still sleeping and that under no circumstances could they be disturbed. They had unwittingly created an international incident. The newspaper headlines screamed out the great insult – "Imelda Stood Up". It was made perfectly clear that the first family of the Philippines felt they had

With a collective sigh of relief, the Beatles return to London

been snubbed. All hell was let loose – their hotel and British embassy were soon besieged with bomb threats, and the local promoter refused to pay them their receipts from the concerts.

The following day, with the controversy still in full swing, the Beatles prepared to make their getaway. Suddenly they began to find themselves victims of every petty bureaucracy imaginable. They were first told that they couldn't leave the country until they had paid income tax on their receipts for the concert – which they still had not been paid. After much discussion,

Brian Epstein paid the bill just so they could get out of the country as quickly as possible. This was easier said than done. Since the row had broken out, all security had been withdrawn. They made their way to the airport, all the time being kicked and jostled by angry Filipinos – both Brian Epstein and road manager Mal Evans received minor injuries.

Finally, with everyone having boarded the plane, there was an announcement that two of the entourage were to report back to the airport terminal: it seemed that the Filipino authorities had "lost" all docu-

mentation regarding the Beatles' arrival. This made them, in effect, illegal immigrants. For the best part of an hour the plane was held up while the correct paperwork was filed. Angry and exhausted, and wondering why they had to keep on doing these tours, they finally departed. When they returned to London, a reporter asked George Harrison what their next move would be. Already dreading the impending American tour, his weary response was, "We're going to have a couple of weeks to recuperate before we go and get beaten up by the Americans." Little did he know.

'Paperback Writer" being performed on Top of the Pops

versation, John talked about his interest in religion, with the remark, "Christianity will go. It will vanish and shrink. I needn't argue with that… We're more popular than Jesus now."

The interview was published without an utterance from the British public. Nearly six months later, on July 19th, an American teenage magazine published Maureen Cleave's interview under the headline banner: "I don't know which will go first – rock and roll or Christianity."

The quote caused a storm and was immediately reported throughout the country. The hard-line American church-goers did not let this pass unchallenged. Radio station after radio station, especially in the Bible Belt states, banned the Beatles' music. Some went even further, organizing public burnings of Beatles records and magazines. As before, John Lennon was thoroughly bemused by the American reaction. How was it that so many people could have been upset by the views of a pop singer?

The Beatles arrived on Thursday, August 11th and immediately held a press conference at the Astor Towers in Chicago. As if they could have thought otherwise, the congregated media only wanted to talk to one Beatle. John explained what he had really meant. In fact, he explained it several times, but all they wanted to know

A MATTER OF CONTEXT

Time after time when celebrities or politicians talk to the press, interviewers highlight a particular quote which, when removed from its original context, can take on a whole new, and sensational, meaning. This can happen so much more easily when a young man renown for delivering sarcastic or humorous one-liners with a completely straight face has his words reported out of context. Such a misunderstanding can hardly have exploded with such force as it did for John Lennon at the end of July 1966.

Earlier in the year, John had given an interview to the Beatles' old friend Maureen Cleave of the London *Evening Standard*. During the course of their con-

God-fearing Americans burn the music of the blaspheming Beatles

was if he was prepared to retract his words. With a puzzled expression and with as good a grace as he could muster under the circumstances, John Lennon apologized. Then, as quickly as the incident had flared up, the matter was more or less forgotten, and the tour went ahead.

A NEW ART FORM

Still battered and bruised from their Far Eastern experience and struggling with their reluctance, the Beatles tried desperately to charge themselves up to play America again. However, in the midst of the periodic gloom that descended upon the Beatles' camp, August 5th, 1966 saw a new milestone. Before leaving for America there was one important development to see through. The fruits of those three months in Abbey Road was about to hit the streets.

Although it was packaged somewhat inauspiciously in a black and white sleeve designed by their old friend from Hamburg, Klaus Voorman, *Revolver* represents for many modern day fans the moment when the Beatles story really starts. For compared to songs they were writing just a few months before, *Revolver* (an earlier working title of *Abracadabra* having been abandoned) represents a quantum leap forward.

The Beatles had reached such heights of popularity that they were now divorced from all notions of normality. Just being a Beatle meant that you couldn't do things that a normal group of working class lads in their mid-twenties usually do – not without creating a public disturbance, anyway. As individuals, they now moved in more sophisticated circles, and their pre-occupations changed.

As Paul had said in an interview earlier in the year, "We've all got interested in things that never used to occur to us… I've got thousands of new ideas." So it was under the influence of a the fledgling hippie underground, LSD, electronic music, experimental cinema and the avant-garde art scene, that a new direction was born. The Beatles, being the Beatles, simply

dragged the rest of the pop world along in their wake.

The differences that *Revolver* brought to the world of pop music were manifold. For one, it was an album born of studio experimentation – many of the songs were created in the studio, the recording process itself shaping the final compositions. There was also little or no thought given to how it would be possible to perform such pieces in a concert environment. And the songs had changed – as writers, Lennon and McCartney had become "serious". They were producing music for a whole new audience – hip, culturally aware young people, no longer teenage girls.

But most of all, it seemed as if they were now working to please themselves. Although they were all so rich that they could easily have retired and lived the rest of their lives in luxury, it seems they still had one thing to achieve; to be taken seriously. If their old audience could follow them – great, if not, too bad.

Revolver was also the authentic dawning of the album as a coherent body of

work, not just a selection of songs thrown together. Whilst the world has long since revised its perceptions of pop music as an art form – few at the time would have seriously regarded even something as revolutionary as Elvis' Sun label recordings as art – *Revolver* was perhaps the first album by a pop group to be seriously treated as a work of art. With *Revolver*, the Beatles paved a the way for a whole new direction in pop music.

In spite of this evident change in priorities, *Revolver* showed that there were still enough fans to take it straight to number one, both in Britain and America. It immediately went on to sell well over two million copies throughout the world.

Revolver also showed the esteem in which the Beatles were held by their peers, becoming possibly the most covered album in pop history. Six of the songs had already been released as singles by 10 different artists before the album even came out, although only 'Got to Get You Into My Life' by Cliff Bennett and the Rebel Rousers (produced by Paul McCartney) managed to get into the Top 10.

Paul and Ringo accept the plethora of awards bestowed on them by Melody Maker

REVOLVER

LABEL:	PARLOPHONE PCS 7009
CD RE-ISSUES:	(UK) CDP 746 441 2; (US) C2-46441-2
PRODUCER:	GEORGE MARTIN
RELEASE DATE:	AUGUST 5TH, 1966

SIDE ONE

TAXMAN

(Harrison)
(2:35)

Revolver showed that the Beatles now had a third highly capable songwriter in their midst. 'Taxman' was written when George, by now in the highest possible tax bracket, found out how much of his income was taken in tax payments by the British government. George sings, "one for you – nineteen for me": in pre-decimal currency, a pound was made up of 20 shillings – for every pound the Beatles earned, they paid 19 shillings and three pence (96p) in income tax.

ELEANOR RIGBY

(Lennon/McCartney)
(2:35)

Revolver was also the album where Paul matched John's output. Released as a double "A" side single (backed by 'Yellow Submarine') on the same day as the album, Paul's 'Eleanor Rigby' is a simple story of loneliness. The main character came to Paul when he passed a wine merchants called Rigby and Evens while visiting Jane Asher who was performing in Bristol. Later it was discovered that a woman of the same name had been buried in 1939 at St

Peter's Church in Woolton, the backdrop for John and Paul's first meeting in 1957. The name may well have lurked in the depths of Paul's mind over the years: as Paul later said, "I was looking for a name that was natural. Eleanor Rigby sounded natural." George Martin's sophisticated baroque string quartet arrangement, creates an air of melancholy desperation that transforms the song into one of the most haunting records to ever grace the top of the hit parade.

I'M ONLY SLEEPING

(Lennon/McCartney)
(2:58)

Maureen Cleave, in her notorious *Evening Standard* piece earlier in the year, had already noted that John Lennon was now "probably the laziest person in England." This is illustrated perfectly in his first song for *Revolver*. The lazily strummed acoustic guitars and chorus melody lagging behind the beat perfectly evoke such as sensation. Although George Martin had used tape effects before (speeding up the piano solo during *Rubber Soul*'s 'In My Life'), 'I'm Only Sleeping' features a backwards guitar solo – achieved by turning round the audio tape, recording the solo, and then turning the tape back

round again. This would become something of standard technique on many psychedelic recordings of the late Sixties.

LOVE TO YOU

(Harrison)
(2:58)

George's second contribution to the album showcases his continued interest in Indian music. George himself plays the sitar, while Indian musician Anil Bhagwat plays the tabla – a percussion instrument.

HERE, THERE AND EVERYWHERE

(Lennon/McCartney)
(2:22)

Thought by many to be Paul McCartney's greatest love song. Again, it was inspired by his relationship with Jane Asher, which now looked to be back on course. It also took into account a new influence on the band – the Beach Boys. Like the Beatles, they were in the process of transforming themselves, and in the form of the fragile Brian Wilson, they also had a composer possessed of equal genius. Paul was especially impressed by the complex harmonic structure of 'God Only Knows' from the classic *Pet Sounds* album – 'Here, There and Everywhere' was an attempt to capture the same atmosphere. Shortly before his death in 1980, John Lennon would declare that it was his favourite song the Beatles ever recorded.

YELLOW SUBMARINE

(Lennon/McCartney)
(2:36)

While many have attempted to furnish it with some mystic or drug-related meaning, Paul's 'Yellow Submarine', sung by Ringo, was simply intended to be a children's song. As such, as Paul says, it had to be "...very easy – there isn't a single big word." 'Yellow Submarine' appeared on the flip side of 'Eleanor Rigby', providing the sharpest possible contrast to that song, and evidence of the Beatles new-found freedom to please themselves. Paul McCartney surely succeeded in his original aim, as there can be few people over 25 years old in the western world who are not familiar with 'Yellow Submarine'.

SHE SAID SHE SAID

(Lennon/McCartney)
(2:33)

John's 'She Said She Said' is another evident sign of his use of LSD. The song came about following an organized acid trip the year before in San Diego with various members of the Byrds and actor Peter Fonda – who would find fame a few years later in the archetypal Sixties drug movie *Easy Rider*. Fonda says, "he [Lennon] heard me say 'I know what it's like to be dead.' He looked at me and said 'You're making me feel I've never been born'."

SIDE TWO

GOOD DAY SUNSHINE

(Lennon/McCartney)
(2:07)

Written by Paul and influenced by another popular American group of the time, the Lovin' Spoonful, who were enjoying their first hit in Britain – 'Daydream' – while the Beatles were recording *Revolver*. Later, John Sebastian, leader of the Spoonful, would admit that it was seeing the Beatles on the *Ed Sullivan Show* that had given him the inspiration to form a group.

AND YOUR BIRD CAN SING

(Lennon/McCartney)
(1:58)

Although it features some inspired multi-tracked guitar playing by George, John surprisingly dismissed 'And Your Bird Can Sing' a number of times in later years. Although it is one of the highlights of this great album, he clearly felt that the song was an insubstantial piece of padding.

FOR NO ONE

(Lennon/McCartney)
(1:57)

Paul's 'For No One' is a poignant flashback to the point where a relationship was about to end. While John had all but stopped writing about such things, Paul McCartney had quietly become a master at detailing difficult emotional issues in a simple and coherent manner.

DR. ROBERT

(Lennon/McCartney)
(2:13)

When asked to identify Dr Robert, Paul replied: "Well, he's like a joke. There's some fellow in New York... we'd hear people say, 'You can get everything off him; any pills you want.' ...[He] cured everyone of everything with these pills and tranquilizers... he just kept New York high."

The true identity of Dr Robert was most likely Dr Robert Freymann, who had a practice on New York's East 78th Street. Many of his clients worked in the fields of art and entertainment, and one of them was John Lennon, who wrote the song. Freymann was struck off in 1975, having been found guilty of malpractice.

I WANT TO TELL YOU

(Harrison)
(2:26)

The third of George's hat-trick of fine contributions to *Revolver*, 'I Want to Tell You' is an attempt to describe the frustration of being unable to articulate your thoughts – another phenomenon associated with the use of acid.

GOT TO GET YOU INTO MY LIFE

(Lennon/McCartney)
(2:26)

"We were influenced by our Tamla Motown bit on this." John was happy to continue his admission: "You see, we're influenced by whatever's going." In fact it was Paul who wrote the song and had the idea of adding a four-piece brass section.

TOMORROW NEVER KNOWS

(Lennon/McCartney)
(2:55)

Perhaps the greatest psychedelic piece ever recorded. Although 'Tomorrow Never Knows' is the final track, seemingly pointing to a future direction the band might take, it was the first song they recorded for the session. Originally referred to as 'The Void', after a line by the acid guru Timothy Leary, 'Tomorrow Never Knows' was a plain and simple effort by John Lennon to attempt to capture the sensation of an acid trip. The song revolves around a raga-type repetitive rhythm – only two chords are used are used in the song – layered with 16 loops of randomly found sounds. John's original idea was that his vocal should be hidden among voices that sounded like a chorus of Tibetan monks chanting on a mountain top.

Although contemporary classical composers such as Karl-Heinz Stockhausen had been experimenting with tape loops and other types of electronic technology for years, 'Tomorrow Never Knows' was to have a profound influence on the psychedelic music of the second half of the decade.

An unreleased version of the song appears as 'Mark 1' on the Yellow Dog *Unsurpassed Masters* bootleg series. This is probably as close as the song got to Lennon's original vision – the tape loops whirring away in the foreground with John's voice, recorded through a Leslie speaker, hidden amongst the malaise. Disturbing stuff.

Timothy Leary (centre): the acid king

Going through the motions: the Beatles give an uninspired performance at Shea Stadium

was nothing remotely unusual about their performance. Well, almost nothing. At 10:00 pm that evening, they came off the stage having played a 33-minute set as uninspired as any of the others, to the

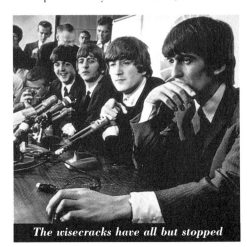

The wisecracks have all but stopped

ENOUGH IS ENOUGH

In spite of this new flush of critical acclaim, the Beatles still found they had to go back to their old jobs – grinning on stage in front of screaming schoolgirls. Now back in the US with John's Jesus quip just about behind them, the Beatles' third US tour was being executed with all the good grace of a group of bored school-children. Instead of taking the opportunity to showcase the new direction of *Revolver*, they chose to go through the motions, churning out the old material the fans wanted to hear, but that the Beatles had grown out of. It all seemed a rather under-whelming exercise. They were playing the same venues as the previous year to mas-sive and enthusiastic audiences, but by now Beatlemania was a thing of the past.

They knew they had reached a plateau of popularity; the last thing they wanted was to repeat the process year after year with diminishing returns. Whatever their fans wanted, the Beatles had changed, simultaneously hitting an all-time high as recording artists and an all-time low as performers. They didn't even bother rehearsing for the tour. They simply grind-ed through their half-hour set, played all the good old hits until their final show on the 29th August, 1966. The venue was Candlestick Park in San Francisco. There

John loses his mop top to play in Richard Lester's How I Won the War

usual ecstatic audience reaction. And they would not set foot on another stage. Ever.

When the Beatles returned to London from America, everyone, Brian included, knew that things were going to be different from now on. They made no immediate plans to record again for three months. The lay-off affected each member differently. John immediately distanced himself from the others, disappearing to locations in Germany and Spain to play a role in Richard Lester's new film production, *How I Won the War*. Perhaps the most charitable description of this film, a satire on the futility of war, is that it was "of its time". During the long breaks between filming, John would become increasingly bored, occasionally putting pen to paper with some yet to be defined Beatle project in mind. Neither film nor John's performance gained many plaudits.

Paul, on the other hand, jumped with typical enthusiasm into London's underground movements. He told the *Evening Standard*, "People are saying things and painting and writing things that are great – I must know what people are doing." His musical activities continued unabated. He took his first tentative steps towards production work – Cliff Bennett and Peter and Gordon, the latter duo featuring Jane Asher's brother, all found success with his support. At the same time he also scored his first feature film, a minor British comedy called *The Family Way*.

George Harrison, always the dark horse of the band, had been quietly hating every second of Beatledom over the past year. He now considered himself to be a serious musician and much of what he had endured as a touring Beatle had become demeaning. It was at a dinner-party earlier in 1966 that George first met Indian sitar virtuoso Ravi Shankar. While in England, Shankar agreed to visit George for some private tuition. The end of "that" US tour offered too great an opportunity to miss – George and Patti disappeared to India for two months. During that time, he studied continuously under Shankar, met with his spiritual advisor and immersed himself in Indian culture and religion. By the time of the couple's return to England, the Beatle

who had shown even less appetite for school work than John Lennon – and that was saying something – developed an insatiable hunger for books on yoga, meditation and all things Indian.

Only Ringo seemed to have achieved anything approaching satisfaction with his life. When the Beatles were in action he would turn up and do his bit, but otherwise he seemed more than happy to disappear into the luxury of his *Sunny Heights* estate to be with Maureen and their new arrival, a son whom Ringo christened Zak.

The Beatles resumed business on Thursday, November 24th, as usual at Studio 2, Abbey Road, and with the ever-present George Martin at the controls. Despite their new personal interests tugging each of them in very different directions, the Beatles remained fiercely loyal to one another.

Each one of them knew that despite the different frustrations of being a Beatle they were each going through, there were still only three other people anywhere in the world who could empathize. That realization reinforced a solid bond.

Jane Asher and Paul, still keeping the media in suspense

Ringo the family man with Maureen and Zak

DEFINING AN ERA

THE BEATLES WERE NOW AT THE PEAK OF THEIR CREATIVE POWER. A SIX-MONTH PERIOD, STARTING IN FEBRUARY 1967, SAW THE RELEASE OF TWO OF POP'S DEFINING SINGLES AND THE MOST FAMOUS LP EVER MADE. THE BEATLES' EVERY MOVE NOW LEFT POPULAR CULTURE CAUGHT UP IN THEIR WAKE.

The remainder of 1966 was devoted mostly to recording a single track. While on location with Richard Lester, John had written yet another song that harked back to his childhood. It was named after a Salvation Army children's home just around the corner from Aunt Mimi's house – *Strawberry Field*. Originally intended to be an album track for an unnamed eighth album, 'Strawberry Fields Forever' initially only appeared on a double A-sided single, backed by Paul's own paean to his Liverpool home, 'Penny Lane'.

As the most complex recording the Beatles would ever make, 'Strawberry Fields Forever' called on George Martin to scale new heights of ingenuity with his armoury of production talents. The song had started out as a simple acoustic ballad, but as the group arrangement evolved, it took on a much "heavier" tone, which John, eyeing from afar the activities of some of the new Californian groups, particularly liked. Over the next month, the Beatles recorded a number of takes of the group arrangement:

November 24th. Take 1.

November 28th. Takes 2-4.

November 29th. Takes 5 and 6. John double tracks vocal to 6 and mixes it down to become take 7.

They then considered the song to be complete, and decided to move on to a song that Paul had been working on, 'When I'm Sixty-Four'. After a few days, John began to re-evaluate 'Strawberry

Fields', worried that it may have veered too far away from his original idea. He asked George Martin to come up with some ideas for an orchestral arrangement. In the meantime, they busied themselves putting together a convoluted rhythm track over which George Martin's arrangement could sit.

December 8th. Takes 9 to 24 (for unknown reasons, takes 8 and 19 never existed). Recording of rhythm tracks for the "orchestral" version.

December 9th. Takes 15 and 24 are edited and mixed down to become take 25.

Percussion overdubs were applied at this point, including backwards cymbals and various Indian instruments.

December 15th. George Martin adds his brilliant arrangement of four trumpets and three cellos to take 25. This is mixed down to become take 26.

December 21st. John adds more vocals and a piano to take 26.

John had one final problem: he liked both finished takes, 7 and 26. He asked George Martin if there was any way the two versions could be cut together. George explained that this would be highly unlike-

Strawberry Field, the inspiration for the greatest single ever made

ly as the tuning and tempo would
inevitably be slightly different. In a modern recording studio with sophisticated
digital time-stretching technology, such a
request would have been quite straightforward, but at that time it could only be
done by manipulating tape recorders –
Martin thought that the effect would be
impossible to achieve.

Nonetheless, on December 22nd, 1966
Martin, along with his engineer Geoff
Emerick, spent a long evening alone at
Studio 2 of Abbey Road experimenting
with the two final takes of 'Strawberry
Fields Forever' to see if there was any
possible way that John's request could be
accommodated. They found to their
amazement that by speeding up take 7
and slowing down take 26 both tuning
and tempo matched. It seemed like a
miracle.

The definitive 'Strawberry Fields
Forever' begins with take seven – the
instantly recognizable "flute" introduction,
played by Paul on the mellotron, a new keyboard instrument that was, in effect, a
precursor of the modern-day digital sam-
pler. Take 7 plays for just under one minute
before cutting seamlessly into take 26.

The single was issued on February
17th, 1967 backed by Paul's 'Penny Lane'
– another Beatles classic. Critics were
quick to hail both songs. But over the
years 'Strawberry Fields Forever has grown
and grown to achieve legendary status. In
the eyes of many, it is the greatest seven
inches of vinyl ever produced. When
viewed in conjunction with the short promotional film that was shot later in the
year – an early video, in effect – the
impact remains electrifying. Never has
there been a set of images that so concise-
ly evoked an era.

In a final irony to the saga, the single
also managed to break a different kind of
record for the Beatles. In spite of the lofty
out-pourings of the music literati,
'Strawberry Fields Forever' became the
Beatles first single since 'Love Me Do' not
to reach the number one spot – it stalled at
number two, behind 'Please Release Me', a
dull ballad by a cabaret singer named
Engelbert Humperdinck.

The Beatles' first release of 1967 changed the face of popular music

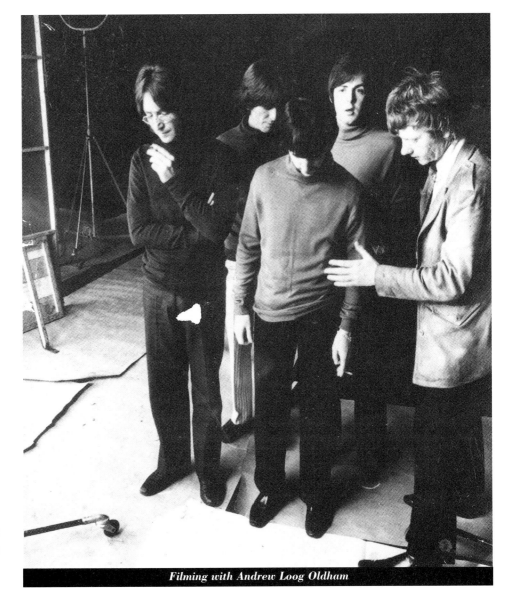

Filming with Andrew Loog Oldham

A STROKE OF GENIUS

The new year kicked off with the Beatles' studio hibernation still in effect. In fact, right up until Friday, April 21st they virtually had a free run of Studio 2 at Abbey Road. Throughout this time they worked and reworked the same material with meticulous precision, ending up with what is without doubt the most influential album in the history of popular music – *Sgt Pepper's Lonely Hearts Club Band*.

So much has been written about this album in the past 30 years that, like the Beatles themselves, it is difficult to review the work with any objectivity. Its musical and cultural significance simply shoot off the scale. The album was conclusive proof that the development shown before and after *Revolver* was no freak occurrence. Again, it displays a supremely confident group at the peak of their creative powers. It also showed beyond doubt, if there was any, that in his usual place – out of the spotlight – George Martin had not only mastered the craft of pop production, he was quietly re-writing the user manual with each passing year. In fact, Martin was so celebrated on the release of the album, that it began to cause a little resentment in one quarter of the band. As Paul later said, slightly overstating his case: "The time we got offended... one of the reviews said, 'This is George Martin's finest album.' We got shook; I mean, we don't mind him helping us... it's a great help, but it's not his album, folks, you know."

Sgt Pepper (as it is invariably abbreviated) started life as a concept album with a general theme of songs that related the Beatles' childhood memories of Liverpool. The first tracks recorded for the session had been 'Strawberry Fields Forever', 'Penny Lane' and Paul's 'When I'm Sixty-Four'. When EMI demanded a new single, the Beatles decided to issue the first pair of tracks. This is essentially as far as the Liverpool theme ever got, and the idea was abandoned. Still wanting to produce a concept work of some sort, Paul came up with the idea of creating a mythical band. "Why don't we make the whole album as

'Strawberry Fields Forever' – *an unsurpassed benchmark in modern music*

A new album hits the streets and a new era begins

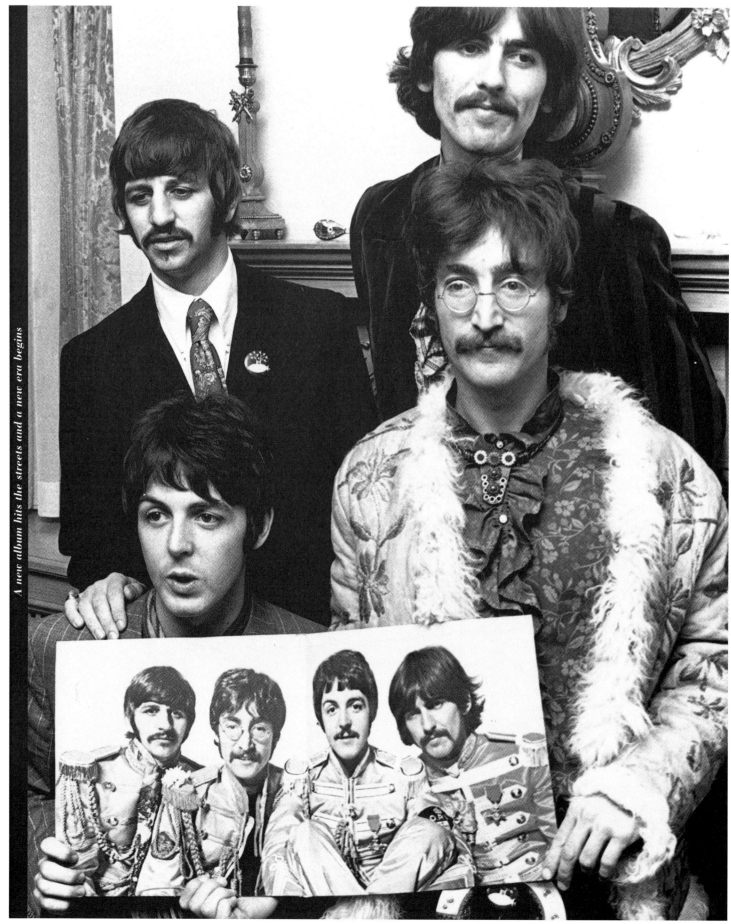

though the Pepper band really existed, as though Sgt Pepper was doing the record?"

The entire album took a total of five months and 700 hours of studio time to record. It cost a record-breaking £25,000. The music throughout reveals a complexity never before heard on a pop album: at this time only the Beach Boys were attempting anything as ambitious. It was seen as a new benchmark in modern music. Despite the complex production, it has become something of cliché to be reminded that the album was recorded on a tape machine with only four tracks.

It was perhaps the first successful pop album where much thought had been put into creating an overall structure. The traditional silence between tracks having been cut down to almost nothing, songs are segued, running into one another. *Sgt Pepper* also brought the Beatles together in a way that they would never be again. It was as if they were prepared to put aside any personal agendas and simply do their best. It even promulgated a genuine Lennon/McCartney collaboration on 'A Day in the Life', the track for which the album would ultimately become so hallowed.

John Lennon in the 'Penny Lane' film

As with their previous effort, *Revolver*, the Lennon and McCartney team were still pulling in very different directions. John's lyrics, aided by a prodigious consumption of LSD, sprawled down an ever more oblique path. His desire to experiment with sound made huge demands on George Martin, and, as a by-product, helped to create a whole new genre of psychedelic music. In contrast, Paul's work was straightforward and craftsmanlike, although, again, it is his musicianship that shines through track after track. His natural understanding of harmony gave an added dimension to his bass sound. If anyone can be said to have led the way forward on this instrument, it was Paul McCartney – in the pop field at least.

A new Beatles album was by now a major media event

SGT PEPPER'S LONELY HEARTS CLUB BAND

LABEL:	PARLOPHONE PCS 7027
CD RE-ISSUES:	(UK) CD PEPPER 1; (US) CAPITOL C2-4644-2
PRODUCER:	GEORGE MARTIN
RELEASE DATE:	JUNE 1ST, 1967

SIDE ONE

SGT PEPPER'S LONELY HEARTS CLUB BAND

(Lennon/McCartney)
(1:59)

It is as if the Beatles knew that, for some, their magnum opus might be considered a little pretentious – the album self-mockingly heralds its own importance with the sounds of an orchestra tuning before it launches into its overture. Paul wrote and sang 'Sgt Pepper's Lonely Hearts Club Band'. Sound effects from Abbey Road's archives were used to give the impression of a live band. The song ends with an introduction to "the one and only Billy Shears" who sings the next number.

WITH A LITTLE HELP FROM MY FRIENDS

(Lennon/McCartney)
(2:41)

The "Billy Shears" in question is Ringo, giving probably his most effective vocal as a Beatle. The song was written by Paul under a working title of 'Bad Finger Boogie'. There have been over a hundred covers of this song – the most successful being a charity number one hit for Scottish group Wet Wet Wet in 1988. On the

reverse of that double "A" sided single, protest singer Billy Bragg could be heard giving an effective (if barely tuneful) rendition of 'She's Leaving Home' (see below).

LUCY IN THE SKY WITH DIAMONDS

(Lennon/McCartney)
(3:45)

The subject of endless speculation, given

The epitome of the Summer of Love

that the initials of the song are LSD. John always denied any drug reference, claiming that the idea came from a painting by his four-year-old son Julian. When asked what the painting was about, Julian replied, "It's Lucy in the sky with diamonds". Paul sometimes found the endless quest for hidden meaning in their work to be beyond belief: "When you write a song and you mean it one way, and then someone comes up and says something about it that you didn't think of, you can't deny it… people came up and said very cunningly, 'Right, I get it. L–S–D,' but we never thought about it." Interestingly, for what is considered by many to be John Lennon and the Beatles at their best, the composer was never satisfied with this version, preferring Elton John's lukewarm 1974 hit single.

GETTING BETTER

(Lennon/McCartney)
(2:47)

A rare Lennon and McCartney collaboration. The inspiration for the song came from their old stand-in drummer Jimmy Nichol, who could often be heard uttering the phrase.

FIXING A HOLE

(Lennon/McCartney)
(2:34) **

Written by Paul, 'Fixing a Hole' is a simple physical/mental analogy. Some have speculated that the song has a drug-related meaning, referring to a heroin fix. Paul was strenuous in his denial: "If you're a junkie sitting in your room fixing a hole, then that's what it will mean to you." As Paul was the Beatle who was always most wary of experimenting with drugs, it would seem highly unlikely that there is any such hidden meaning here.

SHE'S LEAVING HOME

(Lennon/McCartney)
(3:32)

Paul's simple story of a lonely girl who runs away from home to be with her "man from the motor trade", features one of the Beatles most unusual instrumental line-ups. Paul had asked George Martin to score the piece but he had not been available at that time, so Mike Leander stepped in. The Beatles sing but do not play their instruments. Sheila Bromberg plays the harp, accompanied by a nine-piece string ensemble. Paul had taken the inspiration from a story in the *Daily Mirror* newspaper where, "…this girl left home and her father said: 'We gave her everything, I don't know why she left home.' But he didn't give that much, not what she wanted."

BEING FOR THE BENEFIT OF MR KITE

(Lennon/McCartney)
(2:33)

John Lennon took little credit for the lyrics for the number that closed the first side: "It was from this poster that I'd bought in an antique shop… advertising a show which starred Mr Kite. It said the Hendersons would also be there, late of Pablois Fanques Fair. There were hoops and horses and someone going through a hogshead of real fire… all at Bishopsgate… I hardly made up a word." As Paul added later, "…you couldn't make that up!"

A number of interesting sound effects were also added. John intended to create a carnival atmosphere, and wanted to use a fairground steam organ. Such an instrument was not available, so George Martin got hold of a recording of a calliope and cut up the tapes, mixed them up, and reassembled them.

SIDE TWO

WITHIN YOU WITHOUT YOU

(Harrison)
(5:00)

It was now expected that George Harrison would provide an Indian interlude to the proceedings. He duly obliged with his overlong spiritual epic 'Within You Without You'. The song was written at Klaus Voorman's house – George discover-

ing a harmonium in one of the rooms. George is the only Beatle to appear on the track. Other instruments are played by members of the Asian Music Circle, although George Martin added a score for a twelve-piece string section.

WHEN I'M SIXTY-FOUR

(Lennon/McCartney)
(2:36)

The first track on the album to be completed, Paul wrote the song at the age of 16, but dusted it down in honour of his father's sixty-fourth birthday.

LOVELY RITA

(Lennon/McCartney)
(2:40)

Paul tells the story: "I was bopping about on the piano… when someone told me that in America they call parking-meter women 'meter maids'… I was thinking vaguely that it should be a hate song: 'You took my car away and I'm so blue today'… but then I thought it would be better to love her."

GOOD MORNING GOOD MORNING

(Lennon/McCartney)
(2:42)

When composing, John would often have the television on at a very low volume in the background. This sometimes inspired his lyrics: "…I heard 'Good Morning, good

morning'. It was a cornflakes advertisement." So a song was born.

SGT PEPPER'S LONELY HEARTS CLUB BAND

(Lennon/McCartney)
(1:16)

A reprise of the opening track. Ending the "theme" of the album (such as it was), it makes way for that most celebrated epilogue.

A DAY IN THE LIFE

(Lennon/McCartney)
(5:05)

For many, this track represents the pinnacle of achievement for the Beatles. A collaboration with John writing the opening and ending, and Paul penning the middle section. John's song was inspired by two independent events that featured in a copy of the *Daily Mail* newspaper he had found laying around. The first was the death of his friend Tara Brown, an heir to the Guinness family fortune. The second was a light-hearted report that there were an estimated 4,000 holes in the road in Blackburn, Lancashire.

There had been a 24-bar gap in the song when the three sections were linked. Paul suggested to George Martin that an ideal way of closing the gap would be to have an orchestra building up to a

Paul McCartney resented the credit given to George Martin for the success of Sgt Pepper

crescendo, or as John put it, "a sound building up from nothing to the end of the world." Martin hired 40 musicians from the Royal Philharmonic and London Symphony Orchestras and instructed them to play without a score – they were given the highest and lowest notes allowed, but within that framework they could play as they pleased. The songs ends with a crashing piano chord that takes a full 40 seconds before the reverberation fades out.

The lyric "I'd love to turn you on" created a minor controversy. Fearing that it somehow related to drugs, the BBC banned the song. As John said, "This was the only one on the album written as a deliberate provocation. A stick-that-in-your-pipe… But what we want is to turn you on to the truth rather than pot."

The run-off groove

No longer merely a pop group, but commonly considered to be consummate artists, the Beatles' every action was scrutinized in detail for hidden meaning. Never was this more laughably demonstrated than the intrigue surrounding the album's run-off groove. After the piano chord that ends 'A Day in the Life' has finally disappeared the listener is greeted by a collage of backwards sounds that lock

Paul McCartney with Jane Asher

in the final run-off groove. The sounds were tapes of Beatle gibberish, cut-up, reassembled and played backwards. Great speculation ensued. What did it really mean? What were they trying to tell us? One popular story emerged that if you

played the loop backwards it would say "We'll fuck you like Supermen". Paul tried this one out himself and was shocked by the result "…there it was, plain as anything," he exclaimed. Interestingly, he added some other thoughts on the matter: "It plays for hours if your automatic [turntable] doesn't cut off. It's like a mantra in yoga – the meaning changes and it all becomes dissociated from what it is saying. You get a pure buzz after a while because it's so boring that it ceases to mean anything." Sadly, this fascinating experiment can only be performed on the vinyl format – the CD version begins to fade the loop after around ten seconds.

Concept albums

Sgt Pepper is widely considered to be the first pop concept album. Another claimant from the same period is *S. F. Sorrow* by the Pretty Things – one of the greatest, and most underrated, British bands of the Sixties. The recent unearthing of legendary maverick British producer Joe Meek's *I Hear a New World* (credited to Joe Meek and the Blue Men) from 1961, indicates something close to a pop opera, and recording effects that five or six years later would have had even the wildest acid-heads running for cover!

The packaging of *Sgt Pepper* is equally famous in its own right. The idea of having a sleeve that depicted photographs of the Beatles alongside their heroes was Paul's. He said, "…we should have a lot of people who are special to us on the sleeve with us." The idea was met with considerable opposition. EMI hated the idea: to them an album sleeve was not considered to be much more than an advertisement, so anything that obscured their prime selling point – the Beatles, themselves – was a bad thing. Brian Epstein was equally negative about the concept. The band though, were adamant.

Artist Peter Blake was brought in to work on the project with the Beatles. All four members of the Beatles selected the figures that they wanted to include and

Wendy Moger, one of Brian's employees, was given the mammoth task of seeking approval of the living names. Not everyone selected was finally included. Three of John's choices – Jesus Christ, Adolf Hitler and Gandhi – were vetoed on grounds of poor taste. Some things would never change.

Peter Blake and Jann Haworth prepared the life-size montage which was then assembled in the studio of photographer Michael Cooper. The characters were a mixture of cardboard cut-outs and wax figures loaned by Madame Tussaud, the famous London museum. The Beatles themselves are photographed wearing uniforms specially commissioned from Maurice Burman's, the theatrical costumiers – Paul had been talked out of his

original plan to have the Beatles dressed in Salvation Army uniforms.

The cast of characters is listed below. Some remain unknown, but most, with the exception of pop stars and George's Indian gurus, represent heroes from their childhood in the Forties and Fifties:

1. Sri Yukteswar Giri – Indian mystic
2. Aleister Crowley – infamous British occultist
3. Mae West – veteran American actress
4. Lenny Bruce – controversial US comedian
5. Karlheinz Stockhausen – German contemporary composer
6. W C Fields - American vaudeville star
7. Carl Gustav Jung – Swiss pioneer of psychiatry

AN ERA

DEFINING

Not quite there – the Beatles pose in front of Peter Blake's famous montage

8. Edgar Allan Poe – American horror author
9. Fred Astaire – Hollywood film star and dancer
10. Richard Merkin – American artist
11. Binnie Barnes – English actress of the Thirties
12. Huntz Hall – US actor; one of the Bowery Boys
13. Simon Rodia – US artist

14. Bob Dylan – US singer/songwriter
15. Aubrey Beardsley – British Art Nouveau illustrator
16. Sir Robert Peel – British politician, founder of the police
17. Aldous Huxley – British novelist
18. Terry Southern – US author
19. Tony Curtis – Hollywood film star
20. Wallace Borman – US artist

21. Tommy Handley – British radio star of the Thirties
22. Marilyn Monroe – US film star
23. William S. Burroughs – American author
24. Sri Mahavatar Babaji – Indian holy man
25. Richard Linder – US artist
26. Oliver Hardy – US comedian, partner of Stan Laurel
27. Karl Marx – political theorist

28. H G Wells – British author
29. Sri Paramahansa Yogananda – Indian guru
30. Not known
31. Stuart Sutcliffe – early Beatle
32. Not known
33. Dylan Thomas – Welsh poet
34. Dion – American teenage pop star of the Fifties
35. Dr David Livingstone – British missionary and explorer
36. Stan Laurel – British-born comedy star, partner of Oliver Hardy
37. George Bernard Shaw – Irish dramatist
38. Julie Adams – US actress
39. Max Miller – British music-hall comedian
40. Lucille Ball – US film and TV star
41. Marlon Brando – US film star
42. Tom Mix – early American Western star
43. Oscar Wilde – Irish dramatist
44. Tyrone Power – Hollywood film star
45. Larry Bell – US painter
46. Johnny Weissmuller – US Olympic swimming champion who found even greater fame starring in several films as Tarzan of the Apes
47. Stephen Crane – US novelist
48. Issy Bonn – British radio star of the Forties
49. Albert Stubbins – Liverpool footballer
50. Sri Lahiri Mahasaya – Indian guru
51. Albert Einstein – German-born physicist
52. Lewis Carroll – British mathematician, photographer and author of *Alice in Wonderland* and *Through the Looking Glass*.
53. T. E. Lawrence – British archaeologist and military spy, known as "Lawrence of Arabia"
54. Sonny Liston – US heavyweight boxing champion
55-58. Wax dummies of the Beatles
59. Not known
60-63. The Beatles
64. Bobby Breen – British dance band singer
65. Marlene Dietrich – German film star
66. Not known
67. Diana Dors – British film actress of the Fifties
68. Shirley Temple – Hollywood child star.

The whole packaging was unique for the time. Not only was *Sgt Pepper* the first gatefold sleeve, it was the first pop album to include the lyrics of each song printed on the sleeve. Attempts to place some kind of interpretation on the photograph of the Beatles on the back of the sleeve – where Paul can be found with his back to the camera – were rife for a few years after the album's release, especially during the "Paul is dead" rumour the following year. In fact, the mystery is quite simple. Paul was unavailable on the day of the photo shoot and Mal Evans stood in for him.

A further novelty on the album was the inclusion of a cardboard page from which a moustache, badge, picture card, stripes and a supporting stand could be cut out. One final minor curiosity: the sleeve and the spine spell the title as *Sgt Peppers Lonely Hearts Club Band* – with no apostrophe in *Peppers*. Elsewhere, on the song titles and the record labels, the apostrophe is returned. This has doubtless also been a point of debate at some time over the past 30 years.

Sgt Pepper was received, by the public and critics alike, like no other record before. It topped the charts all over the world. On its UK release it went straight to number one and stayed there for six months. Even when it left the Top 30 almost a year later, it continued to make occasional reappearances. By the early Eighties, it had sold over 10 million copies world-wide. This was given a massive boost when the hype surrounding its appearance on CD in 1992 sent it high into the charts all over again.

The critics were, to say the least, fulsome in their praise. To the highest-brows of the high-brow newspapers and magazines it was a genuine work of art. The *Times Literary Supplement* called it "a barometer of our times". In the US, *Newsweek's* Jack Kroll went further, comparing them with T. S. Eliot – in his eyes, 'A Day in the Life' was the Beatles' 'The Waste Land'. As Philip Norman points out in the excellent *Shout: The True Story of the Beatles*, just as there are those who remember exactly what they were doing and where they were the day John F.

Kennedy was assassinated, there is a whole generation who have just as strong a recollection of the first time they heard *Sgt Pepper*. The Beatles had pulled off a pretty neat trick: they were the darlings of the middle-class media; their peers hung on their every move; they were still loved by their former teenage pop audience; their classic commercial tunes appealed to the young and old alike; and what's more, the acid-heads and mystics understood what it was all "really" about.

A good indication of its cultural significance is the increasingly hysterical media stir that inevitably accompanies each anniversary of its release. The tenth anniversary was greeted with reappraisals by the music press and a repromotion package that included a picture-disc of the LP. The twentieth anniversary was too great an opportunity for the media to miss – myriad television programmes and arts magazines all headed with the opening lyric of the album. The twenty-fifth anniversary coincided with the release of a digitally remastered CD version, surrounded by so much industry hype that the album shot back into the charts for yet another stay.

We can only begin to wonder what the entertainment industry will have lined up for us on June 1st, 2017, but it is worth betting that there will be more than a few headlines somewhere that read "It was fifty years ago today".

LOVE AND PEACE

With the fuss surrounding *Sgt Pepper* already in overdrive, within the space of a month the Beatles were ready to make history all over again. A pivotal moment during the summer of 1967 was the first world-wide satellite television linkup. *Our World* was to be a six-hour live television broadcast with 26 participating nations. The total simultaneous television audience would be 400 million. Each nation nominated its greatest names to take part in this historic attempt at world co-operation. Unsurprisingly, the Beatles were invited to represent Great Britain.

The Beatles prepare for their biggest ever audience

A universal message

music, the verses of which were played seven beats to the bar – completely unheard of in pop music. That they managed to turn all of this into a catchy singalong number is testament to their supreme talent as songwriters.

On June 25th, 1967, the broadcast went ahead as planned with the Beatles singing 'All You Need Is Love' "live" over a pre-recorded backing tape. Two weeks later the Beatles 15th single was released – it was their eighth to go straight to the number one spot. Appropriately, it occupied the top of the charts throughout the "Summer of Love". Irrespective of its merits, for many ordinary people, with no great interest in record-buying fashions or music criticism, 'All You Need Is Love' is perhaps the one song that will be remembered as having defined the era like no other.

DEATH OF BRIAN

Now firmly their own men, the Beatles were scaling new heights of creativity. They'd thrown off the shackles of Beatlemania and had developed an influence that was no longer measurable in terms of units shifted. To those in the middle of the action, 1967's "Summer of Love" felt like a genuine revolution – a new frontier – and the Beatles were at the heart of that change.

All of this had begun to pose a problem to Brian Epstein. In his element organizing the minutia of the Beatles working lives during the past five years, and still only in his early thirties, Brian was beginning to feel like an unnecessary part of a machine that was now rolling along happily with its own momentum. It was different when he was managing four clueless young lads: if he wanted them to wear new suits they would; if he wanted them to change their set list, they would; if he told them to tour the Far East, they would. But this was 1967, and while the Beatles unquestionably loved and respected him, they now knew where to draw the line. George Martin remembers an occasion during the *Sgt Pepper* sessions that illustrated the way the balance of power had

Having agreed, the Beatles decided to pen a new song that would receive its world premier on that occasion. A joint composition by John and Paul, 'All You Need is Love' is ample proof, were it needed, that the Beatles now felt no artistic constraints whatsoever. They composed a ponderous, heavily orchestrated piece of

shifted: "When John had finished singing, he [Brian] switched on the studio intercom and said, 'I don't think that sounded quite right, John.' John looked up at him and said in his most cutting voice: 'You stick to your percentages, Brian. We'll look after the music'."

Other areas of Brian's life were now in complete disarray. Merseybeat was now history and of the other acts signed to NEMS, only Gerry Marsden (of the Pacemakers) and a former Cavern employee, Cilla Black, still enjoyed success, and that was veering the way of popular light entertainment – the West End stage or television variety shows. Brian's personal life was as turbulent as ever. Whilst he no longer went to great lengths to hide his sexual orientation, his insistence on picking-up rough young men in London's Piccadilly underground station, and in New York, had provided him and NEMS with more than enough difficulties. The

extent of Brian's "silence" payments can still only be guessed at, but on more than one occasion his prominent position made him an attractive target for extortionists.

Although to the Beatles he had acted in a sensible, almost fatherly way, Brian had leapt into the whole Sixties scene with just as much energy as the rest of the band. However, while it provided John and George with new inspiration, for Brian the haphazard cocktails of pills and alcohol seemed to be consumed more out of unhappiness. At the end of 1966, in a desperate state of depression, he took an overdose of pills. The suicide attempt was not successful. He attempted to find psychiatric help, and checked into a "drying out" clinic. A few months later, in early 1967, he made another unsuccessful bid.

Throughout this unhappy period, he attempted to immerse himself in other interests, returning to his first love – the theatre. NEMS bought the lease on the

Savile Theatre, located in the less fashionable eastern end of London's Shaftesbury Avenue. He immediately subsidized a programme of highly rated, non-profit-making drama and dance productions. But this all still left Brian wanting.

During August 1967, Patti Harrison had read an unprepossessing poster announcing that Maharishi Mahesh Yogi was to give a public lecture. Patti had always accompanied George on his Indian jaunts, and had become every bit as infatuated with Asian culture as her husband. Patti wanted George to persuade the other Beatles to attend the lecture.

So it was, then, that on Thursday 24th April, the Beatles joined a small crowd at the luxury Hilton Hotel, in London's Park Lane. Here they were faced by a little old white-haired Indian wearing a robe, describing in his unusually high-pitched voice, how they would be able to achieve inner peace through meditation. After the

Patti and George – off to see the Maharishi

lecture, they sent word that they would like a private meeting with him – he had been oblivious to their presence during his talk. Such high-profile disciples could not be turned away. The Beatles were immediately invited to join him for the Bank Holiday weekend on a course of indoctrination at University College, Bangor, on the North Wales coast. They asked Brian to join them, but with plans already in place, he reluctantly turned down the offer.

The media got wind of this fast-unravelling story, and were out in force to see the entourage – including Patti, Jane Asher, Mick Jagger and his girlfriend Marianne Faithfull – leaving Paddington railway station. Cynthia Lennon missed the train – she had been held back by a policeman who thought she was a fan. She made her own way. And so it was that the Beatles found inner peace.

Meanwhile, Brian left London to spend the weekend with some friends at Kingsley Hill, his country home. However during the Friday evening he became restless, and announced that he was returning to his house in Belgravia – his Spanish butler Antonio had seen him return and go up to his room. By Sunday, Antonio and his wife Maria became worried that they had heard nothing of him since his arrival, and he was not answering his bedroom intercom. They finally contacted Joanne Newfield, Brian's personal assistant, who, used to such dramas, drove straight over to Belgravia. They called a doctor who advised that the door should be broken down. There they found Brian's body in bed; he had died from an overdose of the bromide-based sleeping drug Carbitol.

Brian's death stunned the world. By the evening, the Beatles, returning from their weekend with the Maharishi, were met by a huge crowd of television cameras. They had sought the advice of their guru, who had told them that as Brian's death was a physical matter, it was not really important. The looks on their faces as they fought their way through the massed ranks of the world's media, told another story – they were visibly devastated. Perhaps Brian never quite realised that, despite often finding himself the butt of a some-

times cruel humour, at heart they knew that he was just as much a Beatle as they were. As John would later say, "Brian was a beautiful guy."

The coroner confirmed that Brian Epstein had indeed died from an overdose of Carbitol. However, his death was registered as "accidental". Brian's sad demise has been the subject of much speculation over the years. It is fair to say that most believe it was no accident; some biographers have even speculated that he fell foul of a murder plot related to Seltaeb's financial problems in America. Although this seems rather far-fetched, barely a year later David Jacobs – the signatory of the Seltaeb deal – was also found dead at his home in Hove, Sussex. A few weeks earlier he had requested police protection claiming that he was "in terrible trouble".

ROLL UP FOR THE MYSTERY TOUR

Brian's death made the Beatles, if anything, even more resolute about controlling their own affairs. Although the world at

large still viewed John as the "leader" of the Beatles, Paul began to assert himself with greater regularity. After a triple triumph of 'Strawberry Fields Forever', *Sgt Pepper* and 'All You Need Is Love', the Beatles could be forgiven for thinking that they were invincible. The project they had just begun as Brian died, was to be a television musical, *The Magical Mystery Tour*. Their credentials as musicians were well beyond dispute, but, would they have made such startling developments without the tutelage and studio expertise of a George Martin? It's doubtful. So the Beatles launched into "The Magical Mystery Tour" like a bunch of first-year film-school students with an unfeasibly large budget. The Beatles wrote, produced, directed, starred in, scored and edited the film. That the outcome was amateurish and over-indulgent, should come as no surprise. Perhaps it is impressive enough that there was an outcome.

The main problem was simply the logistics of organizing such a project. It was precisely the type of thing at which Brian had always excelled. The Beatles wanted to hire Shepperton studios, but

A bridge too far: the Magical Mystery Tour finds it hard to negotiate the country lanes

hadn't realised that it had to be booked months in advance. This was just one example of four young men – for so long protected from the tedious activities of their industry – failing to get to grips with such worldly matters as planning.

The filming was a fiasco. Paul's "story" was inspired by the antics of American "Merry Prankster" Ken Kesey, who, two years earlier had found some notoriety by taking a coach troupe of assorted odd-balls on an acid-crawl of California's endless backwoods. The whole escapade was chronicled with great success by Tom Wolfe in his book *The Electric Kool-Aid Acid Test*. Following the terribly English psychedelia of *Sgt Pepper* with its Victorian and Edwardian regalia, the parochial Paul anglicised the Ken Kesey experience. Viewing it as if it were an English working-class seaside outing, he populated his tour bus with side-show freaks and renegades from the musical hall era. Paul's idea was that the bus would travel around and experience the magic of the English countryside.

Following the flimsiest of scripts, the Beatles hired a luxury coach, selected actors from agency directories and set off to make a film. It all sounded so easy – well, it had been when Richard Lester did it, anyway. As Neil Aspinall, the Beatles' long-standing personal friend, now employed as a road manager, said of the experience, "What we should have been filming was the chaos we caused." With no itinerary to speak of, the coach would go wherever a Beatle wanted it to, always followed by an army of pressmen keen to discover what was going on. Mayhem was caused: to other road users as the coach ambled along tiny country lanes creating traffic jams, or when at the end of day's filming nobody had seen fit to book a hotel for the large entourage. The one phrase in the minds, if not on the tongues, of everyone close to the Beatles was the same – "Brian wouldn't have let this happen!"

When the tour came to an end, the Beatles found themselves with more than ten hours of material. They had originally thought that they could spend around a week editing the film together. In the end,

DEFINING   AN ERA

The beatles launch Magical Mystery Tour with a fancy dress party at London's Royal Lancaster hotel

it took no fewer than 11 weeks to create a one-hour picture.

Of the musical recording sessions, the end of November saw Paul's 'Hello Goodbye' reach number one in the charts, although these days they could no longer guarantee getting there the first week of release. Two weeks later the 'Magical Mystery Tour' was issued. A unique format was chosen for the soundtrack – a pair of seven-inch EPs with a gatefold sleeve and a 24-page booklet telling the story of the film through a series of photographs and cartoon strips. A highly attractive and interesting package, 'Magical Mystery Tour' reached number two in the charts, being held off over the Christmas period by 'Hello Goodbye'.

The critical reaction to the music was generally disappointing. Most agreed that with 'I Am the Walrus', John was still pushing back the frontiers of psychedelia; like his other benchmarks it would influence countless young bands in future. The rest, although it would have been considered extremely good from any other band, was second-rate Beatles. Perhaps they had just overstretched themselves, or Brian's death had cast such a long shadow over the whole proceedings.

If this reception was disappointing, they could not have foreseen the hostility with which their film would be received. It was broadcast by the BBC on Boxing Day. Although filmed in colour – making full use of the psychedelic mood of the day – the BBC chose to show it in black and white. Some 15 million viewers tuned in for what many had hoped would be a visual equivalent to the triumph of *Sgt Pepper*.

The results were a great shock to everyone involved. The following day the British press gave it a unanimous thumbs-down, the critic in the *Daily Express* – a Beatles fan – went as far as to say that in his view there had never ever been such "blatant rubbish" broadcast on British television.

In many ways, the critics overreacted. Whilst it was undeniably no great (or even small) masterpiece, it did have its entertaining moments of pure "Beatleness". In many ways, in fact, it has improved with age, no longer under such pressure of expectation. Also the "pointlessness" at the heart of the film is far more in tune with today's mainstream, although that's not to say that the film was especially ahead of its time, as some have claimed. The Beatles themselves, especially Paul McCartney who was the driving force behind the film, still defend *Magical Mystery Tour* to this day. Then again, this is not so surprising – home movies are usually of most interest to the people that make them.

Just an ordinary guy – Paul waits for a bus outside London's Regents Park

Magical Mystery Tour

RECORD ONE, SIDE ONE

Magical Mystery Tour

(Lennon/McCartney)
(2:45)

Paul wrote most of the title track. It had been recorded in April as a part of the *Sgt Pepper* session, but it was felt that it didn't quite fit in with the overall concept. Later, four trumpeters were hired to overdub the brass section.

Your Mother Should Know

(Lennon/McCartney)
(2:24)

Paul attempts to evoke the mood of the old-time music he grew up with – the sort of thing that Jim McCartney would have played in his band.

RECORD ONE, SIDE TWO

I Am The Walrus

(Lennon/McCartney)
(4:32)

John Lennon's latest psychedelic epic seems to have come about by linking together a number of independent song ideas. Some of the lyrics were written while tripping – Lennon claims that he was influenced to write some sections of the song when he heard a police siren in the distance at his Weybridge home. Other influences on the lyrics are clearly Lewis Carroll and the nonsense-verse writer Edward Lear. Lennon was growing increasingly amused by the degree of interpretation that others had been projecting onto his lyrics. It is clear from later interviews that 'I Am the Walrus' was an attempt to give the Beatle-analysts something to really tax their minds!

As usual, George Martin arranged the strings and brass – eight violins, four cel-

Who are the Egg Men?

los and three horns. The "oompah oompah" backing vocals were performed by members of the Mike Sammes Singers, stars in the firmament of "easy" listening.

RECORD TWO, SIDE ONE

The Fool On The Hill

(Lennon/McCartney)
(2:56)

Written and sung by Paul, who also played piano, recorder and flute. John and George are responsible for the bassy harmonica sounds. The finished track was edited by 90 seconds. It is the most covered song from 'Magical Mystery Tour'; Sergio Mendes enjoyed a US Top 10 hit with his version in 1968, and Shirley Bassey's cover touched the very lowest reaches of the British charts in 1971.

Flying

(Lennon/McCartney/Harrison/Starkey)
(2:14)

Credited to all four Beatles, 'Flying' started out as a simple group improvisation to produce some instrumental background music for the film. John plays the main tune on a mellotron – the electronic noises at the end were tape loops created by John and Ringo. The finished track was approaching ten minutes long, but by the time it reached vinyl it had been pruned to an altogether more manageable length.

RECORD TWO, SIDE TWO

Blue Jay Way

(Harrison)
(3:50)

Blue Jay Way was the name of street in Los Angeles where George and Patti had rented a house during the summer. George wrote the track while he waited for his friend, journalist and former Beatles press officer Derek Taylor, to arrive from London. Taylor was delayed, but not wanting to go to bed until his arrival George wrote the song to keep himself awake.

George plays all the instruments except a cello. Paul joined him for the backing vocals. The track features, among other technological devices, an early appearance of the automatic double tracking (ADT) machine devised by Abbey Road's Ken Townshend.

Additional Notes:

• Although from *Sgt Pepper* onwards Capitol were contractually obliged to issue US albums in the same form as the UK releases, such a rider did not exist for singles. Consequently, *Magical Mystery Tour* was issued in America as an album, with the songs from the EPs on side one and singles from the period making up side two. The additional tracks are 'Hello Goodbye', 'Strawberry Fields Forever', Penny Lane', 'Baby You're a Rich Man' and 'All You Need Is Love' – a contender for the greatest LP side ever. When it was released in America, *Magical Mystery Tour* became Capitol's fastest grossing LP ever, doing over $8 million dollars worth of business in the space of three weeks.

• Two other songs were written for the film: 'Jessie's Dream' and 'Shirley's Wild Accordion'. As far as we can tell, neither was ever recorded.

THE ROT SETS IN

IT WAS PERHAPS INEVITABLE THAT EVEN THE BEATLES WOULD STRUGGLE TO SURPASS THE TRIUMPHS OF THE

PREVIOUS YEAR. HOWEVER, FEW OF THEIR FANS COULD HAVE BEEN AWARE OF THE EXTENT TO WHICH THE

BAND HAD NOW DRIFTED APART.

1968 was to be the beginning of the end. For the Beatles, their long marriage was now showing signs of stress. In spite of periodic efforts to keep things running smoothly, this year was to show that the Beatles were now much less a group than four individuals intent on doing their own thing.

After the fiasco of *Magical Mystery Tour*, the Beatles, seemingly impervious to the need for outside management, decided to push their entrepreneurial flair to the limit. John and Paul rather fancied the idea of being alternative businessmen.

In the middle of 1967 the Beatles had met Simon Posthuma and Marijka Koger, a pair of young Dutch hippie clothes designers. Collectively they called themselves The Fool. On arrival in London earlier in the year, after their own Amsterdam enterprise had failed, they found work as theatrical designers. Having been hired for one of Brian Epstein's Savile Theatre productions, they quickly found their way – by virtue of their status as bona fide "beautiful people" – into the epicentre of the Beatles family. They were soon working almost exclusively for the Beatles; designing the clothes for the *Our World* television spectacle, designing the interior for George's home and painting John's psychedelic Rolls Royce.

In December 1967, The Fool, with a budget of £100,000 from the Beatles, opened up a store, The Apple Boutique – Paul chose the name after a painting by the Belgian artist Magritte – was situated

Crowds are drawn to the opening of the Apple boutique in London's Baker Street

Two London businessmen with their wives

in a four-story house at 94 Baker Street. It would be, as Paul told the world, "A beautiful place where you could buy beautiful things." John's old school friend Pete Shotton was called down from Liverpool to manage the operation.

The boutique was only the start. Their aim was to build an empire where they were in control. There would be no stuffy middle-aged "suits" telling them what to do – all the business decisions would be their own. Next in line was Apple Electronics – one of their more unusual business decisions. John Lennon had met a Greek electronics wizard – at least that's what he had claimed – named Alexis Mardas. "Magic Alex", as John renamed him, would create all kinds of pointless electronic gizmos that John found so fascinating. A particular favourite was the Nothing Box – a small hand-held device which displayed a series of red lights at random – John would spend acid-drenched hours staring at the box, trying to guess which light would come on next. Magic Alex had all manner of wild ideas that the technologically illiterate Lennon found appealing. After criticising as old-fashioned (much to the annoyance of George Martin) EMI's new eight-track studio at Abbey Road, the Beatles hired him to build Apple Studios. Alex told the Beatles that it would be a 72-track tape machine! What's more, sound dividing screens would be replaced by invisible "fields".

From there on the Beatles went Apple crazy. There was Apple Records, Apple Films, Apple Music and Apple Books. The whole operation came under the umbrella Apple Corps Ltd. "It's a pun!" Paul explained helpfully to the press.

A PERIOD OF MEDITATION

With the new business up and running, and a new single 'Lady Madonna' ready for release in their absence, February 1968 saw the Beatles embark on a planned three-month period studying meditation under their guru, the Maharishi Mahesh Yogi. The Maharishi's Indian ashram was situated in Rishikesh, overlooking the River Ganges. In spite of the primitive lifestyle of the region, the Maharishi lived in the relative luxury of a fenced compound. Along with the Beatles and their wives came a fine selection of interested celebrities – Mike Love of the Beach Boys, actress Mia Farrow and hippie folk singer Donovan.

The three months of religious tuition, chanting sessions and transcendental meditation, would prove a testing time for a group of people who had become well used to being pampered. Ringo was the first one to crack. In spite of having taken a large supply of baked beans with him, Ringo and Maureen made their exit after only 10 days and flew back to England – Ringo claimed to have had enough of the spicy vegetarian food. Two months in, Paul and

The Maharishi with his new disciples

Paul and George find inner peace at Rishikesh

John, Cynthia and actress Mia Farrow

as possible about the situation. "We made a mistake," Paul told them: "We thought there was more to him than there was. He's human. We thought at first that he wasn't." And that was that. No more Maharishi.

In spite of this disappointment, the whole experience had been a generally positive one. John in particular used it as a way of overcoming his drug dependency, and the removal from their usual surroundings had been a major creative boost. In all, they came back from Rishikesh with more than 30 new songs.

ENTER YOKO

As the Beatles returned to London little could they have known that a new figure was about to burst into their lives. In 1966, John Lennon had met a Japanese avant-garde artist named Yoko Ono, who had an exhibition in London at the time. Not only had John been attracted to her, he had also appreciated her work and found conversation with her provocatively inspiring. He had intended to collaborate

Jane Asher had also had enough. John and George stayed on but were alarmed at some of the rumours that were beginning to spread. They had already formed the impression that the Maharishi's intended relationship with Mia Farrow was perhaps less spiritual than might have been appropriate for a holy man. When the news broke that a young Californian nurse was alleging that the great one had made sexual advances towards her, John and George too decided that enough was enough.

Returning home, the Beatles faced a barrage of questions from a media keen to make the most of this public humiliation. To their credit, the Beatles were as honest

Conceptual artist Yoko Ono – John immediately detected a like mind

John attends an exhibition of Yoko's work at a Mayfair gallery

148 SETS IN

THE ROT

Yoko is now always at John's side – even when the Beatles are at work

at some future date, but as yet their plans had come to nothing. In the middle of May 1968, with Cynthia away on holiday, John invited Yoko to his Surrey home to work on a series of sound collages. From that day onwards John and Yoko became virtually inseparable. The Beatles had seen nothing like it before – no one had ever managed to break their way in to the inner sanctum. This posed a major crisis for John. While he still cared for "Cyn", he really thought that Yoko – seven years his senior – was his soul-mate.

Her influence immediately began to permeate even the Beatles' most hallowed territory – the studio. Wives and friends had often visited the Beatles while they were recording at Abbey Road, but they would invariably sit in the control room with George Martin and his engineer. Everybody knew it was only the Beatles who were allowed into the "live" room. Not any more. Throughout the subsequent recording sessions, John would sit, guitar in hand, just like he had at any time over the past six years. But now he would have a constant companion at his side, whispering suggestions into his ear. Yoko was always there.

The sessions for the new album were punctuated by a good deal of bad feeling. Not only was Yoko's presence damaging the fragile atmosphere of the studio, Paul began to assert his leadership, often in a heavy-handed way. After criticism about his playing, Ringo, feeling increasingly marginalized, walked out on the band for two weeks. But enthusiastically intending to keep things on course, Paul took over the drumming in his absence. Things became similarly fractious between Paul and George. Only John was oblivious to all of this bad feeling – he had other things to occupy his mind.

Halfway through the recording sessions, on August 26th, 1968, a new single was issued. It was momentous for the Beatles as it was to be their debut release on the new Apple label. The song selected was one that Paul had written while he was visiting Cynthia and Julian Lennon. He says: "I happened to be driving out to see Cynthia. I think it was just after John and

she had broken up, and I was quite mates with Julian... I was going out in my car just vaguely singing this song... 'Hey Jules... don't make it bad.' Then I just thought a better name was Jude."

Even as they were falling apart, the Beatles could still produce timeless material. 'Hey Jude' was an epic lasting over seven minutes. After Paul's simple but uplifting song, the famous singalong chant gradually fades out over a four-minute period. A single of such length was bound to cause difficulties for radio stations – some advised the Beatles that this would necessarily reduce playlist potential. They needn't have worried. 'Hey Jude' would become the Beatles' biggest-selling single of all. Within weeks of release on August 26th, it had topped the charts in Britain, America, Canada, Japan, Germany, Holland, Ireland, Belgium, Malaysia, Singapore, New Zealand, Sweden, Norway and Denmark. It was the biggest-selling single of 1968, and the most performed song for the next three years.

From May until October, the Beatles worked in the studio. Sometimes, in fact, they worked in several studios at the same time. This was to be the hallmark of their next album. Although the band plays together on most of the tracks, it was invariably the composer who would go away and finish it alone. Only Paul, as self-defined overseer, attended studio sessions on every single day.

THE WHITE ALBUM

Inevitably, this was to yield a very different sounding band. In many ways it was their biggest ever change in direction – although not everyone would see it as a major leap forward. The new album would be a polar opposite to their Sgt Pepper triumph. Everything would be pared down to basics. No more brightly psychedelic sleeves – this one would be plain white. No more big sound production jobs – this one would see songs recorded as simply as possible, many of them using the acoustic guitars on which they had been written sitting around the ashram in Rishikesh. As

for the name? Just *The Beatles*.

The sessions for the *The Beatles* – or *The White Album* as it was soon referred to – had yielded well over 30 new songs. That was more than two albums' worth of new material that the Beatles wanted released in a single package. George Martin was worried. To his ears, although there was material of the highest standard, some of it was also, as far as he was concerned, simply not good enough. He pleaded with the Beatles to pare it down to 14 songs that could go on a single album. The Beatles remained adamant.

In retrospect, this could perhaps be seen as the one time that George Martin got it wrong. For all of *The White Album*'s eccentricities – and it does have its weak moments – there has surely never been such a magnificent double album package. Miraculous, given the independent spirit in which it was made, *The White Album* is quite simply a feast of creativity. A band filled with tensions and in-fighting. Four individuals wanting to get their own way. John would later refer to it as their first unselfconscious album.

Unleashed on the world on November 22nd, 1968, *The White Album* quickly became the fastest selling album of all time. It was a major success throughout the world – even reaching number seven in the Swedish *singles* chart. The White Album has now sold something in the region of eight million copies. It was also the biggest selling double-album until the 25-million selling *Saturday Night Fever* soundtrack hit the shops in 1979.

Some of the critics were cautiously positive, feeling slightly let down after *Sgt Pepper*. Others, like the *Observer's* music critic Tony Palmer went into a slightly embarrassing overdrive. He claimed that *The White Album* would "see the last vestiges of cultural snobbery and bourgeois prejudice swept away in a deluge of joyful music making, which only the ignorant will not hear and only the deaf will not acknowledge." Palmer would later make a highly successful career move, directing 1978's 17-part documentary about the history of popular music. The title for this enterprise? 'All You Need Is Love'.

THE BEATLES (THE WHITE ALBUM)

LABEL:	PARLOPHONE PCS 7067–8
CD RE-ISSUES:	(UK) CDS 746 443 8; (US) C2-46443-2
PRODUCER:	GEORGE MARTIN
RELEASE DATE:	NOVEMBER 22ND, 1968

RECORD ONE, SIDE ONE

BACK IN THE USSR

(Lennon/McCartney)
(2:41)

Written by Paul at the suggestion of Mike Love, 'Back in the USSR' was a Soviet equivalent to the Beach Boys' own 'Back in the USA'. Indeed, the chorus features precisely the kind of falsetto backing vocals heard on early Beach Boys hits. Interestingly, both George and John play bass on the track.

DEAR PRUDENCE

(Lennon/McCartney)
(3:35)

Written by John for Prudence Farrow, the younger sister of Mia Farrow. Both sisters were in Rishikesh at the same time as the Beatles. Prudence, against the advice of the Maharishi, would spend unduly long periods in meditation – so much so that she was assigned a full-time nurse. English post-punk band Siouxsie and the Banshees took the song into the Top 10 in 1983.

GLASS ONION

(Lennon/McCartney)
(2:13)

Another of John's digs at those who would ascribe hidden meanings to their songs: "Whatever people make of it afterwards is valid but it doesn't have to correspond with my thoughts… the mystery and shit which is built around all forms of art needs smashing anyway."

'Glass Onion' contains references to a number of previous Beatles songs, written in a way that would seem to be answering questions. For example, he claims that the walrus in 'I Am the Walrus' was Paul. One of the first bands signed to Apple was an Welsh group called the Iveys. Needing a change of name, John had wanted to call them Glass Onion – instead they chose Badfinger after Paul's working title for 'A Little Help from My Friends'.

OB-LA-DI, OB-LA-DA

(Lennon/McCartney)
(3:06)

An early attempt at a white reggae sound written by Paul. The song's title comes from a phrase by Nigerian percussionist Jimmy Scott that apparently means "Life goes on" in Yoruba. John was known to have detested 'Ob-La-Di, Ob-La-Da'. Scottish group Marmalade took the song to number one.

WILD HONEY PIE

(Lennon/McCartney)
(0:53)

A short repetitive chant written and produced entirely by Paul.

A fake microphone fails to keep Ringo's voice off The White Album!

THE CONTINUING STORY OF BUNGALOW BILL

(Lennon/McCartney)
(3:12)

Written by John based on a true incident in Rishikesh. A clean-cut American college boy – Richard A. Cooke III – visited his mother who was attending the same course as the Beatles. The pair went on a hunting expedition and he killed a tiger. John was present when the Maharishi admonished them for their behaviour. On the track, Yoko Ono sings one line of the final verse and joins in with the choruses.

WHILE MY GUITAR GENTLY WEEPS

(Harrison)
(4:41)

Written by George and featuring the superb lead guitar work of his friend Eric Clapton. The song was inspired by George's reading of the *I Ching* – the Chinese book of change.

HAPPINESS IS A WARM GUN

(Lennon/McCartney)
(2:40)

The title and chorus were taken directly from the cover of a gun magazine that belonged to George Martin. John spotted the headline and thought it was too good an opportunity to miss. The other phrases used in the song came about as a result of a communal acid trip with Derek Taylor, Pete Shotton and Neil Aspinall.

RECORD ONE, SIDE TWO

MARTHA MY DEAR

(Lennon/McCartney)
(2:27)

One of Paul's simple love songs, inspired by Martha, his old English sheep dog. Unusually for the Beatles this was not recorded at Abbey Road, but at London's Trident Studios.

I'M SO TIRED

(Lennon/McCartney)
(2:02)

During the time spent with the Maharishi, John found that the amount of time he was spending in meditation meant that he was unable to sleep. He was also missing some of his home comforts – "…curse Sir Walter Raleigh, he was such a stinking get."

BLACKBIRD

(Lennon/McCartney)
(2:18)

Written and recorded by Paul McCartney using an altered guitar tuning. Paul McCartney has said that it was a creative outpouring that saw words and music fall straight into place. Some have also suggested that the song was a metaphor for racial oppression.

PIGGIES

(Harrison)
(2:03)

George's 'Piggies' is a very gentle mocking of middle class behaviour. However, this is not how Charles Manson, a struggling Californian ex-musician, saw it. For him it was a call to arms – the line "What they need's a damn good whacking" took on a whole new meaning. He and his followers went on to commit a series of mass-murders, the most prominent victim being film star Sharon Tate. At one of the murder scenes the word "pigs" was daubed in the victim's blood.

ROCKY RACCOON

(Lennon/McCartney)
(3:32)

Paul's Western scenario – originally called 'Rocky Sassoon' – was written on a rooftop in Rishikesh with some help from John Lennon and Donovan. George plays bass, John plays harmonium and George Martin plays the bar-room honky-tonk piano.

DON'T PASS ME BY

(Starkey)
(3:48)

Ringo's first sole credit as a composer, although it was written and offered to the Beatles five years earlier. Ringo sings and plays piano on this country and western ditty. While Ringo shows no signs of lyrical genius, it does contain the memorable couplet: "I'm sorry that I doubted you – I was so unfair/You were in a car crash and you lost your hair."

WHY DON'T WE DO IT IN THE ROAD

(Lennon/McCartney)
(1:39)

Written by Paul, rather in the style of John Lennon. This snippet features Paul playing everything.

I WILL

(Lennon/McCartney)
(1:43)

Paul plays guitars and sings on his own composition. Ringo plays cymbals and percussion, and John Lennon tapped the rhythm on a piece of wood (or a skull, depending on your source of information). Strangely, this simple song took 67 takes to get right.

JULIA

(Lennon/McCartney)
(2:52)

On the surface, John Lennon's 'Julia' seems to be written about his mother who had been killed in a car accident in 1958. However, some of the phrases used are clearly inspired by his new love Yoko – her name in Japanese means "child of the ocean". John sings and plays the acoustic guitar – Donovan had taught him finger-picking techniques while at Rishikesh.

BIRTHDAY

(Lennon/McCartney)
(2:41)

Paul's rock and roller was written in the studio. Paul has said that 'Birthday' is one of his favourite tracks on the album. John was less impressed: "It's a piece of garbage," he said in 1980.

YER BLUES

(Lennon/McCartney)
(3:59)

John's desperate blues was written at the height of his marital dilemma between Cynthia and Yoko Ono – a situation that he claims made him feel suicidal. On the way back from India, John told Cynthia that he had not been faithful. Within months he and Yoko became inseparable.

MOTHER NATURE'S SON

(Lennon/McCartney)
(2:46)

The song was written by Paul after a lecture by the Maharishi. Paul recorded it at Abbey Road in the early hours of the morning after the other Beatles had gone home. A brass overdub was added later.

EVERYBODY'S GOT SOMETHING TO HIDE EXCEPT ME AND MY MONKEY

(Lennon/McCartney)
(2:25)

To begin with, the song was known as 'Come On, Come On' after the opening lyrics. According to John, "It was about me and Yoko. Everybody seemed to be paranoid except for us two, who were in the glow of love."

SEXY SADIE

(Lennon/McCartney)
(3:13)

John's song of disillusionment with the Maharishi, which had stemmed from rumours of his interest in the Beatles' money and accusations of making sexual advances to women at Rishikesh. The opening lines were originally, "Maharishi, what have you done?" but John was advised to drop the idea on legal grounds.

HELTER SKELTER

(Lennon/McCartney)
(4:28)

For some time, Paul had wanted to produce something raucous and loud. When he read a review of an apparently similar-sounding new single by the Who he was disappointed. When he heard the song – most likely 'I Can See for Miles' – it was nothing like the one he had in mind, so the Beatles went ahead with 'Helter Skelter, the closest they ever got to heavy rock. Charles Manson found the track particularly inspiring. As John said of the whole nasty business: "…I don't know what 'Helter Skelter's' got to do with knifing somebody, I never listened to the words properly, it was just a noise."

LONG LONG LONG

(Harrison)
(3:04)

George sang and played guitar on his song with Paul providing accompaniment on a Hammond organ. What seems to be a simple love song to Patti, was in fact about God.

REVOLUTION 1

(Lennon/McCartney)
(4:13)

A faster, more distorted version of this song had already appeared on the flip side of the 'Hey Jude' single. 'Revolution' is a reply to the arious revolutionary bodies who saw John as a natural ally. The key lyrics are "…change your head… free your mind instead." Responding to criticism of 'Revolution', John said, "I'll tell you what's wrong with it [the world] – people. Tell me one successful revolution. Who fucked up communism, Christianity, capitalism, Buddhism…" John himself confuses the issue on the album by following the line "…count me out", with the word "in".

HONEY PIE

(Lennon/McCartney)
(2:38)

One of Paul's periodic regressions to the old-time music his father used to play. George plays bass and John executes one of his rare guitar solos.

SAVOY TRUFFLE

(Harrison)
(2:52)

The lyrics to George's 'Savoy Truffle' are taken largely from the different kinds of chocolate found in Mackintosh's *Good News* chocolates. The song's inspiration was Eric Clapton who seems to have been giving a prelude to his well-documented future addictions – in this case, it was an obsession for chocolate.

CRY BABY CRY

(Lennon/McCartney)
(3:00)

John's nursery rhyme song was probably inspired by television adverts, and Donovan's hippie folk songs that he had been played in India.

REVOLUTION 9

(Lennon/McCartney)
(8:15)

In its own way, 'Revolution 9' is one of the Beatles' most important tracks. It certainly influenced a generation of experimental musicians. It is also probably the most universally loathed Beatles track.

'Revolution 9' is a disturbing eight-and-a-quarter-minute sound collage assembled by John and Yoko. The individual components are hard to pick out: muffled conversation, a test tape voice repeating "number nine", John and Yoko screaming "right", crowd disturbances,

George and John take a stroll with their new friend, Mike Love of the Beach Boys

Paul playing the piano and orchestral overdubs from 'A Day in the Life'.

John tells the story: "'Revolution 9' was an unconscious picture of what I actually think will happen when it happens… like a drawing of revolution. All the thing was made with loops. I had about 30 loops going, fed them into one basic track… chopping it up, making it backwards… Number nine turned out be my birthday and my lucky number. There are many symbolic things about it, but it just happened, you know… I was just using all the bits to make a montage. I really wanted that released."

So much so, that John presented the others with the idea of releasing it as a single with the somewhat more conventional 'Revolution'. It's hard to imagine how

the public would have reacted, even to such a "B" side – it wasn't music in a sense that many people would have been able to comprehend. John didn't manage to get his way on that issue. In fact, the other three Beatles were even opposed to its appearing on the album, but John held his ground. The more narrow-minded listener will doubtless be relieved that with the advent of the CD reissue, this track can be skipped without the effort of going to the turntable.

GOOD NIGHT

(Lennon/McCartney)
(3:09)

John wrote 'Good Night' as a lullaby for his son Julian. In fact, Ringo is the only

Beatle who appears on the recording, singing it over a thirty-piece orchestra.

Additional Notes:

• The packaging concept for *The Beatles* was created by artist Richard Hamilton. It was his idea that it should be a plain white sleeve. The gatefold package includes a poster with lyrics on one side and a photomontage on the other. There are also four individual portraits of the Beatles taken by photographer John Kelly. The original gatefold sleeve was sealed at the ends and had the openings for the records at the top.

THE ROTTEN APPLE

Without the guiding hand of a Brian Epstein it was becoming increasingly difficult to pinpoint exactly what was going on with the Beatles. The Apple Corps had now taken a leap into the public domain as John and Paul proudly announced the birth of the Apple Foundation for the Arts. The aims would be, as Paul put it, "A kind of Western Communism… we're in a happy position of not needing any more money so for the first time the bosses are not in it for the profit. If you come to me and say 'I've had such and such a dream', I'll say to you, 'Go away and do it'."

The Beatles were planning to be the Medicis of the hippie era – almost. Predictably, the Foundation was inundated with proposals of every possible type that could even vaguely be considered in the realm of the arts: demo tapes, poems, novels, film treatments – every type of invention imaginable. The Apple Foundation was immediately overwhelmed.

With the Apple Corps ballooning by the day, the offices above the Baker Street boutique were now hopelessly inadequate. Neil Aspinall was given the task of finding a new address. Within days the Beatles took over the lease of a five-story Georgian building in London's Mayfair. Number three Savile Row was to become the headquarters for one of the most absurdly unsuccessful business ventures of the era.

While Apple was sprawling uncontrollably before their very eyes, one part of the empire was successful. With music being something the Beatles knew a bit about, it was not surprising that the Apple record label would be a big success. Their very first signing was an American singer song-writer named James Taylor who, in spite of failing to score a hit for the label, would eventually become one of the most successful artists of the early Seventies. Like Taylor, few of the early signings achieved major commercial success – Welsh singer Mary Hopkin, Anglo-Welsh band Badfinger and the Radha Krishna Temple being the exceptions. Apple was, however, responsible for many other fine releases – artists such as Jackie Lomax, Trash, The Hot Chocolate Band (who later found great success as Hot Chocolate), Billy Preston, Modern Jazz Quartet, Doris Troy and English classical composer John Tavener.

1968 also saw the conclusion of a rather tiresome project that had been hanging around for nearly two years – a Beatles animation film. The band hated the idea of the project and deliberately

Apple Corps HQ, 3 Savile Row, Mayfair, London W1.

Just like any other office, really

had very little involvement, agreeing to supply four new songs and a live action sequence to the ending. The results were surprising. In fact, while the fun-loving "Fab Four" that appear in *Yellow Submarine* were by now virtually unrecognisable, the film was something of a triumph of cinema animation. The brightly coloured psychedelic images captured the era with perfection. Even the script – writ-

ten by, among others, a Yale English professor named Erich Segal – amalgamating stories and characters from the *Revolver* and *Sgt Pepper* albums was entertaining and in its own way, quite coherent.

The Beatles attended the premiere of the film. John took the opportunity to do a premiere of his own – his first public appearance with Yoko. *Yellow Submarine* was greeted ecstatically by film and ani-

mation critics. Although the Beatles had little to do with the film's creation, as the *Daily Telegraph* reported, "The Beatles' spirit is here." Alexander Walker of the London *Evening Standard* described it as "The key film of the Beatles' era... a trip through contemporary mythology."

Whilst the film was one of the year's biggest hits in America, it was pretty much killed off at birth in the UK – distributor

With Yoko detaining the real John Lennon, the other three make do

This children's toy – made by Corgi – is now a collector's item

Rank bizarrely choosing not to give it a full release. Whilst the film was widely acclaimed, the Beatles themselves received few plaudits for their four new songs. These seemed to have been knocked out in the studio to fulfill contractual obligations. George's 'Only a Northern Song' is a sarcastic dig at his publishing contract which meant that, as principle shareholders in Northern Songs, John and Paul made more publishing money on George's songs than he did. His other effort 'It's All Too Much' is about his LSD experiences. Paul's 'All Together Now' is a simple children's nursery rhyme. John's 'Hey Bulldog' was recorded and mixed in the space of one afternoon – an indication, perhaps, of the way they felt about it.

BUSINESS GOES ON

As 1968 came to a close, the Apple Corps was, if not yet completely rotten, certainly showing signs of having gone off. Apple Films and Apple Books had yet to release a single product. Apple Electronics, in spite of the heavy subsidy, looked incapable of producing a viable product. The Apple Foundation for the Arts had stalled – there simply were not the resources to even look at the applications let alone judge their worth. The Apple Boutique had been a disaster from day one. So much so that on moving to Savile Row, the Beatles themselves took a decision to close it down – as Paul told the press, "The Beatles are tired of being shopkeepers."

The termination process was a simple one. One evening, the Beatles and their families visited the shop and helped themselves to anything they fancied. The following day they told the world it could do the same. Hundreds of eager shoppers, held in check by a dozen policemen, fought their way through the doors and made off with anything they could lay their hands on.

The Beatles were selling as well as ever, but their business affairs were now well and truly out of control.

Ringo and George under attack from a Blue Meanie

The solution to this problem would ultimately result in their bitterest disagreement. Seen by the media as having a license to print money, there would clearly be no shortage of offers to take over from where Brian Epstein had left off. An early contender in 1967 had been Australian impresario Robert Stigwood. He had initially tried to buy NEMS, although the takeover ended up going the other way. When Brian died, Stigwood tried to raise the capital to buy out Brian's share of NEMS, but when the Beatles made it clear that they didn't want to be managed by him, the plan was scrapped.

Stigwood eventually went on to huge success managing the Bee Gees, and producing *Grease* and *Saturday Night Fever* – two of the biggest movie musicals of all time. His interest in the Beatles didn't end there. In 1978 he produced a musical version of *Sgt Pepper's Lonely Hearts Club Band* starring the Bee Gees with 1977's flavour-of-the-moment Peter Frampton tak-

ing the role of Billy Shears. The film was universally slated and bombed spectacularly at the box office. However, Stigwood astutely realised that a potentially huge market lay in soundtrack albums – Saturday Night Fever" was one of the biggest-selling albums of all time.

The soundtrack to *Sgt Pepper* featured covers of most of the original album, plus 18 other Beatle hits, performed by a selection of stars of the day. Although the album sold in Beatle-like quantities, the briefest of listens would show that whilst they were the most covered band in pop history, it was nigh on impossible to improve on the originals – although funksters Earth, Wind and Fire had a bold stab with their dynamic take on 'Got to Get You into My Life'.

It was Allen Klein, America's foremost showbiz lawyer, who put a halt to Apple's decay. In doing so he would also play a significant role in splitting the band. The Beatles had first heard about Klein as far

back as 1966, when Mick Jagger, by whom Klein had been employed as a business advisor, told the Beatles that although they were selling far more records than the Rolling Stones they were making a lot less money. Although Paul initially suggested that Brian Epstein should speak to Klein, nothing happened. When the Beatles formed Apple, Klein approached them, but at that time they were more interested in doing things for themselves and they didn't even reply to his communications.

Now though, with everything in such a mess, John took the initiative and arranged a meeting. Apparently impressed by the fact that Klein was familiar with John's songs and wasn't a "suit" like all the other business men, John then succeeded in convincing George and Ringo that he should be their representative.

Matters were more problematic for Paul McCartney. The previous year, Paul had become friendly with a New York photographer name Linda Eastman. This was

Linda Eastman – a new face in the Beatles camp

Paul and Linda wed at Marylebone Registry Office in London. They are accompanied by Heather, Linda's daughter from a previous marriage

to be the final straw for Jane Asher, who walked out of Paul's life there and then.

Paul's relationship with Linda flourished and they quickly prepared to get married. Paul was now faced with a tricky family dilemma; Linda's father and brother were partners in the New York law firm Eastman and Eastman. Now Paul wanted them to represent the Beatles. An uneasy alliance was created that allowed everybody to be involved, although Klein was clearly in charge. This did not provide the unified management that the Beatles had been looking for – at every future crossroads the interests of Paul and the others seemed to be at odds. This ultimately provedto be the crack that widened into the band's final demise.

GETTING BACK TO BASICS

Paul was still the motivating force behind the band. He saw himself as a born musician with a strong need to perform in front of an audience. His colleagues didn't quite feel the same way. Paul, concerned that apathy was spreading throughout band, thought that a goal to work towards, maybe a one-off filmed concert performance, might bring some life and enthusiasm into the Beatles. A number of ideas were thrown about. Some were reasonably practical – a series of shows at the Round House in London's Chalk Farm. Others were somewhat surreal – a live broadcast from a stage in the middle of the Sahara Desert. Whilst Paul's impetus hardly brought an overwhelmingly enthusiastic response, the others reluctantly agreed. TV producer Denis O'Dell, who was hired to organise the event, also suggested that rehearsals for the show be recorded for an alternative television documentary.

The taped rehearsals, at Twickenham Film Studios, started off on January 15th. The tensions were palpable from the start. Again, to the annoyance of the others, Yoko never seemed to be more than a few feet away from John. The main problem, though, was that Paul was the only Beatle who really wanted to be there. His annoyance at the antipathy surrounding him

spilled over into arguments about playing. The other three, for their part, were clearly beginning to tire of Paul's over-assertiveness. George in particular became irritated that Paul was telling him exactly how he wanted things played – something that had never really happened in the Beatles. In one incident, filmed for the world to see, an exasperated George, having been told how to play his instrument once too often, just snaps back at Paul, "Look, just tell me how you want me play it and I'll play it, OK?"

Shortly afterwards, George quietly walked out and spent the best part of the next week in Liverpool with his parents. Seemingly oblivious to his absence, the filming and rehearsals went on without him. He eventually returned with as little ado as his departure.

The recording of the new album – still untitled, but referred to as *Get Back* – was scheduled to take place in Magic Alex's new Apple Studios in the basement of Savile Row. At the end of January, the Beatles turned up to start recording only to find complete chaos. Far from the 72-track studio their in-house boffin had promised, the scene was more reminiscent of a home-built electronics laboratory with dozens of tiny loudspeakers placed all around the studio. Despite the dubious-looking surroundings they decided to try some test recordings, but these only confirmed their worst fears. Magic Alex might have possessed an innovative mind, but he was equally incapable of producing anything usable. The next two days were spent undoing Alex's handiwork and hiring mixing consoles from Abbey Road.

The recording went more smoothly than one would have imagined from the rehearsals. As the idea for *Get Back* was to return to a more spontaneous, live type of recording, the Beatles brought in an extra musician – George's friend Billy Preston, an outstanding keyboard player. The presence of an outsider seemed to relax the tensions that had made the Twickenham experience so unbearable. As Paul McCartney said, "You know what it's like when you have company... you try and be on your best behaviour."

UP ON THE ROOF

Meanwhile, plans were being changed behind the scenes. *The White Album* had used up the back-catalogue of new material, and the new songs were taking their time to develop. The budget for filming the live performance couldn't possibly stretch through the recording of an entire album – that could last up to six months. An alternative concert idea, or something, would have to materialise very soon. It was decided that on Thursday 30th January the Beatles would perform an unannounced concert on the roof of their Savile Row headquarters. This would be the live performance that would be filmed.

At lunchtime on the great day, the Beatles took to the impromptu stage, at the top of the building surrounded by family, friends and film crews. The Beatles struck up the opening chords of *Get Back*. Within minutes local office workers began to investigate the noise. Gradually, the narrow roads around Mayfair became more and more congested, until the police inevitably came to investigate the commotion. Finally, after 42 minutes of playing, and distracted by the number of police officers who were by now trying to get them to stop the music, the show came to an end with another version of *Get Back*. After a final crash of the cymbals, with the guitar chords fading, Paul shouts out, "thanks Mo" to Ringo's wife who is applauding wildly. John quips, "I'd like to say thank you on behalf of the group and ourselves and I hope we pass the audition." And that was the Beatles final public performance.

With the filming now over, the Beatles spent the next day duplicating their rooftop performance in the studio for the *Get Back* album. It all seemed so straightforward – they just wanted to record a set of songs like they had on that first day spent at Abbey Road with George Martin. If only it could have been that simple.

After spending much of February trying to finish the album, their enthusiasm – even Paul's – began to dwindle. The Beatles decided to bring in producer Glyn

John and Yoko are granted bail following their arrest for possessing marijuana

John and Yoko – relentless peace protesters

Johns. They handed over the pile of master tapes and invited him to finish it. The Beatles had reached rock bottom – they had recorded an album that they couldn't be bothered to finish. As John says: "We didn't want to know about it anymore, so we just left it… and said 'Here, mix it.' None of us could be bothered going in. Nobody called anybody about it and the tapes were left there. Glyn Johns did it. We got an acetate in the mail."

The results were worse than they had expected; 29 hours of music had been mixed down to a single album. They had wanted it to sound rough, but not this rough. They debated releasing it in that state. John was particularly keen: "I didn't care. I thought it was good to let it out and show people what had happened to us… we don't play together anymore, you know, leave us alone."

They decided to sit on the project for the moment. The only tangible fruits of those sessions in 1969 were a pair of singles. Paul's 'Get Back' was released in April, followed by John's 'The Ballad of John and Yoko', on which John plays guitars and Paul drums and piano. As far as the public were concerned the Beatles could still do little wrong – both singles were, again, world-wide number one hits.

ONE LAST TRY

The coming months saw the Beatles embroiled in legal wrangling of the Klein-Eastman variety. They also started to get more and involved in working on their own projects. John and Yoko were making a name for themselves as peace protesters and continuing the experimental sound

collages such as 'Revolution 9' that so many had hated (or laughed at). Ringo was now actively pursuing his acting career, starring in *The Magic Christian*. George was engaged in production work and Paul simply busied himself writing songs and improving himself as a musician.

Then, in June 1969, Paul McCartney contacted George Martin with an unexpected request. He told George that the Beatles wanted to record an album with him, just like they had done with *Revolver* and *Sgt Pepper*. Martin, although sceptical, agreed to one more try and Abbey Road was block-booked for the first three weeks of July. Once again, everyone was on their best behaviour, put their differences behind them and concentrated on the one thing that had created such a close friendship – and now seemingly the only thing they had left in common – music.

The album was to be called *Abbey Road* – apt as the home of nearly all of their classic recordings. From its release date at the end of September, the album was seized on by fans as undeniable proof that the Beatles were genuinely 'together' again. While *The White Album* had broken records – it was the fastest ever selling album at the time of its release – *Abbey Road* sold in even greater quantities. It went to number one in the UK, not budging for the next five months. Released two months later in the US, it was similarly successful – in fact, at that time, *Sgt Pepper*, *Magical Mystery Tour* and *The White Album* were all still in the Top 100 charts. World sales of *Abbey Road* are now well over 10 million, making it among the biggest selling albums of all time.

The sleeve, again eschewing flashy design conventions of the period, was simplicity itself: a photograph of the four Beatles on a zebra crossing outside Abbey Road studios. The reverse side shows a road sign that reads Abbey Road.

(Strangely, Paul's bare-footed presence was taken as proof of his demise at the time of the "Paul is dead" rumour in America.)

This sleeve made *Abbey Road* the most famous recording studio in the world. Every year thousands of tourists from all over the world still visit the studio as if it were a latterday religious shrine. The new road signs continue to disappear almost the moment they are put up. The graffiti on the walls outside the studio's car park are a constant reminder that as far as icons of popular culture go, the Beatles have only been surpassed by one man – their idol, Elvis.

The critics were also now firmly back on their side. The material on *Abbey Road* showed a new maturity, although it was still closer to pop music than rock – such categorisation was growing increasingly important at this time. On show for the first time were the Beatles as musicians. George's delicate solo playing showed that years of hanging out with Eric Clapton had done him no harm. Even Ringo, for years

the "unmusical" one, was playing with greater confidence than ever – a few minutes from the end of the album he even takes a drum solo. Paul, in the meantime, had become a versatile multi-instrumentalist and skilful arranger.

If *Abbey Road* was to give their public hope for things to come, the Beatles – John in particular, always knew that it would be their last album. If that was to be the case, *Abbey Road* was a pretty special way to go out. Perhaps the revelation of the album was that two of its most beautiful and striking songs – 'Something' and 'Here Comes the Sun' – were both written by George Harrison. For many it was the second side of the album, with its segue of short tracks creating the effect of a mini-opera that captured the imagination. *Abbey Road* ends with the vignette 'The End' in which Paul sings; "And in the end the love you take is equal to the love you make." And with that the Beatles and the Sixties – the decade they had all but created – came to an end.

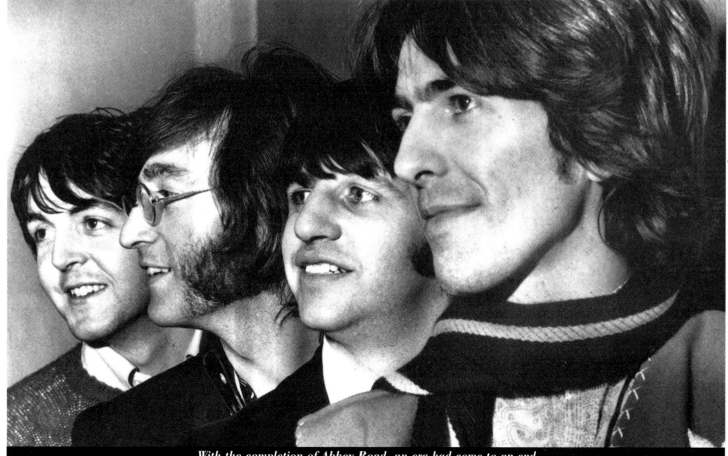

With the completion of Abbey Road, an era had come to an end

ABBEY ROAD

LABEL:	PARLOPHONE PCS 7088
CD RE-ISSUES:	(UK) CDP 746 446 2; (US) C2-46446-2
PRODUCER:	GEORGE MARTIN
RELEASE DATE:	SEPTEMBER 26TH, 1969

SETS IN   THE ROT

164

After their wedding in Gibraltar, John and Yoko spend a few days in Paris

COME TOGETHER
(Lennon/McCartney)
(4:16)

John's composition was written originally as a campaign song for Dr Timothy Leary, who was planning to run for Governor in California. His rival was set to be a former B-movie actor named Ronald Reagan. Leary's campaign had barely started when he was convicted of possessing marijuana.

SOMETHING
(Harrison)
(2:58)

George Harrison wrote this song – dedicated to his wife Patti (who eventually left him for his best friend Eric Clapton) – for inclusion on *The White Album*. Released as a single, although it fared badly by Beatle standards, only just scraping into the Top 5, it has become something of standard, being the second most covered Beatles song after 'Yesterday'.

MAXWELL'S SILVER HAMMER
(Lennon/McCartney)
(3:24)

In John's eyes, 'Maxwell's Silver Hammer' was Paul's "Grandma music" at its worst. According to Paul, "This epitomises the downfalls of life. Just when everything is going smoothly 'bang bang' down comes Maxwell's silver hammer and ruins everything."

OH DARLING
(Lennon/McCartney)
(3:25)

Inspired by the doo-wop singers of the Fifties, Paul "...came into the studios early every day for a week to sing it by myself... I wanted to sound as though I'd been performing all week." In spite of Paul's efforts, John always thought he could've done a better job.

OCTOPUS'S GARDEN

(Starkey)
(2:48)

During a boating holiday in Sardinia, Ringo was told by the ship's captain about the way octopuses lived. This apparently inspired Ringo to write his second song for the Beatles. George felt that Ringo was composing "cosmic songs without noticing it."

I WANT YOU (SHE'S SO HEAVY)

(Lennon/McCartney)
(7:44)

One of the simplest love songs ever written. John says: "This is about Yoko... there was nothing else I could say about her other than I want you, she's so heavy." Annoyed when criticised for being trite, Lennon argued, "When you're drowning you don't say 'I would be incredibly pleased if someone would have the foresight to notice me drowning and come and help me', you just scream."

SIDE TWO

HERE COMES THE SUN

(Harrison)
(3:04)

Written on a sunny afternoon in Eric Clapton's garden, George felt relief at having escaped from a tense business meeting with Allen Klein. 'Here Comes the Sun' is another of George's best-known compositions – it features the first Beatles use of a moog synthesiser. In 1976 Steve Harley and Cockney Rebel took their own version of the song into the British hit parade.

BECAUSE

(Lennon/McCartney)
(2:44)

John's 'Because' is about the early days of his relationship with Yoko. The song's chord structure is inspired by Beethoven's 'Moonlight Sonata' (Piano Sonata No. 14 in C Sharp Minor), which Yoko Ono would play on John's grand piano.

YOU NEVER GIVE ME YOUR MONEY

(Lennon/McCartney)
(3:57)

A song written by Paul in three parts. This is the first of a medley of short or half-finished songs which are segued and take up most of side two.

SUN KING

(Lennon/McCartney)
(2:32)

The song starts with a guitar instrumental that is clearly inspired by Fleetwood Mac's 'Albatross', which had been a hit six months earlier. John originally called the track 'Los Paranoias', most probably because of the random Italian, Spanish and Portuguese words that make up the last verse. It may also be that Lennon is parodying Paul McCartney's French verse in 'Michelle' four years earlier.

MEAN MR MUSTARD

(Lennon/McCartney)
(1:06)

John wrote this in India, inspired by a newspaper story of a man who habitually hid his money away. In the song, John originally wrote about his sister Shirley, but changed it to Pam for the track that followed.

POLYTHENE PAM

(Lennon/McCartney)
(1:18)

At the time, John said he had sung 'Polythene Pam' in a thick Liverpool accent "because it was supposed to be about a mythical Liverpool scrubber dressed up in her jackboots and kilt." Later he admitted that it was a composite of a character from their Cavern days known as Polythene Pat, and a girl he'd met in 1963 with the British beat poet Royston Ellis.

SHE CAME IN THROUGH THE BATHROOM WINDOW

(Lennon/McCartney)
(1:52)

Written by Paul after his St John's Wood house had been broken into by one of the many fans who would loiter outside. These hangers-on would later become immortalised as 'Apple Scruffs' on George's *All Things Must Pass* album.

GOLDEN SLUMBERS

(Lennon/McCartney)
(1:31)

Paul's composition, written at his father's house in Cheshire: "I came across the traditional tune 'Golden Slumbers' in a song book of Ruth's [his stepsister]. And I thought it would be nice to write my own."

CARRY THAT WEIGHT

(Lennon/McCartney)
(1:37)

Sharply edited into the back of the previous track, 'Carry That Weight' was written by Paul, although all four Beatles sing the main tune.

THE END

(Lennon/McCartney)
(2:04)

The number opens uncharacteristically with Ringo's only drum solo. There then follows three guitar solos, one each from John, Paul and George. Finally, Paul's profound lines "the love you take is equal to the love you make" close the lid on the Beatles studio career. It showed, as John said, "if Paul wants to he can think".

• After a gap of 20 seconds, Paul's throwaway 23-second ragtime 'Her Majesty' appears. The song is not listed on the cover of the original issue of the album, although it does appear on the record label.

END OF STORY

As far as three of the Beatles were concerned, that was pretty much that. Paul still wanted to keep things going, though. On one occasion when Paul again tried to push them into playing live, John told the band that he'd had enough. He wanted out. But this was no revelation – after all, Ringo and George had walked out before,

but they always came back. They left things to simmer.

Allen Klein's emergence on the scene had been a dramatic one. He arrived to find Apple Corps in a worse state than he could have imagined. Number three Savile Row was already looking a serious mess and everywhere Klein looked he found an army of paid hangers-on who produced little of any value. Klein scorched his way through Apple Corps instantly writing off

whole departments. Within months he had pared the organisation down to the barest of essentials.

Klein had also found the Beatles contractual affairs in a muddle. The Beatles had mistakenly thought that *Yellow Submarine* constituted the third and final film of their contract with United Artists. They were wrong. Instead of issuing the *Get Back* project as a TV show Klein decided that they had enough material to

turn it into a feature length film that could be sold to United Artists.

Klein's next move was to renegotiate their record deals. This was to be a problem because by now John was insistent that he was leaving the band. Klein asked him to keep silent until he had completed his negotiations. John agreed, although speculation began to increase again in the music press.

The Beatles continued to have little to do with the *Get Back* project – now retitled *Let It Be* after one of Paul's songs on the album. One thing was decided, though: no matter how little they cared about it, the album in its current state was simply not up to scratch. With the Beatles' consent, Klein handed it over to American producer Phil Spector. Spector had found fame in the early Sixties with his production hallmark – the dramatic, heavily orchestrated Wall of Sound that graced hits by, among others, the Ronettes, the Righteous Brothers and Ike and Tina Turner.

The finished version of *Let It Be* is in many ways the Beatles' strangest album. Some of the tracks Spector left in a raw and unfinished state, even leaving snippets of dialogue – mostly John's sarcastic quips. The rest of the album was very heavily doctored with the addition orchestras and brass sections. Even the Beatles were in for a surprise!

Let It Be

LABEL:	PARLOPHONE PXS 1 AND PCS 7096
CD RE-ISSUES:	(UK) CDP 746447 2; (US) C2-46447-2
PRODUCERS:	GEORGE MARTIN, GLYN JOHNS, PHIL SPECTOR
RELEASE DATE:	MAY 8TH, 1970

SIDE ONE

TWO OF US

(Lennon/McCartney)
(3:33)

Paul's 'Two of Us' is a love song to the new woman in his life, Linda Eastman. It was originally recorded by New York group Mortimer, who were signed to Apple, but it was never issued.

DIG A PONY

(Lennon/McCartney)
(3:52)

A song that shows the Beatle state of mind during the *Get Back* sessions. A composite of two of John's songs put together in the studio, 'Dig a Pony' makes little sense at all. In an interview a few months before his death, he announced that it was "another piece of garbage."

ACROSS THE UNIVERSE

(Lennon/McCartney)
(3:43)

A version of this song had already been released in 1968 on a World Wildlife Fund benefit album. John had not liked that take, and wanted to re-record it. The version that found its way onto *Let It Be* features John singing solo with an acoustic guitar, backed by an orchestra and choir.

I ME MINE

(Harrison)
(2:24)

The verses for George's 'I Me Mine' are played in waltz time – apparently inspired by a marching band he saw on television. In the film of *Let It Be* John and Yoko are seen to be dancing to George's performance of the song.

DIG IT

(Lennon/McCartney/Starkey/Harrison)
(0.48)

Edited down from a five-minute jam, John sings about the CIA, the FBI, blues guitarist BB King, and Manchester United football manager Sir Matt Busby.

LET IT BE

(Lennon/McCartney)
(4.02)

Paul's hymn-like *Let It Be* seems to have been a response to the heavy pressure of the additional responsibilities he took on as unofficial leader after Brian Epstein's death. As he said, "I wrote it when all those business problems started to get me down… writing the song was my way of exorcising ghosts." The original version, with John on bass and Billy Preston on organ, had already been a million-selling hit single two months earlier. An alternative version, in which George plays a different guitar passage, is included on the album.

MAGGIE MAY

(traditional)
(0.39)

John and Paul give a brief rambling rendition of a traditional Liverpool folk song.

SIDE TWO

I'VE GOT A FEELING

(Lennon/McCartney)
(3.34)

A composite of two songs, Paul's 'I've Got a Feeling' and John's 'Everybody Had a Hard Year'. Paul sings his part and John his. The song ends with both parts sung at the same time.

ONE AFTER 909

(Lennon/McCartney)
(2.50)

John and Paul wrote 'One after 909' together in 1959 but it had never found its way onto record, although they had recorded it during the same session that had produced 'From Me to You' in 1963. Two versions from that session can be heard on 1995's *Anthology 1* set.

THE LONG AND WINDING ROAD

(Lennon/McCartney)
(3:34)

The song that finally caused Paul to snap. He hated Phil Spector's over-the-top additions, feeling that he had spoiled the documentary nature of the *Get Back* project. Allen Klein's refusal to restore original versions was the catalyst for Paul's public resignation. 'The Long and Winding Road' was issued as a single in the US at the same time as the album came out. Needless to say, in spite of Paul's views, it went to number one, selling 1.2 million copies within two days.

FOR YOU BLUE

(Harrison)
(2:24)

'George's Blues', as it was first known, follows a traditional 12-bar structure. Perhaps the most unusual thing about it is that while all the Beatles were most defi-nitely feeling the blues, George's are, as he says, "happy-go-lucky!"

GET BACK

(Lennon/McCartney)
(3:07)

Already a world-wide hit over a year ago, the album presents a different take, ending with John's words, edited from the ending of the rooftop concert.

Additional Notes:

• *Let It Be* was originally only released in a boxed set that came complete with a book of photographs and dialogue from the film. Six months later, this version was deleted to be replaced by a standard sleeve with no inserts.

• The whole of the *Let It Be* album was brilliantly covered in 1988 by the band Laibach, who hailed from the country formerly known as Yugoslavia. A part of a collective art community, Laibach presented a harsh form of "industrial" music bound up with a seemingly (although one could never be quite sure) serious totalitarian manifesto. *Get Back*, for example, takes the form of a neo-fascist marching song. The whole package opens up some fascinating political issues, and particularly seems to question the relationship between the "Gods" of pop and the hordes who hang on their every word. John Lennon would doubtless have enjoyed every minute of the album.

John decides to leave the Beatles but agrees not to make it public

THE ROT   SETS IN

With the demise of the Beatles imminent, Ringo reflects on an uncertain future

THE FINAL CURTAIN

While three of the Beatles were largely ambivalent, Paul McCartney was mortified – it was his songs that had received most of Phil Spector's alterations. Things had now gone too far – he wrote to Klein insisting that his original versions be put back on. He got no response. In March 1970, he contacted John to tell him that he now intended to leave the group. So, while John had informed everyone of his decision six months earlier, it was Paul who on April 17th sent out a press release – accompanying his debut album *McCartney* – a somewhat pompous and self-important interview announcing "his" decision. The Beatles were now officially dead.

May 20th saw the film premiere of *Let It Be*. Although Jane Asher and Cynthia Lennon were among the celebrities in attendance, there wasn't a single Beatle to be found. Perhaps it was just too much for any of them to take. As John said: "It was hell making the film… even the biggest Beatle fan on earth couldn't have sat through those six weeks of misery. It was the most miserable session on earth."

The film made the tensions that had been growing for the past three years abundantly clear to the world. It is a fascinating exercise in observing group dynamics. Everyone looks thoroughly miserable except Paul McCartney who enthusiastically chivvies the whole facade along. He chatters away endlessly, even though it's quite clear that most of the time nobody is paying attention to a word he's saying.

The final sequence of events turned *Let It Be* into something of a postscript to the Beatles story. Sheer apathy comes through on the album. As for the film? It quite simply shows the sad spectacle of four adults who have grown too far apart to be reconciled. For the Beatles, it was the end of the story.

The final curtain

GOING IT ALONE

SUCH HAD BECOME THEIR STANDING IN POPULAR CULTURE, THE BREAK-UP OF THE BEATLES MADE HEADLINE NEWS ALL OVER THE WORLD. ALTHOUGH FOUR IMMENSELY SUCCESSFUL SOLO CAREERS WERE BORN AS A RESULT, THE MEDIA STILL CLUNG TO THE HOPE OF A BEATLES REUNION.

By the time of the official announcement in April 1970 that an era really had ended, few were completely surprised. All four of the Beatles had already started solo careers. It was inevitable that a band that had been so successful, both with critics and audiences – as a result of which each member was universally known and loved – would spawn solo careers. It was readily assumed that, as two giants of popular music, both Lennon and McCartney would go on to great things – even if John seemed to be, for the time being at least, under the creative spell of Yoko, whom he had now married. Paul, however, as a master of what John would uncharitably call "Grandma music", seemed destined for a long and distinguished musical career.

Things were a little different for the other two. It would be fair to say that although his contributions to the final Beatle albums were of an extremely high standard, less was expected of George

At least two spectacular solo careers were expected

Harrison. Still firmly into Indian religion and culture, George spent more and more time in the company of virtuoso musicians like Eric Clapton.

Ringo, it was supposed, might attempt a few recordings, but if we were to hear much more of him it would more likely be in the film world where his performances in the two Beatle films had shown a fledgling talent with great potential.

However, one thing was guaranteed. For the foreseeable future, anything that involved any of the Beatles would be reported with extreme interest by a media always ready to hold the front page for the two magic words – "BEATLES REFORM". But they would have to wait… and wait… and wait. And so they did – until 10:30 in the evening of December 8th, 1980.

JOHN LENNON – WORKING CLASS HERO

In 1968, John Lennon had finally got together with Japanese avant-garde artist Yoko Ono. Lennon and McCartney had not worked closely together in recent years; Yoko Ono effectively took over his role as John's creative partner. This manifested itself initially in some rather bizarre experiments, not least of which was the first of John's solo efforts.

The first collaboration was *Unfinished Music Number 1 – Two Virgins*, released in 1968. A series of sound collages – in much the same vein as 'Revolution Number 9 – the music itself created little stir. Had they bothered to listen, few pop fans would have even considered it to be music at all. Controversy surrounded the sleeve, which featured John and Yoko in a full-frontal nude photograph. Eventually, the album was only made available placed in a brown paper bag. Surprisingly, given the popularity of the Beatles, if not the uncompromising music, the album only sold around 5,000 copies and was soon deleted.

The following year, the duo ploughed a similar furrow with similar success, on *Unfinished Music Volume II – Life With The Lions*, one side of which was recorded on a cassette recorder during Yoko's failed

pregnancy at Queen Charlotte Hospital. Again, Lennon's bold artistic statement failed to capture a large audience.

In 1969, with the future of the Beatles still unclear, John and Yoko formed the Plastic Ono Band. At this time, they were active propagandists for peace, frequently pulling highly publicised stunts. One such effort was a series of what they termed "Bed-ins", one of which took place at the Queen Elizabeth Hotel, in Montreal, Canada. For 10 days the Lennons' suite became the centre of all manner of media activity. They enjoyed visits from luminary supporters like Dr Timothy Leary and TV crews from all over the world. It was also

the location they chose to record their first single – an anthem for their peace protest, 'Give Peace a Chance'. That it was crudely recorded and badly performed was not the point. In his mind, John was turning the tables on a media that had for so long fed on the Beatles. He was getting his own back. The single was an immediate success, and has proved to be the definitive peace anthem throughout the world.

In 1970, John soon sought to put together a "real" band for future recordings. The most consistent players were Eric Clapton on guitar, Klaus Voorman on bass, and Ringo on drums. Controversial singles like 'Cold Turkey', a song that

A call for peace

John and Yoko, reunited in 1975

titles like 'Mother', 'Isolation', 'Look at Me' and 'My Mummy's Dead' (recorded by John alone on a portable cassette recorder), the subject matter dealt firmly with his troubled childhood in a highly confessional manner. The album came out to a guardedly positive response from the press, but sales were healthy enough to place it in the Top 20. To mainstream Beatle fans it looked like John had returned to something they could understand – "real" songs. When his work was reappraised at the time of his death in 1980, this album was considered by many to be his finest work.

The following year, 1971, was one of John Lennon's most commercially successful. He had installed an eight-track recording studio at his home in Tittenhurst Park. It was here that Lennon, along with Phil Spector, produced his most successful album, *Imagine*. A gentler, more commercial sound, combined with more coherent lyrics, *Imagine* found immediate favour with fans of the Beatles. Not only did it contain the haunting melody and peace anthem of the title track – probably one of the most famous pop songs of all time – it also contains bitter attacks on Paul McCartney in the form of 'How Do You Sleep', and to a lesser extent 'Crippled Inside'. *Imagine* topped the charts on both sides of the Atlantic.

For several years previously, Lennon had been refused entry to America. This was ostensibly as a result of his drug convictions in 1968, although it was commonly conceded that his anti-capitalist, anti-authoritarian and anti-Vietnam War stance had made him an "undesirable" to the Federal authorities. In September 1971, when he was finally given permission to enter the US, John and Yoko flew from Heathrow Airport to New York. Over the coming years, John would face many a long battle with the US immigration authorities, firstly to prevent his deportation, and secondly to acquire the Green Card that would allow him permanent residency in the US. This was finally granted to him in 1976.

John would never return to the UK; he was fed up with the way Yoko was treated

illustrated the agony of drug withdrawal (and that Paul had refused to record with the Beatles) and 'Instant Karma' were all big hits and boosted his anti-establishment rating.

If any further proof of this were needed, in the midst of this batch of hit records, John and Yoko still saw fit to produce their third avant-garde offering, *The Wedding Album* – a souvenir collage of their wedding in Gibraltar the year before. Again, this proved to be altogether too much for mainsteam fans and some critics, one of whom – *Melody Maker's* Richard Williams – inadvertently reviewed two blank sides of EMI test pressings! The review greatly amused John and Yoko, who sent him a telegram saying "…this is the first time a critic topped the artist …we're not joking!"

With the Beatles now a thing of the past, the end of 1970 saw a shift in emphasis in Lennon's music. The messages were still there, but now they were less often wrapped up in chants and sloganeering. After reading *The Primal Scream*, a book by psychiatrist Dr Arthur Janov, John underwent an intense three-week session of therapy under the direction of Dr Janov himself. The underlying principles of Primal Scream therapy are that all neuroses were a result of lack of parental love during early childhood. Dr Janov encouraged his patients to exorcise these ghosts by screaming at the absent parents.

The first tangible fruits of such therapy as far as the outside world was concerned was the album *John Lennon/The Plastic Ono Band*. Not surprisingly, with song

by the UK media. To him they consistently mocked his view that, "She's an artist, and a very serious one."

The albums that followed *Imagine* – *Mind Games* and *Walls and Bridges* – charted out familiar territory, and while his work remained popular, his revolutionary status began to dwindle. This period also saw the beginning of one the most turbulent times in his life. For most of the mid-Seventies, he was frequently estranged from Yoko, and became heavily involved in the excesses of the celebrity alcohol and drug scene.

By the end of the decade John Lennon, seeminged to have finally sorted out his marital problems and found a more settled lifestyle. Just as he had done in his Beatle days, he began to find simple pleasure in just lounging around his luxury apartment at the Dakota Building, overlooking New York's Central Park. He now devoted most of his attention to bringing up his son Sean. With the renewed domestic harmony came a new surge of creativity. He began working on his first album of new material in six years – the only intervening album having been *Rock and Roll*, an album of

his favourite songs from the Fifties.

Double Fantasy was released in November 1980. Whilst it won few critical ovations, it was nonetheless well received and, along with an accompanying single '(Just Like) Starting Over' quickly entered the Top 10 in America and throughout most of Europe. For many it was a sign that one of the great creative minds in popular music was back, and ready to tackle a new decade.

As we all know, this was not to be. On December 8th, 1980, while returning late from a recording session at the Hit Factory, John and Yoko were about to enter the Gothic-styled courtyard of the Dakota Building. A voice from behind called out, "Mr Lennon?". John turned round. Several of shots from a .38 calibre revolver rang out and John fell to the ground. He was rushed to Roosevelt Hospital, but his blood loss had been so great that by the time of his arrival he had already been pronounced dead.

The assassin was a Beatles fanatic named Mark David Chapman. Like Lee Harvey Oswald – John F. Kennedy's assassin – Mark Chapman immortalised himself

through a single act of brutality. And the reunion of the Beatles was laid to rest once and for all.

John's death provided an opportunity to reassess his life and work. Not surprisingly, the record companies were the first to encourage the idea. Within the space of a few months, Lennon's estate enjoyed his greatest ever commercial success as a solo artist, as the new material all leapt to the top of the charts. No sooner had '(Just Like) Starting Over' dropped from the number one position, than it was replaced by the hastily reissued 'Imagine'. One place behind it sat the now perennial 'Happy Xmas (War Is Over)'.

John Lennon's death stunned millions of people around the world. While unquestionably capable of acts of cruelty and selfishness, John had publicly stood out for the most positive aspects of humanity. He preached the true spirit of the Sixties – love, peace and understanding – as vociferously, even belligerently, as anyone. The world may have moved on, and some of those ideals may now seem rather naive, but as philosophies go, there are a whole lot worse that we could embrace.

Liverpool pays a final tribute to one of its greatest sons

PAUL MCCARTNEY – GOING FOR IT

Right from the beginning, it was always thought that if any of the Beatles would enjoy solo success it would be Paul. Even though with each passing year, it was the Lennon contributions to the Beatles that were becoming revered as "old masters", Paul's music had grown to develop a more conventionally commercial edge.

His first effort was the album *McCartney*. Controversial from the beginning, it was scheduled for release at the same time as the Beatles official swan song *Let It Be*. The rest of the Beatles asked Paul if he would postpone its release – he refused and so *Let It Be* was itself put back. *McCartney* was the culmination of Paul's development as a musician over the previous five years.

Whereas the others had started their solo careers with all-star megabands, *McCartney*, as its name suggests, is a result of only one pair of hands, with the exception of the odd vocal contribution from his wife Linda. Recorded over the previous year, in a variety of locations – many of them on a Studer 4-track that Paul had bought for his own use – *McCartney* was given a positive reception, and songs like 'Maybe I'm Amazed' upheld the common view that Paul McCartney might well go on to dominate the Seventies as the Beatles had the previous decade. *McCartney* was an international success, taking the number one spot in the US, but being narrowly held off by Simon and Garfunkel's *Bridge over Troubled Water* in Britain. Even greater success awaited 1971's follow-up album, *Ram*.

In spite of controversy surrounding the banned "political" single 'Give Ireland Back to the Irish', or 'Hi Hi Hi', with its supposed drug references – also banned by the BBC – Paul McCartney's output was characterised by extremely lightweight catchy pop songs with trite lyrics. This was a stark contrast to John Lennon's cathartic soul-mining, and an approach that found greater favour with the public than the music press.

After the Beatles abandoned live work in 1966, it had always been Paul McCartney who was keen to get back out on the road. To this end, in late 1971 he introduced the world to his new band, Wings. His sidemen were Denny Laine, an original member of the Moody Blues, and an unknown drummer – Denny Seiwell. To the bemusement of the music world, Wings also featured a prominent figure on keyboards, although one not associated with music – Linda McCartney.

Wings first album, *Wild Life*, was received by the press with unprecedented hostility. Many couldn't work out what McCartney was up to. *Red Rose Speedway*, attributed in 1973 to Paul McCartney and Wings, fared little better. In spite of the misgivings of the press, however, both albums continued to sell healthily.

What many critics would consider to be Paul McCartney's crowning achieve-

Paul McCartney and Wings

Ebony and Ivory

Denny Laine. Lightweight even by his standards, 'Mull of Kintyre' was a pretty, if rather bland paean to his Scottish home, complete with the sounds of a 21-piece bagpipe band. It was not in the least bit extraordinary. However, what happened next, was. Within two weeks of its release it was holding the UK number one spot – a position it would maintain for the next nine weeks. By the time it had left the Top 30, in February 1978, 'Mull of Kintyre' had sold 2.6 million copies, making it at that time Britain's biggest selling single ever – 900,000 more than its nearest rival: 'She Loves You'. Even more remarkable was the success it enjoyed in America. It didn't even touch the Top 30!

McCartney hung up his Wings in 1979, by which time there had been several line-up changes and two more poorly received albums, *London Town* and *Back to the Egg*. He now resumed working on his own – literally so with 1980's *McCartney II*, where again he played all the instruments. He has since been involved in a number of collaborations, including number one hits with Stevie Wonder – 'Ebony and Ivory' – and Michael Jackson.

In 1984, perhaps with one eye looking back at the *Magical Mystery Tour* debacle, McCartney decided to have another stab at the motion picture world. His self-financed effort, *Give My Regards to Broad Street*, which he also wrote and starred in, was viewed by some as a pop-star ego out of control. It was slated by critics, and bombed at the box office, losing him a sizeable amount of money. However, as one of the richest men in Great Britain it was a luxury he could afford. His ego came into question again in 1991, when he presented *Liverpool Oratorio*, a new classical piece based on his childhood.

For some, McCartney has failed to live up to the high expectations he helped to create in the Sixties. But one fact remains: Paul McCartney has sold more records throughout the world than any other single artist. He continues to enjoy enormous world-wide success although it is now less regular or guaranteed. But a pop song-writer of McCartney's pedigree is always liable to pull off yet another masterstroke.

ment as a solo artist, *Band on the Run*, was issued at the end of 1973. The album was recorded at a studio owned by Cream's drummer Ginger Baker in Lagos, Nigeria. *Band on the Run* was truly a turn up for the books. On release it was given rave reviews by most of the popular music press, although many of the "serious" music scribes were still less convinced, viewing it as "more of the same". The public could not have disagreed more with this viewpoint. A pair of million-selling singles 'Jet' and the title track 'Band on the Run', took the album to number one virtually world-wide. *Band on the Run* would spend over two years in the album charts and, with world sales exceeding six million,

became the seventh biggest-selling album of the decade.

While McCartney's subsequent albums – *Venus and Mars*, *Wings at the Speed of Sound* and the live *Wings over America* triple set – came nowhere near to matching the success of *Band on the Run*, they were still big business, all making number one in America. By the end of 1977, in spite of the punk revolution of the past year, there was little doubt that Paul McCartney, with or without his Wings, was one of the biggest names in the world of popular music.

But Paul surpassed even himself (and the Beatles) with his next single, 'Mull of Kintyre', co-written with his Wings partner

George Harrison – The Dark Horse

George was the first Beatle with a solo release to his name. At the end of 1967 Harrison had agreed to perform the soundtrack to his friend Joe Massot's experimental film *Wonderwall*. It failed to make the charts, as did his second album, the rather unjustly damned *Electronic Sounds*. Released on Apple's subsidiary experimental label Zapple, the album features George experimenting with his newly acquired moog synthesiser. With extended improvisations covering each side, it had been recorded under the guidance and influence of American synthesiser pioneer Bernie Krause (of Beaver and Krause).

Although, on the breakup of the Beatles, it was predicted that John Lennon and Paul McCartney would enjoy major solo success, it was George Harrison that made the early running. In the middle of 1970, he assembled a star-studded line up of friends and session musicians at Abbey Road, this time under the keen eye of producer Phil Spector. The result was *All Things Must Pass*, a triple album boxed set that retailed in the UK for £4 19s 6d (£4.98) – almost double the price of a regular album. Two of the records contained George's new collections of songs and the

Harrison and Clapton at the Bangladesh benefit concert

third contained five extended jam-sessions. The album quickly went to the top of the charts on both sides of the Atlantic. Critics were full of praise – to them it showed that the high standard of his final Beatles contributions was no fluke.

In early 1971, 'My Sweet Lord' was lifted from the album for single release. Within two weeks it had gone to the top of the charts where it stayed for almost two months. It eventually became the biggest selling single of 1971. Both single and album topped the charts simultaneously on both sides of the Atlantic. However, Harrison's dream start was given a severe setback when in March 1971 a US music publisher began a legal battle with Harrison and Apple claiming that 'My Sweet Lord' had plagiarised an American hit of the mid-Sixties – 'He's so Fine' by the Chiffons. The court battle was finally resolved after five tortuous years with Harrison defeated and forced to pay out over a half a million dollars.

But back in 1971 Harrison followed on with another triumph. His long-time friend Ravi Shankar, appalled at the level of starvation in his homeland, approached George with a view to organising a benefit concert for UNICEF – the children's charity who were working under terrible circumstances in Bangladesh. Shankar wanted to raise $25,000.

George threw himself headlong into the

task, quickly organising some of rock's top stars to perform a free benefit concert. All the Beatles were invited – which caused something of a flurry in the music press. Paul, fearing a new outbreak of "Beatles Reform" mania, turned the event down straight away. John, who had agreed to begin with, also pulled out when it became clear that Yoko Ono was not to be one of the guest artists.

On August 1st, 1971, two concerts were performed before an audience of 20,000 at Madison Square Gardens in New York. The first was a raga specially written by Ravi Shankar. For many Westerners, whose total knowledge of Indian music had been George's cross-cultural experiments, this piece would be a genuine introduction the music of India. Whilst it could hardly be said that Asian music has made a big impact in the West, this, for a majority of listeners, was where it first began.

But it was the second concert that everyone had really come to see. This time George performed, taking most of the vocal duties, backed by a 25-piece band that featured, among others, Ringo Starr, Eric Clapton, members of Badfinger, Leon Russell, Billy Preston, Klaus Voorman and spectacularly, Bob Dylan.

Royalties from the concerts raised nearly $250,000. However, the album and film that followed brought in a staggering total of $15 million. Eventually, thanks to

George makes the early running

the corporate greed of the various record companies involved and the intervention of the IRS – the US tax authority – only a small proportion of that money reached its destination, but as a reward for their efforts, George Harrison and Ravi Shankar both received awards from the UNICEF organisation. Nothing like it was seen again until Live Aid, 14 years later.

His follow-up album, 1973's *Living in the Material World*, was seen by most critics as a disappointment, although it did yield another big hit single, 'Give Me Love (Give me Peace on Earth)'. In spite of the lack of critical support, both single and album still hit the top of the US charts – although in Europe George's fortunes began to dwindle.

After such a flying start, George's stamina was beginning to tail off. He started off his own Dark Horse label, which enjoyed a brief success with his first signing, a duo called Splinter. However, his own work took a down turn. The albums released throughout the rest of the Seventies – *Dark Horse*, Extra Texture and *Thirty Three & A Third* – were invariably slammed by the music press and sold in decreasing quantities. Finally, 1979's *George Harrison* album failed to chart at all in the UK, and fared only a little better Stateside.

Since then, George Harrison has kept the lowest profile of the surviving Beatles. He involved himself in the British film industry, his Hand-Made company being responsible for a number of significant comedy films, often the work of his friends from the Monty Python team. He has continued to enjoy periodic success with his increasingly infrequent recordings. A highlight was the album *Cloud Nine*, which spawned 'Got My Mind Set on You', a world-wide hit in 1987.

The following year he founded the Traveling Wilburys – a supergroup featuring the talents of Harrison, Bob Dylan, Jeff Lynne (from ELO), Roy Orbison and Tom Petty. Success was more or less guaranteed but the project's crowning achievement was to return Roy Orbison to the forefront of the pop world before his untimely death in December 1988.

For most of the time, Harrison now seems happy to live the life of a recluse, shut away in his country mansion, never overly exerting himself or over-eager to relive former glories.

However, an increasing tendency to venerate pop stars of old, and with a new generation now interested in the Beatles, it would be premature to write-off the possibility of George Harrison resuming major star status.

RINGO STARR – EASY COME EASY GO

During 1974, John Lennon was reported in a newspaper interview as saying that the only reason the Beatles had stayed together after *The White Album* was because they were worried that Ringo wouldn't be able to do anything on his own. He then went on to remark on the irony that over the

Ringo Starr – The Magic Christian

past year Ringo had probably outsold his own efforts. Based on Ringo's songs and stints at the microphone, few expected great things;as with George Harrison, his successes up to the mid- Seventies came as something of a surprise.

His first album, *Sentimental Journey* was started during 1969. Here, Ringo sings a dozen standards from his childhood, backed by George Martin's orchestra. Although not without charm, it showed, if anyone needed to be told, that Ringo was not one of the world's great balladeers. Critically hammered, it enjoyed a brief stay in the charts, sneaking into the US Top 20 for one week. He followed this with another theme album – this time using some of America's top country and western musicians. *Beaucoups of Blues* was generally given a positive reception, although it barely scraped into the charts. It was beginning to look as if Ringo wouldn't be able to cut it.

Ringo's response was a run of hit singles over the next three years that his former colleagues were unable to match. His 1971 composition 'It Don't Come Easy' was a revelation. Recorded with George Harrison and Klaus Voorman, it hit the Top 5 on both sides of the Atlantic. Closely followed by another Top 10 hit, the solo composition 'Back off Boogaloo' established Ringo and paved the way for a splendidly eccentric pop career.

Ringo's career hit its peak at the end of 1973. A highly rated new single, 'Photograph', co-written with George Harrison, topped the charts in the US. The parent album, *Ringo*, was similarly successful. *Ringo* is of particular significance to Beatles fans in that it is the closest the Beatles ever got to a full reunion. With an all-star line-up, *Ringo* featured not only his three erstwhile colleagues, but Marc Bolan, members of The Band, Steve Cropper, Billy Preston and a host of LA's top session men.

In 1974, a second single – a cover of Johnny Burnette's 'You're Sixteen' – was lifted from the album. This, too, went to the top in the US sending the *Ringo* album shooting back up the charts again. In all, *Ringo* sold over two million copies – a

Ringo and his personality-laden All-Starr Band

figure that his old band wouldn't have been too unhappy with.

Sadly, *Goodnight Vienna*, the album that emerged in November 1974 was a much weaker affair. While it still managed a respectable Top 20 position, it was to be downhill all the way from here. In the early Eighties Ringo found himself in an unthinkable position for a Beatle – a new album but no takers – he couldn't get a record deal.

As many had suspected he would, Ringo also tried his luck in the movie business. In the first half of the Seventies he acted in diverse selection of offbeat film roles: *Son of Dracula*, Frank Zappa's *2000 Motels*, Ken Russell's *Lizstomania*, and the spaghetti Western *Blindman*. He also played the role of a Teddy Boy to great acclaim in the rock'n'roll feature film *That'll Be the Day* (which starred David Essex). Ringo also directed *Born to Boogie*, a film about Marc Bolan of T Rex.

The Eighties were wilderness years for Ringo. By 1979, interest in his musical and film activities seemed to have all but disappeared, and he drifted into a lengthy period of alcohol abuse. Ringo's most notable work during these troubled times was as the narrator of the children's television series *Thomas the Tank Engine*. Along with his new wife, American actress Barbara Bach, Ringo spent the best part of the decade trying to get his act together, finally resurfacing in Paul McCartney's much-reviled *Give My Regards To Broad Street*.

Even after the height of Beatlemania, Ringo always enjoyed immense personal popularity, and although in interviews the Ringo Starr of today can sometimes seem a rather embittered, forgotten man, he remains a strangely charismatic figure. In the early Nineties he tried to restart his musical career with the All Starr band, an unwieldy unit that featured, among others, Todd Rundgren, Joe Walsh, Dave Edmunds, Nils Lofgren and Ringo's son, Zak. Despite the combined talents involved, this project has yet to make any real headway.

REUNIONS AND OTHER MYSTERIES

Until John Lennon's murder in 1980, the music press would report, with dull regularity, rumours that the Beatles would be getting back together. They almost found themselves on the same stage in 1971 for George Harrison's Bangladesh benefit concert. They all played on the *Ringo* album, but not at the same time. By the end of the decade, whilst three Beatle careers were on a downward spiral, Paul McCartney was on top of the world. Nonetheless, the closest they ever managed was a proposed concert for Kampuchean refugees that Paul had initiated. Both George and Ringo had said they were prepared to perform on-stage with Paul. It was John who refused to have anything to do with it. With their personal differences now long in the past, John dismissed the concert: "…we'd just be four rusty old men."

Then there were the mystery stories – the Beatles had reformed, but they were working under an assumed name. One of the most popular of these rumours occurred in 1973 when an unknown Canadian band called Klaatu released a very Beatlesque collection that included the song 'Calling Occupants of Interplanetary Craft', later a hit for the Carpenters. The rumour was fuelled by incidental facts – Klaatu is the name of space traveller in the classic sci-fi film *The Day The Earth Stood Still* – a still from which features on the cover of Ringo's *Goodnight Vienna* album (Ringo's head is superimposed onto the body of Klaatu). Craftily, the band's management – who had never supplied any biographical detail on the band – remained silent, pushing sales of the *Klaatu* album past the quarter-million mark. Eventually the group's identities were made public and the fuss died down. Klaatu made another four albums before disbanding.

Of course, John's death on December 8th, 1980 stopped all such speculation, although more than one person would voice the possibility of a reunion with Julian Lennon taking John's place!

In 1995, thanks to the wonders of technology, the Beatles did record together again – after a fashion. With a market for Beatle rarities and bootlegs still flourishing, Apple decided to issue the *Anthology* series – three two-CD sets that, for the non-bootleg collector at least, give a fascinating new insight into the Beatles' story,

releasing out-takes or alternative versions of some of the most famous songs in the history of popular music.

This development was fascinating in its own right, but they had something else in mind. Much against the wishes of George Martin, who oversaw the *Anthology* project, Yoko Ono submitted two of John's home demos. The idea was to produce two final new Beatles tracks, with the other three playing along to John's home recording. Both would be released as singles.

The first effort, 'Free as a Bird', was not even a complete song – little wonder, then, that whilst admittedly pleasant and catchy, it really is incoherent nonsense. From two of Lennon's verses, under the guidance of producer Jeff Lynne (once the guiding light behind the Electric Light Orchestra, a band who had openly based their entire career on the Fab Four), the other ex-Beatles managed to cobble together something that sounded a little bit like an out-take from the *Let It Be* album. In fact, it sounded more like an out-take from an ELO album.

The second song, 'Pure Love', was at least a finished song, but given that the demo – as with 'Free as a Bird' – dated back to 1977, it is reasonable to assume that John Lennon didn't use them on his final *Double Fantasy* album because he felt them to be sub-standard. The

Anthology series and the two "new" singles have hardly set off the new wave of Beatlemania that some of the media had suggested, but they certainly fared well enough to make the Top 5 in the charts in every major record market in the world.

When asked at the height of Beatlemania how long he thought the Beatles would last, John Lennon's reply was a cautious one: "You can be big-headed and say 'Yeah, we're gonna last ten years,' but as soon as you've said that you think… we're lucky if we last three months." It's now 39 years since the Quarry Men first played their first ramshackle skiffle concerts, yet interest in the band shows no sign of abating.

The success of the *Anthology* series proves the Beatles' enduring ability to cross divides of taste and generation. In the 26 years since their split, successive generations of music fans have continued to buy into the legend of the Beatles. Their classic albums from *Revolver* to *Abbey Road* continue to sell in large numbers.

If any greater proof of the Beatles' enduring appeal were needed, in 1995 readers of a top British music monthly voted *Revolver* the greatest album ever made. The vast majority of those readers were not even born when that album was recorded. Who would bet against a similar result 10, 25 or 50 years from now?

Reunited – the three surviving Beatles and George Martin return to the studio in 1995

CHRONOLOGY

1940

JULY 7TH:
Richard Starkey (Ringo Starr) born.

OCTOBER 9TH:
John Lennon born.

1942

JUNE 18:
Paul McCartney born.

1943

FEBRUARY 25:
George Harrison born.

1957

MARCH:
John Lennon forms the Quarry Men.

JULY 6TH:
Paul McCartney meets John Lennon, who is performing with the Quarry Men. He is invited to join.

AUGUST 7TH:
The Quarry Men play at the Cavern Club – then a jazz and blues venue. Paul McCartney misses the gig because he is away at Scout camp!

OCTOBER 18TH:
First Quarry Men performance featuring Lennon and McCartney.

1958

MARCH:
Paul introduces school friend George Harrison to The Quarry Men. He joins the band several months later.

AUGUST:
The Quarry Men cut their first demonstration record.

1959

NOVEMBER:
The band become Johnny and the Moondogs and reach the final heat stages of *Star Search* – a TV talent contest.

1960

JANUARY:
Stuart Sutcliffe, a friend of John's from art school, wins a painting competition. He spends his prize on a bass guitar and is invited to join the band.

MAY 20TH:
The band become the Silver Beetles and begin a week-long tour of Scotland supporting Johnny Gentle.

AUGUST:
Through promoter Allan Williams the band – now calling themselves the Beatles – are booked to play a three-month residency at a Hamburg night club. They recruit Pete Best as a permanent drummer.

OCTOBER:
The Beatles meet drummer Richard Starkey – also playing in Hamburg with Rory Storm and the Hurricanes. They play together on a recording of 'Summertime' by the Hurricanes' bassist.

1961

FEBRUARY:
The band play their first gig at the Cavern as the Beatles.

MARCH–JULY:
A second engagement in Hamburg. Stuart Sutcliffe leaves the band and remains in Hamburg with fiancée Astrid Kirchherr to study under Eduardo Paolozzi.

AUGUST:
The Beatles play on Tony Sheridan's version of 'My Bonnie' in sessions for orchestra leader Bert Kaempfert.

NOVEMBER:
Brian Epstein sees the Beatles play at

the Cavern Club. The following month he becomes their manager.

1962

JANUARY:
The band audition unsuccessfully for Decca Records. Epstein, deciding they need a change of image, buys them matching suits.

MARCH 7TH:
The Beatles make their radio debut on the BBC's *Teenager's Turn – Here We Go.*

APRIL 13TH:
The Beatles return to Hamburg. They discover Stuart Sutcliffe has died.

JUNE 6TH:
The Beatles record demos with producer George Martin at EMI's studios in Abbey Road, London.

AUGUST 16TH:
Drummer Pete Best is sacked. He is replaced by Ringo Starr.

AUGUST 23RD:
John Lennon marries his girlfriend Cynthia Powell.

OCTOBER 4TH:
'Love Me Do', the debut single is released. It climbs the UK chart slowly, peaking at number 17 in December.

OCTOBER 17TH:
The Beatles make their TV debut on Granada's *People and Places.*

1963

JANUARY 11TH:
'Please Please Me', their second single, is released. It reaches number one on February 22nd.

MARCH 22ND:
Debut album *Please Please Me* is

released. On May 8th it goes to number one, where it stays until November
.

APRIL 12TH:
Third single, 'From Me to You' is released. It tops the chart for six weeks.

AUGUST 23RD:
'She Loves You' reaches the number one spot one week after release. It becomes Britain's best-selling single of all time until Paul McCartney's 'Mull of Kintyre' in 1977.

OCTOBER 13TH:
The Beatles play before the Queen Mother at *Sunday Night at the London Palladium.*

NOVEMBER 22ND:
The second album – *With the Beatles* – goes to the top of the charts where it displaces their debut.

NOVEMBER 29TH:
'I Want to Hold Your Hand' is released. With advance orders of 900,000, it goes straight to number one.

1964

JANUARY 16TH:
'I Want to Hold Your Hand' becomes the band's first number one in the US charts. The top of the American chart is monopolised for the next three months by Beatles singles.

FEBRUARY 9TH:
The Beatles appear on *The Ed Sullivan Show* before a record-breaking TV audience of 73 million.

FEBRUARY 11TH:
The Beatles begin their first American tour, starting in Washington.

MARCH:
'Can't Buy Me Love' is released in UK and US to combined advance orders of over three million.

APRIL 4TH:
The US *Billboard* chart is swamped by Beatles singles: 'Can't Buy Me Love', 'Twist and Shout', 'She Loves You', 'I Want to Hold Your Hand' and 'Please Please Me' hold the Top 5 places.

JUNE 4TH:
The band embarks on its first world tour. Drummer Jimmy Nichol replaces the hospitalised Ringo for the first five dates.

JULY 7TH:
The premiere of the first Beatles film, *A Hard Day's Night.* The album and title track go straight to number one.

AUGUST:
Beatlemania grips the US as the band plays a second American tour.

NOVEMBER 27TH:
A new single 'I Feel Fine' becomes one of the fastest-selling singles of all time. It is the Beatles' fifth consecutive million-seller.

DECEMBER 4TH:
The new *Beatles for Sale* album enters the charts at number one.

1965

APRIL 9TH:
'Ticket to Ride' becomes the Beatles' fifth consecutive single to go straight to the top of the British charts.

JULY 29TH:
Premiere of their second movie, *Help!* The soundtrack album and title track go straight to number one.

AUGUST 14TH:
The Beatles begin their third American tour.

OCTOBER 26TH:
The Queen presents the Beatles with MBEs in the Great Throne Room in Buckingham Palace.

DECEMBER 3RD:
Rubber Soul album and 'Day Tripper' single are released. It signals a change of direction and an attempt to rid the Beatles of their "moptop" image.

DECEMBER 12TH:
The Beatles play their final British tour date, in Cardiff.

1966

JANUARY:
George Harrison marries Patti Boyd (the marriage lasts until 1974).

MAY 1ST:
The performance at the *NME* poll-winners party is their last UK concert.

JUNE:
The US-only *Yesterday and Today* album is withdrawn before release after controversy about the sleeve.

JUNE 10TH:
The Beatles 12th single. 'Paperback Writer' goes to number one.

JULY 4TH:
While touring the Far East a misunderstanding takes place which is reported in the press as a slur on the first lady of the Philippines. Public hostility grows and they are forced to leave the island in haste.

JULY 29TH:
A British interview from six months earlier is reprinted in a US teen magazine – *Datebook*. John Lennon's comments about modern Christianity cause media uproar. US radio stations in the 'Bible Belt' organise record-burning congregations.

AUGUST 5TH:
The seventh album *Revolver* is released to universal acclaim. Almost 30 years later readers of Britain's *Q* magazine will vote it the best album of all time. The same day, the double "A" sided

'Eleanor Rigby'/'Yellow Submarine' is released. It reaches number one in 12 different countries.

AUGUST 12TH:
The final US tour begins in Chicago. The Beatles do not rehearse and play no material from the new album.

AUGUST 29TH:
The Beatles' last-ever concert takes place, at Candlestick Park in San Francisco.

1967

FEBRUARY 17TH:
Double "A" sided 'Penny Lane'/'Strawberry Fields Forever' is released. Although many consider it to be one of the greatest singles ever made, it is the first Beatles single not to top the chart since 1962. It is held off the number one spot by cabaret singer Engelbert Humperdinck.

MAY:
EMI announces that the Beatles have, so far, sold more than 200 million records.

JUNE 1ST:
Sgt Pepper's Lonely Hearts Club Band is released to critical hysteria. A pivotal album in pop history, it sells consistently up to the present day.

JUNE 25TH:
The satellite TV show *Our World* features the debut performance of the new single 'All You Need Is Love'. It is seen by a world-wide audience of 200 million.

AUGUST 25TH:
The band attends a conference of the Spiritual Regeneration League in Bangor, Wales, under the tuition of Maharishi Mahesh Yogi.

AUGUST 27TH:
Brian Epstein is found dead.

NOVEMBER 24TH:
'Hello Goodbye' is released. It achieves global sales of over two million.

DECEMBER 8TH:
Double EP package 'Magical Mystery Tour', the soundtrack to the TV film of the same name, is released.

26TH:
Magical Mystery Tour premieres on TV – it becomes the first Beatles project to be greeted with open hostility.

1968

FEBRUARY:
The Beatles study in India under the instruction of the Maharishi.

MARCH 15TH:
'Lady Madonna' is released. The flip side is George's 'The Inner Light', the first time one of his compositions has featured on a single.

MAY:
John and Paul announce the formation of their own business empire, Apple Corps Ltd.

AUGUST:
Ringo walks out of a recording session in Abbey Road – he returns a few days later.

Cynthia Lennon files successfully for divorce, citing John's adultery with Yoko Ono.

AUGUST 26TH:
'Hey Jude'/'Revolution' is released. Its massive world-wide sales make it the Beatles' biggest selling single.

NOVEMBER 22ND:
The double album *The Beatles* is released. Better known as *The White Album*, it is a collection of individual projects.

1969

JANUARY:
The Beatles begin filming and recording a project intended to get the Beatles "back to their roots". Following a performance on the roof of the Apple Building in Savile Row, London, and the unsatisfactory mixing of the album, the project is shelved.

FEBRUARY:
Allen Klein is appointed new manager of the Beatles.

MARCH:
Paul McCartney marries Linda Eastman.

John Lennon marries Yoko Ono and stages a "bed-in" protest for peace in a hotel in Amsterdam.

APRIL 11TH:
'Get Back' is released. It sells nearly five million copies throughout the world.

MAY 30TH:
The band's first ever stereo single, 'The Ballad of John and Yoko', is released. Only John and Paul play on it. It is the Beatles' final number one.

SEPTEMBER 26TH:
Abbey Road, the final Beatles album to be recorded, is released. With sales of over ten million, it becomes one of the biggest selling albums of all time.

OCTOBER 31ST:
'Something', written by George Harrison, only reaches number five in the UK charts.

NOVEMBER:
John announces his intention to leave the band. Allen Klein persuades him not to go public until business deals have been completed. Lennon agrees to his request.

1970

MARCH 6TH:
'Let It Be' is the final single before the Beatles split. Again, it fails to reach the number one spot.

APRIL 10TH:
Paul announces officially that the Beatles have split.

MAY 8TH:
The *Get Back* project, remixed by Phil Spector, is released under the new title *Let It Be*. In the US it becomes the fastest grossing album up to that point.

1973

APRIL 19TH:
A pair of greatest hits double album packages are released. *The Beatles 1962-1966* and *The Beatles 1967-1970* are among the biggest selling albums of the year.

1976

MARCH 6TH:
All 23 Beatles singles are re-promoted in Britain. One week sees all 23 in the Top 100, four of them ('Paperback Writer', 'Hey Jude', 'Get Back' and 'Yesterday') reach the Top 20.

1977

MAY 6TH:
The Beatles at The Hollywood Bowl is released featuring recordings from their US concerts in 1964 and 1965. The album still managed to make the number one spot.

1980

DECEMBER 8TH:
John Lennon is shot dead in New York by Mark Chapman, a disturbed fan.

1995

DECEMBER:
Interest in the Beatles takes off again. A six-part television series is launched, with the story of the Beatles told through interviews and footage of the period. At the same time, Apple release *Anthology 1* a double album/CD of unreleased material or alternative versions. It is intended as the first of three such packages. It tops the charts.

'Free as a Bird' becomes the first "new" Beatles single in 15 years. It is created in the studio by the surviving Beatles from a half-finished John Lennon song recorded in 1977. The single achieves Top 5 placings in all the major world markets.

1996

MARCH:
Anthology 2 is released. A second "new" single 'Pure Love' is released.

AUGUST:
Anthology 3 is released.

DISCOGRAPHY

				Top UK Chart Position	Top US Chart Position
OCT	1962	LOVE ME DO		17	1
JAN	1963	PLEASE PLEASE ME		1	3
APR	1963	FROM ME TO YOU		1	116
JUN	1963	MY BONNIE		48	–
AUG	1963	SHE LOVES YOU		1	1
NOV	1963	I WANT TO HOLD YOUR HAND		1	1
MAR	1964	TWIST AND SHOUT		–	1
MAR	1964	CAN'T BUY ME LOVE		1	1
MAY	1964	SIE LIEBT DICH		–	97
JUN	1964	AIN'T SHE SWEET		29	19
JUL	1964	A HARD DAY'S NIGHT		1	1
JUL	1964	I'LL CRY INSTEAD		–	25
JUL	1964	AND I LOVE HER		–	12
AUG	1964	MATCHBOX		–	17
NOV	1964	I FEEL FINE		1	1
FEB	1965	EIGHT DAYS A WEEK		–	1
APR	1965	TICKET TO RIDE		1	1
JUL	1965	HELP!		1	1
SEP	1965	YESTERDAY		–	1
DEC	1965	WE CAN WORK IT OUT/			
		DAY TRIPPER		1	1
FEB	1966	NOWHERE MAN		–	3
JUN	1966	PAPERBACK WRITER		1	1
AUG	1966	ELEANOR RIGBY/			
		YELLOW SUBMARINE		1	2
FEB	1967	STRAWBERRY FIELDS FOREVER/			
		PENNY LANE		2	1
JUL	1967	ALL YOU NEED IS LOVE		1	1
NOV	1967	HELL, GOODBYE		1	1
DEC	1967	MAGICAL MYSTERY TOUR		2	–
MAR	1968	LADY MADONNA		1	4
AUG	1968	HEY JUDE		1	1
APR	1969	GET BACK		1	1
MAY	1969	THE BALLAD OF JOHN AND YOKO		1	8

SINGLES:

			Top UK Chart Position	Top US Chart Position
Oct	1969	Something	4	1
Mar	1970	Let It Be	2	1
May	1970	The Long And Winding Road	–	1

EXTENDED PLAYS:

9/63	The Beatles Hits
9/63	Twist And Shout
11/63	The Beatles 1
2/64	All My Loving
6/64	Long Tall Sally
11/64	A Hard Day's Night 1
11/64	A Hard Day's Night 2
4/65	Beatles For Sale 1
6/65	Beatles For Sale 2
12/65	Beatles Million Sellers
3/66	Yesterday
7/66	Nowhere Man
12/66	Magical Mystery Tour (double EP)

ALBUMS:

22/3/63	Please Please Me
22/11/63	With The Beatles
10/8/64	A Hard Day's Night
4/12/64	Beatles For Sale
6/8/65	Help!
3/12/65	Rubber Soul
5/8/66	Revolver
10/12/66	A Collection Of Beatles' Oldies (But Goldies)
1/6/67	Sgt. Pepper's Lonely Hearts Club Band
22/11/68	The Beatles (The White Album)
17/1/69	Yellow Submarine
26/9/69	Abbey Road
8/5/70	Let It Be

RETROSPECTIVES COMPILATIONS:

1973	The Beatles 1962-1966
1973	The Beatles 1967-1970
1976	Rock 'N' Roll Music
	The Magical Mystery Tour
1977	The Beatles At The Hollywood Bowl
1978	The Beatles Collection (box)
1979	Rarities
1980	The Beatles Ballads
1981	The Beatles EP Collection
1982	Twenty Greatest Hits
1995	Anthology 1
1996	Anthology 2
	Anthology 3

INDEX

INDEX

ACKNOWLEDGEMENTS

The publishers would like to thank the following sources for
their permission to reproduce the photographs in this book:

Corbis Bettmann
London Features International
Pictorial Press
Popperfoto
Rex Features.

BIBLIOGRAPHY:

The Ultimate Beatles Encyclopedia – Bill Harry (Virgin)
A Hard Day's Write – Steve Turner (Carlton)
Beatlemania – Bill Harry (Virgin)
Working Class Heroes – Neville Stannard (Virgin)
Paperback Writers – Bill Harry (Virgin)
The Long and Winding Road – Neville Stannard (Virgin)
Shout – Philip Norman (Elm Tree Books)
Beatles In Their Own Words (Omnibus Press)
The Beatles Conquer America – Dezo Hoffmann (Virgin)
The Complete Beatles Chronicle – Mark Lewisohn (Harmony)
The Beatles: The Authorized Biography – Hunter Davies
(Heinemann)
Lennon Remembers – Jann Wenner (Straight Arrow)
Mersey Beat – Bill Harry (Omnibus)
All You Need Is Ears – George Martin (MacMillan)
I Me Mine – George Harrison (Genesis Publications)
The Beatles: It Was Twenty Years Ago (Michael Press)
Various copies of *The Beatles Monthly*